Sacred History, Sacred Literature

R. E. Friedman

Sacred History, Sacred Literature

Essays on Ancient Israel, the Bible, and Religion
in Honor of

R. E. Friedman

on His Sixtieth Birthday

Edited by
SHAWNA DOLANSKY

Winona Lake, Indiana
EISENBRAUNS
2008

www.eisenbrauns.com

The publication of this book was generously assisted by the
University of California, San Diego, Judaic Studies Program

Library of Congress Cataloging-in-Publication Data

Sacred history, sacred literature : essays on ancient Israel, the Bible, and religion in
    honor of R. E. Friedman on his sixtieth birthday / edited by Shawn Dolansky.
        p.   cm.
Includes bibliographical references and indexes.
ISBN 978-1-57506-151-1 (hardcover : alk. paper)
    1. Bible. O.T.—Criticism, interpretation, etc.   2. Judaism—History.
I. Friedman, Richard Elliott. II. Dolansky, Shawna.
BS1171.3.S33   2008
221.6—dc22

                                                                                                    2008040327

The paper used in this publication meets the minimum requirements of the American
National Standard for Information Sciences—Permanence of Paper for Printed Library
Materials, ANSI Z39.48-1984. ⊚™

Contents

Part 1
The Hebrew Bible

Part 2
Source Criticism

Richard Elliott Friedman
An Appreciation

WILLIAM H. C. PROPP

University of California, San Diego

At 60, Richard Elliott Friedman is still young. His step is spry, his humor racy, his imagination fertile. What's more, his eye is still bright, and his skin appears to be adequately hydrated. And why not? He is only halfway to his proverbial 120.

The 60th year is a good midpoint from which to survey past accomplishments and future promise. Professionals in the field know well Friedman's main contributions, some widely accepted, others not yet: the case for the double redaction of Deuteronomy–2 Kings, the case for both a Priestly source and a Priestly redactional stratum in the Torah, the case for the historical tabernacle, the case for a Yahwistic source running from Genesis through 1 Kings, and the case that the Hebrew Bible is unified by a thematic recession of the divine presence. Friedman's contributions are all standard treatments that appear in the bibliography of every serious discussion.

Dick should feel especially proud of leading the fight to incorporate the study of the Hebrew Bible, including the question of its literary antecedents, into the field of Judaic Studies. It was not always so. For several generations of Jewish scholars, the method of Wellhausen was a thing *treyf*, nothing less than an effort to dismantle Judaism. Friedman, in contrast, put the modern, critical study of the Torah and Bible at the heart of the Judaic Studies Program he built at the University of California, San Diego.

Another attribute that has set Dick apart is a sustained effort to make the Bible relevant, though not necessarily in a religious sense. Whether it is bringing the fruits of literary study and philology to an unprecedentedly wide readership with works such as *Who Wrote the Bible? The Disappearance of God, The Hidden Book in the Bible, Commentary on the Torah*, and *The Bible with Sources Revealed* or his current work on how the Bible is applied and misapplied to contemporary moral, political, and nationalist debates, Friedman has never been content to let Scripture grow moldy in its academic container. He is, bar none, the greatest spokesman for the critical, intelligent study of the Hebrew Bible.

At UCSD, our debt to Dick is incalculable. Brought here in 1976 as the first full-time professor of Judaic Studies, he assembled a team of textual scholars, historians, and archaeologists by persistence, force of personality, and personal excellence. Dick created a new center for biblical and Judaic studies in the southwest, on a campus otherwise known principally for scientific research. He organized international conferences; he brought as guest lecturers some of the world's brightest luminaries in Jewish studies. For 30 years he has been the heart and soul of the UCSD Judaic Studies Program.

So, Dick, here is a collection of essays written especially in your honor. But "Festschrift" sounds so stuffy, not like you at all. Let's call it your Party Book, a celebration of your manifold contributions to biblical and Judaic studies on the occasion of your 60th birthday. Enjoy! We can't wait to see what's next.

Abbreviations

General

ANE	ancient Near East
BIN	Babylonian Inscriptions in the Collection of James B. Nies
d.	died
DN	divine name
EA	El-Amarna tablet
Heb.	Hebrew
JPS(V)	Jewish Publication Society (Version)
K	tablets in the Kouyunjik collection of the British Museum
KJV	King James Version
LXX	Septuagint
MT	Masoretic Text
NBC	Nies Babylonian Collection, Yale University
NEB	New English Bible
NIV	New International Version
NJB	New Jerusalem Bible
NKJV	New King James Version
NRSV	New Revised Standard Version
RSV	Revised Standard Version

Reference Works

AB	Anchor Bible
AbB	Altbabylonische Briefe in Umschrift und Übersetzung
ABD	Freedman, D. N., editor. *The Anchor Bible Dictionary.* 6 vols. Garden City, NY: Doubleday, 1992
ARM	Archives royales de Mari
ASOR Dissertation Series	American Schools of Oriental Research Dissertation Series
ASOR Monograph Series	American Schools of Oriental Research Monographs
BAR	*Biblical Archaeology Review*
BASOR	*Bulletin of the American Schools of Oriental Research*
Bib	*Biblica*
BibInt	*Biblical Interpretation*
BR	*Biblical Research*
COD	*Concise Oxford Dictionary*
COS	Hallo, W. W., editor. *The Context of Scripture.* 3 vols. Leiden: Brill, 1997–2003

EncJud	Roth, Cecil, editor. *Encyclopaedia Judaica*. 16 vols. Jerusalem: Keter, 1972
ErIsr	*Eretz-Israel*
GCCI	Dougherty, R. P. *Goucher College Cuneiform Inscriptions*. 2 vols. New Haven: Yale University Press, 1923–33
GKC	Kautzsch, E., editor. *Gesenius' Hebrew Grammar*. Translated by A. E. Cowley. 2nd ed. Oxford: Oxford University Press, 1910
HAT	Handbuch zum Alten Testament
HSM	Harvard Semitic Monographs
IBHS	Waltke, B. K., and O'Connor, M. *An Introduction to Biblical Hebrew Syntax*. Winona Lake, IN: Eisenbrauns, 1990
ICC	International Critical Commentary
IEJ	*Israel Exploration Journal*
JAOS	*Journal of the American Oriental Society*
JBL	*Journal of Biblical Literature*
JM	Joüon, P. *A Grammar of Biblical Hebrew*. Translated and revised by T. Muraoka. Subsidia Biblica 27. Rome: Pontifical Biblical Institute, 2006
JSOT	*Journal for the Study of the Old Testament*
JSOTSup	Journal for the Study of the Old Testament Supplement Series
JSS	*Journal of Semitic Studies*
KTU	Dietrich, M.; Loretz, O.; and Sanmartín, J., editors. *Die Keilalphabetischen Texte aus Ugarit*. Alter Orient und Altes Testament 24. Kevelaer: Butzon & Bercker / Neukirchen-Vluyn: Neukirchener Verlag, 1976
*KTU*²	Dietrich, M.; Loretz, O.; and Sanmartín, J., editors. *Die Keilalphabetischen Texte aus Ugarit*. Alter Orient und Altes Testament 24. Kevelaer: Butzon & Bercker / Neukirchen-Vluyn: Neukirchener Verlag, 1976. 2nd ed.: Dietrich, M.; Loretz, O.; and Sanmartín, J., editors. *The Cuneiform Alphabetic Texts from Ugarit, Ras Ibn Hani, and Other Places*. Münster: Ugarit-Verlag, 1995
OTL	Old Testament Library
RIH	De Rougé, J. *Inscriptions hiéroglyphiques copiées en Égypte*. Études égyptologiques 9–11. Paris: Vieweg, 1877–79
SAA	State Archives of Assyria
SBLDS	Society of Biblical Literature Dissertation Series
UT	Gordon, C. H. *Ugaritic Textbook: Texts in Translation, Cuneiform Selections*. Rev. ed. Analecta Orientalia 38. Rome: Pontifical Biblical Institute, 1998
VT	*Vetus Testamentum*
VTSup	Vetus Testamentum Supplements
ZAW	*Zeitschrift für die Alttestamentliche Wissenschaft*
ZDMG	*Zeitschrift der deutschen morgenlandischen Gesellschaft*

Introduction

SHAWNA DOLANSKY

Northeastern University

It is fairly easy—and commonplace—to acknowledge the contributions of one's teachers to one's scholarship. It is more difficult to demonstrate the degree of one's appreciation for those contributions. It is impossible to repay the debt owed to the very best of those teachers, the kind who influence far more than outward scholarship, whose impact is felt in the development of who an individual *is* as a scholar and in the model one strives for in the maturity of that scholarship.

To call Dick Friedman "my mentor" would capture only part of what I mean. It is true that he supervised my dissertation; he wrote letters of recommendation; he advised me on my research and on my teaching. Through seven years of graduate school and beyond, Dick has been a counselor, an adviser, and most valuably, a good friend.

I was fortunate to have been able to work with Dick from the beginning of my graduate career. With a background in modern European intellectual history, I quickly became lost in Northwest Semitic grammar, cuneiform inscriptions, and pottery typology. The saving grace of my first year of graduate school was a class Dick offered on his book, *The Disappearance of God*, which had just been published. For my first paper in graduate school, I was able to incorporate old friends (Nietzsche and Freud) with new ones in an essay, "Existentialism in the Epic of Gilgamesh." From there, Dick and I worked together on a joint publication (my first), "After-life: The Biblical Silence."[1] When I expressed to Dick my concern with establishing my scholarship in the fields of literature and religious studies in addition to ancient history and biblical studies, he devised a minor field for me, under his supervision, entitled the Bible in Western Literature. While he encouraged the breadth of my interests, he also emphasized the need to "sweat the fine points" and develop depth in my biblical analyses down to minute grammatical details. Through it all, he provided the model for the kind of scholar I wanted to be.

---

1. In *Judaism in Late Antiquity, Part 4: Death, Life-After-Death, Resurrection and the World-to-Come in the Judaisms of Antiquity* (ed. A. J. Avery-Peck and J. Neusner; Leiden: Brill, 2000).

My admiration for his work goes beyond his clever mind, quick wit, reverence for learning, passion for teaching, and his keen eye for both fine detail and larger patterns. Dick is a synthesizer of information at every level—he can take the Bible apart *and* put it back together—and he recognizes the need for both endeavors. He can direct complex syntheses to scholars in a way that they can respect and then explain these complexities with ease to laypeople. He can study a word in the context of a sentence, a chapter, a source, the Torah and then extend his analysis to rabbinic literature, existentialism, Hollywood movies, modern politics, and Zionism. The relationship of disparate parts to the whole goes beyond his knowledge of each of these contexts. In his depth of analysis, Dick is a model of biblical scholarship; in his breadth, he is a model scholar. Dick demonstrates the need for biblical studies to extend far beyond the scholarly study of the Bible to the teaching of that scholarship to non-scholars and the application of that scholarship outside of academia to real life.

This collection of articles by various scholars from biblical studies and beyond samples a variety of areas in which Dick's scholarship has had an impact: the Hebrew Bible and Source Criticism, of course, but also Israel and the Ancient Near East, Archaeology, Jewish Studies, and Religious Studies in general. And they are written by people on whom Dick's impact as a person is at least equal to his influence on them as a scholar.

A 60th birthday is a convenient excuse to pull together a tribute to Dick—brilliant scholar; extraordinary teacher; successful author; warm, caring, and supportive friend—but the real reason is an attempt on my part to say thank you, Dick, for everything.

Part 1
The Hebrew Bible

Ezekiel and the Levites

JACOB MILGROM

The Hebrew University of Jerusalem

The only pericope on the Levites' duties in the book of Ezekiel is found in 44:9–14.[1] As I will show, this text contains several terminological cruces, which have never failed to give engaged scholars a collective exegetical headache and whose resolution has stood in the way of understanding this pericope. This was my experience in my first book, when I analyzed the role of the Levites in the wake of the Korahite rebellions (Numbers 16–18) and referred to Ezekiel's Levites in several footnotes.[2] Except on one point, I have not changed my mind on their resolution; my perspective, however, has altered. Instead of Ezekiel supporting Numbers, I now suggest that Numbers supports Ezekiel.

In this essay, I will show that the function and placement of the priests and Levites in Ezekiel's temple is based on Num 18:3a and 5a, with one distinction: whereas in Num 3:7, 18:3a the Levites and priests share the guarding duties at the entrance to the court, in Ezekiel's temple the Levites and priests are strictly separated; the Levites are in charge of the outer court and all the gatehouses and the priests are in control of the inner court. This is why the priests are assigned both inner chambers (40:45–46) as stations for their armed guards.

First, I must discuss Ezek 40:45–46, because many commentators have assumed that this text actually concerns the Levites:

זה הלשכה אשר פניה דרך הדרום לכהנים שמרי משמרת הבית והלשכה אשר פניה דרך הצפון לכהנים שמרי משמרת המזבח המה בני־צדוק הקרבים מבני לוי אל־ה׳ לשרתו

This is the chamber that faces south for the priests who perform guard duty[3] for the temple, and the chamber that faces north for the priests who perform guard duty for the altar—they are the descendants of Zadok, who alone of the descendants of Levi have access to Yhwh to serve Him.

---

1. The Levitic land allotment is mentioned in 45:5, 48:11–13, which, however, says nothing about their responsibility.

2. J. Milgrom, *Studies in Levitical Terminology: The Encroacher and the Levite, The Term ʿaboda* (Berkeley: University of California Press, 1970) nn. 41, 43, 226, 310, 316.

3. That שמרי משמרת denotes 'perform guard duty' was demonstrated in my *Studies in Levitical Terminology*, 8–16.

The assignment of the northern chambers to the priests שמרי משמרת הבית 'who perform guard duty for the temple' seems erroneous. These allegedly non-Zadokite priests occur nowhere else. Furthermore, their described function is the *ipsissima verba* for the function of the Levites: שמרי משמרת הבית (44:14a). Hence, some scholars reason, the term לכהנים may be an error for ללוים.[4] One of these scholars, Menahem Haran, retains the MT, claiming that לכהנים betrays a slip of the writer's pen. These priests originally sided with King Manasseh and his idolatrous program.[5] The exile of Jehoiachin (597 B.C.E.) left a shortage of Levites in the Jerusalem temple, which Ezekiel tried to fill by demoting the idolatrous priests to Levites.[6]

These Levite solutions must be rejected out of hand. The two chambers are situated in the inner court to which only priests have access. To ascribe one of them to Levites would undermine the basic premise undergirding the architectural structure of Ezekiel's temple: priest and nonpriests invariably occupy discrete spheres.[7] The MT must be correct.

The way to unravel the exegetical knot of Ezek 40:45–46 is first to tackle the problem of the unattested "non-Zadokite" priests who occupy the northern, south-facing chambers. That problem was, in my opinion, definitively laid to rest by Rodney Duke, who posited that the pronoun המה (v. 46b) refers back to both sets of priests, implying that both priestly groups are Zadokites.[8] I would only add two items for support: note that only the Zadokite priests are granted a land allotment (48:11; cf. 45:4), without mention of any other priestly group. Thus, all the priests granted a place in the temple personnel are Zadokites. Also, two sacred chambers for eating the most sacred sacrifices are assigned to the priests 'אשר קרובים לה 'who have access to YHWH' (42:13), an expression that denotes the Zadokites (40:46; 44:15, 16; 45:4). These two chambers are reminiscent of the two chambers in the inner court for the priestly guards (40:45–46). The conclusion is unavoidable: all priests granted a place among the temple personnel in the inner court are Zadokites.

---

4. Even most recently R. Kasher, *Ezekiel*, vol. 2, chaps. 25–48 (Tel Aviv: Am Oved, 2004) 797 (Hebrew).

5. M. Haran, *Temples and Temple Service in Israel* (Oxford: Clarendon, 1978) 104–5. Haran's theory must be questioned on historical grounds: why didn't Josiah remove these idolatrous priests—the more so since they allegedly served in the Jerusalem temple? Moreover, Josiah slaughtered priests of YHWH elsewhere (1 Kgs 13:2; 2 Kgs 23:20)—and they are not even accused of being idolatrous! Would he have not done the same to idolatrous Jerusalem priests?

6. Idem, *Ezekiel: World of the Bible* (Tel Aviv: Revivim,1984) 224–25 (Hebrew).

7. Milgrom, *Studies in Levitical Terminology*, nn. 14, 47.

8. R. K. Duke, "Punishment or Restoration? Another Look at the Levites of Ezekiel 44.6–16," *JSOT* 40 (1988) 61–81, esp. 75.

Ezekiel specifies or alludes to these priests as Zadokites (he probably was one) because in his view the Zadokites were in the main loyal to the priestly tradition (despite 22:26). However, the non-Zadokite priests in the countryside allowed idolatrous elements to penetrate into their cults, and hence, they would have been excluded from Ezekiel's temple.

The next problem was alluded to above: the Levites are assigned the same function as the priests שמרי משמרת הבית 'who perform guard duty for the temple' (44:14a; cf. 45:5). The resolution of this problem, I aver, lies in realizing that the term בית (lit., 'house') means two different things in 40:45 and 44:14. In the architectural chaps. 40–42, הבית refers only to the temple building (21 times). The meaning "temple grounds/sacred precinct/*temenos*" appears beginning with chap. 43. Thus, 40:45 refers to the *priestly* cordon responsible for guarding the temple building (including the altar and inner court, see below) whereas 44:14 refers to the Levitic cordon responsible for guarding the temple gatehouses and the outer court.[9]

But why is there a need for two priestly cordons, one for the temple building and one for the altar (40:45–46), and correspondingly for two priestly chambers for eating their meals and exchanging their clothing (42:13–14)? The answer comes to light after examining two priestly pentateuchal verses:

אך אל־כלי הקדש ואל־המזבח 'to the *sanctuary* vessels and to the *altar*' (Num 18:3b)

משמרת הקדש ואת משמרת המזבח 'guarding the *sanctuary* and guarding the *altar*' (Num 18:5a)

As I noted in 1970, P postulates two areas, hence the necessity for two cordons for priestly guard duty—the (entrance to) the sanctuary (and its sancta) and the altar (and the inner court).[10] Thus, Ezekiel, who bases the reconstruction of his temple on the priestly, pentateuchal prototype (Num 18:1–7), also prescribes two priestly cordons of guards for precisely the same area—the sanctuary building and the altar.

---

9. I. M. Duguid, *Ezekiel and the Leaders of Israel* (Leiden: Brill, 1994) 88 argues that just as the priests are overseers (more precisely, "guards") of the קדש 'sancta' (Num 18:53) and the same term קדש is used for the guardianship of the Levites (Num 3:32), the same fluidity is evidenced with the term בית in Ezek 40:45 and 44:14, the former verse referring to the responsibility of the priests and the latter referring to the Levites. His conclusion is correct but for the wrong reasons. In Num 3:32, Kohatite Levites carry the קדש 'sancta' (v. 3) on the wilderness march. But once the camp rests, the sancta revert to the charge of the priests. Thus, the term קדש does not change in meaning. The Kohatite Levites are given a higher, holier status than the rest of the Levites (cf. Num 18:1) only during the movement of the camp. Besides, one cannot reason from Numbers (P) to Ezekiel: P does not indulge in protean terminology.

10. Milgrom, *Studies in Levitical Terminology*, 14 n. 47.

Thus, there is no conflict between 40:45–46 and 44:14. The latter, which speaks of the Levites as שמרי משמרת הבית (or משרתים את הבית 'who serve the sacred precint/*temenos*', 44:11; 45:4; 46:24), refers only to the Levites' guard duty in the temple gatehouses and Levitic assistance with the laity's animal sacrifices (slaughtering them) in the outer court. In sum, the Levites are not mentioned either by error or design in 40:45–46. This passage deals only with the priestly guards in the inner court. We can now turn to 44:9–14, the only pericope dealing with the Levitic custodial responsibility in the sacred precinct.

My analysis of 44:9–14 begins with a translation, followed by select terminological annotations and discussion.

9 כה־אמר אדני ה' כל־בן־נכר ערל לב וערל בשר לא יבוא אל מקדשי לכל־בן־נכר
אשר בתוך בני ישראל:
10 כי אם־הלוים אשר רחקו מעלי בתעות ישראל [אשר תעו] מעלי אחרי גלוליהם
ונשאו עונם:
11 והיו במקדשי משרתים פקדות אל־שערי הבית ומשרתים את־הבית המה ישחטו
את־העלה ואת־הזבח לעם והמה יעמדו לפניהם לשרתם:
12 יען אשר ישרתו אותם לפני גלוליהם והיו לבית־ישראל למכשול עון על־כן נשאתי
ידי עליהם נאם אדני ה' ונשאו עונם:
13 ולא־יגשו אלי לכהן לי ולגשת על־כל־קדשי אל קדשי הקדשים ונשאו כלמתם
ותועבותם אשר עשו:
14 ונתתי אותם שמרי משמרת הבית לכל עבדתו ולכל אשר יעשה בו:

9 This has the Lord YHWH declared: No foreigner, uncircumcised of heart[11] and uncircumcised of flesh, may enter my sanctuary—including[12] all foreigners who reside among the descendants of Israel.[13]

10 Rather[14] the Levites (shall enter) who defected from me when the Israelites strayed from me [who strayed from me][15] after their idols and they bore/shall bear their punishment.

11 They shall be inside my sanctuary performing guard duty at the gatehouses of the sacred precinct and serving the sacred precinct. They shall be the ones to slaughter[16] the burnt offering and the

---

11. Foreigners are categorically outside of the covenant community. Hence they are not *spiritually* ("uncircumcised of heart") and *physically* ("uncircumcised of flesh") identified as Israelites.

12. For the rendering of לכל, see my *Studies in Levitical Terminology*, 64 n. 237.

13. Even the children of גרים 'foreign residents', whom you have bought, retain the status of permanent slaves (Lev 25:25–26). So, too, even the descendants of resident foreigners retain their foreign status and are banned from entering the sanctuary.

14. כי אם is a strong adversative following a negative sentence, GKC §163a / p. 500.

15. אשר תעו is most likely a gloss. It is omitted in the LXX.

16. Slaughtering the sacrificial animal is the duty of the offerer (Lev 1:5, 3:2). So is flaying, quartering, and washing the carcass (Lev 1:6, 9). Since the slaughtering of the עלה 'burnt offering' was performed inside the inner (northern) gate, it seems probable that the other acts performed on the carcass—flaying, quartering, and washing—were also

well-being offering for the people and it is they who shall attend to them by serving them.

12 Because they (the Levites) used to serve them before the (the people's) idols, which were iniquitous stumbling blocks for the house of Israel, I therefore swore an oath against them—the declaration of the Lord YHWH—and they bore/shall bear their punishment.

13 They shall have no access to me to perform priestly duties for me, nor have access to my sacred or most sacred offerings.[17] They shall bear their shame and the abominations they perpetrated.

14 And I shall appoint them as guards of the sacred precinct (namely, the outer court and the gatehouses), responsible for all its maintenance and all work that is done inside it.

As was the case with 40:45–46, the precise understanding of 44:9–14 will depend on the decipherment of its terminology. The key terms are בֶּן־נֵכר, מקדשי, בית, and ונשאו עונם.

1. בֶּן־נֵכר 'foreigners'. This term has been identified with Gibeonites (Josh 9:27); Solomon's Canaanite slaves (1 Kgs 9:20), referred to as Solomon's slaves among the returnees to Zion (Ezra 2:55, Neh 7:57); the נתינים (Ezra 2:43–54, Neh 7:47–56); and others.[18] I prefer to identify them with the Carites[19] (2 Kgs 11:4) who served as mercenary guards of the palace, and since the temple served as a royal chapel, it was a simple matter for the Carites to take up position there. It is only natural that the illegitimate guards of Solomon's temple/palace, the Carites, should be replaced by legitimate, Torah ordained guards, the Levites.[20]

2. מקדשי 'my sacred precinct'.[21] Only this meaning is attested in Ezekiel, in which this plastic term either denotes "the sacred precinct" of the priests (i.e., the inner court) or "the sacred precinct" of the laity, including

---

done by the Levites. Since the slaughtering of the well-being offering occurred in the outer court, there was no difficulty for all the other preliminary sacrificial acts to be carried out by the offerer.

17. עולה וזבח (lit., 'the burnt and well-being offerings') is the common expression for all the blood sacrifices, including the חטאת 'purification offering' and the אשם 'reparation offering'. Originally, I presume, the עלה 'burnt offering' was the sole expiatory sacrifice, hence the origin of the turn עלה וזבח (Lev 7:8; Josh 22:26, 28, 29; 2 Kgs 5:17; Jer 7:22; 17:28; Ezek 40:42). This last citation (Ezek 40:42) proves that this idiom is an abbreviation of all the blood sacrifices, because three verses earlier (40:39) the same list includes the עולה, the חטאת, and the אשם. This idiom is also found in Num 15:3, 5, but the subject there is the votive and freewill sacrifices, which preclude expiatory sacrifices (i.e., the חטאת or the אשם).

18. See Milgrom, *Studies in Levitical Terminology*, 9.

19. Ibid., nn. 78, 149.

20. Ibid., 9.

21. I discussed this in ibid., 78, 149, where I demonstrated that מקדש in P never means the sanctuary building but only 'the sacred precinct' or 'the sacred objects'.

the Levites (i.e., המקדש החיצון 'the sacred area of the outer [court]' 44:1). In any case, the term מקדש never refers to the temple building.

3. הבית 'the temple grounds, *temenos*' (11, 14). Above, I established that בית in this pericope refers, not to the temple building (its exclusive meaning in chaps. 40–42), but to the temple grounds, the *temenos*—although not in their entirety. The Levites, like the laity, have no access to the inner court, the exclusive domain of the priests. There may be a hairline difference between the Levites and the laity: the Levites have access to the northern inner gatehouse, where they slaughter the laity's most holy sacrifices. But this locus (rather than its function) is no innovation. As temple guards, they are stationed in all the gatehouses. Indeed, their function is defined with precision: משרתים פקדות אל־שערי הבית ומשרתים את־הבית 'performing guard duty at the gatehouses of the sacred precincts and serving the sacred precinct' (44:11a). The latter duty refers to slaughtering the sacrificial animals (44:11b), cooking the meat of the well-being offering (46:24), and probably to other minor ways the Levites could be of assistance to the worshiping laity (44:11b). All this is subsumed under the locus בית, the outer court and the gatehouses.[22]

4. ונשאו עונם (44:10b, 12b). There are two justifiable renderings of this term.

A. "*They (the Levites) will bear their (own) punishment.*" The idiom נשא עון, in which עון means punishment, occurs 27 times (Exod 28:38, 43; Lev 5:1, 6, 17; 7:18; 10:17; 17:16; 19:8, 17; 20:17, 19; Num 5:31; 14:34; 18:1, 23; 30:15; Isa 33:24; Ezek 4:4, 5, 6; 14:10; 24:23; 44:10, 12; Hos 4:8). The "punishment" here is explained twice, following the idiom ונשאו עונם. The Levites are assigned the perilous task of guarding the sanctuary (vv. 11, 14) against all unauthorized incursions, advertent and inadvertent alike. If they fail, the penalty is death by divine agency.[23] Moreover, it falls on the entire Levitic cordon. As for the intrusive prohibition not to serve as priests (v. 13), it is not a punishment, as claimed by the school of Wellhausen,[24] but a statement of the responsibility of the Levites, as based on Num 18:3aβ (see no. 2, below). Indeed, it must be acknowledged that Ezekiel grounds his provisions for the Levites on Num 18:1–7, 23, as follows:

---

22. For this meaning of בית, see 43:11, 12 (2), 21; 44:5, 11, 14; 45:5, 20; 46:24; 48:21; see ibid., 14 n. 47.

23. See my *Leviticus 17–22* (AB 3a; New York: Doubleday, 2000) 1488–90. Whereas the encroacher is put to death by the armed Levitic guards, the failed Levitic guards obviously cannot be killed by human agency, but only by God; see my *Studies in Levitical Terminology*, 21 n. 2; idem, *Numbers* (Philadelphia: Jewish Publication Society, 1990) 342–43, 423–24.

24. J. Wellhausen, *Prolegomena to the History of Ancient Israel* (trans. J. S. Black and A. Menzies; New York: Meridian, 1957) 122–24.

1. The division of the priests into two groupings (40:45–46) is based on ושמרת את משמרת הקדש ואת משמרת המזבח 'you (the priests) shall perform guard duty of the sanctuary and guard duty of the altar' (Num 18:5a), as shown above.

2. The prohibition against Levitic access to the sacred and most sacred objects and to officiate on the altar (44:13a) is based on אך אל־כלי הקדש ואל־המזבח לא יקרבו 'but to the sanctuary vessels and to the altar they (the Levites) shall have no access' (Num 18:3aβ).

3. Levitic guard duty (44:14) is founded on ושמרו משמרתך ומשמרת כל־האהל 'And they shall perform your guard duty and the guard duty of the entire Tent' (Num 18:3aα; cf. 4aβ).

4. The banning of foreigners (בני נכר) from the sanctuary (44:9) is grounded on וזר לא־יקרב אליכם 'the unauthorized should not encroach on you' (Num 18:4b).

5. The priestly guard duty of the inner court (44:15a, 16b) is based on תשמרו את־כהנתכם לכל־דבר המזבח 'you shall guard your priestly obligation in everything regarding the altar' (Num 18:7a).

6. The Levitic responsibility for encroachment upon the *temenos* by the unauthorized (foreigners on the outer court and Israelite laity—including Levites—on the inner court) is founded on והם ישאו עונם 'and they (the Levites) will bear their (own) punishment' (Num 18:23aβ). As pointed out by Duke,[25] the responsibility of the Levites to guard the sanctuary is commensurate with the role of the watchman/prophet in Ezek 3:16–21. Both bear the penalty of death if they fail as guards. Thus guard duty (vv. 11, 14), indeed, bears a punishment. The Levites need be eternally vigilant—their lives are at stake.

However, Ezekiel does not slavishly imitate his Priestly (P) precedent. In two matters he flatly reverses the explicit Laws of P. First, P ordains that priests and Levites share the guarding duty ושמרו משמרתם 'they (the Levites) will perform your (the priestly) guard duty' (Num 18:3aα). The custody of the Tabernacle was neatly divided between the two sacred orders: priests on the inside, Levites on the outside and *both at the entrance*. Ezekiel rejected the latter; priests and laity were sharply divided, and contact between them was strictly forbidden. Priests controlled the inner court, an eight-stepped platform above the outer court where the Levites held sway in the outer court, as well as in all the gatehouses.[26]

---

25. See Duke, "Punishment or Restoration?" 66.

26. However, the priests themselves obviously use the Levite-controlled gates. Therefore, it must be assumed that the prohibition against contact between the two applies

A more radical change in the status of the Levites is contained in Ezekiel's prescription that the Levites (and the priests) are to be allocated territory (48:13–14) when the holy land is redivided among all the twelve tribes. This constitutes an unqualified contradiction of the express prohibition against the Levites (and the priests) possessing any inheritable land (Num 18:20, 24b).

This reading of ונשאו עונם resolves a number of difficulties: (1) It is no longer necessary to follow the erroneous interpretation of Ezek 44:13a, namely, that the prohibition against the Levites officiating (on the altar) implies that hitherto they were priests;[27] Ezekiel is merely applying the Levitic prohibition of Num 18:3bα (no. 2, above). (2) As demonstrated above, there is no need to posit a missing Levitic group in 40:45; Num 18:5a shows that there was a priestly tradition of two groupings of priests in the Tabernacle. (3) The exclusive right and responsibility of the priests to guard the inner court (44:15a, 16b) is not Ezekiel's innovation; rather, it is grounded in Num 18:7a (no. 5, above). (4) The presence of (probably God-fearing) foreign guards (בני נכר) in the sanctuary (cf. 2 Kgs 11:6) may not be a sin in itself but an exegetical extension of the זר 'unauthorized' (Num 18:4b; no. 4, above). (5) The Levites' punishment for their failure to guard the sanctuary (ונשאו עונם, 44:10bβ, 12bβ) is not for their complicity in Israel's idol worship, but the automatic application of their responsibility in guarding the Tabernacle, as explicitly stated in P; namely, they will take responsibility for their errors, והם ישאו עונם 'and they (the Levites) will bear their (own) punishment' (Num 18:23aβ).[28]

B. *"They (the Levites) bore their own punishment."*[29]   The verb נשא occurs either as an imperfect or as a perfect attached to a *waw*. The context invariably bears a future sense; hence, the *waw* is sequential. There is one excep-

---

when the priests are officiating, namely, when they are wearing their sacred and *contagious* vestments. The gate entrances would only be used on entering and exiting, namely when they are not officiating.

27. This is the case either of countrywide small sanctuaries, high places (see Wellhausen, *Prolegomenon*, 124–26), or in the Jerusalem temple (Haran, *Temples*).

28. These strictures also strike at the rendering I offered in *Studies in Levitical Terminology*, 22–32, "They (the Levites) will bear their (the Israelites') punishment." Besides this, I was subsequently convinced by Duguid's argument (*Ezekiel and the Leaders of Israel*, 77 n. 114), who follows R. Whybray, *Thanksgiving for a Liberated Prophet: An Interpretation of Isaiah 53* (JSOTSup 4; Sheffield: University of Sheffield, 1978) 31–57 that the prevention of encroachment is the sin of the Levite guards, and by the rule of Occam's razor this is the simplest and, hence, the most accurate reading. Indeed, I admitted as much when I wrote that the principle "was not vicariousness" (*Studies in Levitical Terminology*, 32).

29. To the best of my knowledge, only M. Fishbane (*Biblical Interpretation in Ancient Israel* [Oxford: Clarendon, 1985] 134) adopts this rendering but without annotation or discussion.

tion: the context of Ezek 44:10, 12 is perfect. It speaks of Israel's past sins, before they were exiled, when they engaged in idol worship. Hence, the initial *waw* is not consecutive but copulative, referring to the time when the Levites bore their punishment, namely, when they were exiled together with their people. Thus, both Israel and the Levites were punished and restored, Israel to its land and the Levites to their former position (according to P) as temple guards.

Therefore, the idiom ונשאו עונם is not a statement about the future, declaring that the Levites will be punished for aiding their fellow countrymen to worship idols. The Levites have paid for their idolatrous collusion. And just as God will restore Israel to its land where they will allot the land among the twelve tribes more equitably (45:1–8, 48:1–29) than in the past (Joshua 15–21), so God will fulfill for the Levites the role that he set out for them in the priestly tradition—to be the temple guards (Num 18:3a, 4a) and assistants to the lay worshipers (Num 16:9). Moreover, Ezekiel is basing himself on a priestly, pentateuchal precedent: the Levite rebel chieftains led by Korah were slain by God (Num 16:35), and the Levites themselves were assigned perilous guard duties in the sanctuary (Num 18:3a, 4a).[30] The Levites' work load, however, undergoes a slight change. They will supplant the lay worshipers as slaughterers of the sacrificial animal, and in stark contradiction to Num 18:24, they will be granted a block of contiguous inheritable property for themselves and their descendants.

Thus, there are two viable interpretations of the idiom ונשאו עונם (Ezek 44:10b, 12b). Each may be subject to challenge. Both, however, share a common basis, which, I aver, is beyond question: Ezekiel construed the function of the Levites and their distinction from the priests largely on the basis of the priestly tradition embodied in Numbers 18. Thus, the Levites were not former priests who were demoted because they colluded with the people in the idol worship. The Levites are merely assuming the tasks assigned to them by the Priestly tradition (P) as guards in the sanctuary (Num 18:3a, 4a). Because Ezekiel posits absolute separation between priests and nonpriests, he takes pains to confine the Levites within the outer court and in the gatehouses. The laity is restricted even further to the outer court, with no access to the gatehouses of the inner court; its erstwhile right of slaughtering its sacrificial animals is transferred to the Levites, and the slaughtering takes place either inside or below the (northern) inner gate. This cultic change, though slight, shows that Ezekiel was not slavishly chained to his priestly tradition. His relative independence of imagination and thought can be demonstrated further by his divergence from

---

30. Cf. also S. L. Cook, "Innerbiblical Interpretation in Ezekiel 44 and the History of Israel's Priesthood," *JBL* 114 (1995) 199.

the tradition, such as in the allotment of land to the Levitic tribe (48:13–14) and in the right granted resident aliens (גרים) to own and bequeath landed property (47:22–23). Thus, Ezekiel was not engaged in abstract hermeneutics when he based the function of the Levites (and the priests) on the theoretical prescriptions of Numbers 18. Rather, he applied himself creatively and innovatively to these priestly precedents as the basis—but not the totality—of his vision of the Levitic (and priestly) functions in the temple.[31]

---

31. See Milgrom, *Studies in Levitical Terminology*, nn. 40–41, 47.

Framing Aaron:
Incense Altar and Lamp Oil in
the Tabernacle Texts

CAROL MEYERS

Duke University

I. Introduction

Most of the second half of the book of Exodus contains information about the construction of the tabernacle in the wilderness. These tabernacle materials are generally understood to comprise two discrete sections. A detailed set of instructions for the fabrication and consecration of the structure itself, all its appurtenances, and an elaborate set of priestly vestments appears in chaps. 25–31. Then, following several chapters (32–34) recounting the golden calf incident, chaps. 35–40 relate the process of amassing the requisite materials, constructing the portable shrine with its furnishings and accoutrements, and dedicating the shrine. These two blocks of materials are variously identified as "command section," "instructions," "directions," or "prescriptive texts" followed by "fulfillment section," "execution," or "descriptive texts."[1]

Since the mid-19th century, most critical biblical scholarship has followed Wellhausen in accepting the main arguments put forward earlier by Popper, who understood the descriptive texts to be a more or less mechanical copying, in a later stage of development by a different author, of the prescriptive texts.[2] Traditional literary and historical-critical approaches generally tended to see the tabernacle accounts as late priestly documents

---

1. See B. A. Levine, "The Descriptive Tabernacle Texts of the Pentateuch," *JAOS* 85 (1965): 307–18; C. Houtman, *Exodus* (trans. J. Rebel and S. Woudstra; Historical Commentary on the Old Testament; 4 vols.; Kampen: Kok / Leuven: Peeters, 1993–2002) 3:308. Although the "descriptive texts" section may in fact be better understood as containing parts of a longer sequence (see n. 3 below), I will continue to use the prescriptive-descriptive terminology for convenience.

2. J. Popper, *Der biblische Bericht über die Stiftshütte: ein Beitrag zur Geschichte der Composition und Diaskeue des Pentateuch* (Leipzig: Hunger, 1862). See the review of literary and traditio-historical analysis in B. Childs, *The Book of Exodus: A Critical Theological Commentary* (OTL; Philadelphia: Westminster, 1974) 329–37.

with no basis in early Israelite tradition. However, such views have subsequently been modified significantly as the antiquity of many of the terms, objects, and practices that appear in the tabernacle materials has become evident. Moreover, traditional approaches have been challenged by the recognition that these blocks of material in Exodus are also part of a larger multi-stage sequence of sanctuary building that extends into Leviticus 8–10 and Numbers 6–7; and it is virtually the same as patterns found in Ugaritic and Mesopotamian building narratives.[3]

Even though the tabernacle texts in Exodus may be part of a larger sequence, the parallel nature of the prescriptive and descriptive sections remains noteworthy and has evoked extensive scholarly comment with respect to the similarities and differences between the two sections. Allowing for the variants that are contingent on the different character of the two sections—such as the change in persons, from second person "you" in the instructions to the third person "they" in the execution[4]—the narratives are strikingly similar. Yet there are divergences. Perhaps the most prominent one is the organization of the materials. The prescriptive section begins with the interior furnishings, moves outward to the structure itself, and then continues to the altar and courtyard; this is followed by information about priestly vestments, and other directions come in what seems to be an addendum. The organizing principle is the degree of holiness; that is, the most holy features are described first, and those in the least holy area—those among the concentric zones of holiness that characterize tabernacle space—come last.[5] In contrast, the descriptive texts follow an architectural or construction logic: the structure comes first, followed by the furnishings and then the surrounding court.

Another significant yet often overlooked difference is the greater interest in the descriptive section in the priesthood in general and in the person of Aaron in particular.[6] This feature will figure in the discussion below, in part 3.

When considering the literary and historical character of the parallel sections, one of the most difficult problems is the location of the incense

3. V. (A.) Hurowitz, "The Priestly Account of Building the Tabernacle," *JAOS* 105 (1985) 21–30; see especially the chart on p. 24. According to this view, chaps. 25–31 are part of a first stage (beginning in 24:15) that contains divine commands, and chaps. 35–40 are seen as one of six (or seven) additional stages of tabernacle building, with the last three (or four) stages appearing largely in Leviticus and Numbers.

4. Other such technical differences are enumerated in Houtman, *Exodus*, 3:308–16.

5. Graded holiness and its spatial correlates are discussed in detail in M. Haran, *Temples and Temple Service in Ancient Israel* (Oxford: Clarendon, 1978; reprinted, Winona Lake, IN: Eisenbrauns, 1985) and P. P. Jenson, *Graded Holiness: A Key to the Priestly Conception of the World* (JSOTSup 106; Sheffield: Sheffield Academic Press, 1992).

6. See my *Exodus* (New Cambridge Bible Commentary; New York: Cambridge, 2005) 225.

altar. As one of the three pieces of golden furniture (along with the lamp-stand and the offering table) in the outer sanctum, it holds pride of place, being positioned directly in front of the curtain (*pārōket*) separating the outer sanctum from the holiest zone where the ark, the holiest object of all, is situated (Exod 40:5). Accordingly, in the section reporting the execution of the instructions, the incense altar appears sequentially after the two associated appurtenances: the table in 37:10–16, the lampstand in 37:17–24, and then the incense altar in 37:25–28.[7] Also, in several other priestly passages (Exod 39:36–38; 40:4–5, 22–27; Num 4:7–11) the incense altar appears together with the table and the lampstand. However, the prescriptive texts do not include the incense altar in that sequence, that is, immediately following instructions for the table and lampstand in Exod 25:23–40. Rather, as shown in the chart below,[8] it appears in 30:1–10 in what seems to be an addendum (chaps. 30 and 31) that comes after the directions for consecrating the priests and the structure. Those directions in turn appear following the instructions for making the tabernacle structure, the altar and the surrounding court, and the priestly vestments. Instructions for the incense altar are thus at considerable remove from the instructions for its associated appurtenances.

The seeming displacement of the directions for making the incense altar from the passage reporting the golden furnishings in the prescriptive texts has been the subject of extensive scrutiny. Indeed, scholars attempting to understand the logic of the arrangement of materials in the tabernacle texts have often viewed the apparently anomalous position of the instructions for making the golden altar as an important issue. However, it is also possible that the position of the instructions for the incense altar is not anomalous at all but rather is the result of a rationale other than the one insisting that it should be grouped with the table and the lampstand in both sections of the tabernacle texts. Such other rationales will be reviewed here. I will then add one modest proposal to them in honor of Richard Friedman's tabernacle wisdom, one of his many significant contributions to biblical studies.

II. Theories about the (Dis)Placement
of the Incense Altar

Wellhausen's hypothesis about the absence of the incense altar from the expected table-lampstand-incense altar sequence, like his ideas about

---

7. Note that the Septuagint omits the incense altar in its translation of Exodus 37, perhaps to balance its absence from chap. 25, but the presence of the incense altar is assumed in the Septuagint's rendering of 40:26; see D. W. Gooding, *The Account of the Tabernacle* (Cambridge: University Press, 1959) 66–69, 76.

8. Adapted from table in my *Exodus*, 225.

Tabernacle Texts

	Prescriptive Section	Descriptive Section
Introduction		
materials	25:1–9	35:4–29
Main section		
ark — MOST HOLY	25:10–22	37:1–9
table — HOLY	25:23–30	37:10–16
lampstand — HOLY	25:31–40	37:17–24
[*incense altar — HOLY — expected place?*]		[*37:25–28*]
structure — over MOST HOLY + HOLY	26:1–37	36:8–38
altar — LESS HOLY	27:1–8	38:1–7
court structure — around LESS HOLY	27:9–19	38:9–20
oil for light [out of place?] — HOLY	27:20–21	[35:8, 28]
vestments for priests	28:1–43	39:1–31
inventory of work and metals	—	38:21–31
Consecration of priests and structure		
Addendum?		
incense altar [out of place?] — HOLY	30:1–10	37:25–28
census ritual	30:11–16	—
laver — LESS HOLY	30:17–21	38:8; 40:7, 30
anointing oil and incense	30:22–38	37:29
appointment of artisans	31:1–11	35:30–36:7
Sabbath observance	31:12–17	35:1–3
[Completion	—	39:32–43]
[Summary: erection and installation	—	40:1–38]

Sequence of information, indicating parallel materials, in the tabernacle texts of Exodus according to the order in chaps. 25–31.

the origins and date of P, long dominated critical biblical scholarship. Chapters 30–31, in his view, contained miscellaneous cultic information and were a later addition to chaps. 25–31. He claimed that the tabernacle was modeled after the Solomonic temple, which would not have had an incense altar (despite the presence of an incense altar, considered a secondary interpolation, in 1 Kgs 7:48) because such items were thought to be cultic developments of the late Preexilic or Exilic Periods. The incense altar was thus absent from the original P but added in chap. 30 by P's successor (P^s) well into the Second Temple period.[9]

These views about the incense altar as well as other aspects of Wellhausen's theories about the tabernacle and P have of course been modified or contested during the course of the 20th century.[10] The archaeological evidence for incense altars dating to the Iron II period now refutes the argument that such items must be later and lends authenticity to both the tabernacle and temple accounts.[11] It also calls into question the traditional scholarly view that the "proper place" for the incense altar in the prescriptive texts is in Exodus 25.[12] If the incense altar as described in Exodus 37 is deemed original to the set of furnishings in P's conception of the interior of the tabernacle, and if those two chapters (25 and 37) are part of a literary whole rather than two separate parts in a long sequence of development, then the omission of the golden incense altar from Exodus 25 implies the presence of a different logic than scholars have assumed. Granted, the governing concept of the prescriptive texts is not the logic of construction, as is the case for the descriptive ones; but holiness as the organizing principle may not be sufficiently fluid by itself to accommodate the omission of the incense table from the section on golden furnishings.

In a significant departure from the view that the instructions for the incense altar in 30:1–10 are an afterthought or displacement, Milgrom asserts that functionality is the determining factor.[13] He divides the descriptive texts into two parts: 26:1–27:19, a blueprint for the tabernacle's construction, and 27:20–30:38, the tabernacle in operation. He notes that the incense altar is described functionally—that is, the instructions for making it (vv. 1–6) are immediately followed by instructions on where it is to be placed (v. 6) and how it is to be used (vv. 7–11). For this reason, he suggests that it is placed in the second part of the instructions because it belongs

---

9. J. Wellhausen, *Prolegomena to the History of Ancient Israel* (repr., Cleveland: World, 1957; German original, 1878) 63–64. See also B. Baentsch, *Exodus-Leviticus-Numbers* (Handkommentar zum Alten Testament 1/2; Göttingen: Vandenhoeck & Ruprecht, 1903) 258–60.

10. See the summary in R. Friedman, "Tabernacle," *ABD* 6:224–25.

11. See, e.g., S. Gitin, "New Incense Altars from Ekron: Context, Typology, and Function," *ErIsr* 23 (Biran Volume; 1992) 43–39; idem, "Incense Altars from Ekron, Israel and Judah: Context and Typology," *ErIsr* 20 (Yadin Volume; 1989) 52–67. M. Haran disputes the identification of these artifacts as incense altars ("Incense Altars—Are They?" *Biblical Archaeology Today, 1990: Proceedings of the Second International Congress on Biblical Archaeology, June-July, 1990* [Jerusalem: Israel Exploration Society and the Israel Academy of Sciences and Humanities, 1993] 237–47), but the consensus holds to the incense-altar identification.

12. As expressed by M. Noth, *Exodus: A Commentary* (trans. J. S. Bowden; Philadelphia: Westminster, 1962; German original, 1959) 234.

13. J. Milgrom, *Leviticus 1–16* (AB 3; New York: Doubleday, 1991) 236–37.

with a set of directions for cultic actions that are done twice daily by the high priest: 27:20–21 deals with bringing lamp oil and kindling light on a regular (*tāmîd*) basis, 28:1–29:37 provides details about the investiture of the priest(s) who will carry out this ritual, and 29:38–42 gives directions for the *tāmîd* offering. Similarly, he notes, the laver and anointing oil are also "omitted" from their "logical" place because the instructions for making them include information about how they are to be used; thus they appear in 30:17–21 and 30:22–38 respectively, after the instructions for the incense altar.

Although the functionality principle argued by Milgrom is compelling, the supposed displacement of the incense stand may reflect another logic, one that takes into account both the holiness ideology of the tabernacle texts and functionality, albeit functionality of a different kind. Haran has amply demonstrated that the prescriptive texts reflect the gradations of holiness that characterized ancient shrines and temples in the ancient Near East.[14] As already indicated, this would imply that the incense altar, as part of the middle zone of the three zones (most holy, holy, less holy), is in fact out of place in the prescriptive texts because it is not grouped with the other two items of the middle zone of "holy" items. However, one other significant difference—beside the presence of directions for using the incense altar and absence of such directions for the lampstand or table— between the instructions for the incense altar and those for the other two appurtenances of the holy zone must be noted. For both the table and lampstand, directions for the vessels and utensils to be used with them are appended to the instructions for these items: for the table, Exod 25:29 = 37:16; and for the lampstand, Exod 25:38–39 = 37:23–24. Also, the instructions in Num 4:9–12 for packing and transporting the vessels of the middle zone include information about the associated vessels of the table and lampstand but not the incense altar.[15]

Why might the utensils have been omitted from the information about the incense altar in both Exodus 30 and 37, especially given the fact that vessels of some sort would have been necessary for the use of the altar as directed in 30:7–10? In another article, I suggested that the special function of the golden altar in relation to principles of holiness must be considered.[16] The incense altar is involved not only in the daily ritual (with incense to be offered on it every morning and evening when the lamps

---

14. See n. 5.

15. Contra J. Milgrom, who suggests that the phrase "all the service vessels" in v. 12 includes the vessels used with the incense altar; see his *Numbers* (JPS Torah Commentary; Philadelphia: Jewish Publication Society, 1990) 27.

16. C. Meyers, "Realms of Sanctity: The Case of the 'Misplaced' Incense Altar in the Tabernacle Texts of Exodus," *Texts, Temples, and Traditions: A Tribute to Menahem Haran* (ed. M. V. Fox et al.; Winona Lake, IN: Eisenbrauns, 1996) 33–46.

were tended) but also in the annual purgation ritual.[17] The latter involves the transfer of blood, which was deemed "most holy to the LORD" (v. 10). The blood was collected as part of a ritual act performed in the less holy zone, the courtyard, and transferred to the holy space directly in front of the ark, which is in the holiest zone. The basins (*mizrāqîm* or *mizrāqôt*) used for bringing blood from the bronze courtyard altar into the tabernacle so that blood could be smeared on the incense altar's horns were likely made of bronze; this means that a vessel made of less holy material would be brought into holy space.[18] As such, it would transgress the zones of sanctity that characterize the tabernacle. In addition, because its role involved a "most holy" substance and because the incense smoke penetrated "most holy" space of the inner sanctum in order to form a cloud over the ark and its cover (Lev 16:12–13), it also had a connection with the holiest zone, which was not the case for either the lampstand or the table.

Thus the incense altar seems to have had an anomalous position with respect to zones of holiness, and perhaps for this reason it does not appear in the expected place in Exodus 25 with the other two golden appurtenances. Its function disrupts the realms of sanctity in the blueprint for the tabernacle; and the prescriptive texts, embodying the concept of graded holiness, consequently present it outside the expected sequence.

Milgrom has objected to this explanation, notably because it involves the claim that the basins were bronze rather than gold.[19] Indeed, it is true that incense was brought inside the inner sanctum in cup-shaped censers, which surely were gold (cf. Num 7:14); and it is inconceivable that a non-golden vessel would be brought into that most holy space with blood for sprinkling on or near the cover of the ark (as in Lev 16:14). However, the atonement rite mentioned in Exodus 30 does not seem to refer to that particular act but rather to blood being brought to the horns of the golden incense altar. In contesting my theory, Milgrom points out that the utensils for the incense altar would have been kept in the outer court rather than with the altar itself, in contrast to vessels for the golden table and lampstand, which were kept with those items; this may have led to a differential treatment of the incense altar. It may be true that the table's golden vessels were kept on it (Exod 25:29), but it is not clear that the golden snuffers and trays for tending the lampstand were set down nearby.

---

17. U. Cassuto (*A Commentary on the Book of* Exodus [trans. I. Abrahams; Jerusalem: Magnes, 1983; Hebrew original 1951] 390) asserts that the inclusion of directions for ritual is why the directions for the incense altar are found in chap. 30 instead of 25.

18. The argument that they were made of bronze involves consideration of details in Zech 9:15, 14:20; 1 Kgs 7:48–50, 15:15; Jer 52:18–19; see Meyers, "Realms of Sanctity," 40–42.

19. J. Milgrom, *Leviticus 23–27: A New Translation with Introduction and Commentary* (AB 3B; New York: Doubleday, 2001) 2083.

III. Another Consideration

Milgrom particularly objects to my claims about the use of a bronze vessel in the annual expiation rite as a source for the placement of the incense altar instructions outside the expected place in Exodus 25. While this objection may not be valid, my earlier claims do need to be modified in another way. The explanation I attached to the putative bronze basin, with respect to the zones of sanctity, did not take into account the fact that instructions for using the altar are included in Exodus 30 but are absent in the directives for the table and lampstand in Exodus 25. That difference, instead of or perhaps in addition to the issue of material and level of sanctity, deserves scrutiny in relation to the role of Aaron.

The prescriptive texts, in contrast to the descriptive ones, manifest great interest in the priesthood and especially in the person of Aaron. The section on priestly vestments, for example, is somewhat more extensive in the prescriptive texts (Exod 28:1–43) than in the descriptive ones (39:1–31). Even more striking is the fact that Aaron's name appears some 16 times in the directions for vestments in Exodus 28 but is virtually absent from the parallel execution section. In the latter (Exodus 39), it appears only twice: once in the introduction, which arguably is part of the inventory that precedes it and not actually part of the vestment passage;[20] and once in reference to the several garments made for his sons as well as for him. Thus Aaron's name does not appear at all in Exodus 39 in relation to the garments made only for him. Moreover, the consecration ceremony of Exodus 29, which follows the vestment section and in which Aaron holds center stage, does not appear at all in the descriptive texts. In contrast, Moses' name appears *seven* times in Exodus 39 but not once in the equivalent vestment section in Exodus 27.

The prominence of Aaron in the prescriptive texts clearly permeates Exodus 28 and 29 and prompts us to attend to what occurs before and after these two Aaronic chapters. Immediately preceding them is a brief unit with various stipulations: the kind of oil to be brought for the lampstand, the place where the light should be kindled (just outside the curtain shielding the ark), and instructions for Aaron and his sons to tend the light "from evening to morning before the Lord" (27:20–21).[21] Immediately following those two chapters is the incense altar passage. After directions for constructing it, its role in the daily and annual ritual is set forth: Aaron is enjoined to offer fragrant incense on it "every morning when he dresses

---

20. Cassuto, *Exodus*, 473.

21. The text refers to a single lamp, perhaps a remnant of an earlier tent-of-meeting tradition incorporated into the tabernacle texts; see my *Exodus*, 232–33 and cf. my *Tabernacle Menorah: A Synthetic Study of a Symbol from the Biblical Cult* (Piscatawny, NJ: Gorgias, 2003; original ed., 1976) 26.

the lamps . . . and when Aaron sets up the lamps in the evening . . ." (30:7–8), and Aaron is then given instructions for the yearly atonement rite. Note that the lamp and incense rituals were performed daily (whereas the weekly bread ritual for the golden table is not mentioned at all in Exodus; cf. Lev 24:5–9) and thus frame the vivid picture of Aaron in Exodus 28 and 29. The mention of "morning" before "evening" in chap. 27 and vice versa in chap. 30 constitutes a chiasm that contributes to the ritual framing of Aaron as chief priest.

In our zeal as scholars to recover the nature and details of the tabernacle, its appurtenances, and its rituals, we sometimes fail to take into consideration the fact that the priesthood and the tabernacle are interrelated concepts in the Priestly sources of the Pentateuch. The complex cultic system set forth in P is as much about priests, what they do, and when they do it, as it is about where they do it and the apparatus and sacrificial items they use. The instructions for building the tabernacle are not simply about the structure and its appurtenances but also about the chief officiant and his daily ritual.

Similarly, we often fail to remind ourselves that our notions of literary structure, the organization of narrative units, and logical sequences may not coincide with the artistry of biblical writers. Thus functionality indeed seems to trump the supposed logic of grouping the holy golden furnishings together in the holiness-oriented directions section, even though they are grouped together in the construction-oriented section, Exodus 37. Milgrom was clearly on the right track in his observations about functionality, whereby the instructions for the incense altar in 30:1–10 should be related to the instructions for lamp oil in 27:20–21 with respect to the *tâmîd* character of the light and incense rituals. But it is also important to account for the insertion of information about the annual expiation offering, which involved vessels and material from the less holy realm and for which the gradations-of-holiness principle is also important. Finally, the extensive information inserted between the lamp oil and incense altar instructions about Aaron's vestments and consecration (chaps. 28 and 29) must be taken into account. These materials can be understood as part of the Aaronic interest of the writer. By framing them with directions for the lamp oil and the incense altar, the writer signifies the integral nature of priesthood, structure, and ritual in the tabernacle texts.[22]

---

22. In support of this understanding, it is instructive to note that in the traditional division of the Pentateuch into portions for weekly synagogue reading, the *parashah* known as T'tzavveh begins with Exod 27:20–21 and ends with Exod 30:1–10. The Babylonian sages who organized the annual cycle of Torah readings understood that the instructions for the lamp oil and the incense altar surrounding information about Aaron formed a meaningful unit.

Necromancy and 1 Samuel 19:22

W. RANDALL GARR

University of California, Santa Barbara

In the beginning, Samuel presides over Saul's inauguration (1 Sam 10:1, 20–24) and accurately predicts what is to come (vv. 5–6, 9b). Then Saul is transformed as he encounters a group of prophets; the spirit of God rushes over him (v. 10bα) and turns him into another man (v. 9aβ).[1] His behavior is suddenly like theirs, and he acts like an ecstatic in their very midst (v. 10bβ; see also v. 11a). The public reacts to this incident with shock and awe: "Is Saul too among the prophets?" (vv. 11bβ, 12bβ).

In the end, Samuel abandons Saul, rejecting him (1 Sam 13:13–14, 15:23b–31a) and even confirming his rival, David, as Saul's successor (16:13a). The spirit of God is gone, too (v. 14a; see also 18:12bβ), and Saul is plagued by an unrelenting evil spirit (16:14b–15) that could make him uncontrollably violent (18:10–11a).

In this unstable condition, Saul comes to Ramah in pursuit of David (1 Sam 19:22–23a). But the spirit of God intervenes (v. 23bαa). Saul again behaves like a raving ecstatic (v. 23bαb) and then proceeds to strip off his royal garb, collapse, and lie naked for a full day and night (v. 24a).[2] This time, the public reacts with incredulity and disgust: "For this reason they say, 'Is Saul too among the prophets?'" (v. 24b). They ridicule Saul's conduct as shocking and awful.[3]

1 Samuel 19 illustrates Saul's downward spiral and, in four successive stories, depicts his dogged resolve to kill David (vv. 1, 2a, 11a, 15b; see also

Author's note: I thank Herbert Huffmon, Jan Joosten, Laura Kalman, and Cynthia Miller for their robust critique of an earlier version of this paper.

1. See Robert R. Wilson, *Prophecy and Society in Ancient Israel* (Philadelphia: Fortress, 1980) 178.

2. Ibid., 182–83.

3. See Simon B. Parker, "Possession Trance and Prophecy in Pre-Exilic Israel," *VT* 28 (1978) 278 with n. 19 in conjunction with J. L. Seeligman, "Aetiological Elements in Biblical Historiography," *Zion* 26 (1961) 151–53 (Hebrew) [repr. in idem, *Studies in Biblical Literature* (ed. Avi Hurvitz et al.; Jerusalem: Magnes, 1996) 23–25 (Hebrew); and as "Ätiologische Elemente in der biblische Geschichtsschreibung," in *Gesammelte Studien zur Hebräischen Bibel* (ed. Erhard Blum; Forschungen zum Alten Testament 41; Tübingen: Mohr Siebeck, 2004) 91–94]. See also André Caquot and Philippe de Robert, *Les livres de Samuel* (Commentaire de l'Ancien Testament 6; Geneva: Labor et Fides, 1994) 236.

vv. 4bαa, 5b, 10aα, 14a, 20aα). David escapes the first attempt when Jonathan convinces his father to relent (vv. 1–7). He escapes the second by dodging a spear that Saul impulsively hurls at him (vv. 8–10). David's third escape, abetted by his wife, is accompanied by a coverup that involves תרפים (vv. 11–17). Michal tricks (רמה) both Saul's messengers and Saul himself into believing that they have captured her husband (v. 17a) by replacing David with a cultic object that is almost always "associated with divinatory practices of some kind" and "likely . . . functioned in necromantic practices."[4] The final escape takes place in Ramah (19:18–20:1a). Saul learns that David is there (19:19) and sends messengers to "take" him (v. 20aα; see also v. 14a). Yet one posse, then another, and then a third are possessed by prophetic ecstasy and rendered ineffective (vv. 20b–21). Furious (v. 22 [LXX] < 20:30aα; cf. 11:6b),[5] Saul goes after David himself (19:23a). But this fourth attempt is thwarted in the same way as the posses' previous three (v. 23b). Saul becomes seized by a fit of madness (v. 24).

The fourth movement in Saul's fourth attempt to capture David begins in 1 Sam 19:22.

> Then he himself [Saul] went to Ramah. He came to the great cistern that is in Secu; he asked, "Where are Samuel and David?" Someone [lit., he] said, "Here, at Naioth in Ramah." (after NRSV)

It is "a peculiar verse . . . whose strangeness induces the reader to weigh the question as to what is up with Saul."[6] For example, Saul seems to "ask for the whereabouts of David and Samuel"[7] even though, in the case of David at least, that information was already known (v. 19).[8] Saul inquires

---

4. T. J. Lewis, "Teraphim תרפים," *Dictionary of Deities and Demons in the Bible* (ed. K. van der Toorn, B. Becking, and P. W. van der Horst; 2nd ed.; Leiden: Brill, 1999) 849a, b. See also Harry A. Hoffner, "אוב ʾôbh," *Theological Dictionary of the Old Testament* (ed. G. J. Botterweck and H. Ringgren; Grand Rapids: Eerdmans, 1974) 1:132; H. Madl, "Die Gottesbefragung mit dem Verb šāʾal," in *Bausteine Biblischer Theologie: Festgabe für G. Johannes Botterweck zum 60. Geburtstag* (ed. Heinz-Josef Fabry; Bonner biblische Beiträge 50; Cologne: Hanstein, 1977) 52–53; and Joseph Blenkinsopp, "Deuteronomy and the Politics of Postmortem Existence," in *Treasures Old & New: Essays in the Theology of the Pentateuch* (Grand Rapids: Eerdmans, 2004) 186.

5. See, e.g., Julius Wellhausen, *Der Text der Bücher Samuelis* (Göttingen: Vandenhoeck & Ruprecht, 1871) 114; and August Klostermann, *Die Bücher Samuelis und der Könige* (Kurzgefaßter Kommentar zu den heiligen Schriften Alten und Neuen Testamentes sowie zu den Apocryphen A/3; Nördlingen: Beck, 1887) 83.

6. J. P. Fokkelman, *Narrative Art and Poetry in the Books of Samuel: A Full Interpretation Based on Stylistic and Structural Analyses* (4 vols.; Studia semitica neerlandica 20; Assen, The Netherlands: Van Gorcum, 1981–1993) 2:277, 279 (reference courtesy of Tremper Longman).

7. Ralph W. Klein, *1 Samuel* (Word Biblical Commentary 10; Waco, TX: Word, 1983) 199.

8. See also K. Budde, *The Books of Samuel* (trans. B. W. Bacon; The Sacred Books of the Old Testament 8; Leipzig: Hinrichs / Baltimore: Johns Hopkins University Press, 1894)

about Samuel even though the prophet is not the object of the search.[9] 'The great cistern' (בור הגדול) is triply strange for its grammar,[10] its uncertain referent,[11] and its absence of a direct translation in the Septuagint.[12] The *hapax legomenon* 'in Secu' (בַשֶׂכוּ) is no less odd, for the same three reasons.[13] In sum, the first step in Saul's final, desperate, and unsuccessful manhunt makes little sense.

A pedestrian interpretation of 1 Sam 19:22 is nonetheless viable. Indeed, it is corroborated elsewhere in the biblical text.

ויבא He came . . . וישאל ויאמר and asked . . . ויאמר Someone said . . .
(1 Sam 19:22)

[Sisera] said to [Jael], ". . . If someone יבוא comes ושאלך ואמר and asks you, 'Is anyone here?' ואמרת you should say, 'No.'" (Judg 4:20)

As in Sisera's hypothetical, this episode has three sequenced components: arrival, query framed by שאל and אמר, and response framed by אמר.[14] From this perspective, then, the episode was unremarkable. Saul came to Ramah, asked for roadway directions, and received a concise, informative reply.[15]

On its own, however, this reading is unproductive and unsatisfying. The reason is simple: this prosaic interpretation does not address the contextual or philological problems in the verse.

But a complementary reading is available, and it develops from the compound frame that introduces Saul's question in 1 Sam 19:22. This frame has a specific function in the Deuteronomistic History.

וישאלו The Israelites inquired of God ויאמרו, "Who should go up first for us into combat with the Benjaminites?" ויאמר Yahweh said, "Judah (should go) first." (Judg 20:18)

67; and Henry Preserved Smith, *A Critical and Exegetical Commentary on the Books of Samuel* (ICC; Edinburgh: T. & T. Clark, 1899) 183 (on v. 19b). Cf. W. Nowack, *Die Bücher Samuelis* (Handkommentar zum Alten Testament 1/4/2; Göttingen: Vandenhoeck & Ruprecht, 1902) 101.

9. Cf. Shimon Bar-Efrat, *I Samuel: Introduction and Commentary* (Mikra le-Yisraʾel; Tel Aviv: Am Oved / Jerusalem: Magnes, 1996) 251 (Hebrew).

10. E.g., Wilhelm Caspari, *Die Samuelbücher* (Kommentar zum Alten Testament 7; Leipzig: Deichert, 1926) 245.

11. Fokkelman, *Narrative Art and Poetry in the Books of Samuel*, 2:279.

12. See Wellhausen, *Der Text der Bücher Samuelis*, 114.

13. See ibid. in conjunction with Moshe Zvi Segal, ספרי שמואל (Jerusalem: Kiryat-Sepher, 1976) קם.

14. For the latter two components, see also Gen 24:47a, 32:30a, and, similarly, 38:21 (all J).

15. In addition to Klein's interpretation quoted above, see Walter Brueggemann, *First and Second Samuel* (Interpretation; Louisville: John Knox, 1990) 145; and Barbara Green, *How Are the Mighty Fallen? A Dialogical Study of King Saul in 1 Samuel* (JSOTSup 365; London: Sheffield Academic Press, 2003) 320, 321.

Like 1 Sam 19:22, this verse is part of a chase scene. The Israelites petitioned their deity for oracular advice. They posed a WH-question of God, and a response came with the requested identification. Like 1 Sam 19:22, the compound frame וישאלו . . . ויאמרו prefaces an oracular query. Evidently, Saul sought David's location by consulting an oracle.[16]

It is unlikely, though, that Saul sought a Yahwistic oracle. Such an oracle specifically indicates its divine addressee in its opening frame. In Judg 20:18, for example, the compound frame addresses "God." Elsewhere, it identifies Yahweh.

> וישאלו The Israelites inquired ביהוה of Yahweh לאמר, "Who should go up first for us to the Canaanites to combat them?" ויאמר Yahweh said, "Judah should." (Judg 1:1–2a)

> וישאל David inquired ביהוה of Yahweh לאמר, "Should I go up to the Philistines? Will you hand them over to me?" ויאמר Yahweh said to David, "Go up; I will very much hand the Philistines over to you." (2 Sam 5:19; see also Judg 20:23, 27–28; 1 Sam 23:2; 30:8)

So too, when the introductory frame is truncated to שאל alone, a Yahwistic oracle names either "God" (e.g., 14:37) or "Yahweh" (e.g., 22:10, 23:4). The absence of this divine addressee in 1 Sam 19:22 suggests that Saul's oracular inquiry was not directed to Yahweh.[17]

There were reasons for soliciting a non-Yahwistic oracle.

> וישאל Saul inquired of God, "Should I go down after the Philistines? Will you hand them over to the Israelites?" ולא ענהו But he [God] did not answer him that time. (1 Sam 14:37)

In that case, Yahweh did not respond because Jonathan had violated Saul's sworn prohibition against food intake (vv. 27–29 < v. 24; see also vv. 38–42). The breach foreclosed oracular communication; unrepaired, the breach made it impossible for the respondent to offer any "divine reassurance" or "public divine legitimation" to Saul's proposed course of action.[18] Saul was on notice that a violation had occurred.[19] Another breach

---

16. In this context, see Claus Westermann, "Die Begriffe für Fragen und Suchen im Alten Testament," *Kerygma und Dogma* 6 (1960) 11.

17. See Morris Jastrow, "The Name of Samuel and the Stem שאל," *JBL* 19 (1900) 89–90; and, more generally, Friedrich Schwally, *Das Leben nach dem Tode nach den Vorstellungen des Alten Israel und des Judentums einschliesslich des Volksglaubens im Zeitalter Christi* (Giessen: Ricker, 1892) 70. See also Madl, "Die Gottesbefragung mit dem Verb *šā'al*," 37.

18. Herbert B. Huffmon, "Priestly Divination in Israel," in *The Word of the Lord Shall Go Forth: Essays in Honor of David Noel Freedman in Celebration of His Sixtieth Birthday* (ed. Carol L. Meyers and M. O'Connor; ASOR Special Vol. 1; Winona Lake, IN: Eisenbrauns, 1983) 358. See also ibid., 356.

19. Kenneth M. Craig Jr., *Asking for Rhetoric: The Hebrew Bible's Protean Interrogative* (Biblical Interpretation Series 73; Leiden: Brill, 2005) 50–55. For other violations, see Pamela Tamarkin Reis, "Eating the Blood: Saul and the Witch of Endor," *JSOT* 73 (1997) 15.

occurred later with Saul's serial attempts to persecute and kill Yahweh's anointed David (see 19:11–15), even after he forswore it (v. 6b). Seeking an oracle that conflicted with the interests of the public or priests was futile. By the end of chap. 19, no legitimate party would be complicitous with Saul's crazed determination to destroy David.[20]

Unlike other illegitimate consultations, though, Saul's solicitation in 19:22 does not mention the oracular technique or goal. The frame does not mention the necromantic אוב or ידעני (e.g., Deut 18:11, 1 Sam 28:7, 1 Chr 10:13), nor does it mention תרפים (Ezek 21:26; see also Zech 10:2). Still, the consultation identified or confirmed David's whereabouts at Naioth in Ramah (see 1 Sam 20:1a).

The nature of this oracular session is linked to the site where it occurred: 'the great cistern' (בור הגדול) in Ramah.[21] The site is not identified, but the definite phrasal qualifier signals that the cistern is at least partially identifiable in a real-world or discourse context. This context is arguably cultic. Granted, "no explicit connection with 'holes' is evident in the Israelite form of necromancy."[22] The connection is inferred.[23] בור is a burial place for the dead (e.g., Jer 41:7). It symbolizes death (e.g., Prov 28:17) and the netherworld (e.g., Isa 14:15). The medium at Endor also saw Samuel's ghost "coming up out of the ground" (1 Sam 28:13), presumably through an opening (see also Isa 29:4). Finally, the Septuagint notes that the cistern (הבור = τὸ φρέαρ) at Mizpah that Ishmael filled with "all [the corpses of the men] he had struck down" was 'large' (φρέαρ μέγα, Jer 48:9; cf. 41:9 [MT]). 'The great cistern' at Ramah, then, was deathly and in this context, known.

As with the great cistern in 19:22, the phrase 'in Secu' (בשכו) also seems locative. In fact, שכו is conventionally understood as a place-name. But its prefixed definite article (בَשכו) could suggest a common noun, instead. Moreover, the noun has a Hebrew cognate: משכית.[24] The word is a rare

---

20. In this context, note Huffmon's dictum: "The role of divination was to provide the correct answer" ("Priestly Divination in Israel," 358).

21. For the phrase structure, see Alexander Borg, "Some Observations on the יום הששי Syndrome in the Hebrew of the Dead Sea Scrolls," in *Diggers at the Well: Proceedings of a Third International Symposium on the Hebrew of the Dead Sea Scrolls and Ben Sira* (ed. T. Muraoka and J. F. Elwolde; Studies on the Texts of the Desert of Judah 36; Leiden: Brill, 2000) 26–39, esp. 32 (on spacial designations).

22. Brian B. Schmidt, *Israel's Beneficent Dead: Ancestor Cult and Necromancy in Ancient Israelite Religion and Tradition* (Tübingen: Mohr Siebeck, 1994; repr., Winona Lake, IN: Eisenbrauns, 1996) 151.

23. See Schwally, *Das Leben nach dem Tode*, 71.

24. For analogous morphological derivatives from final weak roots, see חצי 'half' :: מחצית 'half, middle' (חצה) and רעי 'pasture' :: מרעית 'pasturing, shepherding' (רעה).

"cultic term."[25] It is idolatrous, taboo, and subject to destruction (e.g., Num 33:52, Ezek 8:12). In lithic form, a מַשְׂכִּית can be laid or situated on the ground for the purpose of worship (Lev 26:1). It could be a threshold of some kind,[26] and at Ramah it lay at the gateway to the world below—proper noun or not.

Interestingly, neither בּוֹר הַגָּדוֹל nor שֶׂכוּ appears in the Septuagint. For (עַד) בּוֹר הַגָּדוֹל (עַד), the Greek version has ἕως τοῦ φρέατος τοῦ ἅλω = בְּאֵר הַגֹּרֶן (עַד) '(up to) the well of the threshing floor'. For בְּשֶׂכוּ, it reads τοῦ ἐν τῷ Σεφι = בַּשֶּׂפִי 'in the Sephi'. Each Greek phrase nevertheless confirms that Saul's query in 1 Sam 19:22 was hardly benign.

שֶׂפִי cannot yet be confidently defined.[27] The word refers to a locale—"a hot (Jer 4:11), dry (Isa 41:18) hill where nothing grows (Isa 49:6; cf. also Jer 14:6)."[28] It can also have cultic associations.

> When Jeremiah elsewhere refers to the . . . šĕpāyîm . . . in connection with worship practices, which is only in 3:2 and 21, he does so disparagingly. If the same is intended here [sc., in 7:29], . . . [t]he people are being urged to do their lamenting on the very places they have been frequenting, which are *not* sanctioned by Yahweh and *not* where Yahweh will hear them.[29]

שֶׂפִי, then, is a place to conduct mourning rituals, but it is *not* the place to communicate with God. Despite the elevation associated with the שֶׂפִי (see Jer 3:2), the inquiry in 1 Sam 19:22 (LXX) is cultic, non-Yahwistic, and funerary.

גֹּרֶן is a different matter. It too can be elevated (see 1 Sam 9:11),[30] although it is not usually cultic in nature. Yet it is the locale of an important divinatory contest in the Deuteronomistic History (1 Kgs 22:10 = 2 Chr 18:9).[31] Before undertaking a mission against their Aramean enemy, Kings

25. Jacob Milgrom, *Leviticus: A New Translation with Introduction and Commentary* (3 vols.; AB 3–3B; New York: Doubleday, 1991–2001) 3:2281.
26. Victor Avigdor Hurowitz, "אבן משכית—A New Interpretation," *JBL* 118 (1999) 207.
27. See William McKane, "*špy(y)m* with Special Reference to the Book of Jeremiah," in *Mélanges bibliques et orientaux en l'honneur de M. Henri Cazelles* (ed. A. Caquot and M. Delcor; Alter Orient und Altes Testament 212; Kevelaer: Butzon & Bercker / Neukirchen-Vluyn: Neukirchener Verlag, 1981) 319–35.
28. P. Kyle McCarter Jr., *I Samuel: A New Translation with Introduction, Notes & Commentary* (AB 8; Garden City, NY: Doubleday, 1980) 329.
29. Jack R. Lundbom, *Jeremiah: A New Translation with Introduction and Commentary* (3 vols.; AB 21A–21C; New York: Doubleday, 1999–2004) 1:490–91 (italics added).
30. E.g., Budde, *Die Bücher Samuel* (Kurzer Hand-Commentar zum Alten Testament 8; Tübingen: Mohr Siebeck, 1902) 139; and Smith, *The Books of Samuel*, 183.
31. For the LXX ad loc., see A. Šanda, *Die Bücher der Könige* (2 vols.; Exegetisches Handbuch zum Alten Testament 9; Münster i. Westf.: Aschendorff, 1911–1912) 1:493; and, by implication, Mordechai Cogan, *I Kings: A New Translation with Introduction and Commentary* (AB 10; New York: Doubleday, 2001) 490. Cf. Bernhard Stade and Friedrich Schwally, *The Books of Kings* (trans. R. E. Brünnow and Paul Haupt; The Sacred Books of the Old Testament 9; Leipzig: Hinrichs / Baltimore: Johns Hopkins University Press, 1904) 169.

Ahab and Jehoshaphat sought a divine oracle (1 Kgs 22:5 = 2 Chr 18:4). Bedecked in royal garb and situated at the threshing floor in the administrative center (1 Kgs 22:10a = 2 Chr 18:9a), they gathered hundreds of prophets, posed their question, and received a positive and encouraging response (1 Kgs 22:6 = 2 Chr 18:5). They also witnessed the prophets' stereotypical behavior (1 Kgs 22:10b = 2 Chr 18:9b). Skeptical of the affirmative oracle, however, Jehoshaphat requested a second opinion (1 Kgs 22:7 = 2 Chr 18:6). Micaiah was chosen (1 Kgs 22:8–9 = 2 Chr 18:7–8), and he ultimately conveyed a true oracle that predicted the routing of the Israelite army and the death of its king (1 Kgs 22:17–18, 36–37 = 2 Chr 18:16–17, 33–34). Micaiah then explained why the huge contingent of ecstatic prophets was uniformly wrong (see 1 Kgs 22:13a = 2 Chr 18:12a): they did not possess "the spirit of Yahweh" (see 1 Kgs 22:24b = 2 Chr 18:23b) because an untruthful spirit had tricked them (1 Kgs 22:20–23 = 2 Chr 18:19–22). The verdict disparaged irrational, ecstatic divination at the threshing floor while conceding that it was God-driven.[32]

The scene at Ramah is analogous.[33] After learning of David's location in Ramah (1 Sam 19:19), Saul sent three platoons to snag him (vv. 20–21). Each was neutralized when it made contact with a band of prophets and succumbed to ecstatic contagion. So Saul took matters into his own hands. He came to the threshing floor in Ramah (v. 22aα [LXX]) and, adding the prophetic leader Samuel to his most wanted list, sought a new oracular indication of David's whereabouts (v. 22aβ). The response was reaffirming (v. 22b),[34] encouraging, and true (see 20:1a). But when Saul acted on the information, he too was derailed by infectious ecstasy: "the spirit of God" overwhelmed him, drove him crazy, and deflected his pursuit (v. 23). It invalidated the oracle at the threshing floor and, in the process, left Saul dismantled and unhinged (v. 24a).[35]

---

32. Cogan, *I Kings*, 497, 498.

33. For the connection, see Klostermann, *Die Bücher Samuelis und der Könige*, 83.

34. Fokkelman, *Narrative Art and Poetry in the Books of Samuel*, 2:283–84.

35. The meaning of לפני שמואל (ויתנבא גם־הוא) in v. 24 is puzzling. Read in a spacial sense ('before Samuel'), the phrase has text-critical implications because it disagrees with "the statement in [1 Sam] 15.35 that Samuel would not see Saul again alive" (McCarter, "1, 2 Samuel," in *The HarperCollins Study Bible* [ed. Wayne A. Meeks; New York: HarperCollins, 1993] 448 [ad 19:18–24]; see also Schmidt, *Israel's Beneficent Dead*, 202 n. 292; and, with additional support, Bernhard Lehnart, "Saul unter den 'Ekstatikern' [ISam 19,18–24]," in *David und Saul im Widerstreit—Diachronie und Synchronie im Wettstreit: Beiträge zur Auslegung des ersten Samuelbuches* [ed. Walter Dietrich; Orbis biblicus et orientalis 206; Fribourg: Academic Press / Göttingen: Vandenhoeck & Ruprecht, 2004] 205–6). Another reading is possible, too. It may have a rare comparative sense, as in 1:16 (see Shalom M. Paul, "Psalm 72:5—A Traditional Blessing for the Long Life of the King," *Journal of Near Eastern Studies* 31 [1972] 352 [repr. in idem, *Divrei Shalom: Collected Studies of Shalom M. Paul on the Bible and the Ancient Near East, 1967–2005* (Leiden: Brill, 2005) 52]), in which

The strange episode at Ramah now makes sense. After the תרפים facilitated David's most recent escape (1 Sam 19:11–17), Saul resorted to the
very divinatory technique that had just outsmarted him. He understood
that no orthodox form of consultative divination would compromise David (Yahweh's anointed) or Samuel (the prophetic channel through whom
this status was conferred). Saul knew that he no longer had prophetic support (e.g., 15:23b–29), and he even conceded that an evil spirit emanating
from Yahweh tormented him (e.g., 16:14b, 17), requiring musical exorcism
(vv. 15–17, 23). Frustrated, Saul sought other divine guidance. Clearly,
Samuel's denunciation of oracular תרפים was wasted on him (15:23a). Saul
sought a necromantic medium, inquiring after his estranged ex-patron,
Samuel, as well as his nemesis David. Saul understood that "such [necro-
mantic] practices could produce reliable results."[36]

The question posed by Saul has an ironic twist. Its WH-format was certainly reasonable enough; for example, David would later ask Yahweh to
point him in the right direction.

Afterwards, וישאל David inquired ביהוה of Yahweh לאמר, "Should I go up
into one of the cities of Judah?" Yahweh said, "Yes." ויאמר David said,
"אנה Where should I go up to?" ויאמר He said, "To Hebron." (2 Sam 2:1)[37]

It was also reasonable to request oracular confirmation of what Saul already knew—a reaffirming and reassuring oracle could assuage the fear of
what lay ahead (see 1 Sam 23:2–5). But the reply of the oracle was parodic,
because it recalls Saul's coronation in 1 Samuel 10, when an omen was
sought to locate the king nonapparent (v. 21bβ).

וישאלו They again inquired of Yahweh, "Has someone come here yet?"
ויאמר Yahweh said, "הנה He's here hiding about the baggage." (1 Sam
10:22)

---

case, Saul's demeanor mimicked that of the one Mosaic prophet (see 19:20 in conjunction with 10:12). Saul's elevation and downfall are both bound to Samuel (e.g., Fokkelman, *Narrative Art and Poetry in the Books of Samuel*, 2:280).

36. Mordechai Cogan, "The Road to En-dor," in *Pomegranates and Golden Bells: Studies
in Biblical, Jewish, and Near Eastern Ritual, Law, and Literature in Honor of Jacob Milgrom*
(ed. David P. Wright et al.; Winona Lake, IN: Eisenbrauns, 1995) 326. See also Schmidt,
Israel's Beneficent Dead, 202; Philip S. Johnston, *Shades of Sheol: Death and Afterlife in the
Old Testament* (Leicester, England: Apollos / Downers Grove, IL: InterVarsity, 2002) 157–
58; and Christophe L. Nihan, "1 Samuel 28 and the Condemnation of Necromancy in
Persian Yehud," in *Magic in the Biblical World: From the Rod of Aaron to the Ring of Solomon*
(ed. Todd E. Klutz; Journal for the Study of the New Testament Supplement 245; London:
T. & T. Clark, 2003) 49.

37. See Rannfrid I. Thelle, *Ask God: Divine Consultation in the Literature of the Hebrew
Bible* (Beiträge zur biblischen Exegese und Theologie 30; Frankfurt am Main: Peter Lang,
2002) 60. Cf. Westermann, "Die Begriffe für Fragen und Suchen," 12.

In Saul's ascent, an oracular הנה located the missing king. In Saul's decline (19:22b), it sent him to the place where the new king and his promoter went missing. The irony, however, lies in the question that Saul did *not* put:[38] Saul did not inquire about the basic success of his mission. He did not elicit a strategy or specific instructions for accomplishing his goal, nor did he seek divine sanction. In this sense, then, Saul asked the wrong question. Perhaps he was desperate.[39] Perhaps he was mad.[40] But he consulted a necromancer and received a true divine oracle. The oracle, though, was ultimately useless,[41] because Yahweh had intervened on behalf of David to the mounting disgrace of Saul.

---

38. See Thelle, *Ask God*, 70.

39. See, e.g., Cogan, "The Road to En-dor," 320; and Nihan, "1 Samuel 28 and the Condemnation of Necromancy," 47–48 (on 1 Samuel 28).

40. See Jastrow, "The Name of Samuel," 85 (on Hannah's prayer).

41. See, in this context, John Barclay Burns, "Necromancy and the Spirits of the Dead in the Old Testament," *Transactions of the Glasgow University Oriental Society* 26 (1978) 4 (on 1 Samuel 28).

A Tale of the Prophet and the Courtier: A Responsive Reading of the Nathan Texts

Herbert Bardwell Huffmon
Drew University

Although Nathan is a prominent figure in the texts that narrate the life of David and the early days of Solomon, Nathan's specific roles remain somewhat puzzling. Indeed, there may be several individuals named Nathan active during this period, and questions continue as to the number of distinctive Nathans. My essay will concentrate on the best-attested Nathan, who is commonly identified as Nathan הנביא 'the prophet'. He appears first in 2 Samuel 7 (// 1 Chronicles 17) with the divine promise of a perpetual dynasty for David. He appears again in 2 Samuel 12 in connection with the Bathsheba affair (see also the title of Psalm 51), and he makes a final appearance in Samuel–Kings in the matter of the succession to David's throne, supporting Solomon over against the presumptive heir, Adonijah, in 1 Kings 1. In the first two contexts, Nathan fills the traditional prophetic role: the word of the Lord came to him (2 Sam 7:4), God sent him or sent a message through him (2 Sam 12:1, 25), and he is to say "thus says the Lord" (2 Sam 7:5, 8; 12:7, 11). Nathan carried out these commissions (2 Sam 7:17), and he is duly honored as a prophet in later tradition (Ps 51:2; 1 Chr 29:29; 2 Chr 9:29, 29:25; Sir 47:1).[1] Yet the particular issue in the present discussion is the contrast between Nathan's one and only title, הנביא (a title that certainly fits with much of the tradition), and the wider range of activities ascribed to him. Nathan's words and deeds often belie the role of the prophet, court prophet or not, and better fit the role of adviser or counselor, a title that is not actually used of Nathan. Indeed, many scholars have noted this oddity with Nathan among the prophets, as illustrated by his initial role in 2 Sam 7:1–3 where he appears as a subservient adviser or counselor to the king.[2] Also, as for Nathan's central role in

---

1. In 1 Chr 29:29 and 2 Chr 9:29, Nathan the prophet is identified as the source of royal chronicles.

2. P. K. McCarter notes that Nathan's response is often interpreted "merely as a courtly courtesy, a polite and formal response to the king not necessarily reflecting the speaker's

the succession struggles during the last days of King David, he is described as "the obsequious Nathan of 1 Kings 1, who, bowing and scraping before the king . . . , pleads Solomon's case with every courtly indirection and blandishment."[3]

Neither in 2 Sam 7:1–3 nor in 1 Kings 1 does Nathan, though given the title הנביא, engage in typical prophetic action or use typical prophetic diction. My purpose in this essay is to carefully examine the language used and to establish the understanding of Nathan that is presented to the contemporaries of these texts—a sort of reader/listener response that is based on Nathan's reported words and deeds within the historical-cultural context in which the text was generated.[4]

In 2 Samuel 7, Nathan is conveniently at hand when David, now nicely settled in as king in Jerusalem, comments to him, "Here I am dwelling in a cedar house, while the Ark of the Deity dwells in the midst of the tent." This comment obviously invites a response from Nathan, and it could clearly lead to some form of oracular divination to clarify the appropriate next step for King David. The implication is that the Ark of the Deity should also have a cedar house, one that David would provide, a proposal that typically calls for an appropriate divine confirmation that such a step would be welcome.[5] Nathan's response indicates just such an understanding of the comment by David, that is, as a comment seeking some confirmation, although there is nothing explicit that points to a divinatory procedure. Rather than reporting some form of divination, the text initially merely states that Nathan responds, saying, "All that is in your heart, go (and) do," adding, "because the Lord is with you." Many scholars concur with the judgment of F. M. Cross that Nathan's words reflect "familiar protocol appropriate to Nathan, the subject, speaking to his king."[6] The words

---

considered opinion" (*II Samuel: A New Translation with Introduction and Commentary* [AB 9; Garden City: Doubleday, 1984] 196. More pointedly, D. F. Murray refers to "the obsequious flattery of Nathan's courtly response" and to "the deferential courtier" (*Divine Prerogative and Royal Pretension: Pragmatics, Poetics and Polemics in a Narrative Sequence about David* [*2 Samuel 5.17–7.29*] [JSOTSup 264; Sheffield: Sheffield Academic Press, 1998] 243, 263; see also pp. 33, 160, 314). Murray adds that "under the guise of consulting the prophet Nathan about his project to rehouse the ark, David is actually seeking to manipulate, indeed to coerce, Yahweh" (p. 240).

3. McCarter, *II Samuel*, 196.

4. As John Barton points out, however, "To respond to a parable may be an exercise in reader-response theory, but to reconstruct someone else's response is pure historical criticism" (*Reading the Old Testament: Method in Biblical Study* [revised and enlarged ed.; Louisville: Westminster John Knox, 1996] 213).

5. Michiko Ota, "A Note on 2 Sam 7," in *A Light unto My Path: Old Testament Studies in Honor of Jacob M. Myers* (ed. H. N. Bream, R. D. Heim, and C A. Moore; Gettysburg Theological Studies 4; Philadelphia: Temple University Press, 1974) 403–7.

6. F. M. Cross, *Canaanite Myth and Hebrew Epic: Essays in the History of the Religion of Israel* (Cambridge: Harvard University Press, 1973) 242.

are indeed appropriate for a subject speaking to a king, but they do not seem appropriate for a prophet.[7]

Nathan's phrase "all that is in your heart, go (and) do" has no precise parallel in prophetic announcements, although it is well attested in the words of courtiers. In the Mari and Neo-Assyrian prophetic texts, involving prophets who are frequently cited as receiving royal largess (that is, in some sense, court prophets), it is the king's official reporting the prophetic message who writes to the king "may my lord, in accordance with his deliberation, do what seems good to him" (ARM 26.220) or "may my lord do what seems good to him" (ARM 26.221).[8] The prophetic messages offer assurance and criticism, but they do not give blanket approval to the king. It is the king's officials and underlings who give such approval.[9]

The first part of Nathan's response, "All that is in your heart, go (and) do," illustrates a basic characteristic of kingship. It is none other than the king in particular who can "do what is in his heart." When other persons can "do what is in their hearts" without authorization from a person with higher authority, this can easily lead to disorder. The classic instances are the reports about the gross disorder toward the end of the period reported in Judges, which use a parallel phrase to describe a time "when there was no king in Israel, people did what was proper in their own eyes" (Judg 17:6, 21:25).

The phrase "do what is proper/good in your own heart," like its parallel "do what is proper/good in your own eyes," is appropriate to a king. For example, note the instruction that the early Hittite king Hattushili offers in his bilingual edict to his new son Murshili about how a king should act:

---

7. Cross (p. 242) cites the prophet Micaiah's response to Ahab in 1 Kgs 22:15, echoing the words of the prophetic band (as Micaiah was advised to do by the king's messenger), although the king immediately challenges his agreement, as well as Jeremiah's comments in response to the prophet Hananiah in Jer 28:5, 11, emphasizing that immediate responses may yield to subsequent oracles. But the responses are different in tenor and in context. The king immediately challenges Micaiah's agreement, and Jeremiah is confronting Hananiah, who has all the trappings of prophecy, so Jeremiah initially retreats. That persons such as Nathan may play contrasting roles need not be rejected as imposing schizophrenia, as Cross suggests.

8. For these texts, see M. Nissinen et al., *Prophets and Prophecy in the Ancient Near East* (Society of Biblical Literature Writings from the Ancient World 12; Atlanta: Society of Biblical Literature, 2003) nos. 30 and 31, respectively.

9. For parallel phrases in Neo-Assyrian letters from royal officials and servants, note "Let the king, my lord, do as he pleases" (no. 32) and "The king, my lord, may do as he pleases" (no. 115) in M. Luukko and G. van Buylaere, eds., *The Political Correspondence of Esarhaddon* (SAA 16; Helsinki: Helsinki University Press, 2002); see also nos. 33, 53, 82, 87, 120, 128–29, 134, 138, 142–43, 152, 181, 183, 202. Further references to the SAA will be by volume and text number.

I have given you my words. They shall read this [tablet] aloud in your
presence every month. Thus you will be able to impress my [words] and
my wisdom into (your) heart, [and] to rule successfully over my [sub-
jects] and the high noblemen. If you [observe] an offense in anyone—
whether someone offends before a deity, or someone speaks some (irre-
sponsible) word—consult the assembly. Slander must be referred to the
same assembly. My son, always do what is in your heart.[10]

In a Middle Assyrian letter from an unnamed Babylonian king to (king)
Mutakkil-Nusku, the Assyrian king is told that "You should act according
to your heart (*ki libbika*)."[11] In Babylonian correspondence from the Neo-
Assyrian period, we find the king's servant, Bada, advising "May the king,
my lord, realize all his royal plans according to his heart's (desire)" (SAA
17.101).

The Amarna correspondence offers a number of examples.[12] A letter
presumably from Kadashman-Enlil to Amenophis III, takes up the question
of the pharaoh providing a daughter to wed the Kassite king. The pharaoh
answered, "From time immemorial no daughter of the king of Egy[pt] is
given to anyone." The response is, "Why n[ot]? You are a king; you may
a[ct] according to your heart (*ki libbika*)" (EA 4:4–8). In EA 38, a letter from
the king of Alashiya (Cyprus) to his brother king in Egypt dealing with alleged improper actions by some Alashiyans, the king denies any involve-
ment in the matter but notes that if some Alashiyans were involved, the
pharaoh should send them back, and, says the king, "I will act according to
my heart (*ki libbiya*)." And if it should prove that some Alashiyans were involved in improper behavior, writes the king to the pharaoh, then "You
yourself (should) act according to your heart (*ki libbika*)." In EA 108:57–58,
a letter from Rib-Addi of Byblos to the pharaoh, Rib-Addi complains that
the sons of ʿAbdi-Ashirta are acting improperly, "according to their heart"
(*kima libbišunu*), not in accord with Egyptian policy. However, "if it is the
desire (*libbi*) of the king, the Sun, they will be taken in a day." There is a
similar note in EA 125:40–45, also a letter from Rib-Addi to the pharaoh,
"What are the dogs, the sons of ʿAbdi-Ashirta, that ⟪that⟫ they act according to their heart (*kima libbišunu*) and set fire to the cities of the pharaoh."

---

10. G. Beckman, trans., "Bilingual Edict of Hattushili I," in *COS* 2:15, §22.
11. See J. A. Brinkman, *A Political History of Post-Kassite Babylonia, 1158–722 B.C.*
(Analecta Orientalia 43; Rome: Pontifical Biblical Institute, 1968) 101–4; see also his en-
try, "Mutakkil-Nusku," *Reallexikon der Assyriologie* 8:500 (1997). For the passage cited, see
E. Weidner, "Aus den Tagen eines assyrischen Schattenkoenigs," *Archiv für Orientforschung*
10 (1935–36) 3, line 12.
12. For the Amarna letters (cited as EA), see W. L. Moran, ed. and trans., *The Amarna
Letters* (Baltimore: Johns Hopkins University Press, 1992). For a full edition of the texts,
see J. A. Knudtzon et al., *Die El-Amarna Tafeln* (Vorderasiatische Bibliothek 2; Leipzig:
Hinrichs, 1915). Note that the translations given are intentionally literal.

Acting "according to the heart" is proper for kings; others are supposed to act according to the king's heart.[13]

In the Neo-Assyrian texts there are many parallel statements. SAA 10.349 is a letter of [Mar-Issar] to the king (Esarhaddon) that mentions some repair work about which Itti-Marduk-balatu "wrote to the king, my lord: 'Let them turn the gold (for repairs/work) over to me, and let me act according to my heart (*ki libbiya*).'" For ordinary persons to act "according to their heart," they needed to be acting in accordance with the king's policy or with the king's permission.[14] Alternatively, the king may grant a particular freedom of action to someone, as in the case of David's grant to Barzillai, the Gileadite, who had been helpful to him during his flight from Jerusalem. Barzillai had requested David's favor for the king's servant, Chimham, presumably Barzillai's son: "Do for him according to what is good in your eyes." But David's generous response was, "I will do for him that which is good in your eyes, and anything you choose for me (to do), I will do for you" (2 Sam 19:38–39). Previously, David had told his troops, who had opposed his wish to lead them in battle against Absalom, "Whatever seems good in your (pl.) eyes, I will do" (2 Sam 18:4).

By using the words "All that is in your heart, go (and) do" in 2 Sam 7:3, Nathan also speaks in the manner of a royal adviser, a courtier, not in the manner of a prophet. Kings are specifically the class of people who can do "all that is in their heart" or "all that is good in their eyes," even when the king has been installed by the will of the people.[15] A king has considerable freedom of action; others, at least from the perspective of the king, are supposed to do what is right in the king's eyes. In keeping with the superior status of those who can do what is right in their own hearts, this expression is used in reference to God. For example, in 1 Sam 2:35, God says that "I will raise up for myself a faithful priest, whatever is in My heart and in

---

13. E. Salonen (*Die Gruss- und Höflichkeitsformeln in babylonisch-assyrischen Briefen* [Studia Orientalia 38; Helsinki: Societas Orientalis Fennica, 1967] 106, 114) cites concluding formulas expressing the hope that "the heart of my lord the king be satisfied," as well as opening formulas in which the king reports that he is feeling good together with the hope that the recipient(s) "may be doing well." Additional examples occur in SAA 13.1, 4–6; 16.3–4.

14. For a parallel, note the Persian king's grant of authority to Ezra and his brethren over the (Jerusalem) temple treasury to do "what seems good to you (Ezra) and to your brethren" (Ezra 7:18). Similarly, King Ahasuerus grants to Haman that "the silver (offered by Haman) is given to you as well as the people (the Jews) to do with them as (seems) good in your eyes" (Esth 3:11).

15. Note that Abner, the Israelite general, negotiated an agreement with the elders of Israel and the leading Benjaminites to recognize David as king: he informed David regarding "all that was good in the eyes of Israel and in the eyes of all the house of Benjamin" (2 Sam 3:19). Abner advises David, "They will make a covenant with you, and you can rule over all your soul (נפשך) desires" (2 Sam 3:21).

My soul he will do." And in 2 Kings 10:30, God says to King Jehu, "you have done well to do (what) is proper in your eyes, (and) you have acted according to all that is in My heart, (and) you have done to the House of Ahab according to all that is in My heart."[16] Other occurrences of such phrases include the words addressed to King Saul by his troops when he wanted to press the attack against the Philistines (although Jonathan had violated a ban, as at least some of the army knew), "All that is good in your eyes, do" (1 Sam 14:36). Similarly, Jonathan, the crown prince—thus in the putative position of a king—is told by his arms bearer in response to another proposed assault, "Do all that is in your heart" (1 Sam 14:7); and when the rebellious Jehu pursues the remaining members of the House of Ahab, he is told by the officials of Samaria, "We are your subjects, and we will do whatever you tell us to. We will not proclaim anyone king; (that which is) good in your eyes, do" (2 Kgs 10:5).[17]

Apart from a few other occasions, such as when the phrase is used by the deceptive Gibeonites in speaking to Joshua (Josh 9:25) or by the men of Jabesh-Gilead in tentatively surrendering to the Ammonites (1 Sam 11:10), again addressing a leader or leaders,[18] the phrase is used several other times regarding David himself. While David had gone into hiding from Saul, Saul ended up in a cave where David and his men were concealed, and his men told David, "This is the day of which the Lord said to you, 'I will deliver your enemy into your hands'; you may do for him according to what is good in your eyes" (1 Sam 24:5). Saul's lame (grand)son, Mephibosheth, says to David, "My lord the king is like an angel of the Lord, so do what is good in your eyes" (2 Sam 19:28). In 2 Sam 24:22, Araunah says to David regarding his threshing floor, "Let my lord the king take it and offer up what is good in his eyes."

The above pattern of usage shows that ordinary folk defer to the king or a comparable leader, inviting that person to "do what is right in your heart/eyes,"[19] and the king defers to the deity, as in 2 Sam 15:26 when Da-

---

16. For other examples with God in mind, note Judg 10:15, "Do for us [the Israelites] according to all that is good in your eyes; only save us this day"; and 1 Sam 3:18, "The Lord will do what is good in His eyes." Note also 2 Sam 10:21 // 1 Chr 19:13 (Joab speaking).

17. The situation of the locals who harassed Lot when he protected the visitors (angels) and the abuse and harassment of the householder at Gibeah who sheltered the Levite and his concubine can be addressed in a similar fashion, acknowledging their superior power. The abusers may "do to them (Lot's two daughters or the householder's daughter and the Levites's concubine) what is good in your eyes" (Gen 19:8, Judg 19:24). And Jeremiah similarly defers to the officials and the people, saying, "Do for me according to what is good and proper in your eyes" (Jer 26:14).

18. Cf. also Ezra 5:17, Esth 5:4 ("If it seems good to the king"), and Gen 41:37 ("The word was good in the eyes of Pharaoh and in the eyes of all his servants").

19. An interesting example of deference to a (perceived) leader—though not quite our phrase—is the response of Jonathan, the crown prince, to David: "Whatever your soul says, I will do for you" (1 Sam 20:4).

vid says of God, "Let Him do for me according as is good in His eyes." The king may also choose to be gracious—or desperate—and give authority to others. David did that for his loyal troops when he was fleeing from Absalom and proposed to go into the battle with them but they urged him to stay behind in the nearby city. David said to them, "Whatever seems good in your (pl.) eyes, I will do for you" (2 Sam 18:4). And to one of his supporters, Barzillai the Gileadite, who had entrusted to David his protégé (son?), Chimham, saying, "Do for him according to what is good in your eyes," David responds by saying "I will do for him according to what is good in your (Barzillai's) eyes, and anything you choose for me (David) (to do), I will do for you" (2 Sam 19:38–39).[20]

Prophets, however, apart from the words of Nathan "the prophet" in 2 Sam 7:3, do not speak in this fashion to the king or to others. The words, "all that is in your heart, go (and) do," are the words of a courtier to a king, not a prophet to a king. This phrase is more than a polite formality. It is a fundamental recognition of the special capacity of a king or of someone else in a position of great authority. Prophets are obviously aware of the power of a king, but prophets do not address kings in this fashion. Courtiers, for whom the court is their focus and who are experienced in the realities of the court, do so address the king.[21] The presence of the title "prophet" in 2 Sam 7:1–3 together with the speech of a courtier points to a larger issue.

The continuation of Nathan's response to David in 2 Sam 7:3 uses a more ordinary phrase, "because the Lord is with you." This phrase has been studied intensively by H. D. Preuss and D. Vetter, among others;[22] it expresses the assurance of divine presence and support and as such is very widely attested, whether in the precise fashion of 2 Sam 7:3 "because the Lord is with you" and its variants or in semantic equivalents. Such expressions of assurance are, of course, well attested in prophecy and elsewhere—this is not a distinctive phrase. In 1 Sam 10:7, Samuel says to Saul, "because God is with you," precisely the Chronicler's equivalent (1 Chr 17:2) to the phrase in 2 Sam 7:3.[23] In a slightly different form, God reminds David, "I was with you wherever you went" (2 Sam 7:9 // 1 Chr 17:8). So this assurance, in

---

20. With similar language, Abraham grants authority to Sarah regarding the childbearing Hagar (Gen 16:6); Elkanah grants authority to his wife, Hannah (1 Sam 1:23); Nebuzaradan, the chief of the Babylonian guards, grants Jeremiah freedom of movement (Jer 40:4–5).

21. For example, note the frequent concluding phrase in Neo-Assyrian letters from officials to the king, "may my lord do as he wishes."

22. H. D. Preuss, "'. . . ich will mit dir sein!'," *ZAW* 80 (1968) 139–73; D. Vetter, *Jahwes Mit-Sein: Ein Ausdruck des Segens* (Arbeiten zur Theologie 1/45; Stuttgart: Calwer Verlag, 1971).

23. Compare with Gen 26:28; Exod 3:12; Josh 1:9; Judg 6:16; Isa 41:10; 1 Chr 28:20.

terms of our limited biblical texts, may be expressed by God, by kings, or by charismatic leaders.[24]

A slightly different form, "for I am with you (to deliver you)," is used in the call of Jeremiah (1:8), and similar assurance is frequently cited for Jeremiah (1:19, 15:20, 20:11, 30:10–11, 42:11, 46:28) and is also featured in call narratives for Moses (Exod 3:12), Gideon (Judg 6:16), and Saul (1 Sam 10:7). Comparable assurance is found elsewhere as well.[25]

Such an announcement, expressed in a variety of ways, is also widely attested in the ancient Near East.[26] Within the prophetic texts, we find such expressions as "F[e]ar not, for I have made [you] king, [and I will (!) st]and with [you], and I will deliver you from all [these kings . . .], in the Zakkur inscription from Hamath.[27] From the Neo-Assyrian corpus note "I am Ishtar of Arbela. I will go before you and behind you" (SAA 9.1.1). These are semantic equivalents, though not precise parallels. However, there are many more precise examples in non-prophetic texts, because expressions of divine support and presence abound in ancient Near Eastern texts and are not distinctive to particular roles or genres. The anomaly is this: someone identified as a "prophet" who speaks like a courtier, as does Nathan in 2 Sam 7:3.

Subsequently, in the maneuverings concerning succession to David's throne, Nathan, again identified as הנביא, acts like a court adviser if not a court manipulator.[28] In the contest between Adonijah, the apparent crown prince, and Solomon, the eventual successor, Nathan plays a prominent role. But again he is not involved with revelations from the divine but offers counsel. In response to the initiatives taken by Adonijah and his sup-

---

24. As a wish rather than a declaration—if this is an appropriate distinction—various words of assurance are offered by Jethro to Moses (Exod 18:19), by Moses to the Israelites (Deut 2:7) or to Joshua (Deut 31:23), by the Israelites to Joshua (Josh 1:17), by Saul to David (1 Sam 17:37), by Jonathan to David (1 Sam 20:13), by Abner to David (2 Sam 3:12), by the woman of Tekoa to David (2 Sam 14:17), by David to Solomon (1 Chr 22:16), and by God or an angel to Abraham (Gen 26:3), to Jacob (Gen 31:3), or to Jeroboam (1 Kgs 11:38). The phrase "the Lord be with you" is also an ordinary greeting (Ruth 2:4).

25. Gen 21:20; 26:24; 39:2, 3, 21, 23; Josh 6:27, 14:12; Judg 1:19; Isa 43:2, 5; Amos 5:14; Hag 1:13, 2:4.

26. For a general collection, see H. D. Preuss, "'. . . ich will mit dir sein!'" 161–71; and T. Ishida, *The Royal Dynasties in Ancient Israel: A Study on the Formation and Development of Royal-Dynastic Ideology* (Beihefte zur Zeitschrift für die alttestamentliche Wissenschaft 142; Berlin: de Gruyter, 1977) 90–92, who draws primarily on Neo-Assyrian prophetic texts. The examples could easily be multiplied.

27. See M. Nissinen et al., *Prophets and Prophecy*, 203–7, A.13–14, trans. C. L. Seow.

28. For T. Ishida, Nathan is "the ideologue of Solomon's party" who may even have "fabricated a *coup d'etat* on the part of Adonijah to furnish a pretext for extracting from David the designation of Solomon as his successor," though all for a good purpose ("Solomon's Succession to the Throne of David—A Political Analysis," in *Studies in the Period of David and Solomon and Other Essays* (ed. T. Ishida; Winona Lake, IN: Eisenbrauns, 1982) 175–87; see esp. 177, 179, 187. Ishida's conclusion is that "Nathan was a prophet

porters, Nathan contacts Solomon's mother, Bathsheba, saying, "Come now, let me advise you (אִיעָצֵךְ נָא עֵצָה)," and tells her how to approach King David and seek a formal declaration of succession on behalf of Solomon (1 Kgs 1:12). Once she has done that, Nathan tells her, "I will come in after you and confirm your words." Nathan does as he said he would, following all the proper protocol for a reception by the king, and presents David with his understanding of what Adonijah is doing and the question, "Can this word have come from my lord the king, though you did not make known to your servant (i.e., Nathan) who is to succeed to the throne of my lord the king?" The chapter projects intrigue, if not manipulation and/or manufacture of a royal announcement, but Nathan's words present him as strictly in the role of a royal counselor. Nathan accompanies the group for the anointing of Solomon, but it is Zadok the priest who does the actual anointing in 1 Kgs 1:39, though both Zadok and Nathen are mentioned in 1 Kgs 1:34 and 45, the last specific mention of "the prophet" Nathan in Samuel-Kings.

Prophets are sent to convey a divine word and are not explicitly sent by God to give counsel, which is the particular domain of the wise or the elders.[29] Of course, prophets bringing a divine word may be perceived by others as giving counsel, as in 2 Chr 25:14–16, where God sends a prophet to protest against the king's actions in recognition of Edomite gods, at which time King Amaziah responds, "Have we appointed you a counselor to the king (הַלְיוֹעֵץ לַמֶּלֶךְ נְתַנּוּךָ)? Stop, why should they kill you?" The prophet did not reiterate his message about worshiping other gods, but did say, "I know that God has counseled (יָעַץ) your destruction, because you have done this and have not listened to my counsel (עֲצָתִי)." Here the prophetic word reiterates God's counsel—stop the idolatrous practices!—and is equivalent to giving counsel. And, of course, a king might occasionally initiate seeking counsel from a prophet, as did Zedekiah with Jeremiah (Jer 38:14–16), but Jeremiah replies, "If I tell you, you'll surely kill me; and if I counsel you (אִיעָצְךָ), you won't listen to me." But having been granted immunity, as it were, by the king, Jeremiah offered a word of the Lord. Indeed, prophets might be viewed by others as having special insight, but prophets speak as divine messengers and not as advisory counselors. Proper royal counselors speak for themselves (as with Ahitophel and Hushai, or even with the queen mother, Athaliah; 2 Chr 22:3–4) but not for God.

The possible afterlife of Nathan, however, includes the notice in the special LXX text in 3 Kgdms 2:46h, enumerating Solomon's "cabinet." This

---

who, being disappointed in David, placed his hopes in young Solomon" (p. 187). If so, Nathan manipulates the situation to Solomon's benefit.

29. See Jer 18:18 and Ezek 7:26.

cabinet includes a son of Zadok the priest and two sons of Nathan—perhaps the same Nathan "the prophet"—one of whom is in charge of the district administrators and the other, mentioned at the end of the list, is the counselor (ὁ σύμβουλος). The title "counselor," though attested in the David narratives, is not otherwise included in the cabinet lists.[30]

One path to follow in comprehending Nathan as prophet and counselor/courtier might be to appeal to a contrast between court prophets, who are part of the intimate royal circle, and prophets who are from outside that circle. However, the Mari prophets, who are often recorded as recipients of royal benefactions, do not address the king in the manner of a courtier; that is, they do not use the language of 2 Sam 7:3,[31] nor do they act as Nathan did in 1 Kings 1.

Another path is to consider the fluidity of official roles in the early days of the monarchy of a relatively small state where many separable roles can be accumulated or consolidated by one gifted individual. Samuel is well known as associated with many areas of action, but Samuel has a commensurate list of titles and roles—prophet, man of God, seer, judge. Nathan's contemporary, Gad, is identified as a visionary, a visionary of David, a visionary of the king, a prophet, and as a prophet, the visionary of David. A late indication of this fluidity in role and title may be 1 Chr 29:29, according to which "the deeds [lit., words] of David the king, the former and the latter, behold they are written according to the words of Samuel the seer, and according to the words of Nathan the prophet, and according to the words of Gad the visionary."

So, Nathan is presented in our sources as a prophet by title and as a courtier by rhetoric who gives counsel and who intervenes in court affairs. In 1 Kings 1, the use of titles (or patronyms) is very common for Abiathar and Zadok, which could have influenced the use of the prestige-lending title of "the prophet" for Nathan. Whatever the case, the dual portrait of Nathan in 1 Kings illustrates the multiple paths that versatile individuals might take in a small, fledgling monarchy. There were no precise job descriptions and individuals might bridge the later, more institutionalized role structures.[32]

---

30. Note, however, the references to David's counselors, Ahitophel and Hushai, and the inclusion of the title "counselor" in the list in Isa 3:2–3.

31. Even the Mari prophet, Lupahum, who seems to have the king's confidence in that he receives many royal rewards and is sent on missions by the king to clarify divine reports, never speaks in the manner of a courtier. See the texts in Nissinen et al., *Prophets and Prophecy*, nos. 9, 53, 62.

32. For an interesting reconstruction of a dual nature for Nathan as a Jebusite court official/prophet who also becomes a prophet of Yahweh, see Gwilyn H. Jones, *The Nathan Narratives* (JSOTSup 80; Sheffield: Sheffield Academic Press, 1990).

A Forgotten Cultic Reform?
2 Kings 3:2b

ANDRÉ LEMAIRE

École Pratique des Hautes Études, Paris

One of the characteristics of the historiography of the books of Kings is the importance of the cultic institutions and related reforms.[1] The building of the Jerusalem temple by Solomon (1 Kings 6–8),[2] the cultic reforms of the Judean kings Asa (1 Kgs 15:12), Jehoshaphat (1 Kgs 22:47), Athaliah (2 Kings 11), Joash (2 Kgs 12:1, 17), Ahaz (2 Kgs 16:1, 19), Hezekiah (2 Kgs 18:4), Manasseh (2 Kgs 21:3–18), and Josiah (2 Kings 23) are all well known and have been the object of many studies, especially to contradict or defend their historicity.[3] The same is also true for the cultic reforms of the Israelite kings Jeroboam I (1 Kgs 12:26–33) and Jehu (2 Kgs 10:15–28).

---

1. See H.-D. Hoffmann, *Reform und Reformen: Untersuchungen zu einem Grundthema der deuteronomistischen Geschichtsschreibung* (Abhandlungen zur Theologie des Alten und Neuen Testaments 66; Zürich: Theologischer Verlag Zürich, 1980); R. H. Lowery, *The Reforming Kings: Cult and Society in First Temple Judah* (JSOTSup 120; Sheffield: JSOT Press, 1991).

2. See, for instance, V. Hurowitz, *I Have Built You an Exalted House: Temple Building in the Bible in Light of Mesopotamian and Northwest Semitic Writings* (JSOTSup 115; Sheffield: JSOT Press, 1992).

3. For Hezekiah's reform, see A. F. Rainey, "Hezekiah's Reform and the Altars at Beer-Sheba and Arad," in *Scripture and Other Artifacts: Essays on the Bible and Archaeology in Honor of Philip J. King* (ed. M. D. Coogan et al.; Louisville: Westminster John Knox, 1994) 333–54; N. Naʾaman, "The Debated Historicity of Hezekiah's Reform in the Light of Historical and Archaeological Research," *ZAW* 107 (1995) 179–95; L. Fried, "The High Places (*bāmôt*) and the Reforms of Hezekiah and Josiah: An Archaeological Investigation," *JAOS* 122 (2002) 437–65; A. Lemaire, *Naissance du monothéisme: Point de vue d'un historien* (Paris: Bayard, 2003) 103–13; Z. Herzog, "The Archaeology of the Beersheba Valley and its Implications for the Biblical Period," in *Congress Volume: Leiden 2004* (ed. A. Lemaire; VTSup 109; Leiden: Brill, 2006) 81–102, esp. pp. 96–97.

For Josiah's reform, see N. Lohfink, "The Cult Reform of Josiah of Judah: 2 Kings 22–23 as a Source of Israelite Religion," in *Ancient Israelite Religion: Essays in Honor of F. M. Cross* (ed. P. D. Miller et al.; Philadelphia: Fortress, 1987) 459–75; B. Gieselmann, "Die sogenannte josianische Reform in der gegenwärtigen Forschung," *ZAW* 106 (1994) 223–42; C. Uehlinger, "Gab es eine joschijanische Kultreform? Plädoyer für ein begründetes Minimum," in *Jeremia und die "deuteronomistische Bewegung"* (ed. W. Gross; Bonner biblische Beiträge 98; Weinheim: Beltz Athenäum, 1995) 57–89 (= "Was There a Cult Reform under King Josiah? The Case for a Well-Grounded Minimum," in *Good Kings and Bad Kings* [ed.

Among these many reforms, the cultic reform of King Jehoram of Israel, mentioned very briefly in 2 Kgs 3:2b, does not seem to have attracted many studies. Actually, although mentioned in Hoffmann's book,[4] the action of Jehoram has been presented as "a puzzle."[5] Its description, however, does not seem difficult to understand: "He removed the pillar of Baal (ויסר את־מצבת הבעל) which his father had done." However, the Septuagint and the Vulgate translation is "pillars" (a plural instead of a singular), and since there is no record that Ahab erected a pillar, commentators have proposed to emend the text either to מזבח 'altar'[6] or to אשרה 'sacred tree',[7] comparing to 1 Kgs 16:32–33a. Other commentators underline the fact that this action is attributed to Jehu in 2 Kgs 10:27a. So, this cultic reform appears to have been performed against something that might not have existed or that was eliminated later by somebody else. Is Jehoram's action a phantom? Let us first check the meaning of the sentence, and then we will analyze the historical context in order to appreciate its historicity and meaning.

The verb *swr* generally means 'turn aside'; in the Hiphil conjugation with an object as here, it means 'remove'. As well noted by R. H. Lowery, "In four cases in Kings . . . the causative of *swr* describes a cult purge: Asa removed the idols his ancestors had made (1 Kgs 15:12), the Northern king Jehoram removed the Baal pillar (2 Kgs 3:2), Hezekiah removed the high places (2 Kgs 18:4, 22) and Josiah removed and destroyed Samaria's high place buildings (2 Kgs 23:19)."[8] So, the meaning of this verb is clear, and it seems well adapted to describe a cultic reform.[9]

The object concerned by the reform is presented as מצבת הבעל. This syntagma is only attested again in the Hebrew Bible in 2 Kgs 10:27, and we do not have any other similar sentence with מצבת + divine name. As a *lectio difficilior*, there is no reason to emend the singular to a plural as was done by the versions,[10] probably to generalize under the influence of 2 Kgs 10:27 (cf. also 1 Kgs 14:23; 2 Kgs 17:10, 18:4). So, one can understand the remark

---

L. L. Grabbe; London: T. & T. Clark, 2005] 279–316); Lemaire, *Naissance du monothéisme*, 115–21.

4. Hoffmann, *Reform und Reformen*, 27, 84–86.

5. T. R. Hobbs, *2 Kings* (Word Biblical Commentary 13; Waco TX: Word, 1985) 34.

6. Ibid.

7. Cf., for instance, B. Stade and F. Schwally, *The Books of Kings* (The Sacred Books of the Old Testament 9; Leipzig: Hinrichs / Baltimore: Johns Hopkins University Press, 1904) 185.

8. Lowery, *The Reforming Kings*, 159.

9. See already Hoffmann, *Reform und Reformen*, 84.

10. Against A. Šanda, *Die Bücher der Könige* (Exegetisches Handbuch zum Alten Testament 9/2; Münster: Aschendorff, 1912) 17.

of H.-D. Hoffmann: "Was eine 'masebe des Baal' eigentlich is, bleibt . . . unklar."[11] Various interpretations are possible:

1. One could think of a great rough stone that has been set up as a sacred pillar (cf. Gen 28:18, 31:45, 35:14; Josh 24:26). This stele was one of the three elements, with an altar and a sacred tree, of the traditional sanctuaries / high places that were "removed" by Hezekiah's reform (2 Kgs 18:4a; cf. Deut 12:2–3).[12] It was a symbol of the presence of the deity, eventually of YHWH himself, and there is no reason why such a stele could not have been used to symbolize the presence of Baal.

2. One could think of a low relief representing the deity Baal(/Hadad), like many exemplars of the storm-god reliefs found in northern Syria.[13]

3. One could think of a votive stele, dedicated to Baal with an inscription, or of a commemorative inscription thanking Baal for his help[14] and eventually set up in his sanctuary. This interpretation may have an excellent parallel with the Mesha stele set up in the high place of Kamosh, god of Moab (cf. line 3: *w'š.hbmt.hz't.lkmš*).[15]

Actually, interpretations 2 and 3 could be combined, since the famous Aramaic Melqart stele[16] is a good example of a votive inscription below a relief representing Baal-Melqart,[17] while the Aramaic Zakkur stele[18] is also

---

11. Hoffmann, *Reform und Reformen*, 85.

12. Lemaire, *Naissance du monothéisme*, 103–13.

13. See, for instance, A. Vanel, *L'iconographie du dieu de l'orage dans le Proche-Orient ancien jusqu'au VIIe siècle avant J.-C.* (Cahiers de la Revue Biblique 3; Paris: Gabalda, 1965) esp. 111–58.

14. See already Hobbs, *2 Kings*, 34.

15. See, for instance, J. C. L. Gibson, *Textbook of Syrian Semitic Inscriptions*, vol. 1: *Hebrew and Moabite Inscriptions* (Oxford: Clarendon, 1971; hereafter abbreviated *TSSI*) 74–75; K. A. D. Smelik, "1. Moabite Inscription," in *The Context of Scripture*, vol. 2: *Monumental Inscriptions from the Biblical World* (*COS* 2) 137.

16. See W. Pitard, *Ancient Damascus* (Winona Lake, IN: Eisenbrauns, 1987) 144; idem, "The Identity of the Bar-Hadad of the Melqart Stela," *BASOR* 272 (1988) 2–31; E. Puech, "La stèle de Bar-Hadad à Melqart et les rois d'Arpad," *Revue biblique* 99 (1992) 311–34; E. Lipiński, *The Aramaeans: Their Ancient History, Culture and Religion* (Orientalia Lovaniensia Analecta 100; Leuven: Peeters, 2000) 215; W. T. Pitard, "The Melqart Stela," *COS*, 2:152–53.

17. See C. Bonnet, *Melqart: Cultes et mythes de l'Héraclès tyrien en Méditerranée* (Studia Phoenicia 8; Leuven: Peeters, 1988) 132–36.

18. H. Donner and W. Röllig, *Kanaanäische und aramäische Inschriften* (3 vols.; Wiesbaden: Harrassowitz, 1966–1969) no. 222; Gibson, *TSSI* 2, no. 5; A. Lemaire, "Joas de Samarie, Barhadad de Damas, Zakkur de Hamat: La Syrie-Palestine vers 800 av. J.-C.," *ErIsr* 24 (Malamat Volume; 1993) 148*–57*; Lipiński, *Aramaeans*, 254–55; A. Millard, "The Inscription of Zakkur, King of Hamath," *COS*, 2:155.

a good example of a commemorative inscription engraved below a probable representation of the high god "Iluwer," probably to be identified with Baalshamayin.[19] These archaeological parallels from the end of the 9th or beginning of the 8th century B.C.E. reveal that such a stele dedicated to a deity would not be out of place in Israel at about the middle of the 9th century as was already well noted by E. Dhorme.[20]

In 1 Kgs 3:2b, the stele is explicitly presented as made by the father of Jehoram, that is, King Ahab. Most commentators noted that there is no mention of this action of Ahab in the book of Kings, because in 1 Kgs 16:32–33a it is only said that Ahab set up an altar in the Temple of Baal that he built in Samaria and that he made the Asherah. However, one should underline that this silence of 1 Kgs 16:32–33a about a Baal stele does not contradict explicitly the statement of 1 Kgs 3:2b for two reasons:

1. As is well known, the historiography of the book of Kings does not pretend to be exhaustive, and the usual formula at the end of each reign makes an explicit reference to the royal annals for further information.
2. If one adopts interpretation 1 for the stele, one could expect that this Baal stele should be mentioned in addition to the altar and the Asherah in 1 Kgs 16:32–33a. But this is not the case if interpretation 2 and/or 3 are preferred since, in this case, as a votive or commemorative stele, this stele would have been set up well after the building of the temple, probably toward the end of Ahab's reign. One could think, for instance, of a votive or commemorative stele set up after the battle of Qarqar (853) to thank the deity for the coalition's victory against Shalmaneser III.[21]

Thus far, the sentence of 3:2b seems to be clear and easily understandable, especially if we interpret the Baal stele as a votive or commemorative stele. However, we must also explain the presentation in the MT of 2 Kgs 10:26–27 that apparently attributes the destruction of the Baal stele to King Jehu in 841 B.C.E.:

> They brought out the steles of the temple of Baal and they burned it. They pulled down the Baal stele and they pulled down the temple of Baal.

---

19. Cf. also the colossal statue of Hadad where the inscribed statue is designated by the same Aramaic word *nṣb* as in the Melqart and Zakkur stele.

20. E. Dhorme, *L'évolution religieuse d'Israël I: La religion des Hébreux nomades* (Brussels: Nouvelle société d'éditions, 1937) 160–63; J. A. Montgomery and H. S. Gehman, *A Critical and Exegetical Commentary on the Books of Kings* (ICC; Edinburgh: T. & T. Clark, 1951) 358; J. Gray, *I and II Kings: A Commentary* (2nd ed.; OTL; London: SCM, 1970) 482.

21. The participation of Phoenician and Aramean partners in the battle could explain the dedication to a regional high god. See the possible parallel of the Melqart stele.

This text is fraught with difficulties and variant readings. There are at least two obvious difficulties:[22]

1. In v. 26 the steles are burned (verb שׂרף), while in v. 27 the stele is pulled down (verb נתץ). This seems incoherent. Furthermore, the use of the verbs is strange, since it is the only place where they are used with מצבה as the object. Actually, in this context, one expects שׂרף to be used with Asherah as the object[23] and נתץ, which is the opposite of בנה,[24] with altar (מזבח),[25] house or temple (בית),[26] or else eventually במה (2 Kgs 23:8, 15; 2 Chr 31:1; 33:3) or walls (2 Kgs 25:10; Jer 39:8, 52:14; 2 Chr 36:19).

2. The object pronominal suffix of the verb שׂרף is singular while מצבות is plural.

In these conditions, it is not surprising that in v. 26 a few Hebrew manuscripts and the versions have read the singular מצבת rather than the plural. At the opposite in v. 27, a few Hebrew manuscripts and the Palestinian Greek have the plural instead of the singular.[27] Furthermore, *byt* is missing in v. 26 in the primitive Septuagint, while v. 27bα is lacking in a few Hebrew manuscripts and the Vaticanus.

Taking into account all these difficulties and variants and following B. Stade,[28] the primitive Hebrew text could well have read something like:

They brought out the *Asherah[29] of the temple of Baal and burned it,[30] and they pulled down the *altar[31] of Baal and they pulled down the temple of Baal.

---

22. See, for instance, P. Buis, *Le livre des Rois* (Sources bibliques; Paris: Gabalda, 1997) 221–22.

23. See 1 Kgs 15:13; 2 Kgs 23:6, 15.

24. Cf. D. J. A. Clines, *The Dictionary of Classical Hebrew* (8 vols.; Sheffield: Sheffield Academic Press, 2001) 5:816.

25. Exod 34:13; Deut 7:5, 12:3; Judg 2:2; 6:28, 30, 31, 32; 2 Kgs 23:12; 2 Chr 31:4; 34:4, 7.

26. Lev 14:45; 2 Kgs 11:18, 23:7; Isa 22:10; Jer 33:4; Ezek 26:12; 2 Chr 23:17.

27. Cf. D. Barthélemy, *Critique textuelle de l'Ancien Testament: 1 Josué, Juges, Ruth, Samuel, Rois, Chroniques, Esdras, Néhémie, Esther* (Orbis biblicus et orientalis 50/1; Fribourg: Édition Universitaires / Göttingen: Vandenhoeck & Ruprecht, 1982) 397.

28. "Miscellen. 10. Anmerkungen zu Kö. 10–14," *ZAW* 5 (1885) 275–97, esp. 278–79.

29. C. F. Burney, *Notes on the Hebrew Text of the Book of Kings* (Oxford: Clarendon, 1903) 306; Stade and Schwally, *The Books of Kings*, 232; K. D. Fricke, *Das Zweite Buch von den Königen* (Die Botschaft des Alten Testaments 12/2; Stuttgart: Calwer, 1972) 136. The objection of Gray, *I and II Kings*, 558, followed by Barthélemy, *Critique textuelle*, 397–98, has no textual or archaeological basis: we have no attestation of a wooden מצבה.

30. See, for instance, the NEB (1970).

31. See Burney, *Notes on the Hebrew Text*, 306; Stade and Schwally, *The Books of Kings*, 233; Montgomery and Gehman, *Commentary*, 416; Gray, *I and II Kings*, 558; Fricke, *Das zweite Buch*, 136; G. H. Jones, *1 and 2 Kings* (New Century Bible; 2 vols.; Grand Rapids:

Later on, an addition in the margin also mentioning מצבת הבעל was inserted once, instead of the mention of the Asherah (in v. 26) as the object
of the verb שׂרף, and a second time, instead of מזבח, as the object of the
verb נתץ. Even though the restoration of this primitive Hebrew text is
conjectural, it is clear that the two attestations of the word מצבה in 2 Kgs
10:26–27a are textually problematic[32] and that there was probably some
transformation in the pre- or proto-masoretic tradition.

In addition to this difficult textual problem, we must critically analyze
the probable historical situation connected originally with the removing
of the Baal stele. If this mention was original in the revolution of Jehu, it
seems very difficult to see how and why it was later attributed to King Jehoram, who was regarded a bad king (3:2aα: ויעשׂה הרע בעיני יהוה) and was
killed by Jehu so that the historiography of the Jehu Dynasty and, later on,
of the reform movement, probably tended to attribute to Jehoram bad, not
good, actions. Conversely, if this mention is original in Jehoram's reign,
one can understand that this good action was later attributed to king Jehu
by the historiography of the Jehu dynasty, all the more easily because Jehu
was responsible for the destruction of the temple of Baal in Samaria.

The removing of the Baal stele is therefore very probable and historically connected with the reign of King Jehoram as reported in the notice of
1 Kgs 3:2b.[33] Can we determine its religious meaning?

On one hand, today it is clear that Ahab and his sons/dynasty were not
true partisans of Baal and still recognized YHWH as their national god.[34]
This is especially true of Jehoram. In fact, he is never accused of personal
infidelity to YHWH. Even though he did not like the "true" prophets, as
shown by the story of Micaiah son of Yimlah (1 Kgs 22:8–26) and Elisha
during the joint Moabite campaign (2 Kgs 3:4–27), he did consult them. Elisha himself seems to have no grievance against Jehoram himself, only
against the attitude of his "father and mother" (2 Kgs 3:13). This seems to
be confirmed by the fact that Jehu does not reveal any ground for complaint against Jehoram himself but only against his mother Jezebel and his
father Ahab (2 Kgs 10:22, 25–26, 34). Finally, even though he is judged as a
bad king by the historiography of the books of Kings, because he followed

---

Eerdmans / London: Marshall, Morgan & Scott, 1984) 2:471. This primitive text was
probably echoing back to 1 Kgs 16:32–33a.

32. The vote for the MT in 2 Kgs 10:26–27:3 "C" and 1 "B" (Barthélemy, *Critique textuelle*, 397–98) is a good sign of that.

33. With M. Cogan and H. Tadmor, *II Kings* (AB 11; Garden City, NY: Doubleday,
1988) 43: "There is good reason to accept . . . the reliability of the present reference to a
dedication by Ahab of a pillar to Baal"; against H.-D. Hoffmann, *Reform und Reformen*,
86: "Dennoch wird man hinter 2 K 3,2 keine historische Nachricht vermuten dürfen."

34. See, for instance, W. Thiel, "Ahab," *ABD* 1:100–103.

the tradition of Jeroboam son of Nebat like all the kings of Israel,[35] it is still emphasized that he was "not like his father and mother" (2 Kgs 3:2).

On the other hand, according to 2 Kings 10, Jehoram apparently did not destroy the Temple of Baal with Baal's asherah and altar (2 Kgs 10:26–27 emend.), which his father Ahab had made, probably for his wife "Jezebel daughter of Ethbaal/Ittobaal king of the Sidonians" (1 Kgs 16:31–32). It is likely true that, as long as Jezebel lived, Jehoram showed much respect to her and had no reason to destroy her Baal Temple in Samaria.[36]

Given these conditions, why remove the Baal stele? It is difficult to tell, but we may propose a working hypothesis. First, this stele was probably set up *outside* the Baal Temple and thus could not be justified by the desire to show diplomatic respect for the cult of a foreign queen. Furthermore, as we have seen above, this Baal stele may have comprised a relief of the god Baal, eventually with a votive or commemorative inscription. If so, this stele was likely seen as an attack against the Israelite traditions of monolatry and aniconism. This was especially true if this stele comprised also a votive or commemorative inscription by Ahab as king of Israel.

If this working hypothesis is accepted, the cultic reform of Jehoram in 2 Kgs 3:2b was very limited indeed, but it may have served to deprive us of a royal stele with a relief and inscription set up by Ahab.

---

35. This critical appreciation is probably connected with the redaction during Hezekiah's reign; see my "Vers l'histoire de la rédaction des livres des Rois," *ZAW* 98 (1986) 221–36 (= "Toward a Redactional History of the Book of Kings," in *Reconsidering Israel and Judah: Recent Studies on the Deuteronomistic History* [ed. G. N. Knoppers and J. G. McConville; Sources for Biblical and Theological Study 8; Winona Lake IN: Eisenbrauns, 2000] 446–61, esp. pp. 450–53).

36. In 2 Kgs 3:2b, there is no hint about the location of the Baal stele: there is no indication that the Baal stele destroyed by Jehoram had been set up in the Baal Temple of Jezebel.

Scribal Error and the Transmission of 2 Kings 18–20 and Isaiah 36–39

BRADLEY ROOT

University of California, San Diego

The synoptic parallel in 2 Kings 18–20 and Isaiah 36–39 provides modern scholars with a good opportunity to study the transmission and corruption of texts in the ancient world. This parallel makes a good test case to study textual transmission because: (1) We have a rough idea of when the two textual traditions diverged; (2) both versions of the accounts have been transmitted in the various textual traditions of the Bible; (3) there are some variations between the accounts that are widely accepted as resulting from deliberate expansion or redaction;[1] (4) there are also some variations between the traditions that can be easily explained as resulting from scribal error; and (5) we have a complete text of the Isaianic version of the account from the Dead Sea Scrolls that includes a few instructive examples of scribal error.

Based on the evidence from these parallel accounts, I will attempt to defend the assertion that much of the textual corruption in the texts was the result of unintentional scribal mistakes, and not intentional expansion or redaction. After this, I will draw some preliminary conclusions about when scribal errors are more and less likely to be corrected.

Although much scholarship has been written about the development and transmission of 2 Kings 18–20 and Isaiah 36–39, most studies fail to seriously consider scribal error as a major source of textual divergence. Instead, these studies usually argue that the differences were the result of purposeful revision or expansion by later scribes.[2] While some of the differences in Isaiah 38–39 can certainly be attributed to the insertion of

---

1. The addition of "Hezekiah's psalm" (Isa 38:8–20) and the alterations to the surrounding material are widely regarded as the results of secondary expansion or redaction in the Isaianic tradition: Joseph Blenkinsopp, *Isaiah 1–39* (AB 19; New York: Doubleday, 2000) 481–86; Christopher R. Seitz, *Zion's Final Destiny: The Development of the Book of Isaiah: A Reassessment of Isaiah 36–39* (Minneapolis: Fortress, 1991) 167–71.

2. See Hans Wildberger, *Isaiah 28–39: A Continental Commentary* (trans. Thomas H. Trapp; Minneapolis: Fortress, 2002) 359–493; Seitz, *Zion's Final Destiny*; Brevard S. Childs, *Isaiah* (Louisville: Westminster John Knox, 2001) 259–87.

Hezekiah's psalm,[3] there are still some significant differences between the accounts in Isaiah and 2 Kings that cannot be attributed to redactional activity with a high degree of confidence.

After excluding the differences that are a direct result of the insertion of the Psalm of Hezekiah,[4] I count 45 major disagreements between these two accounts that are responsible for a 140-word difference.[5] Of these 45 variants, 11 are possible cases of haplography or dittography, but 34 cannot be easily explained as having resulted from scribal errors.[6] These latter 34,

---

3. The redactor would have had to make some changes to the psalm's immediate surroundings in order to make his new text flow properly and to eliminate contradictions between the account from 2 Kings and the psalm. I count two major changes to the text (apart from the insertion of the psalm itself) that are probably the result of such redactional activity: 2 Kgs 20:6–9/Isa 38:7 (31 words)—2 Kgs 20:6–9 was moved to Isa 38:21–22 and modified to fit its new context; 2 Kgs 20:9–11/Isa 38:8 (22 words)—Isaiah omits עשׂר מעלות ... אל־יהוה וישב הלך הצל and replaces it with הנני משׁיב. For an in-depth analysis of the Isaianic redaction, see Marvin A. Sweeney, *Isaiah 1–39* (Grand Rapids, MI: Eerdmans, 1996) 491–505, and Seitz, *Zion's Final Destiny*, 163–71.

4. I count two major differences: (1) the insertion of the psalm itself, and (2) the relocation of 2 Kgs 20:6–9 to the end of the psalm. These two variant readings contain 179 words.

5. By *major disagreement* I mean any instance in which the two accounts are different by at least one whole word. I did not count instances in which the word order differs, such as 2 Kgs 19:2/Isa 37:2, which disagree as to the word order of the last three words of the sentence (2 Kings reads הנביא בן־אמוץ and Isaiah reads בן־אמוץ הנביא). Neither did I include instances in which the variant readings look or sound similar enough to be mistaken for each other, such as 2 Kgs 20:12/Isa 39:1 (Isaiah reads מרדך but 2 Kings reads בראדך), because such errors are both too common and too minor to be included in this article's discussion.

6. These 34 variants are as follows: 2 Kgs 18:13/Isa 36:1—Isaiah adds ויהי (1 word); 2 Kgs 18:21/Isa 36:6—only 2 Kings has עהת (1 word); 2 Kgs 18:21/Isa 36:6—only 2 Kings has לך (1 word); 2 Kgs 18:22/Isa 36:7—only 2 Kings has בירושׁלם (1 word); 2 Kgs 18:23/Isa 36:8—only 2 Kings has את (1 word); 2 Kgs 18:27/Isa 36:12—only 2 Kings has אליהם (1 word); 2 Kgs 18:29/Isa 36:15—only 2 Kings has מידו (1 word); 2 Kgs 18:30/Isa 36:15—only 2 Kings has את (1 word); 2 Kgs 18:32/Isa 36:17—only 2 Kings has ארץ זית יצהר ודבשׁ וחיו ולא תמתו ואל־תשׁמעו אל־חזקיהו (11 words); 2 Kgs 18:32/Isa 36:17—only Isaiah has חזקיהו (1 word); 2 Kgs 18:34/Isa 36:19—only 2 Kings has הנע ועוה (2 words); 2 Kgs 18:35/Isa 36:20—only Isaiah has האלה (1 word); 2 Kgs 18:36/Isa 36:21—only 2 Kings has העם (1 word); 2 Kgs 19:4/Isa 37:4—only 2 Kings has כל (1 word); 2 Kgs 19:9/Isa 37:9—only 2 Kings has הנה (1 word); 2 Kgs 19:16/Isa 37:17—only Isaiah has צבאות after יהוה (1 word); 2 Kgs 19:19/Isa 37:20—only 2 Kings has נא (1 word); 2 Kgs 19:19/Isa 37:20—only 2 Kings has אלהים after יהוה (1 word); 2 Kgs 19:20/Isa 37:21—only 2 Kings has שׁמעתי (1 word); 2 Kgs 19:31/Isa 37:32—only Isaiah has צבאות after יהוה, but some manuscripts of 2 Kings agree with Isaiah (1 word); 2 Kgs 19:37/Isa 37:38—only Isaiah has בניו (1 word), but many manuscripts of 2 Kings agree with Isaiah or have בניו as the *Qere*; 2 Kgs 20:2/Isa 38:2—only 2 Kings has את (1 word); 2 Kgs 20:4/Isa 38:4—only 2 Kings has ישׁעיהו לא יצא העיר התיכנה (5 words)—this could be an instance of haplography by homoeoarcton if the scribe confused the י with the ו of the following word.; 2 Kgs 20:5/Isa 38:5—2 Kings says שׁוב where Isaiah says הלוך (1 word); 2 Kgs 20:5/Isa 38:5—only 2 Kings has נגיד־עמי (2 words); 2 Kgs 20:6/Isa 38:5—only Isaiah has יוסף (1 word); 2 Kgs 20:9/Isa 38:7—2 Kings says כי where Isaiah says אשׁר (1 word); 2 Kgs 20:9/Isa 38:7—only Isaiah has הזה (1 word); 2 Kgs 20:11/

however, are almost all one- or two-word variants and are only responsible for 37% of the difference between the parallel accounts.[7] The bulk of the difference[8] (63%) comes from the 11 variants that could have been caused by scribal errors. These variants are as follows:

- *2 Kings 18:14–16/Isaiah 36:1 (60 words)*—Isaiah omits all 3 verses
  This is probably a case of whole word haplography since the simplest explanation is that the scribe's eye skipped from וישלח at the beginning of 2 Kgs 18:14 to וישלח at the beginning of 2 Kgs 18:17.[9]
- *2 Kings 18:17/Isaiah 36:2 (5 words)*—Isaiah omits תרתן ואת־רב־סריס ואת
  This is probably a case of haplography by double-letter homoeoteleuton since the scribe's eye could have skipped from the את before תרתן to the last to letters of the segment's final word, ואת.
- *2 Kings 18:17/Isaiah 36:2 (3 words)*—2 Kings repeats ירושלם ויעלו ויבאו
  This is most likely a case of dittography.[10]
- *2 Kings 18:17/Isaiah 36:2 (2 words)*—Isaiah omits ויעלו ויבאו
  This omission is probably the result of triple-letter homoeoarcton. The scribe's eye would have skipped from the first three letters of ויעלו to the first three letters of ויעמד.[11]
- *2 Kings 18:18/Isaiah 36:3 (3 words)*—Isaiah omits ויקראו אל־המלך
  This is probably a case of haplography by double-letter homoeoarcton. The scribe's eye could have skipped from the first two letters of ויקראו to the first two letters of ויצא.
- *2 Kings 18:28/Isaiah 36:13 (1 word)*—Isaiah omits וידבר
  This could be a case of double-letter homoeoarcton, since the scribe's eye could have skipped from the first two letters in וידבר to the first two letters in the following word, ויאמר. However, it is more

---

Isa 38:8—only Isaiah has בשמש (1 word); 2 Kgs 20:14/Isa 39:3—only Isaiah has אלי (1 word); 2 Kgs 20:16/Isa 39:4—only Isaiah has צבאות after יהוה (1 word).

7. These variants contain 52 words of the 140-word difference between the texts.

8. These variants contain 88 words of the 140-word difference.

9. To my knowledge, the only scholar who raises this possibility is A. S. Herbert in *The Book of the Prophet Isaiah: Chapters 1–39* (Cambridge Bible Commentary; Cambridge: Cambridge University Press, 1973) 196–97. This example, however, looks strikingly like Emmanuel Tov's textbook example of parablepsis. In his book on text criticism, Tov's first example of parablepsis is the omission of Jer 21:36–37 in some manuscript traditions (*Textual Criticism of the Hebrew Bible* [Minneapolis: Fortess, 2001] 238).

10. It appears that there were two independent corruptions at the same point in the traditions of Isaiah and 2 Kings: dittography in the Kings tradition and haplography in the Isaianic tradition (see the next example). As a result, neither text preserves the original reading.

11. For a more detailed treatment of the differences between 2 Kgs 18:17 and Isa 36:2, see my discussion below, p. 55.

likely that וידבר was intentionally omitted from Isaiah because וידבר and ויאמר are redundant.

- *2 Kings 18:33/Isaiah 36:18 (1 word)*—Isaiah replaces ההצל הצילו with ההצילו
  This could be a case of haplography by homoeoarcton. The presence of an extra ה at the beginning of הצילו suggests that the scribe began by writing the ההצ of ההצל, but skipped from the הצ of ההצל to the הצ of הצילו.
- *2 Kings 19:11/Isaiah 37:11 (1 word)*—Isaiah omits את
  This is probably a case of haplography by homoeoarcton. The scribe's eye would have skipped from the א in את to the א in אשׁר.
- *2 Kings 19:24/Isaiah 37:25 (1 word)*—Isaiah omits זרים
  The simplest explanation for this omission is that the scribe's eye skipped from the last two letters of מים to the last two letters of זרים (double-letter homoeoteleuton).
- *2 Kings 19:35/Isaiah 37:36 (3 words)*—Isaiah omits ויהי בלילה ההוא
  Isaiah's omission could be the result of the scribe's eye skipping from the first two letters of ויהי to the first two letters of ויצא (double-letter homoeoarcton).
- *2 Kings 20:5/Isaiah 38:5 (8 words)*—Isaiah omits רפא לך . . . בית יהוה והספתי
  The copyist's eye may have skipped from the final letter of הנני to the final letter of והספתי (homoeoteleuton).

It may be argued that, since many Hebrew words have similar beginnings or endings, the fact that an omitted section begins or ends with the same letters as one of the surrounding words is not significant enough to imply the occurrence of haplography. On the contrary, it is precisely this repetitive textual environment that makes haplography more likely.[12] Furthermore, if the similarity between the beginning of an omission and the beginning of the word that follows the omission, or the ending of an omission and the ending of the word immediately preceding the omission were mere coincidence, the variants bearing the signs of haplography should include both long and short variants in a similar proportion to variants that could not have been the result of such scribal errors. This, however, is not the case. Only one-fourth of the variants in the Kings–Isaiah parallel could

---

12. David Noel Freedman and Shawna Dolansky Overton, "Omitting the Omissions: The Case for Haplography in the Transmission of the Biblical Texts," in *Imagining Biblical Worlds: Studies in Spatial, Social and Historical Constructs in Honor of James W. Flanagan* (ed. David M. Gunn and Paula M. McNutt; JSOTSup 359; London: Sheffield Academic Press, 2002) 99–116, esp. 109; David Noel Freedman and Jack R. Lundbom, "Haplography in Jeremiah 1–20," *ErIsr* 26 (Frank Moore Cross Volume; 1999) 28.

have been caused by haplography or dittography, but six of the eight variants consisting of three or more words could have been caused by these scribal errors. These data suggest that the signs of scribal mistakes do not appear randomly among the textual variants.

The reader should note that it is certainly possible that any of these variants could have been caused by something other than scribal error. As I mentioned above, it seems quite likely that the omission of וידבר from Isa 36:13 is not the result of haplography, but of deliberate omission. In this case, the fact that both the omitted word and the one that follows start with וי is probably just a coincidence. However, in most of the cases noted above, scribal error is both the simplest and most likely cause of the textual corruptions.

It would be difficult, for example, to explain why a later scribe would intentionally add or omit variants such as תרתן ואת־רב־סריס ואת (2 Kgs 18:17/ Isa 36:2) or ויקראו אל־המלך (2 Kgs 18:18/Isa 36:3) from Isaiah. Conversely, it is easy to see how, once these words were accidentally omitted from the Isaianic tradition, their absence would go unnoticed. The missing words from Isa 36:2 are part of a compound direct object, but since the omitted words are followed by a name that still serves as the direct object in the corrupted version of the text, the omission of these words does not create a problematic reading. In Isa 36:3, the omitted text comprises a complete independent clause. Since it is followed by another independent clause, this omission does not create a problematic reading either. Later readers would, therefore, have had no reason to suspect that either of the verses in question lacked anything unless they carefully compared the text with its counterpart in Kings.

Moreover, it is even difficult to find a strong reason why a scribe would have chosen to omit a more substantial section such as 2 Kgs 18:14–16. One common argument by those who think that this is an intentional omission is that Hezekiah's capitulation and payment of tribute to Sennacherib in vv. 14–16 contradicted Isaiah's message that Jerusalem could only be saved by trusting in God.[13] The editor of Isaiah, so the argument goes, had to omit these verses to keep his narrative consistent. This argument, however, does not hold up to close scrutiny because in 2 Kings, Hezekiah's tribute fails to save Jerusalem. Furthermore, Isaiah's text does include a different example of Hezekiah's "shameless" foreign policy of trusting in the strength of foreign kings.[14] In order to maintain that the omission of 2 Kgs 18:14–16 was intentional, scholars would have to assume that an

---

13. Wildberger, *Isaiah 28–39*, 361, 386. For a summary of other attempts to explain this variation between the two versions, see Seitz, *Zion's Final Destiny*, 48–66.

14. Isaiah 39.

incompetent redactor edited this selection. It is a simpler solution to assume that the omission is the result of a common transcriptional mistake.

To be sure, there are cases in which the modern scholar has at his disposal sufficient evidence to suggest an editorial intent. The striking similarity between many of the Deuteronomistic pericopes in Judges–2 Kings, for example, provides considerable support to the theory that the same redactor penned them all. Similarly, because Chronicles tends consistently to expand and condense the material from Samuel and Kings, scholars have a good foundation to suggest that individual differences between Kings and Chronicles were the result of deliberate editorial choice. While scholars must always consider the possibility that an ancient redactor intentionally expanded or abridged his source in order to suit his theological or political biases, we should keep in mind that such theories require the critic to attribute a hypothetical motive to the redactor who made such changes. This need to establish a motive usually sets up a burden of proof so heavy that the modern scholar cannot satisfy it.

Unless there is a clear pattern or a substantial reason to assume the presence of deliberate editorial alterations, scholars should try to explain textual variations as unintentional mistakes before speculating in regard to which motives may have inspired such textual discrepancies. For each of the above examples, there is a valid mechanism that may have facilitated scribal mistakes. In such situations, the critic may propose that the change was accidental without having to establish a motive. This is because scribal errors were both common and unintentional.

Although there is still a debate in our field as to how much textual corruption can be attributed to scribal error, the evidence from ancient manuscripts demonstrates that such errors were relatively common. Scholars have examined scribal errors committed in the Dead Sea Scrolls, and they have found that haplography was a frequent mistake and dittography was a less frequent (but still not uncommon) occurrence.[15]

Although modern researchers have noted both the frequency of scribal errors and that some errors were fixed by later scribes who were probably proofreading the manuscripts, they have not paid sufficient attention to how often textual corruptions were corrected or preserved in these manuscripts. The *Isaiah Scroll*, which contains all of Isaiah 36–39, is an ideal test case for studying the quality controls that ancient scribes would have had in place to correct such mistakes. Since the transcription made by the primary scribe of the *Isaiah Scroll* was corrected by a different hand, modern

---

15. W. F. Albright, "Some Remarks on the Song of Moses in Deuteronomy XXXII," *VT* 9 (1959) 339–46.

readers can develop a more accurate understanding of how the copy editing process worked in the ancient world.[16]

A survey of the scribal errors in chaps. 36–39 of the *Isaiah Scroll* yields some interesting results. The original transcription of the *Isaiah Scroll* contained 24 major differences (99 words) from the MT:

- Nine of these variants (79 words) could have resulted from scribal error. Five of these 9 (60 words) were corrected by a second scribe,[17] and 4 of them (19 words) are preserved in the manuscript.[18]
- Six variants[19] (9 words) disagree with the MT of Isaiah but agree with 2 Kings.
- Nine additional variants[20] (11 words) agree with neither Isaiah nor 2 Kings and cannot be easily explained as the result of scribal error. All of these are only one- or two-word variants.

It is important to note that not all of these mistakes may have been made by the scribe who copied 1QIsaᵃ. William Brownlee has argued persuasively that many of the omissions made by the first scribe are the result of omissions in the manuscript from which he copied. In fact, the scribe sometimes appears to have been aware of this problem since he frequently

---

16. Here, I am using the term *copy editing* in its original sense: the process of ensuring that a copy of a manuscript was made accurately. Today, because technology allows us to make perfect copies of a document, we use the term to refer to the process of checking a document for minor errors of spelling and grammar.

17. 4QIsaᵃ 37:5–7—first scribe omitted all of the three verses—homoeoarcton (. . . וי- - וי) (39 words); 37:14—first scribe omitted החזקיה after ויפרושה—homoeoteleuton (ה- . . . . ה-) (1 word); 37:17—first scribe omitted ואת־ארצם before ונתן—homoeoarcton (ו- . . . ו-) (2 words); 37:31—first scribe omitted פליטת בית־יהודה after ויספה—homoeoteleuton (ה- . . . . ה-) (2 words); 38:21—first scribe omitted all of vv. 21–22—two word haplography (יהוה בית) (16 words).

18. Isa 36:11—4QIsaᵃ omits אל־רב־שקה after ויואה—probable homoeoteleuton (ה- . . . . ח-) (3 words); 37:29—4QIsaᵃ is missing אלי התרגזן יען at the beginning of the verse—2-word haplography (אלי התרגזן) (3 words); 38:11—4QIsaᵃ is missing one יה from the sequence יה יה-—whole-word haplography (1 word); 38:19—4QIsaᵃ repeats v. 19 and the first 2 words of v. 20—dittography (12 words).

19. Isa 36:7—4QIsaᵃ adds בירושלם to end of verse—4QIsaᵃ agrees with the MT text of 2 Kings (1 word); 37:11—4QIsaᵃ adds את after שמעתה—this agrees with 2 Kings and suggests that haplography occurred in the MT tradition (1 word); 37:20—4QIsaᵃ has אלהים after יהוה—this agrees with 2 Kings (1 word); 37:25—4QIsaᵃ has זרים after מים—this agrees with 2 Kings and suggests that haplography occurred in the MT tradition (1 word); 38:6—adds עבדי למעני ולמען דוד to the end of the verse—probable harmonization with 2 Kings (4 words); 39:2—4QIsaᵃ has כול before בית—this agrees with 2 Kings (1 word).

20. Isa 36:2—4QIsaᵃ adds מאודה after כבד—expansion? (1 word); 36:4—4QIsaᵃ adds זה יהו after חזקיה—probable gloss (2 words); 36:4—4QIsaᵃ adds אתה after אשר—(1 word); 36:4—4QIsaᵃ adds בו to end of verse—(1 word); 36:11—4QIsaᵃ replaces -אל with עם—(1 word); 36:16—4QIsaᵃ adds את twice (once after each איש)—(2 words); 37:9—4QIsaᵃ includes both variants from Kings and Isaiah to read וישב וישמע—probable conflation (1 word); 38:18—4QIsaᵃ adds ולוא after יהללכה—(1 word); 39:6—4QIsaᵃ adds יבואו—(1 word).

left blank spaces in his own manuscript so that these omissions could be filled in by someone else.[21] This is significant because it suggests that the copy editor of 1QIsa[a] used multiple manuscripts to check the accuracy of the *Isaiah Scroll* (where else would he have gotten the omitted text?).[22] Moreover, the fact that the copy editor inserted three variant readings or glosses that were left out by the first scribe further suggests that he checked the scroll against multiple manuscripts.[23]

It is not clear how representative 1QIsa[a] is of the quality controls employed by ancient Jewish scribes, and any conclusions drawn from such a small data set can only be considered preliminary and tentative. Nevertheless, it is significant that the data from the *Isaiah Scroll* are consistent with those from 2 Kings 18–20 and Isaiah 36–39 in the MT. An analysis of the data suggests that haplography and dittography are probably responsible for most of the significant textual corruptions. The evidence from 1QIsa[a] also suggests that the practice of checking a newly copied document against multiple manuscripts was an effective—though far from perfect—form of quality control. The copy editor restored 60 words that had been accidentally omitted by the first scribe, and his inclusion of the "plusses" from other manuscripts only resulted in three variants (five words) that cannot be found in the MT. Nevertheless, the copy editor still failed to correct three omissions and one case of dittography,[24] either because he missed them himself or because these variants existed in all of the manuscripts he consulted. It is also noteworthy that the copy editor himself omitted a word when he inserted Isa 38:21–22, and that this omission appears to have been caused by haplography (by the copy editor or by someone else earlier in the transmission history).[25]

Because the copy editor corrected omissions that were most likely made in the manuscript from which the first scribe copied, and because one of the scribes placed several dots above some of the variant readings that are not found in the MT, it seems probable that many of the omissions that one copy editor missed would have been caught by a later copy editor when the document was again copied. In other words, an analysis of the

---

21. William Hugh Brownlee, "The Manuscripts from Which DSI[a] Was Copied," *BASOR* 127 (1952) 16–21.

22. Emanuel Tov argues that some of the documents at Qumran may have been revised and corrected to conform to an authoritative copy of the same composition; *Scribal Practices and Approaches Reflected in the Texts Found in the Judean Desert* (Studies on the Texts of the Desert of Judah 54; Leiden: Brill, 2004) 223–25.

23. The reader should note that some of the variant readings in the *Isaiah Scroll* that are not found in the MT have several dots above them. This also suggests that more than one manuscript was used to check the accuracy of the scroll.

24. See n. 19 above.

25. 38:21—copy editor omitted ישׁאו after ישׁעיהו—homoeoarcton (-ישׁ . . . . -ישׁ) (1 word).

evidence from 1QIsa[a] suggests that the copy editing process used on the *Isaiah Scroll* would have caught both old and new omissions so long as the scribes had access to documents that preserved the omitted text. Although it is not yet clear how common this process of copy editing was in the ancient world, it is clear that such a process could only work with established texts that had already been copied several times. Newer documents and documents that were a scribal community's only copy of a work could not have been checked in such a manner. Furthermore, because many later scribes would have had much of the Bible memorized, they would have been more likely to catch textual corruptions once a text came to be regarded as Scripture. Therefore, it seems that textual corruption may have been more likely to take place in the early stages of a text's transmission and in the early stages of a local manuscript tradition.

This insight may help to explain why Isaiah suffered from more textual corruptions than 2 Kings. By the time the material from 2 Kings was inserted into Isaiah, Kings had probably been standardized and had achieved a sufficiently esteemed status to ensure that copies of the work would be subject to quality controls that would correct many instances of scribal error.[26] It is unlikely, however, that the scribe who first appended this material to Isaiah would have had similar quality controls in place because his main goal was not merely to copy an existing text, but to innovate. Once these chapters had become a part of Isaiah, it seems unlikely that copy editors would have checked the document against the parallel text in 2 Kings instead of just checking it against other copies of Isaiah. Furthermore, if, as most scholars think, chaps. 36–39 were added to the book before Deutero-Isaiah was added,[27] then there was at least one additional opportunity for textual corruptions in Isaiah to have been preserved.

Since a later scribe would have added Deutero-Isaiah to an existing transcription of First Isaiah, his text would have likely reflected only the textual tradition of his transcript. All descendants of that edition of Isaiah (i.e., all editions that included Deutero-Isaiah) would have preserved the textual corruptions of this specific manuscript tradition. In short, the text of Isaiah preserves more textual corruptions than that of 2 Kings because the transmission of our version of Isaiah has a more isolated transmission history (i.e., checked against fewer manuscript traditions) than our version of Kings. These conditions of the transmission of Isaiah suggest that early

---

26. The fact that Chronicles used Kings as a source in the early Second Temple period and that someone inserted material from Kings into Isaiah either before or at the same time that Deutero-Isaiah was added to the text suggests that the book of Kings was already highly esteemed by the early postexilic period.

27. Blenkinsopp, *Isaiah 1–39*, 458–61. Willem A. M. Beuken, *Isaiah: Vol. 2, part 2: Isaiah 28–39* (Leuven: Peeters, 2000) 1–5.

scribal mistakes were likely to have been preserved in all subsequent versions of Isaiah. It is therefore likely that most of the discrepancies between Kings and Isaiah were the result of errors that occurred early in the transmission of Isaiah. These findings, of course, support the theory that this portion of Isaiah is dependent on 2 Kings.

These findings may also have important implications for the evaluation of variants in the manuscript traditions of the Old Testament. Many have argued, for example, that the shorter LXX version of Jeremiah, which probably had a more isolated transmission than MT, is more authentic than the longer version in MT, which they argue contains many glosses and expansions.[28] Jack Lundbom, however, has argued that many of the differences between the short version of Jeremiah in the LXX and the long version in the MT are the result of haplography in the LXX tradition and not expansion in the MT tradition.[29] The evidence presented in this article appears to support the arguments of Freedman, Lundbom, and Dolansky Overton that the accuracy of the longer readings should be preferred when the shorter readings could have been the result of haplography.[30]

Because (as this article has argued) the book of Jeremiah is likely to have suffered from more uncorrected scribal errors in its early stages of its transmission (i.e., before it became standardized and widely circulated) than in its later stages, it is quite possible that early corruptions of the text could account for many of the differences between the LXX and MT. If the earliest copies in the LXX tradition contained a number of omissions (which is quite possible given the number of omissions in just four chapters of Isaiah), then these corruptions would have been preserved in all subsequent copies because the more isolated manuscript tradition behind the LXX would probably have preserved these accidental omissions. Of course, individual manuscripts in the MT tradition would probably have suffered from similar corruptions during the copying process, but the less isolated transmission history of MT would have caused most of the accidental omissions to be corrected as the scribes compared manuscripts from various traditions.

As I noted above, this paper's conclusions are only tentative. Similar research needs to be conducted on a larger data-set in order to confirm these findings. Nevertheless, it seems clear that copy editing played a substantial role in shaping the different manuscript traditions of the Bible.

---

28. Tov, *Textual Criticism*, 320–21.
29. Jack R. Lundbom, *Jeremiah 1–20* (AB 21a; New York: Doubleday, 1999) 57–62.
30. Freedman and Overton, "Omitting the Omissions," 114–15; Freedman and Lundbom, "Haplography in Jeremiah 1–20," 28–30, 37.

Empirical Taxonomy and the Hebrew Bible

A. Dean Forbes

Palo Alto, California

Introduction

Humans are quintessential pattern recognizers. Indeed, so developed is our penchant for detecting patterns that we too often infer their presence in error. To help us avoid faulty inferences, *mathematical pattern recognition* has been devised, a well-developed branch of machine learning with its own professional societies, textbooks, and journals.[1]

Not surprisingly, pattern recognition underlies much biblical research, although it is typically done in an informal manner.[2] If we are fortunate, skill, intuition, and method all help us avoid recognizing and interpreting "patterns" that are actually random accidents;[3] that is, we are able to avoid interpreting *random noise* as *meaningful signal*.[4]

Richard Friedman has honed his pattern recognition skills as he has identified the sources making up the Torah (Friedman 1998; 2003). Proper assessment of his work would require wide-ranging analysis, analysis too extensive to convey in a limited Festschrift contribution (see Forbes 1992).

Instead, in this essay, I will focus on *empirical taxonomy*. The basic question is this: *Given just a computer-manipulable pointed text of the Hebrew Bible, can anything useful be said about the word classes of Biblical Hebrew?*

Author's note: This contribution, especially in its later portions, draws substantially upon Forbes forthcoming. All of the figures here included are from that paper, some slightly modified, and are used with the permission of Gorgias Press.

1. Pattern recognition comes in three flavors: structural, statistical, and hybrid.

2. So far as I know, only my 1995 essay *formally* and *programmatically* uses statistical pattern recognition methods to address a biblical problem. In that paper, I state and execute a plan of attack to classify Hebrew poems on the basis of part-of-speech incidence patterns.

3. *Ramsey theory* shows that complete disorder is impossible, so that large collections of objects *must* contain very regular patterns. See Graham and Spencer (1990) for a fascinating exposition of the theory.

4. *The Bible Codes* (Drosnin 1997) provides a classic example of pattern recognition gone awry. All manner of prophecies are read from a biblical text, suitably transformed by skipping consonants. Example: In the data that purport to have predicted the ascendancy of Clinton to the presidency six months before the election (Drosnin 1997: 32), I also find predicted Clinton's rise (?) to become the head of Fiat Corp. Stay tuned. . . .

61

Word Classes

Word Classes in Linguistics

The vast majority of linguists would agree with Radford when he asserts that "all grammatical operations in natural language are category-based" (1997: 29). Grammatical categories (word classes) are thus central to linguistics.[5] But their treatment by linguists ranges from unsatisfyingly terse to very full. The terse approach is exemplified by Chomsky, who early and often was content to posit a quartet of word classes, defined in terms of a pair of binary features: *noun* [+N, -V], *verb* [-N, +V], adjective [+N, +V], and preposition [–N, –V].[6] In recent years, for a variety of reasons, interest in word classes has greatly intensified. Useful, wide-ranging discussions can be found in Brown and Miller 1999, Vogel and Comrie 2000, and Baker 2003.

Of growing interest are the questions as to whether word classes may overlap (be *mixed*) and whether they may be heterogeneous (be *gradient*). For a full discussion of these issues from the perspective of general linguistics, see Aarts et al. 2004. For a discussion with respect to the Hebrew lexicon, see Forbes 2005.

A standard terminological distinction will prove useful below. It is usual to differentiate between *lexical categories* and *functional categories*. According to Radford (1997: 38):

> [N]ouns, verbs, adjectives, adverbs and prepositions are **lexical categories** (because the words belonging to these categories have lexical/ descriptive content) whereas particles, auxiliaries, determiners, pronouns and complementizers are **functional categories** (because words belonging to these categories have an essentially grammatical function).

> A parallel distinction is often made between *open* and *closed classes*:
> *open*—large, elastic classes of (often inflected) content words
> *closed*—small, fixed classes of function words.

Word Classes in Biblical Hebrew

In the standard grammars of Biblical Hebrew, word classes are treated very cursorily. After providing Richter's list of six basic word classes for Hebrew (verb, nomen [substantive, adjective, and numeral], verbal noun, proper name, pronoun, and particle [adverb, preposition, conjunction, and modal word]), Waltke and O'Connor comment: "It is not our purpose to defend a particular list, however, but rather to point to the usefulness of a word-class approach, despite its mixed origins" (1990: 64–68).

---

5. In this essay, I use *(word) class*, *(word) category*, and *part of speech* interchangeably.
6. See Baker 2003: 1–3 for a trenchant critique of the Chomsky tradition in this area.

Joüon/Muraoka (2006) sequence through these five major categories: definite article, pronouns (demonstrative, interrogative, relative, and personal), verbs, nouns, and "particles" (adverb, preposition, conjunction, and interjection).

Van der Merwe et al. (1999: 53–59) work with ten traditionally-defined "word categories/classes": verbs, nouns, adjectives, prepositions, conjunctions, adverbs, predicators of existence, interrogatives, discourse markers, and interjections.

These classes are pretty standard. The divergences arise when one examines how various words are actually classified. Consider, for example, יֵשׁ 'there is'. Waltke and O'Connor (1990: 72) classify it as a "quasiverbal indicator." Joüon/Muraoka (2006: 541) call it an "adverb of existence." Van der Merwe et al. (1999: 320) label it a "predicator of existence." So what class is it? Or put more operationally, with what other word(s) does it have affinities?

Word-Class Definition

Of the four common ways of inferring word classes (meaning, derivation, inflection, and distribution), meaning is unreliable (Trask 1999: 280):

> Though popular in the past, this criterion is rejected today, since it is hopelessly misleading: lexical categories are syntactic categories, not semantic ones, and the meaning of a word is at best no more than a rough guide to its likely word class.

For Biblical Hebrew, word-class assignment based on *derivation*—on a word's "ability to take word-forming affixes to yield other words" (Trask 1999: 281)—is of little use, since derivational affixes are few.

Approaches based on *inflection* are powerful, especially for lexical categories (open classes). But these approaches require considerable knowledge of Biblical Hebrew. Powerful though it can be, in this essay I will not carry out inflectional classification.

I will rely entirely on word *distribution* for classification. On distributional classification, Trask (1999: 281) comments:

> A word is assigned to a part of speech on the basis of its distribution, the range of syntactic positions in which it can occur. Though not much favoured in the past, this criterion is probably the most important of all today.

For this elementary analysis, *different* spellings are considered to result in *different* words. For example, כְּדָוִיד, כְּדָוִד, כְּדָוִד, בְּדָוִיד, בְּדָוִד, בְּדָוִד, דָּוִד, דָּוִיד, דָוִד, דָוִיד, וְדָוִד, וּלְדָוִד, לְדָוִיד, לְדָוִד, and וְדָוִיד (all forms attested in the Hebrew Bible) are 14 different words, not one word ('David') exhibiting 14 different spelling and prefix combinations. The advantage of proceeding in this manner is that one need not perform morphological analysis. The disadvantage is that word frequencies are reduced, lessening the confidence that one can place in the results.

A Distributional Approach to Word Classification

The Basic Data

The Text—The *Kethiv* text of B19[a], omitting all Aramaic verses.

The Words—A sequence of consonants and vowels, preceded and followed by a space, *maqqep*, or verse ending.[7] There are 300,669 individual words ("tokens") and 51,286 different words ("types").

The Context Array—Quantitation of word distributions has been investigated by word taggers and others (Manning and Schütze 1999: 341–80; Schütze 1997). The simplest approach involves analyzing the contexts in which each word occurs. One first forms the *context array* for the Hebrew Bible, an array of 300,669 rows, one for each individual word. Table 1 shows the beginning of the context array. The fourth column (headed *focus*) holds the complete text of the Hebrew Bible. Each row of the fifth column (headed *n-1*) holds the word that precedes the focus word (to its left). Each row of the third column (headed *n+1*) holds the word that follows the focus word. And so on for the second (*n+2*) and first (*n+3*) columns. From right to left, the columns thus hold the pre-context, focus word, post-context, post-post-context, and post-post-post-context.[8]

Table 1. Incipit of the Context Array

n+3	*n+2*	*n+1*	*focus*	*n–1*
אֵת	אֱלֹהִים	בָּרָא	בְּרֵאשִׁית	
הַשָּׁמַיִם	אֵת	אֱלֹהִים	בָּרָא	בְּרֵאשִׁית
וְאֵת	הַשָּׁמַיִם	אֵת	אֱלֹהִים	בָּרָא
הָאָרֶץ:	וְאֵת	הַשָּׁמַיִם	אֵת	אֱלֹהִים
וְהָאָרֶץ	הָאָרֶץ:	וְאֵת	הַשָּׁמַיִם	אֵת
הָיְתָה	וְהָאָרֶץ	הָאָרֶץ:	וְאֵת	הַשָּׁמַיִם
תֹהוּ	הָיְתָה	וְהָאָרֶץ	הָאָרֶץ:	וְאֵת
. . .	. . .	. . .	. . .	. . .

---

7. This definition obscures the fact that the identification of some words in manuscripts requires knowledge of Biblical Hebrew. Words run together, and the existence of *maqqep*s can be uncertain. Further, cantillations are ignored. So my assertion that I work from *just the text* is an idealization.

8. I found that using one word before and three words following the focus word gave the most coherent results (Forbes 2005).

Characterizing the Local Contexts

Quantitating the Local Context. To enable computational analysis, the context information must be quantitated. One can add up for each focus word how often each word is found in the four context positions and tally the counts. Study is complicated by the fact that for statistical analyses to yield reliable results, sample sizes cannot be too small. To ensure that sample sizes are adequate, I follow Schütze (1997: 34) and work with the 250 most-frequent word types. Table 2 shows the 20 most-frequent word types, each preceded by its incidence count for the Hebrew Bible. (Note that Aramaic verses have been omitted.) Many of the other frequent word types will appear in the tree diagrams shown below.

Table 2. Twenty Most-Frequent Focus Words

6,718	אֵת	3,482	עַל	1,797	וְאֵת	1,044	הַמֶּלֶךְ
6,007	יהוה	3,248	לֹא	1,583	וְלֹא	1,029	עַד
4,808	אֲשֶׁר	2,559	כָּל	1,283	בְּנֵי	1,027	לוֹ
4,344	כִּי	2,259	יִשְׂרָאֵל	1,229	בֶּן	934	הָאָרֶץ
3,540	אֶל	1,964	וַיֹּאמֶר	1,130	אִישׁ	905	מֶלֶךְ

For each of the 250 highest-frequency word types, there are four 250-entry lists of counts. Laying these lists side-by-side, one obtains a 250-row by 1,000-column array of counts holding the context information. The challenge, then, is to use these data, and nothing more, to infer affinities among the 250 high-frequency focus-word types.

The list for pre-context word types preceding a given focus word discloses how often each high-frequency word is that focus word's pre-context. As an example, consider the first 5 focus words in Gen 1:1 (Table 1). The first 2 words in the verse are not high-frequency words, and so do not enter into consideration. The 3rd word (אֱלֹהִים) is the 31st in frequency. But since its pre-context is not of high frequency, no count in its pre-context list will be incremented from zero to one. The 4th word (אֵת) is 36th in frequency. Since, in this instantiation, it is preceded by אֱלֹהִים, the count in the 31st row (corresponding to אֱלֹהִים) of the pre-context list for אֵת is incremented by one. The 5th word (הַשָּׁמַיִם) is 181st in frequency. It is preceded by אֵת and so the 181st row of the pre-context list for הַשָּׁמַיִם is incremented by one. And so on.

The (Veiled) Methods of Classification

Robust inference of focus word affinities on the basis of counts of nearby high-frequency words requires careful choice and validation of technique. One must address technical issues such as: kind of learning, type, and specifics of clustering. I have discussed these matters at some length with ample references to the relevant technical literature (Forbes forthcoming). For present purposes, it must suffice simply to state that classification is carried out by *agglomerative average-linkage hierarchical clustering using the Manhattan metric*, and the result of classification is a tree diagram wherein focus words that have affinities in terms of the contexts in which they appear show up as leaves on nearby branches in the classification tree.[9]

Results

Classification yields a quite large tree of 250 leaves (Forbes forthcoming). To give readers an idea of the nature of the results, I display five subparts of the master tree, five sub-trees. A few comments are warranted.

Figure 1: (i) כֵּן is a possible interloper among the substantives in this subtree. It is usually considered adverbial (Waltke and O'Connor 1990: 396). (ii) The normal and pausal forms of *Jerusalem* are separated. (iii) Note where the *defective* and *plene* spellings of *David* join the sub-tree.

Figure 2: Note that 3 prefixed forms of כָּל are part of the free-standing preposition sub-tree. See Forbes 2005.

Figures 3–4: The main surprise in these figures is that the sub-trees are so sparse.

Figure 5: Here the clustering seems to have misfired. In addition to 18 preposition-plus-pronoun-suffix words, 8 other words seem to be inappropriately included.

Final Comments

We have seen that data clustering based solely on counts of nearby words gathers together many words judged similar by traditional knowledge-intensive criteria. Given the utter simplicity of the input data, these automatic results are an encouraging beginning.

But the clustering algorithms also produce some unacceptable word groups. These oddities must be eliminated via more subtle and inclusive analysis. In my forthcoming essay, I show that this is possible by carrying out distributional analysis of morphologically-segmented texts.

Given the inadequacy of some of the output clusters, it is clear that much work remains to be done if empirical taxonomy is ever to advance our knowledge of the syntax of Biblical Hebrew. But the outlines of how that work should proceed are clear.

---

9. The classification tree is analogous to the family tree, much loved by genealogists. In our case, words that are "contextually close together" share sub-trees.

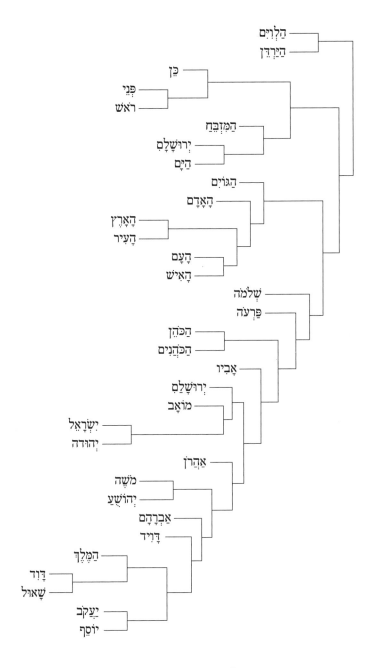

Fig. 1. Substantive Sub-Tree.

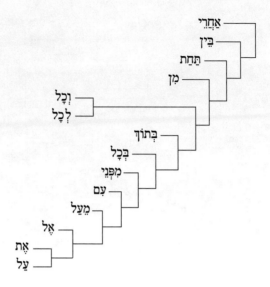

Fig. 2. Preposition Sub-Tree.

Fig. 3. Particle Sub-Tree.

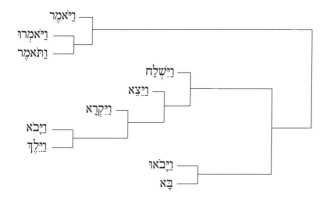

Fig. 4. Verb Sub-Tree.

Bibliography

Aarts, Bas
  2004   *Fuzzy Grammar.* Oxford: Oxford University Press.
Baker, Mark C.
  2003   *Lexical Categories: Verbs, Nouns, and Adjectives.* Cambridge: Cambridge University Press.
Brown, Keith and Jim Miller, eds.
  1999   *Concise Encyclopedia of Grammatical Categories.* Oxford: Elsevier.
Drosnin, Michael
  1997   *The Bible Codes.* New York: Simon & Schuster.
Forbes, A. Dean
  1992   Statistical Research on the Bible. Pp. 185–206 in vol. 6 of *ABD.*
  1995   Shards, Strophes, and Stats. Pp. 310–21 in *Fortunate the Eyes That See: Essays in Honor of David Noel Freedman in Celebration of His Seventieth Birthday.* Edited by A. B. Beck et al. Grand Rapids: Eerdmans.
  2005   Squishes, Clines, and Fuzzy Signs: Mixed and Gradient Categories in the Biblical Hebrew Lexicon. Pp. 105–39 in *Syriac Lexicography I.* Edited by A. Dean Forbes and David G. K. Taylor. Piscataway, NJ: Gorgias.
  forthcoming   Distributionally-Inferred Word and Form Classes in the Hebrew Lexicon: Known by the Company They Keep. In *Syriac Lexicography II.* Edited by Peter Williams. Piscataway, NJ: Gorgias.
Friedman, Richard E.
  1998   *The Hidden Book in the Bible.* San Francisco: HarperSanFrancisco.
  2003   *The Bible with Sources Revealed.* San Francisco: HarperSanFrancisco.

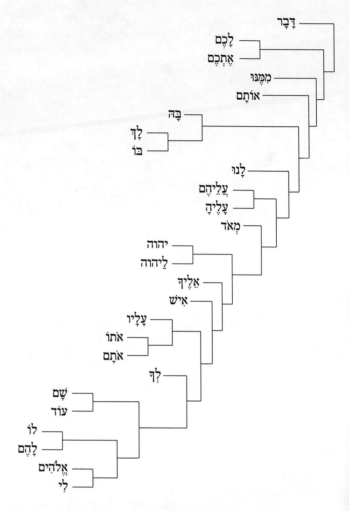

Fig. 5. "Mixed-Bag" Sub-Tree.

Graham, Ronald L., and Joel H. Spencer
    1990   Ramsey Theory. Pp. 112–17 in *Scientific American*. July: 112–17.
Joüon, Paul, and Takamitsu Muraoka
    2006   *A Grammar of Biblical Hebrew*. Revised English edition. Rome: Pontif-
            ical Biblical Institute.
Manning, Christopher D., and Hinrich Schütze
    1999   *Foundations of Statistical Natural Language Processing*. Cambridge,
            MA: MIT Press.

Merwe, C. H. J. van der, et al.
  1999 *A Biblical Hebrew Reference Grammar*. Sheffield: Sheffield Academic Press.
Radford, Andrew
  1997 *Syntax: A Minimalist Introduction*. Cambridge: Cambridge University Press.
Schütze, Hinrich
  1997 *Ambiguity Resolution in Language Learning: Computational and Cognitive Models*. Stanford: CSLI.
Trask, R. L.
  1999 Parts of Speech. Pp. 278–84 in *Concise Encyclopedia of Grammatical Categories*. Edited by K. Brown and J. Miller. New York: Elsevier.
Vogel, Petra M., and Bernard Comrie, eds.
  2000 *Approaches to the Typology of Word Classes*. Berlin: de Gruyter.
Waltke, Bruce K., and Michael P. O'Connor
  1990 *An Introduction to Biblical Hebrew Syntax*. Winona Lake, IN: Eisenbrauns.

Place-Names as Superlatives
in Classical Hebrew

H. G. M. Williamson

University of Oxford

As is well known, Classical Hebrew has no separate adjectival form to express the superlative. This does not mean, of course, that the superlative cannot be expressed, and the standard reference grammars give a full account of the ways in which this may be done (e.g., GKC §133; JM §141). Over fifty years ago, D. Winton Thomas first gave systematic attention to the use of words for "God" and "death," or the like, as expressions of the superlative (cf. English "bored to death").[1] This fact was already recognized by some of the medieval rabbinic commentators, and Thomas's proposals have by and large been favorably received.[2] My suggestion in this essay is that under certain circumstances place-names may serve the same purpose, and I will provide some possible examples of this.

Unlike the examples that Thomas studied, for a place-name to serve as a superlative requires that it go through two stages of semantic development.[3] First, something linked originally to a particular place or region gives its name to a whole class of the same. A Homburg hat no longer has to be made in the German town of that name any more than a Jersey cow has to live in the Channel Islands. This first development is extremely common, of course, and examples could be multiplied without difficulty. Second, however, it occasionally happens that the force of the place-name

---

1. D. W. Thomas, "A Consideration of Some Unusual Ways of Expressing the Superlative in Hebrew," *VT* 3 (1953) 209–24; see too his related articles, building on or extending his initial arguments: "Some Further Remarks on Unusual Ways of Expressing the Superlative in Hebrew," *VT* 18 (1968) 120–24; "The Use of נצח as a Superlative in Hebrew," *JSS* 1 (1956) 106–9; "צלמות in the Old Testament," *JSS* 7 (1962) 191–200.

2. See, for instance, P. P. Saydon, "Some Unusual Ways of Expressing the Superlative in Hebrew and Maltese," *VT* 4 (1954) 432–33; S. Rin, "The מות of Grandeur," *VT* 9 (1959) 324–25; P. A. H. de Boer, "Yhwh as Epithet Expressing the Superlative," *VT* 24 (1974) 233–35; Waltke and O'Connor, *IBHS* 154 n. 33 and 268–69; G. Brin, "The Superlative in the Hebrew Bible: Additional Cases," *VT* 42 (1992) 115–18; J. C. L. Gibson, *Davidson's Introductory Hebrew Grammar—Syntax* (Edinburgh: T. & T. Clark, 1994) 46.

3. Arguably there are some examples in English where an adjective based on the place-name moves directly to a superlative use (e.g., trojan, arctic), but, being adjectives, these have no analogy in Classical Hebrew and are not in the same category discussed above.

develops further into a claim that it represents the best in its class. In these cases the use can only be regarded as that of a superlative in which the geographical force of the name is effectively completely forgotten. Indeed, in a few cases it may even be detached from the original product altogether.

A good example of the latter is the use of the word Champagne. Originally, of course, it was used for a sparkling wine from the Champagne region of France, and from this it developed into a word to refer to any similar sort of wine, regardless of where it comes from. The *Concise Oxford Dictionary*'s rather superior statement "use in sense b is strictly incorrect" is uncharacteristically swimming against the tide of linguistic development. But beyond this generic usage of the word, it has further acquired a second stage of development in popular speech: the sense that it is the best kind of such wine (to which other names are also sometimes attributed), and indeed, it can even be detached from wine altogether. In English parlance, at least, a "champagne moment" can refer to some outstanding incident on the sports field or the like.

Another example that can be cited is Mecca, a place-name from Saudi Arabia, which, as the birthplace of Muhammed, is a place of Muslim pilgrimage. From this, however, it has developed the extended sense of "a place one aspires to visit" (*COD*), and beyond this it can be further used for any place that is deemed to be the best place for someone to visit for some particular purpose: "Salzburg is a Mecca for lovers of Mozart's music."

Inevitably, it is difficult to be certain that examples of this extended usage have been correctly identified in an ancient language without access to native speakers. The best we can hope to do is find potential examples where other contextual considerations indicate that the place-name has become so detached that it serves only as a superlative.

Since we started above with an example based on viticulture, let us continue in the same vein. Isa 5:2 occurs in the well-known Song of the Vineyard. There are difficulties about the identity of the singer in v. 1, but the point of v. 2 is clear—the owner prepared his new vineyard with care:

> He dug it thoroughly and cleared it of stones
> and planted it with "Sorek";
> he built a tower in the middle of it
> and also hewed out a winepress in it;
> he expected it to yield grapes,
> but it yielded diseased grapes.

A very similar use[4] occurs in Jer 2:21:

---

4. Indeed, there is a possibility of direct literary influence; see U. Wendel, *Jesaja und Jeremia: Worte, Motive und Einsichten Jesajas in der Verkündigung Jeremias* (Biblisch-Theologische Studien 25; Neukirchen-Vluyn: Neukirchener Verlag, 1995) 11–29.

I planted you as a Sorek vine,
  a strain tested for purity.
How is it that you have become a rogue vine,
  a vine of unknown strain.[5]

In traditional parlance, the verb 'plant' in both of these passages governs a double accusative,[6] the second of which in each case is שׂרֵק. With the sort of meaning that the word must carry here it occurs nowhere else. Related terms, however, are found also at Gen 49:11 (שׂרקה) and Isa 16:8 (שָׂרֵק). In every case, a type of vine seems to be intended. At Zech 1:8, שְׂרֻקִּים is a color term, and on the basis especially of Gen 49:11, it seems to be some kind of red; for this there is further etymological support.[7] It seems unlikely, however, that color is particularly significant here, since all wine prior to the Hellenistic period in Israel was red.[8] There is also a place-name, נחל שׂרק 'the valley of Sorek' (Judg 16:4), and one may speculate that originally the word denoted a species of vine that originated there or was characteristic of the region; this would seem to have been the understanding of LXX, ἄμπελον σωρηχ.[9] In both the cited contexts, however, the rhetorical emphasis is less upon the type of vine so much as its fine quality, a fact that is underlined by the contrast that follows with something of lesser quality. It would therefore seem reasonable to suggest that in these two passages the point is to emphasize that the owner of the vineyard planted the very best quality vines that he could. The NRSV is therefore justified in dropping the place-name altogether and in translating it with a superlative: 'choice vine(s)'.

My next suggested example occurs only once in the Hebrew Bible: the 'gold of Parvaim' in 2 Chr 3:6 (unparalleled in Kings) is part of the description of Solomon's Temple. The usual view that Parvaim is a place-name, as presupposed already by LXX φαρουϊμ and Tg. פרוים, was challenged by

---

5. The translation is that of W. McKane, *A Critical and Exegetical Commentary on Jeremiah*, vol. 1 (ICC; Edinburgh: T. & T. Clark, 1986) 39, and his commentary may be consulted for justification.

6. Cf. GKC §117ee; Waltke and O'Connor, *IBHS*, 175; to the same effect, Gibson, *Syntax*, 144 explains it more satisfactorily as an adverbial use of the noun.

7. Cf. A. Brenner, *Colour Terms in the Old Testament* (JSOTSup 21; Sheffield: JSOT Press, 1982) 114–15.

8. See C. E. Walsh, *The Fruit of the Vine: Viticulture in Ancient Israel* (HSM 60; Winona Lake, IN; Eisenbrauns, 2000) 106–10, contra O. Borowski, *Agriculture in Iron Age Israel* (Winona Lake, IN: Eisenbrauns, 1987) 104.

9. Contra I. L. Seeligmann, *The Septuagint Version of Isaiah: A Discussion of Its Problems* (Leiden: Brill, 1948) 33 and 59, who thinks rather that ἄμπελον has been added secondarily. It is, of course, common in many languages to name wine after its place of origin (for examples in Hebrew and Aramaic, see J. Naveh, "Unpublished Phoenician Inscriptions from Palestine," *IEJ* 37 [1987] 25–30, esp. pp. 29–30). There seems to be no reason why types of vine should not similarly have been so known.

del Medico.[10] He argued that the temple gold could not all have come from such a place, because elsewhere we are told that some came from Ophir (1 Chr 29:4) as well as other places. On the interpretation offered below, this objection is emptied of all its force, but in fact it is a misguided objection in the first place. On the one hand, there is no need to regard v. 6 as a claim that all the gold of the house was exclusively gold of Parvaim (it explicitly does not include the gold used for the nails in v. 9, for instance), and on the other, as Japhet has shown,[11] it is in any case only one in a number of terms for gold that the Chronicler adds to his Vorlage in an attempt to exaggerate the splendor of the Temple.[12] Del Medico's error is to take one line of later rabbinic interpretation (see below) as being already the Chronicler's own: based on an assumed etymology from *prh*, he renders 'de l'or fructifère' (fruit-bearing gold). But this is not the only such interpretation that the rabbis provided for this word, and it seems certain that, as so often, they were striving to extract significance from what for them had become an obscure term, at best.[13]

A further argument in favor of the likelihood that Parvaim is an ancient place-name comes from its probable occurrence (spelled *prwyn*, as might be expected in Aramaic) in the *Genesis Apocryphon* from Qumran. The text (1QapGen 2:23) is not entirely certain, but the reading of this particular word does not seem to be in doubt; Grelot's reconstruction of the line is *w'zl lh qdmt lprwyn* (with reference to the visit of Methuselah to Enoch), 'and he went straightaway (?) to Parvain (and there he found him)',[14] while Fitzmyer defends the alternative *w'zl l'rk mt lprwyn* 'and he went through the land of Parvaim'.[15] Either way, Parvaim has here become a

---

10. H. E. del Medico, "*Zahab Parwayim*. L'or fructifère dans la tradition juive," *VT* 13 (1963) 158–86. Against the suggestion of A. S. Yahuda, "Hebrew Words of Egyptian Origin," *JBL* 66 (1947) 83–90, esp. 87, to read this as a common noun (dual of Egyptian *pr* 'house', hence "the gold of the best quality, approved by both Egyptian treasuries"; see W. Rudolph, *Chronikbücher* [HAT 21; Tübingen: Mohr Siebeck, 1955] 203). The suggestion appears not even to warrant a mention in Y. Muchiki, *Egyptian Proper Names and Loanwords in North-West Semitic* (SBLDS 173; Atlanta: Society of Biblical Literature, 1999).

11. S. Japhet, *I & II Chronicles: A Commentary* (OTL; Louisville: Westminster John Knox, 1993) 554.

12. This would by no means be the only unusual feature of the Chronicler's description of the Temple, if J. Jarick's analysis is correct; see Jarick, "The Temple of David in the Book of Chronicles," in *Temple and Worship in Biblical Israel: Proceedings of the Oxford Old Testament Seminar* (ed. J. Day; Library of the Hebrew Bible/Old Testament Series 422; London: T. & T. Clark, 2005) 365–81.

13. For this and other objections to del Medico's position, see P. Grelot, "Retour au Parwaim," *VT* 14 (1964) 155–63.

14. P. Grelot, "Parwaïm: des Chroniques à l'Apocryphe de la Genèse," *VT* 11 (1961) 30–38.

15. J. Fitzmyer, *The Genesis Apocryphon of Qumran Cave 1: A Commentary* (2nd ed.; Biblica et Orientalia 18a; Rome: Pontifical Biblical Institute, 1971) 52–53 and 94–95.

strange and remote country, more in the realms of mythical than actual geography, probably to be identified with "the garden of the Righteous," situated "at the ends of the earth," as known from the parallel account in the book of *Enoch* (*1 En.* 106:8; cf. 65:1–5).

The Rabbis, whether or not they were aware of the original significance of the word,[16] used etymology to derive some further meaning from it, linking it either with *pry* 'fruit', and so suggesting that it produced gold fruit (*Num. Rab.* 11:3; cf. *b. Yoma* 21b and 39b),[17] or linking it with *pr* 'a young bull', suggesting that the color of the gold was like the blood of bulls (*b. Yoma* 45a). *Cant. Rab.* 3:10 refers to both interpretations and, interestingly, *Exod. Rab.* 35:1 does as well, within a wider context that further links light and gold, which *b. Sanh.* 103b explains by way of gold as a substitute for the sun. Of these developments, however, our passage in Chronicles gives no hint.

In reality, the location of Parvaim is uncertain. Two main suggestions have been canvassed in the past, both based on the writings of the 10th-century Arabic historian Hamdani.[18] Less likely is *farwa* in southwest Arabia; more likely is *el-farwain* in northeast Arabia, although there is no evidence that this was the site of a gold mine.

If already, by the time of the *Genesis Apocryphon*, the name was open to speculation bordering on the mythical, the possibility seems worth considering that even at the earlier time of the Chronicler the geographical sense was more or less forgotten and "gold of Parvaim" had become proverbial for the finest gold. That is certainly what the Chronicler intends to convey in the context, as the immediately preceding clauses make clear, "[he] covered it with fine gold. . . . He adorned the house with settings of precious stones." Perhaps significantly, it is also the way in which the Vulgate, *aurum probatissimum*, understood it, and Peshiṭta's *dahbā ṭābā* is comparable. There is thus much to be said for including this as an example of a place-name used as a superlative.

The suggestion might be raised that Ophir itself should also be included in this category. The occurrence of the name on an ostracon from Tell

---

16. See Grelot, "Retour," 160 n. 3.

17. This derivation seems also to have been familiar to the author of the apocryphal text published as the "Traité des Vases" by J. T. Milik, "Notes d'épigraphie et de topographie palestiniennes," *Revue biblique* 66 (1959) 550–75, esp. 567–75.

18. See more fully E. L. Curtis and A. A. Madsen, *A Critical and Exegetical Commentary on the Books of Chronicles* (ICC; Edinburgh: T. & T. Clark, 1910) 325; G. N. Knoppers, *1 Chronicles 1–9* (AB 12; New York: Doubleday, 2004) 277. R. North, "Ophir/Parvaim and Petra/Joktheel," in *Fourth World Congress of Jewish Studies: Papers*, vol. 1 (Jerusalem: World Union of Jewish Studies, 1967) 197–202, suggested identifying Parvaim with Ophir, but this does not help further settle its location, because the site of Ophir is itself uncertain; cf. D. W. Baker, "Ophir," *ABD* 5:26–27.

Qasile, *zhb.'pr.lbyt.ḥrn.*[ ] *š 30*,[19] suggests that still in the 8th century B.C.E. it was recognized as at least a type of gold, if not one from a specific locality. There are indications, however, that Ophir might have moved into our third category (place-name used as a superlative), both because of its common biblical use in passages that emphasize the fine quality of the gold (e.g., Isa 13:12,[20] Ps 45:10, Job 28:16) and because it can be used on its own, without the noun for gold (whether *zhb* or *ktm*) needing to be mentioned (Job 22:24). "Gold of Ophir" is thus certainly used proverbially, but whether we can say that it has definitely moved into the category of superlative remains uncertain.

A final example is the use of the place-name Bashan, the extensive plateau some 2,000 feet above sea level and to the east of Galilee. It is a fertile region, making it suitable for agriculture and pasturage (Mic 7:14). Oaks are mentioned in the same region (Isa 2:13, Ezek 27:6, and Zech 11:2) and are likely to have grown in the western part of the plateau (the Golan Heights). It is, however, best known for the quality of its cattle, the famous "cows of Bashan."

At first sight, this appellation might seem to be no more than a reference to a type of cow, just like the Jersey cows referenced in my opening comments. Closer inspection, however, suggests that the use may have gone one step further.

In the first place, we should note that Bashan is used to refer to more than just cattle. Cows (Amos 4:1) and bulls (Ps 22:13) admittedly fit that category, but in two other passages we are clearly invited to take a wider view. Deut 32:14 is part of a passage describing God's bountiful provision for his people in the land that he gave them. It includes the words עם־חלב כרים ואילים בני־בשן ועתודים, which the NRSV renders 'with fat of lambs and goats; Bashan bulls and goats'. The combination elsewhere of כרים, אילים, and עתודים (Isa 34:6, Ezek 27:21, and 39:18) suggests, alternatively, that בני־בשן should be construed not as a reference to bulls but in apposition with and explanatory of אילים 'goats', thus indicating that they are the finest in their class. The matter is admittedly uncertain,[21] but the second interpretation receives support from Ezek 39:18, which refers to rams, lambs, goats, and bulls, and then qualifies the whole list as "fatlings of Bashan, all

---

19. Cf. G. I. Davies, *Ancient Hebrew Inscriptions: Corpus and Concordance* (Cambridge: Cambridge University Press, 1991) 86 (no. 11.002).

20. See on the use here the brief but suggestive remarks of E. A. Seibert, "Harder than Flint, Faster than Eagles: Intensified Comparatives in the Latter Prophets," in *Inspired Speech: Prophecy in the Ancient Near East: Essays in Honor of Herbert B. Huffmon* (ed. J. Kaltner and L. Stulman; JSOTSup 378; London: T. & T. Clark, 2004) 286–301, esp. 293–94.

21. See the cautious discussion in P. Sanders, *The Provenance of Deuteronomy 32* (Oudtestamentische Studiën 37; Leiden: Brill, 1996) 172–75.

of them." Even on the first view, however, the use of the rather general בני־בשׁן is itself an indication that we are moving away from a mere designation of a class.

Secondly, as well as referring Bashan to "fatlings" (which clearly takes us beyond the realm of cattle alone), the final phrase of Ezek 39:18 is cast in such a way as to make the point that Bashan is effectively superlative in use. The list of animals is itself metaphorically descriptive of "the mighty . . . the princes of the earth," and the point of the whole, climaxing with "fatlings of Bashan all of them," is to exaggerate the depiction of the forces of Gog in such a way as to magnify the nature of their defeat. With this in mind, if we return to the other passages that link animals and Bashan, then we are not surprised to find that there seems to be a similar, if not quite so marked, rhetorical emphasis in each of those cases as well. I conclude that it is probable that the designation "of Bashan" has passed from being merely a generic description of a type of cow to having a broader, superlative use.

Because of space constraints I cannot explore additional examples here, though I have noted several other possible candidates. Given Dick Friedman's delight in words and word play, I trust he will enjoy thinking up a few more.

The Real Formal Full Personal Name
of the God of Israel

DAVID NOEL FREEDMAN ל״ז

University of California, San Diego

In Western culture, names can be changed with a nominal filing fee and are nothing more than identification labels that differentiate between individuals. In the ancient Near East, however, a person's name had much deeper significance, embodying the whole person and even one's power. The noun *šēm* ('name') can also mean 'self' or 'essence', and some ancient peoples believed that to know the name of an object would mean gaining mastery over it. A name change could be given prophetically in order to signify an alteration in character, destiny, or status, as with the patriarchs: Abram to Abraham (Gen 17:5) or Jacob to Israel (Gen 32:28).[1]

Patriarchal names such as Isaac, Jacob, and Joseph are typically hypocoristic; that is, they consist of an imperfect form of the verb and its pronominal subject, the third-masculine singular in the case of men. The implied nominal subject in all such cases is a divinity, and generally speaking the god intended is El, the chief of the pantheon in the Northwest Semitic region. Depending on the exact form of the name, it expresses a prayer—either a blessing or a petition—or an action. Thus the names given may be explained as follows:

Yiṣḥāq-ʾēl = 'may or let El laugh (in triumph or derision)'
Yaʿăqōb-ʾēl = 'may or let El protect (?) [the child]'
Yôsēp-ʾēl = 'may El increase abundantly [the fruitfulness of the land]'

In this essay, I will argue that the word *Yahweh* is a verb with a third-masculine-singular-pronominal prefix and that the implied nominal

---

1. My colleague William Propp has traced the exchange of power behind the gods' disclosure of names to humans: "in later magical folklore both Jewish and gentile, God possesses a secret name (not 'Yahweh'), the knowledge of which confers some of his power upon humans; it was supposedly engraved, for example, on Moses' staff. Humans in the Bible, then, are understandably eager to learn the names of deities, and the latter are understandably chary of disclosing them." William Propp, *Exodus 1–18* (AB 2; New York: Doubleday, 1999) 224. Also see B. H. Porter and S. D. Ricks, "Names in Antiquity: Old, New, and Hidden," in *By Study and Also by Faith: Essays in Honor of Hugh W. Nibley* (ed. J. M. Lundquist and S. D. Ricks; 2 vols.; Salt Lake City: Deseret, 1990) 1:501–22.

subject is the great high god, El.[2] The sequence *Yahweh* ʾēl actually occurs in eight places in the Bible. Let us examine some of the passages in which this combination occurs and thus test the hypothesis.

As we proceed with this inquiry, a number of questions must be asked, and if possible, answered:

1. What is the grammatical form of this word? Many, if not most scholars, have treated the Tetragrammaton as a verb, and this has been true of the scholarly tradition to which I belong. Both Paul Haupt and W. F. Albright did so, and so far as I am aware, their students, my colleagues, and I have followed in this pattern.

2. If the Tetragrammaton is a verb, then it must be parsed as a third-masculine-singular prefix or imperfect form of a root originally *HWY → *HWH → HYH, meaning 'to be', 'become', or 'come to pass'. The prefix form may be translated as a future tense or, in the particular vocalization of the name *Yahwēh*, as a jussive or a preterite form.

3. The conjugation of the verb form. The choice here is either Qal or Hiphil. In the Hebrew Bible, the Masoretes recognized a Qal form (that is, a simple tense) but not a Hiphil (that is, a causative form). Nevertheless, it has been argued (and I think correctly) that a causative form of this verb can be assumed for the Bible.

4. If the form is a verb, then it will contain both the verb and the pronoun subject, and we would translate: 'He will cause to be' or 'Let him bring about' or 'He has brought into existence'.

5. What is the noun subject implied by the pronoun? There are many names of this sort in the Hebrew Bible, and in particular, we may point to patriarchal names such as Jacob, Isaac, and Joseph, all of which have the same structure as Yahweh. It is also recognized that these names are abbreviated and that in each case the unwritten subject is a deity. Again, it is most likely that the unnamed deity is El, the chief god of the Canaanite pantheon.

Thus, the full name of those mentioned above would have been Jacob-El, Isaac-El, Joseph-El, and so forth. We may therefore conclude that the full name of our deity was Yahweh-El, which should then be translated: 'May El create', 'Let El create', or 'El has created'.

---

2. See W. F. Albright, "The Name Yahweh," *JBL* 43 (1924) 370–78; idem, "Further Observations on the Name Yahweh and Its modifications and Proper Names," *JBL* 44 (1925) 158–62. For more recent examples, see the introduction to the Anchor edition of *From the Stone Age to Christianity* (Garden City, NY: Doubleday, 1957) 15–16; and W. H. Brownlee, "The Ineffable Name of God," *BASOR* 226 (1977) 39–46.

History of the Name:
Patriarchal to Personal

In orthodox language, *běnê-ʾělōhîm* ('children of God') is a descriptive term referring to the function of angels as messengers (*malʾākîm*). In a polytheistic Greco-Roman, Indo-European, or Mesopotamian context, the "archangels" would be called "lesser deities." In the monotheistic climate of Israel, lesser deities become created "messengers" in the service of El. Some of the angels are known by their proper names, such as the archangels named in various passages (Michael, Gabriel, Ariel, Uriel). The *ʾēl* predicate indicates that the names are archaic and predate the age of Moses.

Each of the archangels, with the inclusion of Yahweh among them, represents a different aspect or attribute of El. Michael (*mîkā-ʾēl*) 'Who is like El' is a rhetorical statement suggesting that El is without comparison, the uncontested supreme deity. Gabriel (*gabrî-ʾēl*) means 'El is my warrior'. Ariel (*arî-ʾēl*) means either 'Lion of El' or 'El is [my] Lion', referencing El as his defender, and Uriel (*urî-ʾēl*) means 'God is my light'.

If our analysis of the name Yahweh is correct, this would put him in the pantheon along with the other *malʾākîm*, lesser deities that were called archangels in the monotheistic Hebrew tradition. The old God is not overthrown as in Greco-Roman mythology, although echoes of a primeval battle are resonant when Yahweh destroys monsters.[3] Ultimately, the overthrow of El is finessed, and the two gods are merged. The anomalous combination Yahweh Elohim,[4] which is commonly understood as an artificial construction or a mixture of sources, may be the survival of the prose equivalent of the poetic Yahweh El with the same original meaning, 'God creates'.

Yahweh is the deity in whom the creative aspect of El is manifest. The root of Yₕwₕ is the verb *hyh*, which appears as a Hiphil imperfect third-masculine singular, to be translated 'He causes to be, he brings into existence; he brings to pass; he creates'. In Exodus, the form *ʾehyeh* is a secondary development: the first-person equivalent of the Tetragrammaton, which is now vocalized as a Qal form in the Masoretic Text: 'I will become what I will become'. The Masoretes did not acknowledge a causative form of the verb, which would mean: 'I bring into being', 'I create what I create'. Thus, Yahweh El exemplifies and expresses the creative aspect of the chief God. This aspect of El is affirmed by Melchizedek, the king of Salem, in Gen 14:19, when he says, "Blessed is Abram of El-Elyon, Creator of heaven and earth." The name *El* figures prominently in the patriarchal stories in

---

3. Isa 27:1, Ps 74:12–15.
4. Gen 2:4, 7, 8, 9, 15, 16, 18, 19, 21, 22; 3:1, 8 (bis), 9, 13, 14, 21, 22, 23.

the book of Genesis.[5] In Genesis 14, when Abraham says, "El Elyon creator of heaven and earth," the emphasis is on "most high."

Exodus 3:13–15

There are several passages in which God reveals his personal name to Moses, including Exod 3:13–15, the first recorded in the Hebrew Bible. While the name *Yahweh* is treated as a proper noun in practically all of its occurrences, when God responds to Moses' specific question, he uses a first-person verb form, which is presented as equivalent to the Tetragrammaton.

> (13) And Moses said to the God, "Behold, I am coming to the sons of Israel, and I will say to them, 'The God of your fathers has sent me to you,' and they will say to me, 'What is his name?' What shall I say to them?"
> (14) And God said to Moses, "I will become what I will become [*'ehyeh 'ăšer 'ehyeh*]." And he said, "thus shall you say to the sons of Israel, *'Ehyeh* has sent me to you.'"
> (15) And God said again to Moses, "Thus you shall say to the sons of Israel, 'Yahweh the God of your fathers, the God of Abraham, the God of Isaac, and the God of Jacob has sent me to you.' This is my name forever and this is my designation for (endless) generations."

The least that can be said about this presentation is that the form of the name given in the first person is regarded as verbal and is pointed by the Masoretes as a Qal imperfect first-person singular. The traditional translation, 'I am that I am', is simply wrong, but it reflects accurately the rendering of the Septuagint here, *egō eimi ho ōn*, literally, 'I am the one who is'. The Hebrew equivalent would be *'ănî 'ănî hû* 'I, I am'.[6] The first-person pronoun is repeated and is followed by the third-masculine-singular pronoun. 'He' serves here as the copula, so a literal reading would be 'I, I am he' (*'ănî hû'*), but a better translation of Deut 32:39 would be 'I am I', the ultimate expression of self-existence. Before Albright, Paul Haupt's solution was to emend the second *'ehyeh* so the expression read: *'ahyeh 'ăšer yihyeh* ('I cause to be what comes into existence').

At the same time, this verbal form is also treated as a subject noun of yet another verb in the combination: ''HYH has sent me'. The parallel clause in v. 15 has Yahweh as the subject of the same verb, showing that Yahweh and 'HYH are equivalent.

---

5. In the composite Torah and in JE, the name *Yahweh* is used at the time of Enosh (Gen 4:26; Propp, *Exodus 1–18*, 223).

6. Deut 32:39: "See now that I, I am, and there is no god beside me. I, I put to death and I bring to life. I have smashed and I, I will heal."

A close reading of the name in its proposed restored form avoids the need for textual emendation.[7] Unemended, the formula in Exod 3:14, *'eh-yeh 'ăšer 'ehyeh*, falls into the category of idem per idem constructions common to both Hebrew and Arabic. Where the means to be more explicit do not exist, the second verb serves as a predicate and thus, like a cognate accusative, emphasizes the verbal action (e.g., Exod 16:23, "What you bake, bake"; and "What you boil, boil"). In Exod 3:14, the personal name occurs three times, twice as a first-person verb and once as a noun with a prosthetic *'alep*, probably elative in force.

Despite the Creator God's preeminence in Israel from patriarchal times, in the context of Exodus, the principal emphasis is on the merciful intervention and the saving action of the God of the Fathers on behalf of his oppressed people. Significance is given to the theme of Yahweh's *šēm* ('name') which, as William Propp insightfully observes, connotes "his fame, posterity, memorial, concept and essence," the revelation of which precedes the great redemptive act of the exodus.[8] The important conclusion is that the name as described here is treated as a verb.

Exodus 6:2–3

And God spoke to Moses and he said to him, "I am Yahweh, and I appeared to Abraham, to Isaac, and to Jacob as El-Shadday, but [by] my name Yahweh I did not make myself known to them."

According to the P source, the name *Yahweh* was not known or used by the patriarchs, whose preferred designation for the deity was *El*, along with various qualifying epithets. So the God of the fathers is El, who should be identified with the great high god of Canaanite mythology, often qualified by descriptive terms reflecting aspects and attributes of the deity:

1. *'ēl šadday*—(from Akkadian *šaddu*) 'El of the mountains'
2. *'ēl 'elyôn*—'El, the most high', which places him at the head of the pantheon
3. *'ēl 'ôlam*—which reflects his immortal status.

---

7. P. Haupt, "Der Name Jahwe," *Orientalistische Literaturzeitung* 12 (1909) 211–14. In contrast, *The International Standard Bible Encyclopedia* contends that, although reading *'ehyeh* as a Hiphil conjugation "is attractive and has had much support, it is doubtful for two reasons. First, there is no known example of *hāyâ* in the Hiphil. Second, on the only occasion where an apparent attempt is made to explain the name (Ex. 3:14), Yahweh's character and acts as Israel's redeeming, covenant God, not His role as Creator, are indicated." *International Standard Bible Encyclopedia* (ed. Geoffrey W. Bromiley; Grand Rapids: Eerdmans, 1979) 2:507.

8. Propp, *Exodus 1–18*, 36.

Only later is Yahweh equated with El and, while the throne of heaven is not shared by the two gods, the lesser deity, Yahweh, assumes the preeminent position once his name becomes interchangeable with El's.

Deuteronomy 32

In Deut 32:7–9, "The Song of Moses," we have a classic collocation of El the Most High, who apportions gods and nations, and Yahweh, whose particular responsibility is the nation of Israel. The historical linguistic context of Deut 32:7–9 offers an important reading of God's name:

> (7) Remember the days of old,
>   Consider the years of generation after generation.
> Ask your father and let him inform you,
>   your elders and let them tell you.
> (8) When the Most High apportioned the nations,
>   when he parceled out human beings,
> He established the boundaries of peoples,
>   according to the number of the sons of God.[9]
> (9) For the portion of Yahweh is his people,
>   Jacob is the lot of his inheritance.

A reasonable reading of this passage would indicate that El Elyon, in his role as the principal deity of the pantheon, has assigned each of the nations to one of the members of his heavenly court, and specifically, that Yahweh (El) has Israel as his special people and vice-versa.

Exodus 34:6–7

The most important passage for our purposes is Exod 34:6–7, which is even more explicit in its use of the complete form of the name of God than either Exodus 6 or Exodus 3. In a running debate between Moses and God on the propriety of God's intentions and behavior, God announced in Exod 33:17–23 that he would reveal his personal name to Moses but added this reservation: "And he said, 'You are not able to see my face because anybody who sees me will not survive'" (Exod 33:20). Then Yahweh says:

> Behold, I have a place, and you shall stand upon the rock, and it will happen when my glory passes by that I will place you in the cleft of the rock, and I will make my hand cover you until I pass by. Then I will remove my hand, and you will see my back side, but my face will not be seen. (Exod 33:21–23)

---

9. The Masoretic Text reads 'the sons of Israel', but the Septuagint, strikingly supported by texts from Qumran, preserves a more original reading that reflects a widespread belief that each nation had a tutelary deity or angel that served as its guardian.

God's face shines so brightly that humans cannot stand it. Moses will receive the full revelation of God without the death-wielding rays. Moses hides in the cleft of a rock, and God passes by so Moses will see his back but not his face.

We find the continuation and the climax in Exod 34:6–7: "And Yahweh passed in front of his face, and Yahweh called, 'Yahweh El is most compassionate and most gracious, longsuffering, and great in mercy and truth.'"

The nature of the Mosaic God is described at length with a series of adjectival modifiers that recall litanic formulations of the earliest period. It is difficult to say how much of this material could have originally belonged to the name of God. Some of these formulas go back to patriarchal times, but much is distinctively Mosaic, as the biblical tradition itself makes clear. [10]

The repetition of Yahweh is a unique occurrence in the Hebrew Bible. For our purposes, the important part of this passage is the phrase *wayyiqrā' Yahweh Yahweh 'ēl raḥûm wĕḥannûn*. What are the proper grammatical analysis and syntactic connections? The most natural way to read this sentence is as follows:

wayyiqrā' Yahweh	and Yahweh called out
Yahweh-'ēl	Yahweh-El
raḥûm wĕḥannûn	is most compassionate and most gracious

But it is also possible to separate Yahweh from El and render it as follows:

wayyiqrā' Yahweh	and Yahweh called out
Yahweh El raḥûm wĕḥannûn	Yahweh is a compassionate and gracious God

Scholars who do not treat the second "Yahweh" as a component of the complete name of God, "Yahweh El," translate "Yahweh Yahweh El" in its indefinite form as 'a god' and, therefore, they consider the adjectives to be attributive. Alternately, the complete name of God is also overlooked when the passage is translated by leaving out the copula altogether, so it reads: 'Yahweh, Yahweh, God merciful and gracious'. [11]

---

10. See my "Name of the God of Moses," *Divine Commitment and Human Obligation: Selected Writings of David Noel Freedman* (Grand Rapids: Eerdmans, 1997) 82–87.

11. Admittedly, one way to increase one's bibliography is to write from two sides of an issue. While I have not contended against all of my previous arguments, I have reversed my opinion on a few matters, one of which is the name of God in this passage. At the time of my 1955 inauguration as Professor of Hebrew and Old Testament Literature at Western Seminary in Pittsburgh, the commonly held view was that El was the name of God. It never occurred to me that it could be anything else. When I published my inaugural address, I translated Exod 34:6: "Yahweh; Yahweh is God, compassionate and gracious, etc." My exegesis continued: "The proclamation begins with the name of God, Yahweh, and continues with a series of qualifying adjectives [. . .]." The five attributes cited in the article "God Compassionate and Gracious" are compassion, grace, patience,

In order to read the first "Yahweh," the second "Yahweh," and the "El" in third position as three synonymous forms of the subject, God, the succeeding adjectives would have to be attributive. In Hebrew, adjectives are classified as either predicates or attributes. In the example "the good man," "good" is attributive. This is easy in English, but not in Hebrew, which does not use a copula; this means the attributive adjective always follows the noun and agrees in gender, number, and definiteness.

In the case of a predicate, such as the position of "good" in the phrase "the man is good," the adjective does not have an article, and it is always indefinite; it usually precedes but often follows its subject. The position is less important. In Exod 34:6–7, "Yahweh El," like all proper names, is definite. If Yahweh-El is definite, the following adjectives are indefinite, so they must be predicate.

Properly speaking, the name itself is found in the third-person formula in 34:6: "The compassionate and gracious God creates what he creates." This parallels the first-person formula adapted for divine utterance in Exod 3:14 and Exod 33:19, where the same verbal roots are used: "I create what I create, and I am gracious to whom I am gracious, and I show mercy to whom I show mercy." Therefore, the correct translation of 34:6–7 is 'Yahweh cried out, "Yahweh El is compassionate, gracious, longsuffering, ready to forgive"'. From that point on in the passage, all commentaries are in agreement.

The question turns on whether El is a proper noun, the name of the chief god of the Northwest Semitic pantheon, or a generic term for deity, followed by a series of attributive adjectives or epithets. I think it is at least equally justifiable to read the list of qualifiers as predicates, and this may be a better resolution of the grammatical connections. The point is that all of the qualifiers are indefinite, while the subject is unquestionably definite, namely, Yahweh, the God of Israel. I believe that in this pivotal passage, we have the complete form of the formal personal name of the God of Israel: Yahweh El.

There are a number of other passages in which the sequence Yahweh El occurs. Of the eight possible instances, only a few qualify for serious consideration. Let us look at them.

Psalm 10:12

There are two options for reading this colon:

1. *Qûmâ Yahweh*   Arise, O Yahweh;
   ʾēl nĕśāʾ yādekā   El, raise your hand.

---

loyalty, faithfulness. D. N. Freedman, "God Compassionate and Gracious: Inaugural Address," *Western Watch* 6 (Pittsburgh: Western Seminary, 1955) 6.

2. *Qûmâ Yahweh-'ēl*   Rise, Yahweh-El;
   nĕśā' yādekā   raise your hand.

A case can be made for either rendering. On the one hand, each colon would begin with an imperative second-masculine-singular verb. The subject then would go with the first verb and the object with the second. Alternatively, we could argue that the structure is chiastic, with verb followed by verb and then subject followed by verb:

Qûmâ Yahweh/'ēl nĕśā' yādĕkā

Psalm 31:6[5]

In Ps 31:6, the second colon has the sequence:

pādîtâ 'ôtî Yahweh   You have redeemed me, Yahweh,
'ēl 'ĕmet   God of truth.

While it might be possible to read the divine name as Yahweh-El, that would leave the final word *'ĕmet* in grammatical limbo.

Psalm 94:1

In Ps 94:1, the sequence Yahweh El is only apparent, because the terms belong with different colons:

'ēl nĕqāmôt Yahweh   God of [my] vindication is Yahweh;
'ēl nĕqāmôt hôpîaʿ   God of [my] vindication has shined forth.

Conclusion:
Naming Names

The additional data drawn from several passages in which Yahweh and El are collocated do not add much to the case but leave it pretty much as it stands in the light of key passages such as Exod 3:14–15, 6:1–2, and principally Exod 34:6.

If the Tetragrammaton, YHWH, is a verb in the earliest biblical tradition, then it has a pronominal subject that is expressed, and behind it a subject-noun. From the passages in Exod 3:6, 6:2–3, and 34:6–7, it seems clear that *Yahweh* was originally a verb for which the proper subject was El. Despite its obvious Canaanite associations, the name *El* is deeply rooted in Israelite tradition. The anomalous combination Yahweh-Elohim (Genesis 2–3) may be the extant prose equivalent of the poetic or formulaic Yahweh-El, both meaning 'God creates'.

A close reading of the passages in Exodus reveals that the original full name of the God of Israel was *Yahweh-El*, which focuses attention on the High God as creator (1) of the whole universe of time and space, (2) in particular, of his people, Israel.

Part 2

Source Criticism

Leitwort *Style and Literary Structure in the J Primeval Narrative*

RONALD HENDEL

University of California, Berkeley

> Somewhere, parently, in the ginnandgo gap between antediluvious and annadominant the copyist must have fled with his scroll.
>
> —James Joyce, *Finnegan's Wake*

The *Leitwort* style of biblical narrative was first clearly elucidated by Martin Buber, the existentialist philosopher and popularizer of Jewish mysticism. From my (admittedly biased) view, this was his most important contribution to civilization. He wrote:

> By *Leitwort* I understand a word or word root that is meaningfully repeated within a text or sequence of texts or complex of texts; those who attend to these repetitions will find a meaning of the text revealed or clarified, or at any rate made more emphatic. As noted, what is repeated need not be a single word but can be a word root; indeed the diversity of forms often strengthens the overall dynamic effect. I say "dynamic" because what takes place between the verbal configurations thus related is in a way a *movement*; readers to whom the whole is present feel the waves beating back and forth. Such measured repetition, corresponding to the inner rhythm of the text—or rather issuing from it—is probably the strongest of all techniques for making a meaning available without articulating it explicitly.[1]

Buber argued that the *Leitwort* style is a distinctive literary technique for the production of meaning in biblical narrative. Hermann Gunkel had earlier pointed to the repetition of key words as part of the economy of biblical narrative, but he attributed these traits as much to the primitive quality of the ancient Hebrew mind as to deliberate literary artistry.[2] Buber much

---

1. M. Buber, *"Leitwort* Style in Pentateuchal Narrative," in Buber and F. Rosenzweig, *Scripture and Translation* (trans. Lawrence Rosenwald; Bloomington: Indiana University Press, 1994; German original, 1936) 114.

2. H. Gunkel, *Genesis* (Macon, GA: Mercer University Press, 1997; German original, 3rd ed., 1910) xl: "As a rule, quite in contrast to our sense of style, the expression is repeated with the recurrence of the substance so that the same word often runs through

more convincingly demonstrated that the *Leitwort* style is a deliberate technique, a constitutive feature of biblical poetics. In recent years Robert Alter, Meir Sternberg, and others have revived Buber's discovery and contributed to our understanding of this literary phenomenon.[3]

In what follows, I wish to trace some of the intersecting webs of *Leitwörter* in the J portion of the Genesis primeval narrative (Genesis 1–11). To some scholars, attention to the biblical sources of Genesis may seem quaint or unliterary. In contrast, I would agree with those who maintain that the interplay between source and discourse is a crucial dimension of a thorough literary analysis and that we need to develop forms of attention sensitive to the mixed voices in the text.[4] Studies of Genesis that claim to discern literary patterns without paying attention to source distinctions are generally unconvincing, tending to blur or harmonize important frictions in the text. A complex reading that takes into account the many-layered senses and histories of the text is a worthwhile and perhaps necessary goal.

In both the J and P layers of the primeval narrative of Genesis 1–11, the *Leitwort* style creates a unifying literary texture that is perceptible and effective within each source *and* in the composite text. In the following I will limit my remarks to the J text, in which the *Leitwort* style has several overlapping effects. First I will consider the way *Leitwörter* are used to link successive stories, thereby creating a unified narrative sequence out of what were probably previously disparate and unconnected stories. Within the J composition, what Buber calls the "back and forth" movement of the *Leitwort* style serves to join together the stories in a coherent sequence and

---

the narrative like a red thread. . . . Undoubtedly, this practice originally arose because of the poverty of the language. The narrators, however, whose narratives are available to us, adapt this style because they can thereby reproduce their impression of the account's unity."

3. R. Alter, *The Art of Biblical Narrative* (New York: Basic Books, 1981) 92–112; M. Sternberg, *The Poetics of Biblical Narrative: Ideological Literature and the Drama of Reading* (Bloomington: Indiana University Press, 1985) 390–427; see also Y. Amit, "The Multi-Purpose 'Leading Word' and the Problems of Its Usage," *Proof* 9 (1989) 99–114. Amit observes that there are "two separate functions of the leading word: sometimes it appears throughout a story as a key word, and sometimes it can be seen as a connective" (p. 109). I would add that these are not necessarily separate functions; as I will show, the *Leitwörter* in Genesis 1–11 often do both.

4. See R. E. Friedman, "Sacred History and Theology: The Redaction of Torah," in *The Creation of Sacred Literature: Composition and Redaction of the Biblical Text* (ed. Friedman; Berkeley: University of California Press, 1981) 25–34; J. Barton, *Reading the Old Testament: Method in Biblical Study* (2nd ed.; Louisville: Westminster John Knox, 1996) 237–46; D. M. Carr, *Reading the Fractures of Genesis: Historical and Literary Approaches* (Louisville: Westminster John Knox, 1996) 4–15; and my remarks in "Tangled Plots in Genesis," in *Fortunate the Eyes That See: Essays in Honor of David Noel Freedman* (ed. A. B. Beck et al.; Grand Rapids, MI: Eerdmans, 1995) 35–51.

binds the stories together. Second, I will explore how the *Leitwort* style creates intertextual links between stories that are not successive. In several instances, as scholars have noted, the web of *Leitwörter* indicates a larger literary structure, yielding a doubled sequence in which several stories are "twinned" with another, most notably the Garden of Eden with the Flood, and to a lesser extent, Cain and Abel with the Curse of Canaan, and the Sons of God with the Tower of Babel. Close attention to the *Leitwort* style illuminates the compositional strategies of the J source in creating a unity out of a prior diversity, and in shaping the intertextual effects in the movement from Creation to Flood to Abraham.

My analysis of these *Leitwort* effects builds on the work of numerous scholars, not only Buber and Gunkel, but also Umberto Cassuto, whose commentary on Genesis 1–11 pays close attention to the *Leitwort* style,[5] and Jack Sasson, along with several others who have commented on the doubled narrative sequence of the primeval narrative.[6] Most of the instances of *Leitwörter* addressed below have been noted previously, but it is useful to gather them together to expose a key dimension of the poetics of the primeval narrative.

It is a pleasure to offer this study in honor of Richard Friedman, who has done so much to clarify and refine our understanding of the biblical sources and to join this understanding with a sophisticated reading of the text.

1. The Leitwort *Effect in Successive Stories*

An important effect of the *Leitwort* style in the J primeval narrative is to bind successive stories together more richly, such that there is a sense of narrative continuity beyond mere temporal succession. In order to gauge the compositional significance of these links, I will first consider

---

5. U. Cassuto, *A Commentary on the Book of Genesis* (trans. Israel Abrahams; 2 vols.; Jerusalem: Magnes, 1961–64; Hebrew original, 1944–49).

6. J. M. Sasson, "The 'Tower of Babel' as a Clue to the Redactional Structuring of the Primeval History (Genesis 1:1–11:9)," in *The Bible World: Essays in Honor of Cyrus H. Gordon* (ed. G. Rendsburg et al.; New York: Ktav, 1980) 211–19, reprinted in *I Studied Inscriptions from before the Flood: Ancient Near Eastern, Literary, and Linguistic Approaches to Genesis 1–11* (ed. R. S. Hess and D. T. Tsumura; Winona Lake, IN: Eisenbrauns, 1994) 448–57; R. L. Cohn, "Narrative Structure and Canonical Perspective in Genesis," *JSOT* 25 (1983) 4–5; G. A. Rendsburg, *The Redaction of Genesis* (Winona Lake, IN: Eisenbrauns, 1986) 7–25; Carr, *Reading the Fractures*, 235–40; idem, "βίβλος Γενέσεως Revisited: A Synchronic Analysis of Patterns in Genesis as Part of the Torah (Part Two)," *ZAW* 110 (1998) 327–34, 342–44; and somewhat differently, S. Niditch, *Chaos to Cosmos: Studies in Biblical Patterns of Creation* (Chico, CA: Scholars Press, 1985) 59–69; and H. J. L. Jensen, "Über den Ursprung der Kultur und der Völker: Eine transformationskritische Analyse von Komplementarität und Verlauf in der jahwistischen Urgeschichte," *Scandinavian Journal of the Old Testament* 2 (1987) 36–45.

the indications that these J stories were not linked in succession in the narrative traditions (which may have been primarily oral) that served as J's narrative source. Gunkel pointed out a number of such indications, that is, logical gaps or inconcinnities, which cumulatively indicate that "the old legends did not originally exist in the current combination, but each existed independently in oral tradition."[7] Some of these gaps or contradictions are the following:

1. "Cain knew his wife" (Gen 4:17). The problem, as commentators have noted for millennia, is that no woman has yet been born for Cain to marry.[8] This is a problem that the J narrative does not address.[9] It is arguably a problem that only arises in the sequencing of the stories, that is, when originally independent stories were joined in chronological order. The problem of Cain's wife is not a problem that arises in the Cain and Abel story itself, it only becomes one when this story is the immediate sequel to the Garden of Eden. This problem inspired colorful solutions by early interpreters, usually involving a sister of Cain and Abel.[10]

2. A similar problem obtains regarding the existence of other people at the time of Cain. In Gen 4:14, Cain protests his punishment on the grounds that "whoever finds me will kill me." Presumably he is not referring to his parents. This creates the problem of what the 17th-century heretic Isaac La Peyrère called "the pre-Adamites."[11] In other words, the Cain and Abel story conflicts with the Garden of Eden story in requiring that other human families exist at the time of Adam and Eve.

3. Yahweh's punishment of Cain, that he be a 'wandering vagrant' נע ונד in the land of 'Wandering' נד (4:12, 16), coexists uneasily with the following statement that he "built a city" (4:18). This activity implies a settled, urban existence. The friction between the Cain cursed to wander and the urban Cain is arguably another indication of originally distinct stories joined together.

4. Another inconcinnity is the cultural legacy of Cain's descendants: Jabal is the father of all pastoralists, Jubal is the father of musicians, and Tubal-Cain the father of metalworkers (4:17–21). Since according to the

---

7. Gunkel, *Genesis*, 2; see also J. Wellhausen, *Prolegomena to the History of Israel* (Edinburgh: Black, 1885; German original, 2nd ed., 1883) 315–17.

8. N. Wyatt notes ("Cain's Wife," *Folklore* 97 [1986] 88–95) that according to the narrative sequence of the J text, Cain's wife must have been Eve!

9. Note that the P genealogy in Gen 5:4 does cover this exigency: "[Adam] begat sons and daughters."

10. J. L. Kugel, *Traditions of the Bible: A Guide to the Bible as It Was at the Start of the Common Era* (Cambridge: Harvard University Press, 1998) 148–49.

11. I. La Peyrère, *Prae-adamitae* (1655); see R. H. Popkin, *Isaac La Peyrère (1596–1676): His Life, Work, and Influence* (Leiden: Brill, 1987).

narrative sequence the flood must end these lineages, the problem arises as to how these lineages and their associated cultural activities persist after the flood. Hence, the account of Cain's descendants as culture heroes conflicts with its placement before the Flood story.

5. A similar problem of continuity through the flood is posed by the existence of the Nephilim. According to Gen 6:4, "the Nephilim were on the earth in those days, and also afterwards." The "also afterwards" seems to be a nod forward to Num 13:33, when the Nephilim are once again on the earth. This inconvenient fact conflicts with the flood story, in which "all that remained (alive) were Noah and those with him on the ark" (Gen 7:23, J). The persistence of the Nephilim is a problem (which the J story seems briefly to acknowledge) that arises when this story is placed before the flood.

6. A problem of temporal and logical sequence also occurs between the J portion of the Table of Nations and the Tower of Babel story. The distribution of the descendants of Noah into an ethnic and geographical diversity in Genesis 10[12] sits uneasily with the initial ethnic and geographical unity in the Tower of Babel story. The Tower of Babel story begins, "The whole earth had one language . . . and they found a valley in the land of Shinar and they settled there" (Gen 11:1–2). But in the previous chapter, the lineages of Noah's sons had already become a linguistic and geographical diversity spread over all the earth. The abrupt shift from ethnographic diversity to unity seems to be a problem that arises in the literary sequencing of the two accounts.

7. The building and naming of the city of Babel in 11:1–9 also sits uneasily with the previous naming of Babel as Nimrod's capital city in 10:10. And further, if we are to assume that Babel is the first city built, then it sits uneasily with the attribution of the building of the first city to Cain in 4:17. These, too, are frictions that appear to be a product of the literary sequence.

These and other logical and narratological difficulties in the J primeval narrative indicate that the stories circulated independent of their current literary sequence in Israelite tradition prior to their textual crystallization. (A clue of a different type is the apparent truncation of the story of the Sons of God and the Daughters of Men, where only the bare outlines of the story are told in 6:1–4 and the rest of the story suppressed.)[13] The J writer created a unity out of this diversity by recounting them in sequence,

---

12. The J portion is 10:8–19, 21, 24–30.

13. See recently R. S. Hendel, "The Nephilim Were on the Earth: Genesis 6:1–4 and its Ancient Near Eastern Context," in *The Fall of the Angels* (ed. C. Auffarth and L. T. Stuckenbruck; Leiden: Brill, 2004) 11–34.

in a distinctive and brilliant narrative voice, laced together with *Leitwörter*. The most notable *Leitwörter* that weave together the successive stories are as follows.

Garden of Eden with Cain and Abel [14]

(a) וידעו כי עירמם הם　'They knew that they were naked' (Gen 3:7)

והאדם ידע את חוה אשתו　'The man knew Eve, his wife' (4:1)

וידע קין את אשתו　'Cain knew his wife' (4:17)

וידע אדם עוד את־אשתו　'Adam knew his wife again' (4:25)

The *Leitword* ידע 'to know' echoes throughout the Garden of Eden story in its various nominal and verbal forms. When the first couple eat from the fruit of the "Tree of Knowledge (דעת) of Good and Evil," they indeed become like gods, "knowing (ידעי) good and evil" (3:5, 22), but ironically their new knowledge is most immediately perceptible as consciousness of their own bodies: "They knew (וידעו) that they were naked" (3:7). This aspect of carnal knowledge (which is only one of several dimensions of this knowledge) is resumed at the beginning of the Cain and Abel story when "the man knew (ידע) Eve, his wife." This particular pursuit of knowledge yields the first children, whose sibling relationship becomes the focal point of the story. Knowledge is not the major theme of the Cain and Abel story (though compare 4:10 with 3:8) and serves primarily as a verbal and thematic transition from the Garden of Eden story. This transitional effect recurs in 4:17, "Cain knew (וידע) his wife," introducing the story of Cain's descendants, and in 4:25, "Adam knew (וידע) his wife again," returning the story to the first parents and the line that will lead to Noah and Abraham.

(b) ואל אישך תשוקתך　'and to your husband will be your desire,
　　　והוא ימשל־בך　and he will rule over you' (3:16)

ואליך תשוקתו ואתה　'and to you will be its desire, and you must
　　　תמשל־בה　rule over it' (4:7)

Yahweh's punishment of Eve and his moral admonishment of Cain have overlapping diction. The operative *Leitwörter* in these two divine speeches are 'desire' תשוקה and 'rule' משל, foregrounding the complexities of desire and discipline—between male and female spouses and within the human soul. For Eve this is a punishment, because she previously desired the forbidden fruit and gave it to her husband, despite Yahweh's prohibition.

---

14. On the verbal echoes that link Genesis 3 and 4, see most fully Cassuto, *Genesis*, ad loc.; and W. Dietrich, "'Wo is dein Bruder?' Zu Tradition und Intention von Genesis 4," in *Beiträge zur Alttestamentlichen Theologie: Festschrift für Walther Zimmerli* (ed. H. Donner, R. Hanhart, and R. Smend; Göttingen: Vandenhoeck & Ruprecht, 1977) 98–100.

Yahweh's speech-act enacts a punishment that corresponds to her transgression. Henceforth she will desire the man, and he will rule over her— these are structures of the new (patriarchal) world order. In continuity and difference, Cain is caught in the conflict between his own desire— kindled by jealousy and anger—and his moral self-governance. The verbal and thematic linkages of desire and rule place Eve and Cain in a complicated analogy, as subjects addressed by Yahweh regarding the difficult consequences of their moral choices.

(c)   ארור אתה מכל־הבהמה   'Cursed be you, more than all the animals' (3:14)

ארורה האדמה בעבורך   'Cursed be the soil because of you' (3:17)

ארור אתה מן־האדמה   'Cursed be you from the soil' (4:11)

The curses on the snake and the soil in the Garden of Eden story verbally recur in the curse of Cain. In each case, Yahweh announces the curse with the *Leitwort* ארור 'cursed be . . .', and the following words, אתה מן and מן האדמה, from the first two curses are combined in the third. The snake is cursed 'more than' or 'apart from' מן all the other animals, meaning that he, in contrast to all the other animals, bears a curse. The soil in turn is cursed 'because of you' (that is, the man), and as a result he will have to have to earn his living by hard agricultural toil. This punishment reverses the man's earlier life of ease in the Garden, as a consequence for his eating the forbidden fruit, and defines a new harsh relationship between אדם 'man' and אדמה 'soil'. The diction of the curse of Cain echoes that of the snake (ארור אתה מן in both cases), while severing his livelihood 'from the soil' (מן האדמה). Previously, Cain was a farmer; now the soil will not yield its strength for him. In the repetition of *Leitwörter*, the curses of the snake and Cain foreground the common isolation of the two criminals, and Cain's alienation from the soil extends the problematic relationship between אדם and אדמה. The soil was cursed because of man, now Cain is cursed in relation to the soil. The reversal of subject and object in 3:17 and 4:11 makes an artful link in the painful relationship between man and the soil, now stained by a brother's blood.

(d)   ויגרש את־האדם   'He banished the man' (3:24)

הן גרשת אתי   'You have banished me' (4:14)

The conflicts in the two stories end with Yahweh banishing the humans—Adam and Eve from the Garden, Cain from the soil. The verb 'to banish' גרש makes these two endings clearly echo each other, suggesting that in some sense Cain's exile is a repetition and intensification of Adam and Eve's exile. This *Leitwort* establishes a thematic continuity by joining the punishments of the first humans to the universal fear of banishment and exile—a common plight in the ancient world and a complex theme in the JE texts. [15]

(e)   גן בעדן מקדם   'a garden in Eden in the east' (2:8)

        מקדם לגן עדן   'east of the Garden of Eden' (3:24)

        קדמת עדן   'east of Eden' (4:16)

After the banishment of Adam and Eve, Yahweh stations fierce monsters 'east of the Garden of Eden' to guard its entrance, and Cain is banished to wander 'east of Eden'. The repetition of the *Leitwörter* קדם and עדן reverse the idyllic quality of the earlier scene when Yahweh planted 'a garden in Eden in the east' (2:8). The word קדם means 'east' in these phrases, but it can also mean 'antiquity, ancient days', a second meaning that hovers over the stories. The word עדן means something like 'abundance, bounty (of food and other provisions)', which is precisely what the Garden provides its dwellers. Adam and Eve are cast outside of the bounty of the Garden, and they cannot reenter. Cain is perhaps doubly banished from this bounty, since he must wander like a vagabond, cut off from the life-giving soil. In this repetition of *Leitwörter*, Cain's fate clearly echoes Adam and Eve's.

Sons of God with Flood

(f) . . . ויהי כי החל האדם לרב   'When humans began to increase . . .

        ויראו . . . כי טבת   and (they) saw . . . that good' (6:1–2)

        וירא יהוה כי רבה רעת האדם   'Yahweh saw that the evil of humans had increased' (6:5)

The chain of *Leitwörter* that link these stories have some dramatic inversions of meaning: 'humans' אדם, 'increase' רבב, 'saw' ראה, and the opposition of 'good' טוב and 'evil' רע. In the Sons of God story, against the backdrop of the increase of humans, "the Sons of God saw that the daughters of men were good (i.e., beautiful)" (6:2). The Flood story begins with these words recurring in a different and menacing way: "Yahweh saw that the evil of humans had increased" (6:5). The subject shifts from the Sons of God to Yahweh, and what the subject sees shifts from the beauty of human women to the evil of the human heart. The increase of humans and the lusty perception of the Sons of God contrasts with the increase of human evil and the moral perception of Yahweh,

---

15. See B. D. Sommer, "Expulsion as Initiation: Displacement, Divine Presence, and Divine Exile in the Torah," in *Beginning/Again: Toward a Hermeneutics of Jewish Texts* (ed. A. Cohen and S. Magid; New York: Seven Bridges, 2002) 26–33.

who will proceed to eliminate the multitude of humanity. In many ways, these two sequential stories seem to be logically unconnected (note the problem of the persistence of the Nephilim addressed above); Wellhausen colorfully calls Gen 6:1–4 a "strange erratic boulder" in its literary context.[16] The verbal echoes at the beginnings of the two stories provide some measure of stylistic continuity and thematic heightening in the transition from one story to the next.

Curse of Canaan with Tower of Babel

(g)   ומאלה נפצה כל־הארץ   'From these the whole earth scattered' (9:19)

פן־נפוץ על־פני כל הארץ   'Lest we be scattered over the face of the whole earth' (11:4)

ויפץ יהוה אתם משם   'Yahweh scattered them from there over
על־פני כל־הארץ   the face of the whole earth' (11:8)

As noted above, the origins of the diversity of peoples is addressed twice in the J primeval narrative, once in the genealogy of Noah's sons in the Table of Nations and again in the Tower of Babel story. This doubling seems indicative of the diversity of traditions that are combined in the J text. This diversity also provides an instance for a verbal link between the beginning of the Curse of Canaan, where Noah's three sons are again introduced, and the Tower of Babel story, where the men of Babel reveal their motivation for building the city. This link is effected by the related verbal roots נפץ and פוץ 'to scatter'. In the first story, the narrative comment that "from these [Noah's sons] the whole earth scattered" (9:19) is proleptic, preparing the future. These words echo in the speech of the men of Babel, who fear such a future: "lest we be scattered over the face of the whole earth" (11:4). By use of the *Leitwort* style, the text creates a sense of thematic continuity—of prediction and fulfillment—out of what may otherwise seem a narrative inconcinnity. At the end of the Babel story, this future, of course, comes to pass: "Yahweh scattered them . . ." (11:8).

Tower of Babel with Call of Abraham

(h)   ונעשה־לנו שם   'Let us make ourselves a name' (11:4)

ואגדלה שמך   'I will make your name great' (12:2)

The transition between the primeval narrative and the Abraham narrative is a key turning point in Genesis. The repetition of the *Leitwort* שם 'name, fame, glory' in 11:4 and 12:2 effects a counterpoint and link at

---

16. Wellhausen, *Prolegomena*, 317.

this narrative hinge.[17] The men of Babel desire an enduring name and so
proceed to build the city and tower, but their hubris results in their own
dispersion and the destruction of their monuments. Rather than making
themselves a name, they ensure their ephemerality and namelessness. In
contrast, Abraham achieves a great and enduring name the right way, by
Yahweh's election and by Abraham's righteousness (doing "as Yahweh
told him," 12:4). Abraham is successful where the men of Babel failed,
hence his name endures. There are other significant inversions of *Leitwörter* at this juncture, most notably, as Hans Walter Wolff observed, from
the fivefold repetition of ערר 'to curse' in the primeval narrative to the
dense fivefold repetition of ברך 'to bless' in Gen 12:2–3.[18]

2. The Leitwort *Effect in Paired Stories*

The biblical reading tradition established by the Babylonian rabbis divides Genesis 1–11 into two portions (פרשות), with the caesura at "These
are the generations of Noah" (Gen 6:9). In recent years, scholars have perceived that there is also a parallelism of sequence and theme in these two
sections. Jack Sasson astutely elucidates this doubled structure:

> [T]he episodes culled from Hebraic traditions of early history were con-
> ceived in two matching sequences. . . . Each one of these sequences de-
> scribes the manner in which man was removed progressively from the
> realm of God [viz., Garden of Eden and Flood—R.H.], in which he initi-
> ated fraternal (and hence human) strife [Cain and Abel and Curse of
> Canaan], divided into tribal and national groupings [Cainite and
> Shemite genealogies and the Table of Nations], attempted to restore his
> divine nature or gain access to the divine realm, but was foiled in this
> by God [Sons of God and Tower of Babel]. In each case, it is the conse-
> quence of this *hubris* which launched God into a decision to particular-
> ize his relationship with man. In the first case, God destroys mankind,
> allows it to survive through his choice of Noah, but almost immedi-
> ately recognizes (Gen 8:21) that His measure was a shade too drastic.
> . . . [In the second case,] [d]istressed by man's repeated attempt to un-
> balance the cosmological order, and no longer allowing Himself the
> option of totally annihilating mankind, God finally settles on one indi-
> vidual, uproots him from his own kin, and promises him prosperity
> and continuity in a new land.[19]

---

17. L. Ruppert, "'Machen wir uns einen Namen . . .' (Gen 11,4): Zur Anthropologie
der vorpriesterschriftlichen Urgeschichte," in Ruppert, *Studien zur Literaturgeschichte des
Alten Testaments* (Stuttgart: Katholisches Bibelwerk, 1994) 124–42.

18. H. W. Wolff, "The Kerygma of the Yahwist," in W. Brueggemann and H. W. Wolff,
The Vitality of Old Testament Traditions (2nd ed.; Atlanta: John Knox, 1982) 54–55. The
occurrences of ערר are 3:14, 17; 4:11; 5:29; 9:25.

19. Sasson, "Tower of Babel," 456–57. Cf. the expansion of Sasson's thesis in Rendsburg, *Redaction of Genesis*, 7–25.

Sasson argues that this thematic and literary structure was the product of the redactor of Genesis, who combined the J and P texts. David Carr has rightly noted, however, that this dual structure exists already in the pre-Priestly primeval narrative, which indicates that this literary structure is a feature of the earliest written crystallization of these stories.[20] The combination of the J and P primeval texts does not obscure this dual structure, since Creation and Flood (each followed by genealogies) also form a two-part structure in the P primeval narrative.[21]

This large-scale structure of the J primeval narrative can be schematized as follows, including the transition to Abraham:

Garden of Eden	Flood
Cain and Abel	Curse of Canaan
Genealogies	Genealogies
Sons of God	Tower of Babel

Abraham

This structure can be represented thematically as follows:

Beginning; encroachment and exile from divine realm	Destruction and new beginning
Strife among sons	Strife among sons
Social differentiation	Social differentiation
Encroachment of human/divine	Encroachment of human/divine

New Beginning

The *Leitwort* style plays an important role in this literary structure, creating a series of intertextual links between the "twinned" stories. In particular, there is a dense set of interlinking *Leitwörter* between the Garden of Eden story and the Flood story. There are less prominent *Leitwörter* linking the story of Cain and Abel with the Curse of Canaan, the two genealogical sequences, and the Sons of God with the Tower of Babel. All of these links create a degree of intertextuality that binds the stories and sequences into a complex literary unity. The primeval era divides into the antediluvian and postdiluvian eras (as it also does in Mesopotamian tradition),[22] but it also anticipates—by theme and *Leitwörter*—the transition

20. Carr, *Reading the Fractures*, 236; idem, "βίβλος," 342–43.

21. For example, E. Blum, *Studien zur Komposition des Pentateuch* (Berlin: de Gruyter, 1990) 289–93. I should note that Rendsburg (*Redaction of Genesis*, 103–6) takes the dual structure in Genesis 1–11 as an argument against the standard model of J and P sources in this text, a proposal that I find unconvincing; see previous note.

22. Cf. the Mesopotamian expression *lām abūbi* 'before the flood' and W. W. Hallo, "Information from before the Flood: Antediluvian Notes from Babylonia and Israel," *Maarav* 7 (1991) 175–76.

from the unresolved problems of primeval times to the story of Abraham.[23] The major *Leitwort* correspondences in this dual structure are as follows:

Garden of Eden with Flood

(a) ארורה האדמה בעבורך   'Cursed is the soil because of you.
בעצבון תאכלנה   In painful labor you shall eat from it' (3:17)

ומעצבון ידינו מן־האדמה   'From our painful manual labor on the soil
אשר אררה   which [Yahweh] has cursed' (5:29)

לקלל עוד את־האדמה   '[I will no longer/never again] curse the soil
בעבור האדם   because of man' (8:21)

The cluster of *Leitwörter*, 'curse' ארר/קלל, 'the soil' האדמה, 'because of' בעבור, and 'painful (labor)' עצבון create an intertextual echo-chamber in 3:17, 5:29, and 8:21. This collocation of words and the human fate they represent are first sounded in Yahweh's punishment of the man in the Garden of Eden (see above, part 1). In Yahweh's curse, the easy relationship between אדם 'man, human' and אדמה 'soil' is sundered.[24] Because of the man's perfidy, he will be alienated from his source and will have to work the cursed soil in hard labor. This is one of the painful conditions of life outside of Eden.

The birth of Noah in 5:29 picks up these words and ideas and in Lamech's naming speech promises relief from this curse. Based on the wordplay of נח 'Noah' and נחם 'relief', Lamech proclaims that Noah will "provide us relief from our work, and from our painful manual labor on the soil which Yahweh has cursed." This prediction lingers in the background of the ensuing Flood story. Noah's invention of wine is no doubt a partial fulfillment of this promise (9:20–21), but the most verbally direct fulfillment is in Yahweh's words in 8:21.

---

23. In this respect, I find unconvincing the argument that the J primeval narrative is compositionally independent of the Abraham story; so F. Crüsemann, "Die Eigenständigkeit der Urgeschichte: Ein Beitrag zur Diskussion um den 'Jahwisten'," in *Die Botschaft und die Boten: Festschrift für Hans Walter Wolff* (ed. J. Jeremias and L. Perlitt; Neukirchen-Vluyn: Neukirchener Verlag, 1981) 11–29; Carr, *Reading the Fractures*, 241. Some of the inconcinnities between the primeval narrative and the Abraham cycle pointed out by Crüsemann are akin to the inconcinnities within the primeval narrative itself (see above, pp. 96–97), and in my view pertain to the divergent traditions that the J source weaves together.

24. On the thematics of אדם and אדמה in the J primeval narrative, see P. D. Miller Jr., *Genesis 1–11: Studies in Structure and Theme* (Sheffield: JSOT Press, 1978) 37–42; E. Zenger, "Beobachtungen zu Komposition und Theologie der jahwistischen Urgeschichte," in *Dynamik im Wort* (ed. E. Zenger and J. Gnilka; Stuttgart: Katholisches Bibelwerk, 1983) 48–50; and below, pp. 108–109.

At the end of the J Flood story, Yahweh proclaims his new resolution: "I will no longer/never again curse the soil because of man, for the inclinations of his heart are evil from his youth" (8:21). This momentous statement clearly sounds the same *Leitwort* cluster as the curse in Eden and the birth of Noah (varying ארר with קלל, both meaning 'to curse'),[25] but it is not entirely clear how it should be understood. There is a verbal ambiguity in Yahweh's words, לא־אסף לקלל עוד את־האדמה, which can mean either 'I will no longer curse the soil' or 'I will never again curse the soil'.[26] The former meaning would mean that the curse is annulled and that this consequence of Adam's transgression is forgiven. But this would suggest that agricultural labor is no longer hard and painful, which belies human experience and undermines the etiological aspect of the curse in Eden. The latter meaning would most naturally apply to a one-time event, presumably the Flood, now described as a punctual curse on the earth that will never again recur. This makes sense contextually, since Yahweh in the next clause clearly promises never again to send a Flood, but it seems an odd meaning given the previous prominence of Yahweh's curse on the soil (האדמה).

Buber's comment that the *Leitwort* style "is probably the strongest of all techniques for making a meaning available without articulating it explicitly" has a powerful corollary here, in that the meaning of *Leitwörter* is often inexplicit and multivocal. In this case, the sense of לא אסיף לקלל עוד את־האדמה can be parsed in two different but equally acceptable ways. The *Leitwörter* echo the curse on the earth in Gen 3:17, which was earlier brought into relation with Noah in 5:29, and hence it argues for 'I will no longer curse the soil'. Perhaps agricultural labor will no longer be quite so hard, and Noah's promised relief has come to pass. But the following clause in 8:21 has the same construction, לא אסף עוד, which clearly means 'I will never again (destroy all life as I have done)'. This parallel phrasing suggests that the first clause be read 'I will never again curse the soil', in which case this punctual curse, capable of repetition, most naturally refers to the Flood. I would suggest that this multivocality does not need to be resolved one way or the other, but that the *Leitwort* style allows it to be both. There is a lingering ambiguity in Yahweh's promise, which suggests rather than explicitly defines its meaning. This is one of the literary virtues

---

25. Note the collocation of the two verbs in Gen 12:3: ומקללך אאר 'And those who curse you, I will curse'.

26. See the arguments of R. Rendtorff, "Genesis 8,21 und die Urgeschichte des Jahwisten," in Rendtorff, *Gesammelte Studien zum Alten Testament* (Munich: Chr. Kaiser, 1975) 188–97; O. Steck, "Genesis 12,1–3 und die Urgeschichte des Jahwisten," in *Wahrnehmungen Gottes im Alten Testament: Gesammelte Studien* (ed. O. Steck; Munich: Chr. Kaiser, 1982) 119–24; D. L. Petersen, "The Yahwist on the Flood," *VT* 26 (1976) 442–44; Crüsemann, "Eigenständigkeit," 24; and the commentaries.

of the *Leitwort* style, and it contributes to the residue of ambiguity at the end of the J Flood story. The curse of Eden seems to be ameliorated, though this is not quite clear, even as Yahweh reconciles himself to the persistence of human evil.

Cain and Abel with Curse of Canaan

(b)   ארור אתה   'Cursed are you' (4:11)

          ארור כנען   'Cursed is Canaan' (9:25)

Three creatures are directly cursed in the J primeval narrative: the snake, Cain, and Canaan. The repetition of ארור אתה in Gen 3:14 and 4:11 (treated above, [c], p. 99) place the snake and Cain in relation in two successive stories. Noah's speech-act "Cursed is Canaan" creates an intertextual link between the non-successive stories of Cain and Canaan. This verbal echo rests within the larger parallel structure of the two stories.[27] Both deal with the sons of the human protagonists of the previous story, and one of these sons commits an offense and is cursed. The details are different—fratricide differs from shaming one's father, and the curse issues from Yahweh in one story and from Noah in the other. Nonetheless, the cursing of a son creates a sense of recurrence and adds to the accumulation of curses that provides the backdrop for the blessing of Abraham.

Genealogies

(c)   ולשת גם־הוא ילד   'To Seth also was born' (4:26)

          ולשם ילד גם־הוא   'To Shem also was born' (10:21)

The genealogies after the stories of Adam's and Noah's sons are linked verbally by their begettings (Qal of ילד in J) and also by the stylistic repetition in 4:26 and 10:21, in which the Qal passive of ילד recurs in a distinctive but slightly varied sequence. Seth (שת) and Shem (שם) have similar sounding names, and they are both apical ancestors of the Israelites, that is, at the top of the genealogical branch that descend to Israel. Thus it may be thematically apt that their acquisition of heirs echoes in the *Leitwort* style of these two verses.

Sons of God with Tower of Babel

(d)   בנות . . . . בני־האלהים   'the sons of God . . . the daughters of men'
          האדם   (6:2, 4)

          בני האדם   'the sons of men' (11:5)

---

27. Cohn, "Narrative Structure," 5; Rendsburg, *Redaction of Genesis*, 14; Carr, *Reading the Fractures*, 236–37.

There is a verbal similarity of the protagonists in these two stories: the 'Sons of God' (בני האלהים) and the 'daughters of men' (בנות האדם) in 6:1–4, and 'the sons of men' (בני האדם) in 11:5. The latter expression (usually translated idiomatically as 'men, humans') is used only here in the primeval narrative and effects what Christoph Uehlinger calls "a latent *Leitwort* association" between the two stories.[28] These phrases also suggest that these daughters and sons of האדם (literally, 'the man', i.e., Adam), are up to no good, which the two stories show to be the case. Like the Sons of God and the daughters of men in 6:1–4, "the sons of men/Adam" in 11:5 threaten the boundary between the divine world and the human world, and Yahweh responds with a punishment that restores this boundary, diminishes human power, and establishes new limits for the human world.

(e)   אנשי השם   'men of name/fame' (6:4)

        ונעשה־לנו שם   'Let us make ourselves a name' (11:4)

        ואגדלה שמך   'I will make your name great' (12:2)

The *Leitwort* שם 'name, fame, glory' links the story of the Tower of Babel with the Call of Abraham (as observed above, [h], pp. 101–102), and also effects a horizontal link between the Tower of Babel and the Sons of God.[29] The semidivine offspring of the Sons of God and the daughters of men are described in 6:4 as "the heroes of old, the men of fame" (lit., 'name' שם). The nature of this fame is left unspecified. But as men of 'name', these mysterious heroes achieve what the men of Babel desire (11:4). These semidivine heroes are also called the Nephilim, which literally means the 'fallen ones', perhaps hinting at their famous deaths.[30] The ambiguous fame of the Nephilim places them in relation to the hubristic desire for fame by the men of Babel. Both provide a negative foil for Abraham, whose "great name" is achieved by Yahweh's election and by Abraham's righteousness. The Nephilim and the men of Babel are antitheses to Abraham—their "fame" is that of antiheroes, and we do not know their names, whereas Abraham is the genuine hero, whose name and glory endures.

---

28. C. Uehlinger, *Weltreich und "eine Rede": Eine neue Deutung der sogenannten Turmbauerzählung (Gen 11,1–9)* (Freiburg: Universitätsverlag, 1990) 569; also Rendsburg, *Redaction of Genesis*, 20. Uehlinger and Rendsberg also point to החל 'to begin' as a *Leitwort* linking the two stories, though I would describe this as a broader linkage among several "beginnings" in the primeval narrative (4:21; 6:1; 9:20; 10:8; 11:6).

29. Rendsburg, *Redaction of Genesis*, 20–21; Uehlinger, *Weltreich*, 569; Carr, *Reading the Fractures*, 187.

30. R. S. Hendel, "Of Demigods and the Deluge: Toward an Interpretation of Genesis 6:1–4," *JBL* 106 (1987) 21–22.

Conclusion

The *Leitwort* style has significant effects in the J primeval narrative. Most of the stories placed in sequence are more richly bound in continuity by the thematic connections sounded by the *Leitwörter*. The sequence as a whole has a twinned or two-paneled aspect, effected particularly by the cluster of *Leitwörter* that resound in the Garden of Eden and the Flood stories, and less prominently by those that link the other twinned stories. Several of the *Leitwörter* also anticipate the turning point from the primeval narrative to the patriarchal narrative, announced by the call of Abraham in 12:1–3, which serves as a major narrative hinge in Genesis.

With Abraham, the genealogical focus of the narrative narrows to a single line, that of Israel and its immediate kin.[31] The primeval narrative is a mythic representation of the human condition and serves as a backdrop to the story of Israel. It begins with a single line with Adam and Eve, branches out into the multitude of humanity, then returns to a single line with the Flood, and branches out again. But the branching is problematic each time. The Flood is only a temporary solution, and Yahweh renounces it. Abraham and his line become the lasting solution.

At the same time that the primeval narrative is a prelude to Abraham, it is also a searching inquiry into the nature of human existence, cast in the mythic idiom of a representation of origins.[32] For example, consider the *Leitwort* pair of אדם and אדמה 'man/human' and 'soil, earth' (addressed above, [1c], p. 99 and [2a], p. 104). The first human is made from the soil and learns at the end of the story that he must return to it. Human mortality is connected to our origins and nature as "earthy" creatures, yet our mortality was only made clear as we were expelled from paradise. In other words, death is both inevitable (by our nature as אדם made from the אדמה)[33] and somehow joined to our ancestors' moral choices and imperfec-

---

31. See the remarks of Carr ("βίβλος," 327–47) on this "structural pattern in Genesis: the way its semantic focus expands and contracts along genealogical lines."

32. The genre "myth" is aptly described in this sense by A. Dundes (*Sacred Narrative: Readings in the Theory of Myth* [Berkeley: University of California Press, 1984] 1): "A myth is a sacred narrative explaining how the world and man came to be in their present form." See further H.-P. Müller's treatment of the mythic functions of the J primeval narrative in "Mythische Elemente in der jahwistischen Schöpfungserzählung," in Müller, *Mythos-Kerygma-Wahrheit: Gesammelte Aufsätze zum Alten Testament in seiner Umwelt und zur Biblischen Theologie* (Berlin: de Gruyter, 1991) 3–42, esp. 34–42.

33. The mortality of humans, even in their creation, is strongly suggested by the phrase 'dust from the earth' עפר מן־האדמה (Gen 2:7), since עפר 'dust, loose earth' is commonly used in expressions of mortality; e.g., עפר ואפר 'dust and ashes' (Gen 18:27, J) and the proverb-like statement in Gen 3:19, 'For dust you are, and to dust you will return'; see D. R. Hillers, "Dust: Some Aspects of Old Testament Imagery," in *Love and Death in the Ancient Near East: Essays in Honor of Marvin H. Pope* (ed. J. H. Marks and R. M. Good; Guilford, CT: Four Quarters, 1987) 105–9.

tions. Both senses inhere in the relationship between humans and death, signaled by the *Leitwort* style and the story's outcome. Similarly, our human destiny as agriculturalists is connected to our material bond with the soil, but it is also connected with our ancestors' flawed behavior, which renders humans unfit for paradise. Our sexual drives and differences are also related to our nature as אדם, since at first there was only one human (inchoately male),[34] and the first woman was built from his rib. Male and female strive to reunite, to become אדם once more, to gain the primal plenitude, a taste of paradise. From this reunion comes new life, hence the woman is called 'Life' (חוה). But giving new life is painful, it is the painful labor meted out to the woman, just as subsistence agriculture is the hard labor of the man. Both forms of אדם share hard labor, in complementary ways. For אדם to survive on the אדמה requires the tools of civilization, so Yahweh gives the humans sturdy clothes (3:21), Cain and his descendants create new forms of civilized life (cities, shepherding, metal tools, and music; 4:17–22), and Noah, as an איש האדמה 'man of the soil', discovers wine (9:20). There is anxiety and fear but also much good that derives from the relationship between אדם and אדמה. What a modern philosopher might analyze as the condition of our "being-in-the-world" (Heidegger) is, in some important respects, articulated in the primeval narrative's portrayal of the deep relationship of אדם and אדמה.[35]

The J primeval narrative is a profound, complex, and sometimes disturbing treatment of the origins and deep structures of humans existence and the world we inhabit. Humans are created for paradise, but do not last there long. We are troubled and unruly creatures, capable of knowledge and virtue, but also driven to violence and evil. We are "like gods," in some respects, but are also earthy and chaotic, often at cross-purposes with Yahweh and with each other. How this unruly world of great extremes comes into being is the burden of the primeval narrative. How to improve this troubled world is what happens next.

---

34. See recently, A. Brenner, *The Intercourse of Knowledge: On Gendering Desire and 'Sexuality' in the Hebrew Bible* (Leiden: Brill, 1997) 12; P. A. Bird, *Missing Persons and Mistaken Identities: Women and Gender in Ancient Israel* (Minneapolis: Fortress, 1997) 164–65.

35. Cf. H.-P. Müller's definition of the function of myth ("Mythos und Kerygma: Anthropologische und theologische Aspekte," in Müller, *Mythos-Kerygma-Wahrheit*, 201): "Der Mythos beantwortet die Frage, warum Seiendes bzw. das menschliche Dasein durch einen Sinn legitimiert wird."

How Moses Gained and Lost the Reputation of Being the Torah's Author: Higher Criticism prior to Julius Wellhausen

MICHAEL M. HOMAN

Xavier University of Louisiana

Introduction

The first five books of the Bible, known collectively as the Torah (in Hebrew) or the Pentateuch (in Greek), contain some of the most famous and influential stories ever composed: Creation, Adam and Eve in the Garden of Eden, Noah and the Flood, Abraham and his family's adventures along the Fertile Crescent, and Moses leading the Israelites out of Egyptian bondage, first to Mount Sinai where they received the Law and then toward the promised land. But who wrote these passages? Millions of religious Jews, Christians, and Muslims believe that God dictated all of these stories to Moses, who then wrote them down on five scrolls. Nevertheless, Bible scholars understand the role of Moses and other humans in this process to be much more complicated.

Higher Criticism and Wellhausen

The stories as they now appear in the Torah represent the work of many authors and editors, some who worked as early as the 12th century B.C.E.,[1] others who lived as much as a century after the Babylonian Exile of 586 B.C.E.[2] Scholars are able to determine this by using a method similar in

---

Author's note: For Dick Friedman, the greatest teacher I've ever had.

1. See Frank Moore Cross, Jr. and David Noel Freedman, *Early Hebrew Orthography: A Study of the Epigraphic Evidence* (New Haven: American Oriental Society, 1952); and *Studies in Ancient Yahwistic Poetry* (SBLDS 21; Missoula: Scholars Press, 1975).

2. For an excellent summary of the authors and editors of the Torah, see Richard E. Friedman, *Who Wrote the Bible?* (Englewood Cliffs, NJ: Prentice Hall, 1987); "Torah (Pentateuch)," *ABD* 6:605–22. Against the recent idea that the entire Hebrew Bible is the product of the Hellenistic world or later, see William G. Dever, *What Did the Biblical Writers Know and When Did They Know It?* (Grand Rapids: Eerdmans, 2001).

principle to the way archaeologists compare changes in forms in order to date ceramic artifacts. For the past 100 years, archaeologists have established a reasonably solid sequential typology by rigorously recording, cataloging, and comparing ceramic artifacts. Thus, an expert can examine pottery fragments such as a jar handle or a cooking-pot base and correctly determine the century and general area in which the object was created. Similarly, historical linguists can date writings, including those in the Bible, by closely examining language. Bible scholars have gradually been able to assign dates to biblical passages by not only looking at the historical context of biblical passages but also by comparing grammar, orthography (spelling), and word usage to other ancient Near Eastern writings.

This linguistic determination of the date of composition works in English literature as well. For example, consider the following two passages:

> You seem to understand me, by each at once her chappy finger laying upon her skinny lips: you should be women, and yet your beards forbid me to interpret that you are so.
>
> (Shakespeare's *Macbeth*, 17th century C.E.)

> wuldres Wealdend woroldare forgeaf, Beowulf wæs breme, blæd wide sprang, Scyldes eafera Scedelandum in.
>
> (*Beowulf*, ca. 11th century C.E.)

Readers easily can determine that the two quotations were written in the past by different authors in separate times. They can also perhaps recognize that the first passage uses a type of English popular in the Elizabethan period and that it was composed long after the second, which uses a form of Old English. A similar amount of time (approximately 500 to 600 years) separates the earliest Hebrew passages in the Torah from the latest.

For centuries, scholars meticulously examined and dissected the Torah, over time grouping grammatically and ideologically similar passages into the following four theoretical authors, known as J, E, P, and D (see table on p. 113). Various editors and scribes combined the documents known as J, E, P, and D into the Torah that we have available today. This theory is known as the Documentary Hypothesis, and the academic endeavor to determine which author wrote various biblical passages is known as Source Criticism, or alternatively, Higher Criticism. In contrast, Lower Criticism (also called Textual Criticism) attempts to determine what original biblical writings might have said by examining all available textual witnesses, such as the Septuagint, the Masoretic Text, and the Dead Sea Scrolls. Thus, Lower Criticism might be interpreted as the foundation upon which Higher Criticism is built. In fact, Higher Criticism was the earliest critical methodology applied to the Bible.

Name of source	Stands for	How it got that name	Date of composition	Background
J	Jahwe	German form of Yahweh, God's most personal name. This author frequently uses "Yahweh" in narration.	Ca. 9th–8th century B.C.E.	J lived in the southern kingdom of Judah, and wrote stories involving talking animals, dreams, and sex. Much of J involved women and women's issues, and because this was the only author who was not a priest, some have argued J could have been a woman.[a]
E	Elohim	This author only calls God Elohim until the time of Moses.	Ca. 9th–8th century B.C.E.	E lived in the northern kingdom of Israel prior to its destruction by Assyria in 721 B.C.E. This author was a priest belonging to a group claiming descent from Moses.
P	Priestly	Passages attributed to this author mostly focus on matters important to the priesthood, such as sacrifice and the Tabernacle.	Ca. 7th–6th century B.C.E.	P was a priest in Jerusalem claiming descent from Aaron, and thus, there are no sacrifices in P until Aaron was inaugurated (Exod 40:13). P calls God "El" or "Elohim" until Exod 6:3, when God revealed His divine name Yahweh.
D	Deutero-nomic	Named after the book of Deuteronomy, most of which this author wrote.	Ca. 6th century B.C.E.	D was a Judean priest affiliated with King Josiah, and he witnessed the destruction of Jerusalem in 586 B.C.E. Many have noticed a connection between D, the prophet Jeremiah, and his scribe Baruch.[b]

a. Friedman, *Who Wrote the Bible?* 86.
b. Ibid., 146–49.

One name, above all others, has been linked to Higher Criticism. Many refer to him as the "Father of the Documentary Hypothesis."[3] His name is Julius Wellhausen (1844–1918), and he was something of a polymath. The son of a Lutheran pastor in 19th-century Germany, Wellhausen received

---

3. Friedman, *Who Wrote the Bible?* 25.

his doctorate in Theology and Semitics from the University of Göttingen (1870). Later, he published on several topics, including the origins of Islam, Christianity, and Judaism as well as linguistics, but it was his seminal book entitled *Prolegomena zur Geschichte Israels* (*Prolegomena to the History of Israel*)[4] that forever changed the discipline of biblical studies. In *Prolegomena*, Wellhausen masterfully synthesized the works of previous scholars and established a clear and convincing argument that the Torah consisted of separate documents written centuries apart.

Much has been written about Wellhausen and the history of Higher Criticism subsequent to *Prolegomena*.[5] Far less research has focused on the traditions of how many came to regard Moses as the Torah's author in the first place and the subsequent scholars who questioned this idea and who paved the road for Wellhausen. The current article seeks to address this gap.

How Moses Gained the Reputation of Being the Torah's Author

Not one passage in the Torah claims that Moses was the author of Genesis through Deuteronomy, with one apparent exception:

> And Moses wrote this *Torah*, and gave it to the priests the sons of Levi, who carried the Ark of the Covenant of Yahweh, and to all the elders of Israel. And Moses commanded them, "At the end of every seven years, at the appointed time of the year of release, at the feast of Tabernacles, when all Israel comes to appear before Yahweh your God at the place which He will choose, you shall read this *Torah* before all Israel in their hearing. . . . When Moses had finished writing the words of this *Torah* in a scroll, to the very end, Moses commanded the Levites who carried the Ark of the Covenant of Yahweh "Take this scroll of the *Torah* and put it by the side of the Ark of the Covenant of Yahweh your God, that it may be there for a witness against you." (Deut 31:9–11, 24–26)[6]

In order to understand the meaning of the above passage, some background on the Hebrew word "Torah" is in order. Originally the Hebrew term *tôrâ* came from a word meaning "to throw" or "to shoot." However, "Torah" is the causative form of this word, and thus means "law," or more accurately, "instruction." In fact, words etymologically related to "Torah"

---

4. The book was first published as *Geschichte Israels* in 1878. A second revised edition in 1883 used the title *Prolegomena zur Geschichte Israels*.

5. See Ronald E. Clements, *A Century of Old Testament Studies* (London: Lutterworth, 1983) and Rolf Rendtorff, "The Paradigm is Changing: Hopes and Fears," *BibInt* 1 (1993) 34–53.

6. See other passages, such as Exod 17:14 and 24:4, which say that Moses wrote specific laws, but nowhere in the Torah does it state that Moses wrote the entire Torah. See Jakob Petuchowski, "The Supposed Dogma of the Mosaic Authorship of the Pentateuch," *The Hibbert Journal* 57 (1958–59) 356–60.

that mean "instruction" are used more than 200 times in the Hebrew Bible, and often they refer to specific teachings. For example, in Num 6:13 we read instructions about what a Nazirite (one who is dedicated to God) can and cannot do. These instructions are called the "Torah of the Nazirite." Similarly, regulations concerning the sacrifice known as the Guild Offering are called the "Torah of the Guild Offering" (Lev 7:1), just as instructions about leprosy are called "Torah of the Leper" (Lev 14:57). Therefore, Moses' "scroll of the Torah" in Deut 31:26 did not refer to the first five books of the Bible; rather, it referred only to the preceding instructions found in Deuteronomy 12–28, a section known as the Deuteronomistic Law Code. In fact, it was the purported discovery of this very "scroll of the Torah" in the Temple that initiated King Josiah's religious reforms in 621 B.C.E. (2 Kings 22–23). Moreover, the language used in Deuteronomy 12–28, as well as the historical and theological context, all suggest a date of composition at some point between the 7th and late 6th centuries B.C.E.[7] Thus, many scholars believe that Josiah himself, or a close aid, had a hand in the composition of the "scroll of the Torah" designated to Moses in Deuteronomy 31. In short, the "Torah" that Moses wrote according to Deuteronomy 31 included only 16 chapters of laws, as opposed to five books, and these 16 chapters of laws as they are now recorded were not written until centuries after Moses' death.

So, how did Moses receive credit for being the author of the entire Torah? It happened gradually. One of the first references to Moses' being the composer of a passage in the Torah appeared in 2 Kgs 14:6, where the author mentioned that King Amaziah did not execute the children of those who attacked Judah, referencing a law in Deut 24:16 by citing "as it is written in the scroll of the Torah of Moses." Shortly thereafter, in the 5th century B.C.E., the idea began to emerge that the first five books of the Bible, in their entirety, were directly connected to Moses. Thus, Ezra the priest, as commanded in Deut 31:9–11, read at the Water Gate the "scroll of the Torah of Moses" (Neh 8:1).[8]

Attributing writings to earlier, more famous predecessors was a common feature of ancient literature.[9] This trend further developed during the intertestamental period in which historical persons were linked directly to the founding of nations (ca. 400 B.C.E.–50 C.E.—the time between the completion of the Hebrew Bible and the earliest writings of the New Testament). Just as Aeneas was interpreted to be the founder and lawgiver of

---

7. See Jeffrey C. Geoghegan, "'Until this Day' and the Preexilic Redaction of the Deuteronomistic History," *JBL* 122 (2003) 201–27.

8. Note also the references to the so-called "scroll of Moses" in Ezra 6:18; Neh 13:1.

9. The first time a Jewish author identifies himself as an author is in the Wisdom of Ben Sira (Ecclesiasticus), Sir 50:29, written in the 2nd century B.C.E.

Rome in Virgil's *Aeneid*, Moses came to be seen as the composer of the Torah, which was Second Temple Israel's national epos and the basis for its legal code. Similarly, about this time the idea arose that King David wrote
the Psalms, Solomon authored Song of Songs, Proverbs, and Ecclesiastes,
and Ruth and Esther wrote the books bearing their names.

The tradition of Moses being the author of the Torah came to be firmly
ingrained by the 1st century C.E. Thus, in the New Testament, Jesus spoke
of "the law of Moses" when referencing a law in Lev 12:3 (John 7:23) or
when referencing the entire corpus of laws (Luke 24:44).[10] More specifically, in Mark 12:26 Jesus cited "the book of Moses" when he quoted Exod
3:6, in which God told Moses "I am the God of Abraham, and the God of
Isaac, and the God of Jacob." From then on, it became official Church doctrine that Moses wrote the complete Torah. Similarly, Josephus and Philo
of Alexandria claimed that Moses was the author of the Torah.[11] However,
even at this early date, there seemed to be a question about how Moses
could possibly have written the final chapter of Deuteronomy, which recorded Moses' death and burial. Thus Josephus and Philo went to great
lengths to explicitly state that Moses was an extraordinary prophet who
wrote passages even about his own death. Even so, the fact that they addressed this specific issue illustrates that people were already raising objections to the idea that Moses authored the Torah in its entirety.

The Earliest Critics

The earliest known written reference in which an author questioned
Mosaic authorship of the Torah occurred in The Apocalypse of Ezra, also
known as 2 Esdras. Most scholars believe that this Apocryphal book was
composed in the late 1st century C.E. In the book, the angel Uriel reveals to
the reader mysteries of the world, many critical of Rome. In chap. 14, Ezra
prays for guidance to write the Torah. According to the author of 2 Esdras,
the original Torah was destroyed in the Nebuchadnezzar fire that ravaged
Jerusalem and destroyed the Temple in 586 B.C.E. Ezra prays to God:

> If I have found favor before You, send the Holy Spirit into me, and I will
> write everything that has happened in the world from the beginning,
> the things which were written in Your Torah, that people may be able
> to find the path, and that those who wish to live in the last days may
> live. (2 Esd 14:22)

---

10. Notice that in the Talmud the rabbis commonly say "The Holy One, blessed be
He, said to Moses . . ." and then quote something that is not in the Torah. See Marc
Bregman, "Pseudepigraphy in Rabbinic Literature," online: http://orion.mscc.huji.ac.il/
symposiums/2nd/papers/Bregman97.html.

11. Josephus, *Ag. Ap.* 1:37–40; *Ant.* 4.8.48; Philo, *Mos.* 2.291.

God then commissioned Ezra and five other men, and after drinking a cup of "something like water, but colored like fire" (14:39), Ezra and the five men wrote 94 books that God dictated. Twenty-four of these were the books of the Hebrew Bible,[12] but 70 books were to be reserved as secret apocalyptic books for the wise. Remarkably, the author of 2 Esdras, writing nearly 2,000 years ago, claimed something upon which nearly all Bible scholars now agree: Ezra played a role in the formation of the Torah as we now have it.

Questions regarding Moses' authorship of the Torah can also be found in the Babylonian Talmud. A famous talmudic passage, Tractate *Baba Batra* 14b, focused on who wrote various books of the Bible. The rabbis claimed that Joshua wrote the book of Joshua, David authored the Psalms, and Samuel composed the books of Samuel, Judges, and Ruth. They further stated that Jeremiah wrote Jeremiah, Kings, and Lamentations, while Hezekiah "and his colleagues" wrote Isaiah, Proverbs, Song of Songs, and Ecclesiastes. Regarding the Torah, however, a debate arose surrounding two issues: (1) how could Moses have written the final verses of Deuteronomy that recorded his death and burial, and (2) how could Moses have written the story of Balak and Balaam (Numbers 22–24), because this story recorded events to which Moses clearly was not a witness. Rabbi Simeon said God dictated the entire Torah to Moses, including the parts about Balaam. Typically Moses heard the dictation, repeated it, and then wrote it down. But now, with the somber final eight verses about his death (Deut 34:5–12), Moses wrote with tears in his eyes without repeating. Nevertheless, Rabbi Judah claimed that Moses wrote the entire Torah *except* the final eight verses, which he attributed to Joshua. This debate illustrates that at this early date even some talmudic rabbis, among the earliest and most learned biblical scholars in history, questioned the orthodoxy of Mosaic authorship of the complete Torah.

Early Christians also doubted Mosaic authorship, as seen in the Clementine *Homilies*. The Clementine *Homilies* were composed by anonymous Christians in the 3rd century C.E., though traditionally the *Homilies* were attributed to Clement of Rome (ca. 30–101 C.E.), the fourth pope of the Catholic Church (after Peter, Linus, and Anacletus). The *Homilies* consisted of a fabricated debate between Peter and Simon the Magician. In these debates, Peter argued that the Hebrew Bible contained both divine truth as well as much that was false. The *Homilies* sought to distance Moses from

---

12. Twenty-four books are counted as follows: 5 in the Torah, 8 in the Prophets (Joshua, Judges, 1 and 2 Samuel [as one book], 1 and 2 Kings [as one book], Isaiah, Jeremiah, Ezekiel, and the Twelve [as one book]) and 11 in the Writings (counting Ezra–Nehemiah as one book and 1 and 2 Chronicles as one book).

passages that the authors viewed as objectionable, such as God being portrayed as anthropomorphic, Noah being drunk, and Abraham having three wives (2.52; 3.55–57). Moreover, the authors of the Clementine *Homilies* noticed that Moses could not have written the passages about his death and that these same passages used the identical writing style as earlier passages (3.47). They decided that Moses was such a great prophet that he even foresaw that one day the Torah would disappear, only to be rediscovered by Josiah. Thus he purposefully did not write it himself. Rather, he dictated it to 70 elders, and the Torah, according to the *Homilies'* authors, was not written down until long after Moses died. Then about 500 years later, the original Torah was found lying in the Temple during King Josiah's reign, only to be destroyed a short time later in the burning of Jerusalem at the hands of Nebuchadnezzar in 586 B.C.E. So, according to these early Christians, Moses never wrote the Torah, and much of what is found in the Torah today postdates 586 B.C.E.

The philosopher Porphyry (233–309 C.E.), like the authors of the Clementine Homilies, argued that the entire Torah, and not just the final chapter of Deuteronomy, postdated Moses. Porphyry was born in Tyre and studied in Athens and then Rome under Plotinus. Porphyry is best remembered for his letter *On Abstinence from Killing Animals*, in which he attempts to persuade a friend to return to a vegetarian diet because animals have souls. However, in the field of biblical criticism, Porphyry made two remarkable discoveries. First, he wrote that the book of Daniel was not written during the Babylonian Exile, when the stories are set, but much later during the time of Antiochus IV (2nd century B.C.E.). This conclusion is shared by most Bible scholars today. Second, he wrote that:

> Nothing which Moses wrote has been preserved. For all his writings are said to have been burned along with the Temple. All that bears the name of Moses was written 1180 years afterwards, by Ezra and those of his time.[13]

While Christian scholars such as Origen (185–253 C.E.) and Jerome (ca. 345–420 C.E.) did not go as far as Porphyry in completely denying Mosaic authorship, they both noticed that it was too simplistic to believe that Moses was the only human to have a hand in the entire Torah as it now existed. Origen attributed inconsistencies in the Torah as God's way of giving deeper meaning to the wise.[14] Jerome concluded, "Whether you wish to say that Moses is the author of the Pentateuch, or that Ezra re-edited it, in either case I make no objection."[15]

---

13. Preserved in the writings of the Christian scholar Macarius, *Apocriticus* 3.3.
14. Origen, *Dialogue with Heraclides*, 12.20.
15. Jerome, *The Perpetual Virginity of Blessed Mary: Against Helvidius*, 7.

Middle Ages

During the Middle Ages, questions regarding Moses' alleged authorship of the Torah surfaced again. This subject was brought up by Heloise (ca. 1100–1164), the brilliant student and wife of Peter Abelard (ca. 1079–1142). Abelard and Heloise's romance and its unfortunate conclusion (Abelard was castrated by thugs Heloise's uncle hired) was one of the most famous in the Middle Ages. Despite their misfortunes, the correspondences they wrote show that both were well educated and excellent critical thinkers. Some have even argued that Abelard was the first to use theology in the modern sense of the discipline, using reason in matters of faith. Abelard famously stated, "By doubting we come to inquiry; by inquiring we perceive the truth."[16] Frequently, Abelard applied this method to biblical studies. One of Abelard and Heloise's correspondences is known as *Problemata Heloise* (*Problems of Heloise*).[17] These consist of a collection of 42 questions raised by Heloise and her fellow nuns about theology and Scripture, which Peter Abelard eruditely answered. In question 41, Heloise and her companions asked Abelard if the end of Deuteronomy was written by someone other than Moses, or by Moses using a prophetic spirit. Abelard's solution claimed that the entire Hebrew Bible was destroyed by a fire. Citing Bede's commentary on the book of Ezra, Abelard explained that Ezra rewrote the Bible and added many things to clarify issues for the reader. Abelard pointed out that there were similar additions in the Gospels. For example, the author of Matt 27:46 added a translation of the Hebrew phrase *'elî 'elî lāmā 'azabtānî* ('My God, my God, why have you forsaken me?'). Finally, Abelard brought up the fact that Jerome's book *Lives of Famous Men* included Jerome himself, implying that obviously somebody other than Jerome described Jerome's death.

Gradually, questions surrounding Moses' authorship expanded beyond the final verses of Deuteronomy. For example, the Jewish scholar Hiwi al-Balkhi published a rationalist critique of the Bible in 9th-century Persia. He wrote 200 reasons why the Bible was not the divine word of God, exposing biblical contradictions and explaining miracles as the causes of natural phenomenon. Thus, he claimed that the parting of the Red Sea during the Exodus was the result of tidal flow. Unfortunately, his original work does not survive today. However, the large number of people who refute him testifies to his influence.[18] The most famous Bible critic of the Middle Ages,

---

16. *Sic et Non* (*Yes and No*).

17. An English translation of all 42 problems with Abelard's solutions can be found in Elizabeth Mary McNamer, *The Education of Heloise: The Methods, Content, and Purpose of Learning in the Twelfth Century* (Mediaeval Studies 8; Lewiston, NY: Edwin Mellen, 1991).

18. See, for example, Israel Davidson, ed., *Saadia's Polemic against Hiwi al Balkhi* (New York: Jewish Theological Seminary, 1915).

Abraham Ibn Ezra (1089–1164), even cited al-Balkhi by name nearly three centuries later. However, Ibn Ezra voiced his disapproval of al-Balkhi's controversial conclusions by changing the gentilic al-Balkhi to *haKalbi* (Hebrew for 'the dog'). From these refutations by Ibn Ezra and others, scholars are able to reconstruct about one-third of al-Balkhi's original 200 criticisms. It is not known if he specifically questioned the idea that Moses wrote the Torah.

Ibn Ezra, despite calling al-Balkhi names, seems to have reached many of the same conclusions regarding Mosaic authorship. Ibn Ezra argued that biblical verses portraying an anthropomorphic God were not to be taken literally.[19] But instead of blatantly questioning orthodox interpretations of biblical passages, a dangerous undertaking in medieval Europe, he often wrote in code. For example, Gen 12:6 states, "And the Canaanite was then in the land." Ibn Ezra wisely noticed that the phrase was likely written at a later date, in a time when there were no Canaanites in the land. Ibn Ezra, rather than openly questioning how Moses could have written that verse, instead argued that "It appears that Canaan, the grandson of Noah, took from another the land which bears his name; if this be sage, and let him who understands it keep silence."[20] Another of Ibn Ezra's famous cryptic criticisms arose from his commentary on the verse: "These are the kings who reigned in the land of Edom, before any king reigned over Israel" (Gen 36:31). The point is that the phrasing implies that the passage was written at a time when kings *did* reign over Israel, namely, centuries after Moses. Ibn Ezra quoted a man he called Isaac (perhaps Isaac ben Solomon Israeli, a 9th–10th-century physician, philosopher, and Bible scholar in Egypt) who said that this chapter was written in the 9th century B.C.E. near the reign of Jehoshaphat. Ibn Ezra wrote that Isaac (Hebrew *yiṣḥaq* 'he laughs') was a good name for this commentator, because "everyone who hears his interpretation will laugh at him."[21] Ibn Ezra even recommended that Isaac's book be burned and argued the awkward position that the king in the verse referred to none other than Moses. Ibn Ezra, however, also suspected post-Mosaic additions to the Bible.

The passage that seems to have troubled Ibn Ezra the most was "These are the words that Moses spoke to all of Israel beyond the Jordan" (Deut 1:1). Ibn Ezra noticed the improbability that Moses wrote this, because Moses never crossed the Jordan River; moreover, none of the Israelites in the audience with Moses had crossed the Jordan. Thus, the author of this passage was likely writing in Israel and setting the story on the other side

---

19. Ibn Ezra, *Commentary* on Gen 1:26.
20. Ibid., Gen 12:6.
21. Ibid., Gen 36:31.

of the Jordan River. But Ibn Ezra cloaked this conclusion in a coded message. He wrote that if one might come to understand five items, "Then you shall know the truth regarding this verse."[22] The five items are as follows:

1. The mystery of the 12,
2. Moses wrote,
3. the Canaanites were then in the land,
4. it shall be revealed on the mountain of the Lord,
5. behold, his bed is a bed of iron.

It was not until six centuries later that the scholar Baruch Spinoza (1632–77) printed a solution to Ibn Ezra's riddle. (Puzzle fans might try to solve the meaning of these five references before reading below.) In the end, writing in code did not keep Ibn Ezra free from controversy. Many exegetes of the Bible after Ibn Ezra have avoided his commentaries, as do some orthodox Jewish scholars today.

Reformation and Enlightenment

Arguments against the idea that Moses wrote the Torah expanded during the Reformation as more scholars engaged in biblical criticism. Andreas Carlstadt (1480–1541), a colleague of Martin Luther at the university in Wittenberg, concluded that Moses did not compile the entire Torah.[23] Carlstadt used as evidence the conclusions of earlier scholars that Moses could not have written about his own death. Carlstadt, too, pointed out that the final chapter of Deuteronomy was written in the same style as the preceding chapters. His conclusions, as well as his influence, rekindled the theory that *all* of the Torah was composed by authors living after Moses. For Carlstadt, the authors of the Torah used written notes from Moses as well as other sources, but they also added their own material. This conclusion was shared by Hugo Grotius (1583–1645),[24] a Dutch jurist who wrote annotations to all of the biblical books, and the Calvinist Isaac de La Peyrère (1594–1676),[25] whose book was confiscated and destroyed, and who was forced to convert to Catholicism and recant before the pope.

The critical examination of the tradition that Moses wrote the Torah reached unprecedented heights in the work of Thomas Hobbes (1588–1679). Hobbes, in chap. 33 of *Leviathan*, argued that the titles of biblical books do not tell us the authors' names. He pointed out that nobody

---

22. Ibid., Deut 1:1.
23. Andreas Carlstadt, *De canonicis scripturis*.
24. Hugo Grotius, *Annotationes in Vetus et Novum Testamentum*.
25. Isaac de La Peyrère, *Systema theologicum ex praeadamitarum hypothesi*, and idem, *Prae Adamitae* 4.1.

believes that Ruth wrote the book of Ruth. Hobbes, like his predecessors, argued the unlikelihood that Moses wrote passages about his own death. Further, Hobbes pointed out that passages such as "no one knows the location of his [Moses'] tomb until this day" (Deut 34:6) were written in a day long after Moses.[26] Hobbes followed Ibn Ezra in believing a post-Mosaic date of composition for the passage "And the Canaanite was then in the land" (Gen 12:6). He concluded, "It is therefore sufficiently evident that the five books of Moses were written after his time, though how long after it be not so manifest."[27] But Hobbes did not divorce Moses from all of the passages in the Torah; he said that Moses did write much of the legal code from Deuteronomy 11 to 27.

Like Hobbes, Spinoza doubted Mosaic authorship but went further than earlier critics. Spinoza believed that Ibn Ezra was the first to question Mosaic authorship, and in chap. 8 of *Tractatus Theologico-politicus* (1670), Spinoza provided biblical verses and explanations for Ibn Ezra's five cryptic clues:

1. *The mystery of the 12* (Deut 27:1–8, *or* Deut 27:15–26, *or* Deut 34:1–12). Here Spinoza was not certain about Ibn Ezra's reference and posited three possibilities. The entire Torah of Moses was said to have been written on the stones of an altar (Deut 27:1–8; Josh 8:32), which according to the Rabbis, consisted of 12 stones. Spinoza suggested that the entire Torah was much too large to fit on 12 stones, so the original Torah was small, and someone could have later written all five books. Second, Spinoza speculated that perhaps the 12 referred to the 12 curses in Deut 27:15–26, which could not have been in the Torah because Moses ordered the Levites to read the curses *after* the recital of the law, in order to bind the people to its observance *after* the Torah was recited. Spinoza implied that first the Torah would have to be recited to the people, as commanded in Deut 31:11, and then later these 12 curses would be in place to make sure people kept the laws. Third, Spinoza posed what today seems to be the best explanation for Ibn Ezra's code: that it refers to the 12 verses that make up the last chapter of Deuteronomy, which tell of Moses' death and burial.

2. *Moses wrote* (Deut 31:9). For Spinoza, an author other than Moses composed this verse because if Moses wrote it, one would expect it to be in the first person. Therefore it sounds like another is recording the deeds of Moses.

---

26. For a detailed examination of the phrase "until this day," see Geoghegan, "'Until This Day' and the Preexilic Redaction of the Deuteronomistic History," 201–27. Similarly, Hobbes argued that Joshua was written long after the person, also based on the phrase "until this day."

27. Thomas Hobbes, *Leviathan* (ed. Richard Tuck; Cambridge: Cambridge University Press, 1996) 262.

3. The Canaanites were then in the land (Gen 12:6).   Abraham and his family leave Haran "and they set forth to go to the land of Canaan" (Gen 12:5). Gen 12:6 and 13:7 states, "At that time the Canaanites were then in the land." Spinoza argued that this must have been written after Moses, when the Canaanites were driven out and no longer possessed the land. Thus, it sounds like Canaanites were not in the land at the time that this verse was composed.

4. It shall be revealed on the mountain of the Lord (Gen 22:14).   Abraham named the mountain upon which he nearly sacrificed Isaac: "Yahweh will reveal, as it is said to this day, 'On the mountain of Yahweh it shall be revealed'" (Gen 22:14). Traditionally, the location of this event was Mount Moriah, where Solomon would later build the Temple. However, according to Spinoza, it was not named "the mountain of Yahweh" until after the Temple was built. Thus, the verse was a reference to Solomon's Temple, which was built long after Moses.

5. Behold, his bed is a bed of iron (Deut 3:11).   When Moses retold the history of the wilderness wanderings to the Israelites, he mentioned the defeat of Og, the king of Bashan. In the passage, Og was said to own a large iron bed in the Ammonite city of Rabbah. It would seem, Spinoza pointed out, that this relic would more likely have been discovered in the time of David, who conquered Rabbah of Ammon (2 Sam 12:26–31). Knowledge about the bed, according to Spinoza, was not obtainable until after the reign of David.

In addition to his explanations of Ibn Ezra's five coded phrases, Spinoza also expanded on Ibn Ezra's criticism of Gen 36:31, which told of kings of Edom "before any king reigned over Israel." This implied that the passage was written at a time when kings ruled over the Israelites, or at least a knowledge that one day after Moses, Israel would have a king.

Spinoza added some of his own evidence questioning Mosaic authorship. Moses, as in the common phrase "And Yahweh spoke to Moses," was often addressed in the third person. The Torah also provided many details about Moses in the third person, such as "Moses was the meekest of men" (Num 12:3). But suddenly in Deut 2:1, Moses declared "Yahweh told me," and shortly thereafter the author again switched to the third person. This stylistic change indicated to Spinoza that more than one author was at work, a theory reinforced by other factors. Not only did Deuteronomy 34 record Moses' death, but his burial and the 30-day mourning period were both described. The Torah also compared Moses to later prophets (Num 18:15, Deut 34:10), indicating that it was written after the tenure of these prophets. Spinoza additionally noticed that certain names were anachronistic, such as Abraham pursuing his enemy to Dan even though the site was not given this name until long after Joshua. Earlier, the site was known as Laish (Gen 14:14, Judg 18:29).

Spinoza concluded, "it is thus clearer than the sun at noon the Pentateuch was not written by Moses but by someone who lived long after Moses."[28] Elsewhere he wrote, "the belief that Moses was the author of the Pentateuch is ungrounded and even irrational."[29] Spinoza also asserted that Genesis through Kings was the work of one historian, who Spinoza identified as Ezra. Ezra used notes from Moses but changed them to fit events in his own time. Yet Spinoza did attribute certain portions of the Torah to Moses, such as the book about a war against the Amalekites (Exod 17:4), "The Book of the Wars of God" (Num 21:12), the laws in the "Book of the Covenant Moses read before the Israelites" (Exod 24:4), and the "Book of the Torah of God" (Deut 1:5, 29:14, 31:9). Spinoza published his findings anonymously, though it was no secret that he was the author of *Tractatus*. For expressing these ideas, in 1656 Spinoza was excommunicated from his synagogue in Amsterdam.

Jews and Protestants were not alone in their questioning of Mosaic authorship. The French Catholic priest Richard Simon (1638–1712) wrote in his *Histoire critique du Vieux Testament* that "Moses cannot be the author of all the books attributed to him." Simon developed a theory that a public scribe guild kept records and passed them down through generations. Thus, according to Simon, the Hebrew Bible was a gradual compilation that eventually underwent a much later final redaction. He was the first to call attention to biblical doublets, which are stories that are told twice, such as creation in Genesis 1 and then again in Genesis 2 or Abraham naming Beer Sheba twice (Gen 21:25–31, 26:26–35). Simon noticed that these doublets had a diversity of narrative style that must be the work of two different authors. Simon's edition was confiscated and destroyed just months after it was published. Several theologians objected to his findings, and he was expelled from the Oratory in Paris. Simon became a parish priest and published several later works using a pseudonym, but these were not as influential as his earlier *Historie*.

Thomas Paine (1737–1809), famous for his influence and support of the American and French revolutions, also bitingly mocked the idea that Moses wrote the Torah. In 1793, Paine was imprisoned in Paris because he did not advocate executing Louis XVI. While there, Paine began writing and distributing the deist text *The Age of Reason*. He carefully examined both the Hebrew Bible and the New Testament and systematically argued that all of the books of the Bible were obvious forgeries in that they were

---

28. Spinoza, *Tractatus*, chap. 8.
29. Ibid.

not written by the person after whom they were named. Regarding Moses, Paine said that the Torah was written centuries later by Hilkiah the priest and Shaphan the scribe. Paine further quipped that the Torah was written by "some very ignorant and stupid pretenders to authorship."[30] Paine wrote that Deuteronomy was written by a Jewish priest fond of tithes. Furthermore, Paine disputed the biblical claim of Moses being the meekest man on earth (Num 12:3), arguing that Moses in fact "was one of the most vain and arrogant of coxcombs."[31]

The "Older" Documentary Hypothesis

In the 18th century, the systematic analysis of detailed biblical passages produced what is now referred to as the "Older" Documentary Hypothesis: the theory that the Torah was composed of two or three parallel strands, or documents. For example, Henning Bernhard Witter (1683–1715), a pastor in Hildesheim, was the first to point out that different sources used a different name for God.[32] Thus, Witter noticed that the first creation account in the Torah, Gen 1:1–2:4, called God "Elohim," and that in the second creation account (Gen 2:5–25), God was referred to as "Yahweh."

The person most responsible for the birth of the Documentary Hypothesis was Jean Astruc (1684–1766), a French professor of medicine and the personal physician for Louis XV. Astruc's religious upbringing was complicated, to say the least. He was the son of a Calvinist minister of Jewish origin who converted to Catholicism one year after the birth of his son. In 1753 Astruc published *Conjectures sur les mémoires dont il paroit que Moyse s'est servi, pour composer le livre de la Génèse* (*Conjectures concerning the original memoranda which it appears Moses used to Compose the Book of Genesis*). But instead of questioning Mosaic authorship because of the description of Moses' death, Astruc focused on earlier periods. He was puzzled as to how Moses wrote material about Abraham and people who lived long before Moses. Like Witter, Astruc noticed that different sources seemed to call God by different names. Astruc identified two major sources, which he referred to as "mémoires." Source A used the name "Elohim" for God, and Source B used "Yahweh." Astruc argued that Moses used these two sources in composing Genesis. Astruc could not fit all of Genesis into these two sources, so he theorized that there were 10 additional fragments of lesser importance scattered throughout Genesis. He concluded that Moses set the two sources and 10 fragments in four columns side-by-side, but at a later date all four columns were mistakenly combined. This combination is what produced

---

30. Thomas Paine, *The Age of Reason*, 2.1.
31. Ibid.
32. Henning Bernhard Witter, *Jura Israelitarum in Palaestinam*, 1711.

anachronisms and difficulties. Approximately half of Astruc's book consists of his re-creation of what he believed to have been the original four columns that Moses had at his disposal. Astruc published the monograph anonymously, although everyone knew Astruc was the author.

Astruc wrote in the book's preface:

> This work was written some time ago, but I hesitated to publish it lest the so-called liberals should abuse it to diminish the authority of the Pentateuch. I showed it to a man well educated and zealous for religion, and he dispelled my scruples, assuring me that my conjectures... could not be but advantageous to the cause of religion.

The intense backlash that Astruc expected did not come. Though this was the only book he published on the Bible, the book was very influential with theologians of his day, to his surprise. However, Astruc's theory would have disappeared had it not been for a German Bible scholar named Johann Eichhorn, who masterfully applied the theory to the entire Torah.

Eichhorn (1752–1827) was a professor of Oriental languages at Jena. He went beyond simply matching biblical passages with sources. Eichhorn attempted to discern linguistic, stylistic, and theological characteristics from each source.[33] Initially, Eichhorn shared Astruc's idea that Moses wrote the Torah by using two main sources and a few fragments—for Eichhorn, three to five in number. However, he later changed his mind and suggested that the Torah was composed of three primary sources that were not combined by Moses but by a later, unknown redactor. Eichhorn believed that this redactor chose sources based on their completeness of the account. Eichhorn was the first to use the term *Higher Criticism* and the first to name the sources "E" (for *Elohim*) and "J" (for German *Jahwe*, English *Yahweh*) due to the respective names for God that each source utilized.

The Fragmentary and Supplementary Hypotheses

In the late 18th century, scholars further dissected the Torah and many concluded that it was not composed of sources but, more accurately, it consisted of a vast number of larger and smaller fragments independent of one another with no continuity. Later, an editor connected these sources together under one heading. This theory came to be known as the Fragmentary Hypothesis. Its main proponents were Alexander Geddes (1737–1802) in England and Johann Severin Vater (1771–1826) in Germany. Geddes was a Catholic priest from Scotland. He argued that the authors of the

---

33. Johann Eichhorn, *Einleitung in das Alte Testament* (*Introduction to the Old Testament*), 1780–83.

fragments belonged to two different circles or schools: one using the divine name Yahweh, the other Elohim.[34] Alternatively, Vater understood the Torah's main fragment to be the laws of Deuteronomy. Vater argued that these laws were composed in the 10th century during the reigns of David and Solomon. Additional historical and legal sections were later added gradually, with the process ending in the period of the Exile. Vater counted at least 38 different fragment sources. Some of these sources, Vater argued, were as early as Moses, but the final product was not redacted until about 586 B.C.E.[35]

In time, the Supplementary Hypothesis grew out of the Fragmentary Hypothesis. The process began with a book review by Heinrich Ewald, but shortly thereafter it was made famous in Ewald's book *Die Komposition der Genesis Kritisch unter Sucht* (*The Composition of Genesis under Critical Examination*), published in 1823. Ewald concluded that the Hexateuch (Genesis through Joshua) was a work by an author that called God "Elohim," although this author used older sections, such as the Decalogue. Later, a parallel document was composed, but this one used the divine name Yahweh. Somebody later added the material of the Yahweh source to the original Elohim work but always gave precedence to the original work, thereby supplementing it. Though Ewald began the theory, he later ended it as well. In his book *Geschichte Israels* (*History of Israel*) published between 1843 and 1855, Ewald suggested that, instead of fragments, there were at least two continuous documents using Elohim. Consequently, he combined the Supplementary Hypothesis with the older Documentary Hypothesis.

The "New" Documentary Hypothesis

With the death of the Supplementary Hypothesis, most scholars returned to the notion that the Torah was composed of documents. Such scholars included Hermann Hupfeld (1796–1866), who in his book *Die Quellen der Genesis und die Art ihrer Zusammensetzung* (*The Sources of Genesis and the Nature of Their Combination*) argued that there were three narrative strands in Genesis. Hupfeld showed that the source that used the divine name Yahweh was a continuous narrative, while the source that used the divine name Elohim was actually two sources. Hupfeld claimed that the Yahweh source was the last of the three to be written. Also, he asserted that the book of Deuteronomy was a separate source entirely. At a later date, a redactor combined all of these documents into one unit.

---

34. Alexander Geddes, *Critical Remarks on the Hebrew Scriptures*, 1800.
35. Johann Vater, *Commentar über den Pentateuch*, 1802–5.

Another influential Bible scholar in Germany was Wilhelm de Wette (1780–1849). His dissertation at the University of Jena argued that Deuteronomy could not have been written before the 7th century and that Deuteronomy was the law book found in the Temple during Josiah's reign. Thus, DeWette argued, Deuteronomy was somehow to be connected with Josiah rather than Moses. DeWette published *Beiträge zur Einleitung in das Alte Testament* (*Contribution on the Introduction in the Old Testament*) and took a middle position between the Documentary and Fragmentary hypotheses. He claimed that the Torah consisted of a large document running from Genesis through Numbers that used the name Elohim. However, many people added fragments to this long continuous narrative.

Next to Wellhausen, it was Karl Heinrich Graf (1815–69) who was most responsible for the modern Documentary Hypothesis. In fact, before Wellhausen, scholars used to refer to it as Graf's Hypothesis and labeled Graf the "Father of the Documentary Hypothesis," though that title today is most often associated with Wellhausen. In the early 1830s, Graf's teacher and friend Eduard Reuss argued that the basic document in the Torah, what scholars would later call P (for *Priestly*), was in fact the latest source. The Dutch scholar Abraham Kuenen further argued that this source was created after the exile of 586 B.C.E. This theory culminated in Graf's publication *Die geschichtlichen Bücher des Alten Testaments* (*The Historical Books of the Old Testament*) in 1866. Graf argued that Deuteronomy did not presuppose the laws and narratives of P, and therefore P must have been written after Deuteronomy. For Graf, J was the oldest source, dating from the 9th century B.C.E. The Elohistic author wrote a short time thereafter. These authors reflected the prophetic spirit of their times—a time, Graf argued, before the Israelite religion was burdened by so many ritualistic laws. The author of Deuteronomy composed a legal code for Josiah's religious reforms in the 7th century B.C.E. Finally, Graf contended, the Priestly author came up with laws to control rituals after the exiled Jews returned to Israel in the 5th century B.C.E.

Ultimately, the Documentary Hypothesis was formulated by Julius Wellhausen (1844–1918), who combined the work of these previous scholars and masterfully argued in favor of the Torah being composed of four documents. Like Graf and others, it appears that much of what drove Wellhausen in his argument was an anti-Jewish desire to liberate Israelite antiquity from what he perceived to be the burden of later Jewish law. That is, Wellhausen loved the stories of David, Saul, Ahab, and Elijah and believed the legal codes were not in the same spirit. In his preface to *Prolegomena*, Wellhausen wrote "in the summer of 1867 [he was 23], I learned through Ritschl that Karl Heinrich Graf placed the Law later than the Prophets, and almost without knowing his reasons for the hypothesis, I was prepared to accept it: I readily acknowledged to myself the possibility of understanding Hebrew antiquity without the book of the Torah."[36]

Today, the academic discipline of biblical studies has changed a great deal. Many new critical methods, such as Literary Criticism, Feminist Criticism, and Narrative Criticism, provide tools for scholars to gain new insights from the Bible.[37] Even so, Higher Criticism, the first critical method applied to the Bible, continues to be one of the most dominant and important methods used by academic experts of the Bible. Scholars still debate dates for various authors of the Bible and argue about which passages belong to which of the sources. These remarkable discoveries regarding authorship of the Torah came gradually through the inquiries and insights of some of the most brilliant minds of the past 2,000 years.

Ps and Qs

The source today known as P changed names several times in the history of the Documentary Hypothesis. In Germany, it was originally called the *Grundschrift* 'base writing' or *Urschrift* 'original writing'. Alternatively (and because this source refers to God using the divine name Elohim until God revealed the personal name Yahweh to Moses [Exod 6:3]), some early scholars referred to the source as "the first Elohist." They originally believed this source to be earlier than the other source that used the divine name Elohim, today known as E, though Wellhausen, following Graf, argued the opposite chronology. But instead of *Grundschrift* or its other names, Wellhausen called this source Q, an abbreviation of *quattuor* (four). This was the fourth source to be identified, as well as the source of the four covenants, those God made with Adam, Noah, Abraham, and Moses. The source in its entirety Wellhausen called RQ, for redacted quattuor. Wellhausen kept the terms Q and RQ until the third edition of *Prolegemena*. From then on, he dropped the abbreviation Q in favor of P, and it has been known as P "until this day."

Moses and Homer

All people, including Bible scholars, are products of their environment. Where and when we work creates real influences on our conclusions, due in part to the reciprocal nature of research. This point was brought up by

---

36. Julius Wellhausen, *Prolegomena to the History of Ancient Israel with a reprint of the article, "Israel," from the Encyclopedia Brittanica* (preface by W. Robertson Smith; Gloucester, MA: Peter Smith, 1973) 3.

37. See, for example, Steven L. McKenzie and Stephen R. Haynes, eds., *To Each Its Own Meaning: An Introduction to Biblical Criticisms and Their Application* (Louisville: Westminster John Knox, 1999).

Umberto Cassuto, a conservative though influential Bible scholar who famously critiqued the Documentary Hypothesis. In 1941, Cassuto published *The Documentary Hypothesis and the Composition of the Pentateuch*.[38] In this work, Cassuto pointed out many startling similarities between the academic study of the Bible and the academic study of Homer's epic poems *The Iliad* and *The Odyssey*. For example, the theories that both the Bible and Homer's poems were composed of separate documents later compiled began, for the most part, in early 18th-century France. It was during this time that Jean Astruc published *Conjectures sur les mémoires originaux don't il paroit que Moyse s'est servi pour composer le livre de Génèse* and argued that Genesis consisted of two main documents with subsidiary sources. And 18th-century France also produced Abbé d'Aubignac, who published *Conjectures académiques ou dissertations sur l'Iliade*. Aubignac argued that the *Iliad* was not written by Homer but was a collection of poems that were originally unrelated. Astruc and Aubignac have both been called the "Father" of their disciplines, both used the word "Conjecture" in their titles, both reached similar conclusions, and neither was an expert in biblical or Homeric studies.

In both disciplines, French amateurs were followed by German professional scholars who systemized their predecessor's lay opinions. In the Bible's case, Eichhorn published *Einleitung in das Alte Testament* between 1780 and 1783. Similarly, Friedrich August Wolf wrote the treatise *Prolegomena ad Homerum* in 1795. Both works were called a *Prolegomena (Introduction)* and reached similar conclusions: they argued that independent documents served as the basis of the Pentateuch and Homer. Then, at the onset of the 19th century, the Fragmentary Hypothesis dominated both fields. Scholars argued that the Torah and Homer were composed of many scrolls that at first existed independent of the others. This theory was replaced in the 1830s by the Supplementary Hypothesis: scholars in both fields argued for the existence of ancient basic documents that later generations gradually completed by adding and redacting. This doctrine did not last long in either academic discipline, and scholars returned to the idea that the Bible and Homer's poems were composed of separate documents. German scholars such as Ulrich von Wilamowitz-Moellendorf again systematically argued that Homer's epics were composed from datable documents separated by centuries. Wilamowitz-Moellendorf was a friend and colleague at the University of Greifswald with Julius Wellhausen, who argued the same was the case for the Torah.

---

38. Umberto Cassuto, *The Documentary Hypothesis and the Composition of the Pentateuch: Eight Lectures* (trans. Israel Abrahams; Jerusalem: Magnes, 1961) [Hebrew, 1941].

Both disciplines dissected the texts and pointed out similar features: repetitions, duplications, contradictions, linguistic and stylistic variations. Cassuto pointed out that similar parallels exist in the study of Indian epic poetry and Middle Age epic poetry, though he did not go into detail. Today, while the Documentary Hypothesis plays a major role in biblical studies, it is rarely invoked in the study of Homer.

How Was the Bible Written?
Reflections on Sources and Authors in
the Book of Kings

ROBERT R. WILSON

Yale University

Surely one of the most influential of Richard Friedman's many publications has been *Who Wrote the Bible?* In it, Friedman explained to nonspecialists why biblical scholars believe the Hebrew Bible to be made up of various literary sources coming from different authors and time periods in Israel's history. At the same time, he reminded specialists in the field why the traditional literary approach is still useful in the face of numerous challenges to it.[1]

Since the publication of Friedman's book, scholars have reached a growing consensus that the Hebrew Bible is in fact a scribal production, the result of the work of literary specialists writing over a long period of time. However, there is still much scholarly disagreement over when this writing was done and which individuals or groups were responsible for it.[2] Furthermore, scholars are still at odds over exactly how the compositional process might have worked, with some scholars claiming that the scribes who wrote the Bible were primarily creative authors who were not strongly influenced by earlier oral or written materials, and other scholars claiming that much preexisting material was included, even though this material might have been edited to varying degrees by the scribal authors.[3] This

---

1. Richard Elliott Friedman, *Who Wrote the Bible?* (New York: Summit Books, 1987).

2. Among the most recent contributions to the debate, see in particular William M. Schniedewind, *How the Bible Became a Book* (Cambridge: Cambridge University Press, 2004), which argues a relatively traditional view of Israel's literary history. On the ancient Near Eastern background of scribal production, see David M. Carr, *Writing on the Tablet of the Heart* (Oxford: Oxford University Press, 2005). For an alternative view that would assign a relatively late date to the compositional process, see Philip R. Davies, *Scribes and Schools: The Composition of the Hebrew Scriptures* (Louisville: Westminster John Knox, 1998).

3. For a recent exploration of the role of editors in ancient literary composition, see John Van Seters, *The Edited Bible: The Curious History of the "Editor" in Biblical Criticism* (Winona Lake, IN: Eisenbrauns, 2006).

question of the use of preexisting material is particularly acute in the book of Kings, where traditional stories and archival data seem to have been involved in the process of writing the book. Especially problematic have been the prophetic stories in Kings, which often appear to be poorly integrated into their context in the Deuteronomistic History. As a way of celebrating Richard Friedman's interest in literary history, the following remarks will reexamine the problem of the prophetic stories, and in this way, I will try to shed some light on the larger issue of how ancient scribes treated their literary sources.

For centuries, readers of the Bible have considered the book of Kings to be a coherent literary work, a continuous narrative, organized chronologically, that traces the story of the kings of Israel and Judah from the end of David's reign to the fall of Jerusalem during the reign of Zedekiah. However, this perception of literary coherence does not mean that readers considered Kings to be a completely original literary creation. Rather the book was recognized to be a work that used preexisting literary sources, whether oral or written, and readers assumed that these sources were to some degree the basis of the author's account. Kings itself mentions some of these sources, and it refers readers to them for additional information. With the rise of critical biblical scholarship in the 19th century, scholars began to suggest that other unnamed sources were used by the writer of Kings as well. It should not come as a surprise, then, to discover that scholars also began to suspect that the prophetic stories in Kings existed in some form before their incorporation into their present literary context.

Several different kinds of observations led to this conclusion. First, scholars noted the distribution of the prophetic stories within the book of Kings. On purely descriptive grounds, the stories appear to be of two different types. First, some of the stories are part of a prophecy-fulfillment schema, which helps to unify portions of the book. In this schema, a prophet delivers an oracle against a person or a place, and when the prophecy is fulfilled, the author duly notes the fulfillment, referring back to the original prophecy. This schema seems to begin in 1 Kgs 13:1–10, where an unnamed Man of God from Judah delivers a judgment oracle against the sanctuary at Bethel, and the fulfillment of this oracle in the time of Josiah is recorded in 2 Kgs 23:15–18. Outside of this case, which may be secondary, such prophecy-fulfillment notices appear only in the reigns of the Northern kings from the time of Jeroboam I (1 Kgs 14:7–16) to the end of the Omride dynasty (2 Kgs 10:17). At the end of the story of the Omride wars, the prophecy-fulfillment pattern is modified and extended when God personally (and unexpectedly) places a limitation on Jehu's dynasty (2 Kgs 10:28–31), and the fulfillment of this divine oracle is noted in 2 Kgs

15:12. However, strictly speaking, no prophet appears in this case. Later in Kings, the prophet Isaiah delivers a long oracle to Hezekiah, and the prophetess Huldah delivers an oracle to Josiah. Both oracles are fulfilled according to the narrative, although the characteristic fulfillment formula is lacking in both cases. In summary, then, the prophecy-fulfillment schema seems to be restricted to the accounts of the reigns of Northern kings and never appears in the material dealing with the kings of Judah. All of this could suggest that the motif is part of a block of material dealing with the North that was used by the writer of Kings to fill out the Northern portion of the dual history.

The second group of prophetic stories lies at least partially outside of the prophecy-fulfillment schema, although some prophets appear in both groups of stories. This second group contains narratives dealing with the interaction between prophets and the Ephraimite kings. These stories deal with both political and religious issues, although some of the stories simply focus on the aggrandizement of the prophet or the prophetic office. These stories begin with Ahijah's anointing of Jeroboam and the legitimation of the Northern Kingdom (1 Kgs 11:29–39), an act that is reinforced by Shemaiah's oracle to Reheboam (1 Kgs 12:22–24). Most of the remaining stories of prophetic activity in Kings have to do with the Northern Kingdom and the story of the overthrow of the Omride dynasty. The bulk of this material is found in the Elijah/Elisha stories (1 Kings 17–2 Kings 10), the Micaiah ben Imlah story (1 Kings 22), and a story coming out of the Aramean wars that involved several unnamed prophets (1 Kgs 20:35–43). Outside of this block of material, the only substantial references to prophets in Kings are to Isaiah and Huldah. In short, the narratives about prophetic activity are focused roughly on the same part of Kings that contains the prophecy-fulfillment schema.

The originally independent character of the prophetic stories, particularly the Elijah/Elisha stories, was suggested to early critical scholars on several grounds. First, there was linguistic evidence. The stories seem to be written in a different dialect of Hebrew than are the stories about the Judean kings, a fact that gave rise to the suggestion that the Elijah/Elisha stories were in a Northern or Ephraimite dialect.[4] The difference in dialect suggested that the stories were not written by the same author who composed the remainder of Kings.

---

4. This distinct dialect was already noticed by early scholars such as Wellhausen and was commented on in detail by C. F. Burney, *Notes on the Hebrew Text of the Books of Kings* (Oxford: Clarendon, 1903). A thorough treatment of the issue appears in Gary A. Rendsburg, *Israelian Hebrew in the Books of Kings* (Bethesda, MD: CDL, 2002), where a full bibliography may be found.

A second line of argument focused on the contents of the Elijah/Elisha stories.[5] First, the religious behavior narrated in the stories did not seem to reflect any knowledge of Deuteronomy, which De Wette had already argued should be identified with the book found in the temple in the time of Josiah. Wellhausen, accepting de Wette's identification, noted that the final version of Kings must have been written after the discovery of Deuteronomy, since the history includes an account of the finding of the book during Josiah's reign. Yet the Elijah/Elisha stories do not seem to know of Deuteronomy's requirement of sacrifice only in the central sanctuary or of Deuteronomy's interest in Levites as legitimate priests. Thus, Wellhausen reasoned, the prophetic stories must be older than Deuteronomy and therefore earlier than the final form of Kings. Second, to Wellhausen and other early scholars, who believed that Israelite religion reached its height in the ethical admonitions of the prophets, the prophets described in Kings seemed decidedly archaic and "primitive." In the prophetic stories in Kings, miracles of the most improbable sort abounded, while in the later writing prophets, miraculous behavior was rare to nonexistent. In the stories in Kings, ethical behavior was rarely talked about or even exhibited, while in the writing prophets, ethical behavior was the main point, according to most 19th-century scholars. This fact also suggested that the stories in Kings must be earlier than their present literary context. They were non-Deuteronomic survivals from an earlier stage of Israel's literary history and had not been modified by later Deuteronomistic scribes.

With the advent of Hermann Gunkel's form-critical method, a new approach to the antiquity of the prophetic stories was developed. By analyzing the stories in the light of common folklore motifs, scholars argued that the stories were close to the early oral stage of Israelite prophecy and thus a good source of information about the earliest stages of this religious phenomenon. This approach has been revived in the recent work of Alexander Rofé, who has provided a thorough analysis of the form of the prophetic stories.[6]

In short, by the end of the 19th century and the beginning of the 20th, a scholarly consensus had emerged that the prophetic stories in Kings, and

---

5. The following account of research on the book of Kings is based on Thomas Römer and Albert de Pury, "Deuteronomistic Historiography (DH): History of Research and Debated Issues," in *Israel Constructs Its History: Deuteronomistic Historiography in Recent Research* (ed. Albert de Pury, Thomas Römer, and Jean-Daniel Macchi; Sheffield: Sheffield Academic Press, 2000) 24–141 [French original 1996]. This article also contains a full bibliography of the discussion. Many of the significant contributions to the debate are reprinted in Gary N. Knoppers and J. Gordon McConville, eds., *Reconsidering Israel and Judah: Recent Studies on the Deuteronomistic History* (Sources for Biblical and Theological Study 8; Winona Lake, IN: Eisenbrauns, 2000).

6. Alexander Rofé, *The Prophetical Stories* (Jerusalem: Magnes, 1988).

in particular the Elijah/Elisha stories, were older blocks of material that antedated their present literary setting and therefore did not share much with the thought of the book of Kings as a whole. They were simply there to fill out the history of the Northern Kingdom, and they were integrated into their larger context through the use of various formulas supplied by the writer of Kings. Although these formulas might reflect the views of their later scribal authors, the material contained in the prophetic stories themselves did not.

However, this consensus began to change with Martin Noth's 1943 publication on the Deuteronomistic History.[7] Noth argued that a single exilic author created a Deuteronomistic Historical Work that extended from Deuteronomy through Joshua, Judges, and Samuel and finally ended with the book of Kings. Within this large work, the Deuteronomistic theological perspective was expressed in a number of different ways but was particularly noticeable in long speeches inserted at various important points in the narrative. Although the work was the creation of a single exilic author, Noth also believed that there were later additions. He also allowed for the possibility that the primary author included preexisting blocks of material that were not necessarily Deuteronomistic. Noth is often vague about the nature and origin of these preexisting blocks, but apparently at least portions of the Elijah stories were among them. Still, Noth argued, everything in Kings was in some sense Deuteronomistic, and he refused to rule out the possibility that the Deuteronomistic scribal author might have reworked earlier prophetic stories in some way.

Noth's proposal immediately created a reaction in the scholarly community, and over the years a huge scholarly literature has developed challenging or supporting the thesis or suggesting modifications. This literature is too complex to summarize briefly, but it is safe to say that most modern scholars believe that there are two or three Deuteronomistic editorial layers in Kings, some of which involve the prophetic stories explicitly. However, the dating of this editorial activity varies. Some scholars argue for a first Deuteronomistic edition of Kings in the period of Hezekiah or Josiah, although there is a growing tendency to place the writing of the book in the exilic or early postexilic period. Furthermore, most scholars maintain that the scribal authors shaped their material from a Deuteronomistic point of view, although some claim that in the prophetic stories the shaping was restricted to the formulas used to incorporate earlier stories into the overall narrative of Kings.

---

7. Martin Noth, *Überlieferungsgeschichtliche Studien* (Tübingen: Niemeyer, 1943). The first portion of Noth's book is translated into English in *The Deuteronomistic History* (2nd ed.; Sheffield: JSOT Press, 1991).

Even this brief survey of the nature of the prophetic stories in Kings suggests that scholarship on the subject has not reached any consensus on the possible Deuteronomistic character of the stories or on the ways in which the Deuteronomistic scribal authors or editors might have gone about their work. On the one hand, all scholars who accept the notion that Kings is in some way Deuteronomistic accept the fact that the prophetic stories are now in Kings and that this fact either makes them Deuteronomistic or at least gives them a role to play in the Deuteronomistic book. Such an observation, however, is not particularly helpful if there is no accompanying analysis of the role that the stories currently play in the overall Deuteronomistic shape of the book, and to date such analyses are rare. To be sure, a fair number of scholars have argued that the prophetic stories are Deuteronomistic because they have been incorporated into Kings through the use of Deuteronomistic formulas, particularly the prophecy/fulfillment formulas. Furthermore, it has been argued that these formulas play an overarching role in giving Kings some sort of Deuteronomistic structure, although it is worth noting that most scholars who mount this argument treat only the formulas dealing with the history of the North, so the formulas are hardly an overarching structure for the whole book. However, in the end it is unclear how far the formulas reach into the prophetic stories with which they are connected, so it remains unclear how far the "Deuteronomizing" of the stories extends or how the scribes actually dealt with their inherited material.

On the other hand, there is a relatively small group of scholars that sees the prophetic stories as an originally independent body of material, probably created to describe and celebrate prophetic opposition to the dynasty of Omri. According to this view, the stories originally described prophetic efforts to undermine the Omri dynasty and to overthrow the worship of Baal that the members of the dynasty encouraged. The stories would have originally reached their climax with the successful overthrow of the dynasty and the enthronement of Jehu, together with the eradication of Baal worship. In some versions of this theory, the political and religious themes are separated into two sets of stories, which have now been combined, either in an original pre-Deuteronomistic cycle or by the editor of Kings. In any case, the stories are now where they are in Kings, perhaps, because they were the only sources that the Kings writer(s) had for this period. The sources for Judah were very different, thus accounting for the shift of focus in Kings after the fall of Samaria. In this account of the prophetic stories, the original function and shape of the stories are still clearly visible, and they have only loosely been incorporated into the History. The Deuteronomistic formulas dealing with the change and evaluation of reigns and the prophecy/fulfillment formulas have been used to incorporate the stories, but the stories themselves remain fundamentally non-Deuteronomistic and basically untouched by the scribal authors of Kings, thus accounting for the disjunctures between the religious views of the prophetic stories and those of the Deuteronomists.[8]

In order to probe further into the question of techniques used by the Deuteronomistic authors or editors to incorporate the prophetic stories into Kings, it would be necessary to examine all of the stories in detail, a task that cannot be accomplished in a short paper. However, a beginning can be made by exploring the degree to which Deuteronomistic language and theology penetrate the stories themselves. The most basic way to accomplish this task is to see what influence, if any, the book of Deuteronomy had on the shaping of the prophetic stories. If Noth is correct that Deuteronomy is intended to lay out the ideological grounds for the Deuteronomistic History, then the prophetic stories should show some resonance with Deuteronomy if they have in fact been given some Deuteronomistic shaping. For the purpose of this exploration, it will be assumed that Deuteronomy is a literary unity, although many scholars claim that this is not the case.

Scholars have traditionally gone about the job of determining influence in several different ways. First, they have recognized influence when they see material quoted from another book. In this case, we would look for quotations from Deuteronomy in the prophetic stories in Kings. Unfortunately, there are few to none. The only clear quotations occur in the reflections on the history of the Northern Kingdom in 2 Kings 17 and in the description of the reign of Manasseh in 2 Kings 21. Neither one of these passages can be considered a prophetic story.

Lacking direct quotations, scholars have tried a second method to determine influence: they have looked for distinctive vocabulary. In this case, they would look for words or short phrases that are characteristic of Deuteronomy and then try to locate those words and phrases in the prophetic stories in Kings. Using the list of Deuteronomistic vocabulary items in the appendix to Moshe Weinfeld's study of Deuteronomy and the Deuteronomistic School, it quickly becomes clear that there is no characteristic vocabulary shared between Deuteronomy and the prophetic stories between 1 Kings 17 and 2 Kings 10.[9] This material in Kings may share a

---

8. This point of view is held by Rofé, *Prophetical Stories*; Mordechai Cogan, *1 Kings* (AB 10; New York: Doubleday, 2001); Marsha C. White, *The Elijah Legends and Jehu's Coup* (Atlanta: Scholars Press, 1997); and Werner Gugler, *Jehu und seine Revolution* (Kampen: Kok Pharos, 1996), among others.

9. Moshe Weinfeld, *Deuteronomy and the Deuteronomistic School* (Oxford: Clarendon, 1972; repr. Winona Lake, IN: Eisenbrauns, 1992) 320–65.

type of Northern Hebrew dialect, but that dialect cannot be said to be Deuteronomic.

Therefore, scholars have traditionally turned to a third way of recognizing influence, the discovery of shared motifs. In this case, they have tried to discover motifs from Deuteronomy in the prophetic stories in Kings. Therefore, I will first look at motifs thought to be characteristic of Deuteronomy and then determine whether or not those motifs can be found in the Elijah/Elisha narratives.

Relative Monotheism. The insistence that Israel has only one God, Yahweh, and that Israel is to worship only that God, is, of course, one of Deuteronomy's hallmarks. To be sure, all of scripture is monotheistic, but Deuteronomy seems to lay particular stress on this principle. The emphasis of the prophetic stories in Kings on relative monotheism is clear, although it is not always clear that Deuteronomy is the source for this emphasis. However, there are some clear instances of probable Deuteronomic influence, particularly in the story of Elisha's contest with the prophets of Baal on Mount Carmel (1 Kgs 18:20–46).[10] In addition, this story seems to illustrate a Deuteronomic call for Israel to choose Yahweh, a call of the sort described in Deut 11:26–30 (and also Joshua 24). In the Elisha stories, the fight against Baal worship is clearest in the account of its eradication from the land after the Jehu revolution. However, it is worth noting that many of the prophetic stories, particularly in the Elisha collection, do not deal with this theme at all, a fact to which I will return later.

Treaty Terminology and the Exodus. In Deuteronomy, the special relationship between Yahweh and Israel is described using language and concepts drawn from ancient Near Eastern treaties. God's fidelity to Israel is grounded in the Exodus and the promises to the ancestors. Israel in return is bound by treaty to obey God's commandments (Deut 5:2; 7:12; 8:1, 6, 11; 11:8, 13; 12:1). The prophetic stories in Kings do not seem to reflect this treaty imagery, and, outside of the story of Elijah's visit to Horeb (1 Kings 19), Exodus references are scarce.

Centrality of Worship. Deuteronomy restricts worship to a single place that the Lord will choose (Deuteronomy 12). The prophetic stories in Kings show no knowledge of this requirement.

Centrality of the Levites. Deuteronomy argues that Levites should have altar rights at the central sanctuary. It also seems to prefer them as priests and to assign them governmental functions as well (Deut 18:1–8). The prophetic stories in Kings show no interest in this topic.

---

10. R. A. Carlson ("Élie à l'Horeb," *VT* 19 [1969] 416) has gone so far as to call this narrative a literary summary of Deuteronomism.

Cult and Festivals.   Deuteronomy has a number of cultic peculiarities, none of which are reflected in the prophetic stories in Kings.

The Nature of the Judicial System.   Deuteronomy favors a local judicial system as the court of first instance, with a major role in the process reserved for local elders (Deut 16:18–20, 17:8–13; chaps. 19–25). Such a local system seems to be envisioned in the Naboth story in 1 Kings 21, although it is likely that the Kings story at this point is reflecting common practice and not reflecting Deuteronomic influence.

The Power of the King.   Deuteronomy assigns only a limited role for the king (Deut 17:14–20), although there is no prohibition on kingship per se. The prophetic stories do not challenge the monarchical system, although they do challenge the right of certain dynasties to exist. The Naboth story (1 Kings 21) does indicate a sensitivity to abuses of royal power.

The Role of the Prophet.   Deuteronomy is unusual in that it is the only part of the Torah that legislates about prophets, and the figure of the prophet seems to have occupied a major role in the Deuteronomic state. The characteristics of the Deuteronomic prophet are outlined in Deut 18:9–22. In this passage, a variety of mediums and intermediaries are banned from the Deuteronomic state, and communication between the human and divine worlds is assigned solely to the prophet, who is to have several important characteristics: (1) the prophet is to be "like me" [i.e., like Moses]; (2) the prophet is chosen by God, a fact which would seem to rule out becoming a prophet by any means other than direct divine choice [i.e., the law would seem to ban hereditary prophets, or prophetic "schools" to train prophets (apprenticeship), or one prophet designating another except through a divine command]; (3) the prophet must be native born. The prophet is to faithfully deliver the divine word, which God puts directly in the prophet's mouth. Because the prophet speaks only the divine word, people are required to obey it. However, the prophet must be careful only to speak the divine word. Prophets who speak in the name of other gods or who speak a word that God did not speak are liable to the death penalty. Israel is told that it can recognize the word that God has not spoken because that word will not come to pass or come true. By implication, then, the genuine word of Yahweh is one that always comes true.

This Deuteronomic notion of the prophet is elaborated further in Deut 13:1–5, which considers a case of a prophet advocating the worship of other gods. As in Deut 18:20, such prophets are not considered to be trustworthy, even though they supply omens or portents that actually take place. In this case, claiming prophetic authority by means of acts of power is not necessarily an indication of genuine prophetic status. Such prophets can still be false if they advocate the worship of other gods, and such prophets must be killed and so removed from the Deuteronomic state.

Unlike some of the other characteristic themes of Deuteronomy, the regulations concerning prophecy seem to have had a deep influence on at least some of the prophetic stories in Kings. Furthermore, that influence permeates the stories and is not confined to formulas incorporating the stories into the Deuteronomistic History.

The influence of Deuteronomy is clear in the prophecy/fulfillment formulas, where the point of the formula is to illustrate that the prophecies were true because what they predicted actually happened. This is the test that Deuteronomy demands of true prophecy, and repeated emphasis on it in Kings seems to reflect the thought of Deuteronomy.

It is also clear that the Deuteronomic views on prophecy deeply influenced the stories about Elijah, who in a number of ways is made to resemble Moses, thus illustrating the Deuteronomic claim that true prophets are to be like Moses. The resonance in Kings between Elijah and Moses has been noticed by a number of scholars, and the evidence cannot be treated in detail here.[11] However, one should note particularly Elijah's flight from Ahab, which is narrated in a way to resemble Moses' flight from Egypt. Elijah's interactions with the widow are the result of God's direct command. The prophet is portrayed in the stories as fulfilling the divine will and not acting on his own (1 Kings 17). In 1 Kings 18, the references to Moses and Deuteronomy in the story of the contest on Carmel have already been noted. In 1 Kings 19, the portrayal of the prophet's flight to Horeb is filled with Mosaic references, and Elijah receives new divine words on Sinai just as Moses received them earlier.

While there may be clear references to Moses as prophet in the Elijah story, such references quickly disappear in the Elisha stories, and that prophet does not seem to be portrayed in the narrative as acting in the Mosaic style. While Elisha seems to fit the Mosaic pattern at the beginning of the cycle, he seems to act more on his own as the stories proceed. Unlike Moses and Elijah, Elisha does not always act solely at the command of God but uses divine power for his own purposes, as a false prophet might do. In some of the stories he creates problems that he then has to solve, and he personally takes credit for his actions, rather than recognizing God as the source of the power the prophet controls. At times he uses his power to aid the illegitimate Israelite kings and at times even helps Israel's enemies, something that is certainly un-Deuteronomic. In short, the stories about

---

11. See particularly Robert P. Carroll, "The Elijah-Elisha Sagas: Some Remarks on Prophetic Succession in Ancient Israel," *VT* 19 (1969) 400–415; and Carlson, "Élie," 385–405. It is interesting to note that resonances with Deuteronomy's views on prophecy are also found in the book of Jeremiah. The prophet Jeremiah is sometimes associated with the authorship of Kings (so Friedman, *Who Wrote the Bible?* 117–35).

Elisha are increasingly negative and eventually form a contrast with the stories about Elijah.

A number of scholars have recently commented on the differences in the portrayals of Elijah and Elisha in the two sets of stories and have offered explanations, ranging from the suggestion that the differences are simply part of the underlying stories themselves to the suggestion that the author of Kings is deliberately trying to make fun of prophets and to denigrate their office.[12] However, it appears that the different portrayals of the two prophets are deeply ingrained in the way that the underlying stories have been shaped by the writer of Kings, so it is likely that the two portrayals are deliberate and serve some function in the overall shaping of Kings. Furthermore, this sort of thorough shaping suggests that the scribal authors of Kings made more modifications in their preexisting material than many scholars suppose. However, the questions of whether the thorough shaping of the prophetic stories was peculiarly Deuteronomic and what larger role it might have played in the book of Kings as a whole are issues that require further investigation.

---

12. For representative explanations of the differences in the portrayals of the two prophets, see Wesley J. Bergen, *Elisha and the End of Prophetism* (Sheffield: Sheffield Academic Press, 1999); Paul J. Kissling, *Reliable Characters in the Primary History: Profiles of Moses, Joshua, Elijah, and Elisha* (Sheffield: Sheffield Academic Press, 1996); and David Marcus, *From Balaam to Jonah: Anti-prophetic Satire in the Hebrew Bible* (Brown Judaic Studies 301; Atlanta: Scholars Press, 1995) 43–65.

Part 3

Israel and the Ancient Near East

The "Biblical" Origins of Passover

JEFFREY C. GEOGHEGAN

Boston College

> . . . no shepherdess, but Flora
> Peering in April's front. This your sheep-shearing
> Is as a meeting of the petty gods,
> And you the queen on't.
>
> —Florizel to Perdita
> Shakespeare, *The Winter's Tale*, Act 4, Scene 4

Scholars have long conjectured that aspects of Israel's Passover ultimately derive from a springtime shepherding rite or festival. The comments of Roland de Vaux are, in many ways, still representative:

> Passover was the springtime sacrifice of a young animal in order to se-
> cure fecundity and prosperity for the flock. . . . It may have been a feast
> celebrated when the tribe struck camp before setting out for the spring
> pastures. . . . It was, in a more general way, an offering for the welfare
> of the flock, like the old Arab feast which fell in the month of Rajab,
> the first month of the spring.[1]

The most common comparisons to Israelite Passover are, as de Vaux's
comments indicate, "old Arab" or Bedouin practices, such as *fidya*, with its

---

Author's note: Part of the research for this essay was carried out during a sabbatical leave
granted by Boston College during the 2007–8 academic year. I wish to thank William P.
Leahy, S.J., President of Boston College, and Kenneth R. Himes, O.F.M., Chair of the Theology Department, for their generosity in providing this leave.
   1. R. de Vaux, *Ancient Israel: Religious Institutions* (2 vols.; New York: McGraw-Hill,
1965); French original, *Les institutions de l'Ancien Testament* (Paris: Cerf, 1958 [vol. 1],
1960 [vol. 2]) 2:489. For similar views, see more recently J. W. McKay, "The Date of Passover and Its Significance," *ZAW* 84 (1972) 435–47; B. N. Wambacq, "Pesaḥ-Maṣṣôt," *Bib*
62 (1981) 499–518; H. Cazelles, "Les fêtes de printemps," *Monde de la Bible* 43 (1986) 6–7;
S. E. Loewenstamm, *The Evolution of the Exodus Tradition* (trans. B. J. Schwartz; Jerusalem:
Magnes, 1992) 189–218; G. Dell'Orto, "L'origine della pasqua," *Parole di vita* 3 (1997) 4–
9; Z. Weisman, "Reflections on the Transition to Agriculture in Israelite Religion and
Cult," in *Studies in Historical Geography and Biblical Historiography: Presented to Zechariah
Kallai* (ed. G. Galil and M. Weinfeld; VTSup 81; Leiden: Brill, 2000) 251–61.

ritual sacrifice and apotropaic blood rites.[2] These comparisons are, to be sure, important for situating Israelite practices within their larger cultural and, especially, anthropological context.[3] Yet, they do not account for other elements central to Passover, such as the despoiling of one's debtor or the release of slaves. Moreover, these comparisons are at somewhat of a temporal and, to a lesser degree, geographical remove from ancient Israel. Therefore, rather than look outside of ancient Israel for the pastoral celebration hypothesized by scholars, I would suggest that it has been preserved in the biblical text all along. The number of common elements between Passover, on the one hand, and Israelite sheepshearing, on the other, makes this the most likely candidate for the shepherding festival contributing to Israelite paschal practices. Before looking at the biblical evidence, we would be well advised to make a brief survey of sheepshearing and shepherding festivals in the ancient world.

Sheepshearing and Shepherding Rites in Antiquity

When one considers the importance of flocks to many ancient (and modern) societies, it is not surprising to find rituals attached to their successful production and reproduction. Along with providing milk and meat for food, flocks produce *wool* for use as shelter, as clothing, and in trade. As a result, not only sheep in general, but *sheepshearing* in particular occupies a prominent place in the lives and literatures of ancient peoples. At Ugarit, for example, shearers are mentioned several times in provision lists, and a comparison of their wages indicates they were quite valuable to the royal court.[4] Similarly, at Babylon, shearers are included on the royal payroll and reference is even made to a shearing sponsored by the royal house.[5] A little further afield, Hesiod (8th–7th century B.C.E.), in his *Works and Days*, discusses the days on which it is most fortuitous to shear one's flock,[6] and Varro (116–27 B.C.E.) in his *Rerum Rusticarum* notes that since sheep are not only shorn but also born and milked in the spring, gifts of milk and meat are presented to Rumina, goddess of nursing mothers, during this season.[7] When one adds to these references the numerous tallies of wool in economic records throughout the ancient Near East and Mediterranean

---

2. On the parallels between *fidya* and Passover, see most recently W. H. C. Propp, *Exodus 1–18* (AB 2; New York: Doubleday, 1998) 434–36.

3. For a general anthropological analysis of Passover, see D. Bergant, "An Anthropological Approach to Biblical Interpretation: The Passover Supper in Exodus 12:1–20 as a Case Study," *Semeia* 67 (1994) 43–62.

4. *UT* 1084:30; 1099:4, 26.

5. E.g., *GCCI* 1 93:3; BIN 1:14, 17; AbB 2:48–52. Compare with the present-day Royal Command Shearing Performance in Napier.

6. Hesiod, *Works and Days*, l.770–75.

7. Marcus Terentius Varro, *Rerum Rusticarum* 2.11.5.

basin, then the importance of shearing to most ancient cultures becomes all the more apparent.

Sheepshearing demands considerable skill and dexterity. As a result, in most times and places, shearers are professionals.[8] Although we lack ancient descriptions of the training involved, modern treatments indicate that it takes up to ten years to gain complete mastery of the skill.[9] After sheep are thoroughly washed and cleaned—a sizable task in itself[10]—the shearer must maneuver the animal in rapidly alternating positions, making swift cuts to remove wool while not inflicting serious injury upon himself or the animal.[11] Any cuts made to the animal have, since ancient times, been treated with various medicinal applications to prevent infection or the spread of disease among the flock.[12] Prior to the invention of modern shears, a skilled hand could shear up to 100 sheep in one day (though the average seems to have been between 30 and 40).[13] With the advent of electric shears, experts now shear up to 300 per day (one about every two to three minutes).

As for the time of shearing, in nearly all times and places it is a springtime event. Mesopotamian catalogues of wool were compiled during the spring Akitu Festival, and tablets at Knossos similarly contain spring shearing records.[14] Spring shearing is due in large part to the natural molting of undomesticated sheep that occurs during this season.[15] Spring also proves the best time for shearing because the warming weather lessens the likelihood of illness to the bare flocks. While some societies have added a fall shearing, usually for economic reasons, the major shearing among modern

---

8. For a general history, see M. L. Ryder, *Sheep and Man* (London: Gerald Duckworth, 1983).

9. For a discussion of the skills and training required, see G. Bowen, *Wool Away: The Art and Technique of Shearing* (New Zealand: Whitcombe & Tombs, 1955; repr. New York: Van Nostrand Reinhold / New Zealand: Whitcombe & Tombs, 1974).

10. E.g., L. Beck (*Nomad: A Year in the Life of a Qashqa'i Tribesman in Iran* [Berkeley: University of California Press, 1991] 283) describes a situation where a flock owner gives the meat of a drowned sheep to the washer in recognition of the difficulty of his task.

11. For descriptions and discussion, see Bowen, *Wool Away*, 22–52; K. Ford, *Shearing Day: Sheep Handling, Wool Science, and Shearing with Blades* (Charlemont, MA: Feet on the Ground Press, 1999).

12. Varro, *Rerum Rusticarum* 2.11.7.

13. S. Hirsch, *Sheep and Goats in Palestine* (Palestine Economic Society 2; Tel Aviv: Omanuth Erez-Israel, 1933) 29–30.

14. Ryder, *Sheep and Man*, 96. Varro (*Rerum Rusticarum* 2.11.6–7) explains that shearing should take place between the spring equinox and summer solstice, when sheep begin to sweat.

15. The removal of wool was done originally by plucking or combing the molting hair, a practice still continued among some communities today (e.g., the Samaritans pluck the paschal lamb in preparation for Passover). Cf. the comments of Varro, *Rerum Rusticarum* 2.11.7.

pastoral communities in Kuwait, Saudi Arabia, Turkey, Iraq, and Israel takes place in the spring, the exact time varying due to custom and climate.[16]

A further consequence of the centrality of flocks to ancient societies is that many cultures held springtime shepherding festivals. These festivals, though differing in detail, commonly included rituals intended to obtain divine favor in order to secure the fertility and well-being of the flocks. Practices of this sort often entailed the ritual slaughter of members of the flock, the application of their blood to animals (individuals or domiciles), and prayers seeking divine protection. Other more celebratory aspects included feasting, drunkenness, ecstatic dancing (frequently in the skins of slain animals), gift-giving, social leveling (or, in some contexts, slave release), and promiscuity (or, in some cases, ritual prostitution). For example, Greek Dionysian rites, though varying in time and place, commonly included sacrifices, feasting, drunkenness, ritual dramas emphasizing the modes of reproduction, and ecstatic dancing by participants in goatskins. These rites were preceded by the Anthesteria, where Dionysus and the king's wife were ceremonially married, gifts were exchanged, slaves were entertained, and prisoners released. Roman Lupercalia similarly included offerings of animals and sacred cakes, feasting, drunkenness, and a ritual race between two youths who, donning the skins of sacrificed goats and smeared with their blood, would strike onlookers with strips of goatskin called *februa* in order to promote fertility.[17] Aspects of these rituals survive to the present day. The Bulgarian Koukeri festival, for example, which most scholars trace to Dionysian rites originating in Thrace, is characterized by feasting, drinking to excess, mock marriages, social inversion, and ritual dancing by masked participants adorned in animal skins or costumes.[18] It is also a spring custom to give *martenitzas* (wool tassels shaped like shepherds) to friends and neighbors.[19]

---

16. For spring shearing in Iran, see Beck, *Nomad*, esp. 285–87. For Kuwait, Saudi Arabia, Turkey, Iraq, and Egypt, see Ryder, *Sheep and Man*, 199–248. For Israel, see Hirsch, *Sheep and Goats*, 29.

17. L. Adkins and R. A. Adkins, *Dictionary of Roman Religion* (New York: Facts on File, 1996; repr. New York: Oxford University Press, 2000) 136.

18. S. Severniak, "Bulgarian Festivals, Old and New," in *Festivals and Cultures* 3/2 (Paris: Unesco, 1976) 82–89. Cf. the Georgian Berikaoba-Keyenoba festival, which has similar rites; J. Rukhadze and G. Chitaya, "Festivals and Tradition in the Georgian Soviet Socialist Republic" in *Festivals and Cultures*, 72–81.

19. See, e.g., Ryder, *Sheep and Man*, 314. Comparable rites seem to lie behind the modern observance of Saint George's day in many parts of Europe, where feasting, gift-giving, communal dancing, the slaughter of a member of the flock, and the decoration of its body with vegetation from the field are common fare. Indeed, the correlation of Saint George's day with the advent of spring has resulted in many springtime rituals and sayings accruing to this famed dragonslayer, including the Russian adage, "George will bring spring," and the Estonian saying, "With his key George makes the grass to grow."

Closer to Israelite soil, Segal provides a useful summary of the modern comparative data:

> Some of the practices at the equinox and solstice that are observed in modern Palestine and the neighbouring countries may well be a survival from ancient times. . . . Among them is the Palestinian ceremony of sacrificing an animal on 1 March and smearing its blood on the doorposts, on the children, and the horses. The same ceremony is performed in the autumn in the Lebanon. In North Africa and in Syria it is the practice to go into the fields at the time of the spring equinox. At the Nebi Musa spring festival in Palestine the pilgrimage to the shrine is accompanied by sacrifices, processions, dancing, and music, new clothes are worn, and gifts exchanged; the festival lasts seven days.[20]

We conclude this necessarily brief and selective survey of sheepshearing and shepherding rites with a prayer offered to Pales, Roman goddess of sheep and shepherds, that aptly expresses the hopes and fears of pastoral communities throughout the ages:

> May I drive back as many sheep as dawn revealed,
> Nor sigh returning with fleeces snatched from the wolves.
> Avert dire famine: let leaves and grass be abundant,
> And water to wash the body, water to drink.
> May I press full udders, may my cheeses bring me money,
> May the wicker sieve strain my liquid whey.
> And let the ram be lusty, his mate conceive and bear,
> And may there be many a lamb in my fold.
> And let the wool prove soft, not scratch the girls,
> Let it everywhere be kind to gentle hands.
> Let my prayer be granted, and every year we'll make
> Huge cakes for Pales, Mistress of the shepherds.
>   (Ovid, *Fasti*, 4.765–76, trans. A. S. Kline)

Sheepshearing in the Bible

Sheepshearing occurs four times in biblical narrative: twice each in both Genesis and Samuel. Because the Samuel material provides the most detailed information concerning this practice in ancient Israel, we will start there.[21]

---

20. For a discussion of the manumission of slaves during spring festivals, especially as it relates to ancient Israel, see J. B. Segal, *The Hebrew Passover: From the Earliest Times to A.D. 70* (London: Oxford University Press, 1963) 125.

21. The analysis provided here follows in outline my earlier treatment of these texts, though with reference to another matter. See my "Israelite Sheepshearing and David's Rise to Power," *Bib* 87 (2006) 55–63.

Sheepshearing in Samuel
David and Nabal, 1 Samuel 25

Most scholars agree that 1 Samuel 25 forms part of a larger apologetic concerned with explaining the many fortuitous events attending David's rise to power.[22] This narrative in particular seems interested in explaining how David went from suppliant to supplanter of Nabal's considerable wealth and property. J. Levenson has also suggested that Nabal was the *rōš bêt ʾāb* or *nāśî* of the Calebite clan and that David acquired this position upon Nabal's death and his marriage to Abigail.[23] Whatever the full implications of David's fortune in this encounter, it is set against the backdrop of sheepshearing and, as a consequence, we are given a unique glimpse into this springtime event.

As an initial observation and one that corresponds to the comparative material, Nabal has hired skilled labor for his shearing. As David says when requesting food: 'I hear that you have shearers' שָׁמַעְתִּי כִּי גֹזְזִים לָךְ (v. 7).[24] Also corresponding to the comparative data, Nabal's sheepshearing includes a festive meal. Indeed, the mere presence of shearers at Nabal's estate allows David to presume that an accompanying feast will follow. As he says via his messengers, "Let my young men find favor in your eyes, for we have come on a festive day. Please give to your servants and to your son David whatever you find at hand" (v. 8). What Nabal has "at hand," we soon discover, is a considerable banquet.[25]

For example, when Abigail hears of her husband's folly in refusing David's request for food, she is able to procure in short order a sizable repast from the festal bounty, including "two hundred loaves of bread, two skins of wine, five dressed sheep, five seahs of roasted grain, one hundred raisin cakes and two hundred fig cakes" (v. 18). That these are intended for Nabal's feast is indicated by their perishable nature, including, it should be noted, "five dressed sheep." Then, upon her return from placating David's wrath, see finds her husband holding a feast 'like the feast of the king' כְּמִשְׁתֵּה הַמֶּלֶךְ (v. 36). While most translations render this phrase figuratively (i.e., "like the feast of a king" [NKJV; NRSV]; "a feast fit for a king" [JPS]; "a princely feast" [NJB]; "a royal feast") the author may have intended it liter-

---

22. For a recent treatment of these events and their contribution to David's ascent, see B. Halpern, *David's Secret Demons: Messiah, Murderer, Traitor, King* (Grand Rapids, MI: Eerdmans, 2001).

23. J. D. Levenson, "1 Samuel 25 as Literature and as History," *Catholic Biblical Quarterly* 40 (1978) 26–27.

24. For the use of *gzz(y)m* to designate skilled laborers, see esp. *UT* 1084:30; 1099:4, 26. Cf. 2 Sam 13:24.

25. Nabal, it seems, downplays the size of his feast by mentioning to David only "meat and water," the bare minimum fare for a sheepshearing meal. Cf. LXX, which changes "water" into "wine," likely due to its central role later in the narrative (v. 28).

ally (i.e., 'like the feast of *the* king').[26] As we will observe momentarily, the royal house did celebrate such a feast. Even if figurative, the excesses of Nabal's sheepshearing are further underscored by his condition during the feast. As the narrator reports, 'Nabal's heart was good upon him and he was exceedingly drunk' וְלֵב נָבָל טוֹב עָלָיו וְהוּא שִׁכֹּר עַד־מְאֹד (v. 36b).[27] Although one might be tempted to attribute Nabal's condition to his base character, as will become evident in the next sheepshearing narrative, drunkenness was an essential, even assumed, part of these events.[28]

A final indication of sheepshearing's significance in ancient Israel is David's description of Nabal's feast as a 'festive day' or יוֹם טוֹב (literally, 'good day'). Although the exact connotations of this phrase are uncertain for this period of Hebrew, it eventually came to denote an official holiday or festival. One reason for this association is the biblical text itself.[29] Esth 9:19 states that the 14th of Adar should be a time of 'gladness and feasting and a festive day' שִׂמְחָה וּמִשְׁתֶּה וְיוֹם טוֹב, giving the raison d'être for the festival of Purim.[30] Consequently, Rashi interpreted the יוֹם טוֹב of Nabal's shearing as Israel's spring New Year's festival, rendering David's request for food as part of his own preparations for this event: 'It is the New Year and we require the festival meal' ראש השנה היה וצריכין אנו לסעודת יום טוב.[31] Similarly, A. Caquot and P. de Robert, in commenting upon David's greeting to Nabal ('To life! And peace to you, and peace to your household, and peace to all

---

26. Favoring the literal translation is the phrase's syntax (construct with the definite article), as well as the use of the phrase כְּ . . . הַמֶּלֶךְ elsewhere. See, e.g., 1 Kgs 10:13; Esth 1:7; 2:18; Dan 11:36; 2 Chr 29:15; 30:6; 35:10, 16. Favoring the figurative reading, however, is that Absalom's feast may also have been described as כְּמִשְׁתֵּה הַמֶּלֶךְ (so LXX and probably 4QSamᵃ). Even so, this does not necessitate against the literal reading, since in the case of Absalom's feast, too, the author may intend to compare it to the shearing usually sponsored by the king. If this is the case, then Absalom's initiative in holding the royal shearing may have more implications for his eventual bid for the throne than is immediately obvious.

27. Cf. the "Thursday of Drunkards," which preceded New Year's in medieval Europe, the festival itself being called the "Feast of Fools"—a fitting parallel to the 'feast of the fool' (מִשְׁתֵּה נָבָל) of this passage.

28. So G. Robinson, *Let Us Be like the Nations. A Commentary on the Books of 1 and 2 Samuel* (Grand Rapids, MI: Eerdmans, 1993) 136: "[Nabal's] folly was coupled with addiction to alcohol."

29. F. Rosenthal ("*yôm ṭôb*," *Hebrew Union College Annual* 18 [1944] 157–76) has argued, e.g., that the use of the phrase to denote an official holiday is postbiblical and that during the biblical period it only means "a merry day of plenty."

30. Cf. מֹעֲדִים טוֹבִים 'good appointed times (i.e., festivals)' (Zech 8:19). Similarly, most modern translations render the phrase in a manner that denotes its festive nature: "a feast day" (NRSV; NKJV), "a festive occasion" (JPS), and even "a festival" (NJB). Cf. the more literal renderings of LXX (ἡμέραν ἀγαθὴν) and Vulgate (*die enim bona*). See *Targum Jonathan*: יומא שירותא.

31. For רֹאשׁ הַשָּׁנָה as the first of Nisan, see Rashi's comments on 1 Kgs 6:1. See also *m. Roš. Haš.* 1:1.

that belongs to you' לְחָי וְאַתָּה שָׁלוֹם וּבֵיתְךָ שָׁלוֹם וְכֹל אֲשֶׁר־לְךָ שָׁלוֹם, which it-self has been understood as reflecting the realities of the New Year[32]) observe: "La démarche de David a lieu, comme on le rappelle en 'un jour de fête,' peut-être une fête annuelle coïncidant avec la tonte et á l'occasion de laquelle David vient réclamer son dû."[33] Whatever the exact implications of this phrase, G. R. H. Wright seems correct in his overall assessment of the significance of sheepshearing to ancient societies:

> As is almost universal in a rural economy sheepshearing was *de rigeur* the occasion for a good time, it was a *Yom Tob* of feasting and hilarity. Furthermore it took place in those parts somewhere about March/April and thus more or less at the time of the Spring equinox, generally the juncture for reckoning the New Year. Therefore in spite of the fact that ancient records give little detailed information in this connection the culture historians always emphasize the religious importance of this festival.[34]

I will return to the potential religious importance of Israelite sheepshearing at the conclusion of this study.

David and Absalom, 2 Samuel 13:23–29

Similar to 1 Samuel 25, 2 Samuel 13 contributes to the overall drama surrounding David's rise to and maintenance of the throne of Israel—only in this particular scene, David's children have taken over centerstage. The chapter begins with Amnon's rape of his half-sister Tamar and ends with Absalom's murder of his half-brother, Amnon as repayment.[35] Because this latter event takes place during sheepshearing, a closer look at Absalom's revenge is required.

It should first be observed that Absalom's feast, like Nabal's, requires the hiring of professional shearers. As Absalom reports when requesting his fa-

---

32. It may be that David's words merely intend to underscore the peaceful intentions of his visit (and thereby further exonerate him from any wrongdoing in what follows). See, e.g., A. F. Campbell, *2 Samuel* (FOTL 8; Grand Rapids: Eerdmans, 2005) 259. However, a number of commentators have noted its appropriateness to an event marking Israel's New Year. Rashi, for example, provides several interpretations of David's greeting, two of which denote blessings for the coming year: 'So may he be shearing (as he is now) in the coming year' כה יהיה לשנה הבאה גוזז, and 'So may the next year be one of living and abiding fortune' כה יהיה לשנה הבאה מזל חי וקים. Similarly, Fokkelman, in summarizing the rabbinic evidence, renders David's salutation: "May you continue to enjoy such prosperity for the year ahead, you and your household and all that is yours!" J. Fokkelman, *Narrative Art and Poetry in the Books of Samuel*, vol. 2: *The Crossing Fates* (Assen, The Netherlands: Van Gorcum, 1986) 484.

33. A. Caquot and P. de Robert, *Les Livres de Samuel* (Commentaire de l'Ancien Testament 6; Geneva: Labor et Fides, 1994) 308.

34. G. R. H. Wright, "Dumuzi at the Court of David," *Numen* 28/1 (1981) 54–63 (57).

35. Dick Friedman's oft-stated adage, "Go try and raise a family," comes to mind. See, e.g., *The Hidden Book*, 37.

ther's attendance, 'Your servant has shearers' גֹזְזִים לְעַבְדֶּךָ (v. 24). Absalom's invitation highlights another parallel with Nabal's shearing: both are royal affairs. Nabal's feast is "like the feast of the king" and Absalom's shearing warrants the presence of the king. Although David ends up refusing Absalom's invitation, it is not due to sheepshearing's insignificance. On the contrary, as David says to Absalom, "No, my son, we must not all attend, or we will be a burden to you" (v. 25). In actuality, David's refusal is likely motivated by his suspicions of Absalom for wanting him at so festive and, hence, vulnerable an occasion. As McCarter observes, "We cannot be sure that the king's courteous but negative response is cautionary, but it is probable that David already suspects Abishalom's ambition and fears him on that account."[36]

McCarter's observations highlight another parallel between Absalom's and Nabal's sheepshearings: both are raucous affairs, characterized by feasting, celebration, and the liberal consumption of alcohol. Indeed, Absalom's plan of revenge against his brother depends upon Amnon's whole-hearted participation in this latter aspect of the festivities.[37] As Absalom says to his associates when plotting his brother's murder: "See now, *when* Amnon's heart is good with wine (כְּטוֹב לֵב־אַמְנוֹן בַּיַּיִן)) and I say to you, 'Strike Amnon,' then you shall put him to death" (v. 28).

Absalom's plan and Amnon's eventual demise point to one final connection between Absalom's and Nabal's feasts: both end in the death of a drunken participant whose downfall paves the way for another's ascent to power. In the case of Nabal's undoing, David acquires significant property and wealth near his eventual first capital, Hebron. In the case of Amnon's death, Absalom becomes next in line for his father's throne. We will return to the significance of these connections below.

Sheepshearing in Genesis
Jacob and Laban, Genesis 31
Genesis 31 recounts the story of Jacob's escape from Padan Aram after serving his father-in-law for 20 years. Although the narrative offers little by way of actual description of sheepshearing, it does, upon closer examination, yield important information about the activities surrounding this event.

First, it should be noted that Jacob's decision to escape during sheepshearing makes good sense in view of our earlier observations about the distractions afforded by this celebration. As von Rad observes: "Die früh-jahrliche Schafschur brachte viele Urbeit, war aber dann auch ein Fest

---

36. P. K. McCarter, *II Samuel* (AB 9; Garden City, NY: Doubleday, 1984) 334.
37. For the other similarities between Nabal's and Absalom's shearings, see esp. Caquot and de Robert, *Les Livres de Samuel*, 500.

(1 Sam 25:1ff., 2 Sam 13:23ff.). Da war Laban mit seinen Leuten mit sich und seinen Ungelegenheiten beschäftigt."[38] At minimum, then, we are to understand that Laban and his sons are too busy supervising the shearing to notice Jacob's escape. More likely, however, we are to imagine that in addition to the business at hand, they are caught up in the festivities of the season.

Second, the timing of Jacob's departure seems apropos if, as the comparative data indicates, this season had known associations with the release or escape of slaves. Certainly Israel's own liberation was connected with this season and, as noted earlier, slave release or, in its tamer form, social leveling were common practices during certain festivals, particularly in the spring.[39] A further suggestion that such associations may have existed in ancient Israel is that Jacob's flight from Laban is cast in a way that mirrors Israel's flight from Egypt, including: both emancipations are effected by God because he has *seen* (ראה) the *afflictions* (עני) of his people (Gen 31:42, Exod 3:7); both Laban and Pharaoh are informed (נגד) of those *fleeing* (בלח), *gather* (לקח) reinforcements and *make pursuit* (רדף), and overtake (נשג) their catch near a mountain or hill country (Gen 31:22–23, Exod 14:5–9); both Jacob and Israel make their flight during the advent of spring (Gen 31:19, Exod 13:4); and both leave their experiences of servitude with considerable wealth (Gen 31:42, Exod 3:21b).[40] Indeed, this last observation highlights another parallel between them: both Jacob and Israel despoil their debtors. This motif is self-evident in the exodus account, where Israel is repeatedly reported to have acquired belongings from the Egyptians during their departure. In the case of Jacob, however, this motif is more subtle yet no less central to the narrative. Immediately following the report that "Laban went to shear his flock," we are informed "and Rachel stole her father's *teraphim* and Jacob stole the heart of Laban the Aramean by not telling him he was fleeing" (vv. 19b–20). Of particular interest is the notice of Jacob's "theft," which has long perplexed commentators since it is both belabored in its diction and inaccurate in its description (Jacob is

---

38. G. von Rad, *Das Erste Buch Mose* (Alte Testament Deutsch; Göttingen: Vandenhoeck & Ruprecht, 1953) 4:268.

39. For a discussion of the manumission of slaves during spring festivals, especially as it relates to ancient Israel, see Segal, *Passover*, 119–20. An echo of slave release in Israel may be heard in the command to allow slaves full participation in its festivals, including and especially the Passover.

40. For allusions to the exodus in the lives of the patriarchs, see, e.g., D. Daube, *The Exodus Pattern in the Bible* (London: Faber & Faber, 1963); R. Alter, *Genesis* (New York: Norton, 1996) 52; R. E. Friedman, *Commentary on the Torah* (San Francisco: HarperCollins, 2001) 53, 103); J. C. Geoghegan, "The Abrahamic Passover," in *Le-David Maskil: A Birthday Tribute for David Noel Freedman* (Biblical and Judaic Studies, UCSD 9; ed. R. E. Friedman and W. H. C. Propp; Winona Lake, IN: Eisenbrauns, 2004) 47–62.

presented as fully justified in leaving with family and flocks for his 20 years of service). Although admittedly conjectural, I would suggest that the repeated reference to Jacob's "stealing the heart of Laban," beyond its possible play on words (*lēb*/*lābān*; *ʾărāmî*/*rîmâ*), plays on a known connection between this season and the settling of old scores, particularly by despoiling one's debtor. After all, such practices are well attested in springtime festivals throughout the ancient and modern world. Moreover, all four biblical sheepshearing narratives contain the motif of settling past grievances by means of despoiling. In view of this evidence, Propp's remarks on despoiling in the context of the exodus account take on added significance:

> The theme of despoiling Egypt may have arisen from a seasonal observance. Exodus envisions children asking, "Why do we slaughter a sheep/goat, eat unleavened bread and consecrate firstborn animals?" (12:26; 13:14; cf. 10:2; 13:8). Perhaps the plundering of Egypt, too, is etiological. Near the equinoxes, many cultures observe carnival holidays with special appeal for the young. Examples from Judaism would be Purim in the spring and *Śimḥat tôrâ* in the fall. In addition, among the folk customs of Passover is the children's "theft" of a piece of *maṣṣâ*, the Afikoman, for ransom. *Possibly, the Israelite paschal ceremony already possessed a carnival aspect.*[41]

As a final observation, Jacob's experience with Laban, beyond its paschal undertones, shares several parallels with David's experience with Nabal. For example, both Laban and Nabal are depicted as prosperous yet parsimonious flock owners. (The fact that Laban's and Nabal's names are the reverse of one another was also thought significant by the rabbis.[42]) In addition, both Jacob and David feel they have been denied proper payment for watching another's flock. Moreover, both Jacob and David seek recompense for their services during the time of sheepshearing. Finally, and perhaps most interestingly in view of the comparative data related to springtime rites, both narratives make reference to servants escaping from their masters. Jacob's escape from Laban during sheepshearing is apparent enough. In the case of David, however, the reference to the escape of slaves does not derive from the action of the narrative but from its dialogue. As justification for refusing David's request for food, Nabal declares, "Today the servants who are breaking away have multiplied, each from the presence of their masters" (1 Sam 25:10). While it is possible that Nabal's words are intended only as a general assessment of the times or, perhaps, as a subtle rebuke of David's actions toward Saul, the seemingly widespread nature of this breaking away ("each servant from the presence of his master"), when combined with Jacob's own actions during this season, leaves open

---

41. Propp, *Exodus 1–18*, 412–13. Emphasis mine.
42. *Yalkut Shimoni, Samuel I 134.*

the possibility that sheepshearing had known associations with slave release or escape in ancient Israel. We will consider the potential significance of these observations after looking at our final sheepshearing narrative.

Judah and Tamar, Genesis 38

The story of Judah and Tamar has generated considerable scholarly discussion, not only because of its more provocative elements (which we will treat below) but also because of its awkward placement in the Joseph cycle, the course of which it seems to interrupt. R. E. Friedman has made an important contribution in this regard, pointing out that Genesis 38 plays an integral role in the development of the theme of "deception for deception" that runs through the Patriarchal narratives and finds its denouement in Joseph, who brings this cycle to an end by choosing to forgive the wrongs committed against him.[43] Genesis 38 also plays an important role in the narrative development of sheepshearing, especially as it relates to the emergence of the Davidic dynasty.[44]

After mourning the death of his wife, Bathshua, Judah leaves for Timnah, where, in keeping with the practice already noted, he has employed professional shearers (v. 12b). On his way to the shearing, Judah employs the services of another professional when he encounters and has sexual relations with a prostitute (vv. 15–16). When Judah later sends payment via his friend, Hirah the Adullamite, he is unable to locate the prostitute and Judah is content to let the matter rest, despite the loss of his promissory deposit of seal, cord, and staff. Several months later Judah is informed that his own daughter-in-law has been "playing the harlot" and is now pregnant. Because she was promised in marriage to his son Selah, Judah condemns her to death. On her way to execution, Tamar sends a message to Judah asking him to identify the items belonging to the one by whom she had become pregnant: Judah's seal, cord, and staff. Realizing his own guilt in the affair, especially in withholding his youngest son, Judah declares, "She is more righteous than I, since I did not give her to Selah" (v. 26).

As noted above, Tamar's somewhat unexpected stratagem for securing her rightful progeny and, perhaps more perplexing, Judah's uninhibited propositioning of a prostitute has occasioned considerable discussion. After all, what would lead Tamar to believe that her father-in-law would enlist the services of a prostitute, and why would Judah not hesitate to do

---

43. R. E. Friedman, "Deception for Deception," *Bible Review* 2 (1986) 22–31.

44. Indeed, here again Friedman has made an important contribution, noting that the motif of sheepshearing both in Genesis and Samuel provides additional evidence for a larger literary project or source spanning from Genesis to Kings (Friedman, *The Hidden Book in the Bible: The Discovery of the First Prose Masterpiece* [San Francisco: HarperSan Francisco, 1998]; for his comments on sheepshearing, see esp. pp. 17, 328).

so?[45] I would suggest that the answer to these questions may be found in the notice that Judah was on his way "to shear his sheep" (v. 13). As noted in our comparative analysis, rituals intended to procure or celebrate the fertility of flocks and fields, including promiscuity or, in some cases, ritualized procreative acts, are common to many springtime festivals. Although the evidence for widespread cultic prostitution in connection with ancient fertility rites has been exaggerated, that Tamar would, upon hearing that her father-in-law was going to shear his sheep, immediately put on the garb of a prostitute and position herself along a road she knew her father-in-law would be traveling, is, at minimum, suggestive.[46] That is, Tamar's promiscuous plan and Judah's ready participation could very well reflect practices known to exist during this season—if not in actuality, at least by reputation or in collective memory.[47]

As a final observation, Friedman and others have pointed out the many parallels that exist between Judah, on the one hand, and David, on the other. For example, just as Judah moves to the region of Adullam (Gen 38:1), befriends a Canaanite named Hirah (Gen 38:1), and marries a woman named Bathshua (Gen 38:2), so David resides among the outlaws of Adullam (1 Sam 22:1), establishes an alliance with the Canaanite king, Hiram of Tyre (2 Sam 5:11) and marries a woman named Bathsheba, who is elsewhere called Bathshua (1 Chr 3:5).[48] Corresponding to this are the

---

45. The suggestion that the notice of Bathshua's death at the beginning of this narrative intends to inform the reader that Judah is in a state of "sexual neediness" is insightful, though perhaps not in the direction intended. More likely, this notice is an attempt, however ineffective, to clean up Judah's actions by making plain that he was unmarried at the time of this event.

46. See, e.g., the recent collection of essays in *Prostitutes and Courtesans in the Ancient World* (ed. C. A. Faraone and L. K. McClure; Madison: University of Wisconsin Press, 2006). See also K. van der Toorn, "Female Prostitution in Payment of Vows in Ancient Israel," *JBL* 108 [1989] 193–205. Whether prostitution in ancient Israel was connected to a religious ritual or merely part of the activities surrounding religious festivals does not affect our observation that Judah's propositioning of a prostitute may have been connected with the springtime festivities of sheepshearing.

47. Cf. Hos 4:13–14. M. M. Homan ("Date Rape: The Agricultural and Astronomical Background of the Sumerian Sacred Marriage and Genesis 38," *Scandinavian Journal of the Old Testament* 16 [2002] 283–92) explicitly relates Judah and Tamar's liaison with the *hieros gamos* of Dumuzi, the faithful shepherd, and Inanna, lady of the date palm (cf. Hebrew *tāmār*). See also Wright ("Dumuzi at the Court of David," 54–55), who comes to a similar conclusion for the story of Amon ("the faithful one") and Tamar ("the date palm"), though his allegorizing of the event seems to go beyond the evidence. See below for a different reconstruction of these events.

48. For similar observations, see J. Blenkinsopp, "Theme and Motif in the Succession History (2 Sam XI:2ff.) and the Yahwist Corpus," in *Volume du Congrès: Genève, 1965* (VTSup 15; Leiden: Brill, 1966) 44–57; G. A. Rendsburg, "David and His Circle in Genesis XXXVIII," *VT* 36 (1986) 438–446, esp. p. 444; Craig Y. S. Ho, "The Stories of the Family Troubles of Judah and David: A Study of Their Literary Links," *VT* 49 (1999) 514–31.

several parallels between Judah's daughter-in-law, Tamar, and the Judahite king's daughter, Tamar. For example, repayment for the injustices committed against both Tamars are obtained during sheepshearing: Tamar entices Judah into a sexual liaison to obtain her rightful progeny, and Absalom invites Amnon to his sheepshearing to repay his sister's disgrace (Gen 38:12; 2 Sam 13:23). Related to this point, both Tamars are involved in, for lack of a better term, "atypical" sexual unions: the former with her father-in-law, the latter with her half-brother.[49] Finally, and perhaps most importantly, the firstborn of Judah and Tamar's sheepshearing liaison is Perez, the eponymous ancestor of the Davidic line.[50] Indeed, the same verbal root (*pāraṣ*) used to describe Perez's actions at birth to obtain the right to sire the royal clan is used also of David and Absalom during their own sheepshearing exploits. David is accused by Nabal of being among those *pāraṣ*-ing from their masters during sheepshearing (1 Sam 25:10), and Absalom twice *pāraṣ*-es upon his father in his attempts to get David and Amnon to attend his sheepshearing (2 Sam 13:25, 27).

　　Although the full significance of these parallels cannot be pursued here, I have argued elsewhere that the connection between sheepshearing and the Davidic dynasty likely arose from actual events related to David's own rise to and maintenance of the throne.[51] As a consequence of the revelry and vulnerability surrounding sheepshearing, David came into possession of considerable land and livestock near what would become his first capital. (David may also have become the *nāśî* of the Calebite clan during this time.) Absalom, too, made an important advance toward the throne during sheepshearing by using its festive atmosphere to remove the successor to his father's throne and, had David been present, perhaps even taking over that throne. These events, as with other events from the life of David,[52] then found expression in the lives of the ancestors, likely, as Fried-

---

49. David's marriage to Abigail may also have resulted in an atypical union, if, as some have argued, she was David's sister (cf. 1 Chr 2:16). See, e.g., J. D. Levenson and B. Halpern, "The Political Import of David's Marriages," *JBL* 99 (1980) 507–18.

50. For additional parallels, see Rendsburg, "Biblical Literature as Politics: The Case of Genesis," in *Religion and Politics in the Ancient Near East* (ed. A. Berlin; Bethesda, MD: University Press of Maryland, 1996) 47–70. See also Ho, "Family Troubles," 514–29.

51. Geoghegan, "Israelite Sheepshearing," 61–62.

52. For example, the "rape" of Jacob's daughter, Dinah (Genesis 34), shares a number of thematic and linguistic parallels with the rape of David's daughter, Tamar (2 Samuel 13). Similarly, both Jacob and David's "fourth" sons—Judah (Genesis 49) and Solomon (1 Kings 2), respectively—inherit the right to rule over their brothers, who are eliminated either by ill-advised sexual exploits (Reuben, on the one hand, Amnon and Adonijah, on the other) or violence (Simeon and Levi, on the one hand, Absalom, on the other). For the parallels between the lives of Jacob and David, see most recently Friedman, *The Hidden Book*, 37–44. For the parallels between Dinah and Tamar, see D. N. Freedman, "Dinah and Shechem, Tamar and Amnon," in *God's Steadfast Love: Essays in Honor of Prescott Harrison Williams, Jr.* (*Austin Seminary Bulletin* 105/2 [1990] 51–63); repr. in *Divine Commitment*

man has argued, as part of the same literary project.[53] The former, that of David and Nabal, influenced the (re)telling of the story of Jacob and Laban, both of which recount the divinely aided despoiling of wealthy but tight-fisted flockowners whose debts come due at shearing. The latter event, that of Amnon and Tamar, found expression in the narrative of Judah and Tamar, both of which involve the vindication of crimes committed against a woman named Tamar and explain or illustrate the *pāraṣ*-ing nature of the Perezite clan in their struggles to rule over their brothers.

Sheepshearing and Passover

In light of the biblical evidence, sheepshearing in ancient Israel was a time of revelry (Nabal and Amnon both get drunk during sheepshearing), trickery (Jacob "steals the heart" of Laban by fleeing during sheepshearing; Absalom tricks Amnon into coming to his sheepshearing), promiscuity (Judah has relations with a prostitute during sheepshearing), and the settling of old scores, often through despoiling (Jacob, Tamar, David, and Absalom all obtain repayment of past debts during sheepshearing). If this picture is accurate, and the common elements among these narratives suggest it is, then this gives Israelite sheepshearings an affinity with many other ancient (and modern) springtime rites and celebrations. Yet, in view of this evidence, how are we to understand the relationship between the celebration of sheepshearing, on the one hand, and the observance of the Passover, on the other, both of which are springtime rites sharing many of the same elements, including the slaughtering and consumption of sheep, the motif of despoiling one's debtors and, perhaps, even an association of servants breaking away from their masters? Are we to imagine that these springtime rites coexisted, in which case their relationship might be likened to the observance within a culture of, say, indigenous festivals and mainstream religious holidays (e.g., Mardi Gras and Easter)? If so, then what happened to the more raucous elements of sheepshearing when Passover gained dominance as a national observance (perhaps during the reigns of Hezekiah and Josiah, though possibly earlier)?[54] Did these elements simply disappear and

---

and Human Obligation (Grand Rapids, MI: Eerdmans, 1997) 485–95. For the several parallels between David and the patriarchs more generally, see the discussion and bibliography in R. de Hoop, "The Use of the Past to Address the Present: The Wife-Sister Incidents (Gen 12:10–20; 20:1–18; 26:1–16)," in *Studies in the Book of Genesis: Literature, Redaction, and History* (ed. A. Wénin; Bibliotheca ephemeridum theologicarum lovaniensium 155; Leuven: Leuven University Press, 2001) 359–69.

53. Friedman, *The Hidden Book*, 3–56.

54. Prior to the centralization efforts of Hezekiah and Josiah, Passover was, as the biblical evidence indicates, a familial or local observance and may have been better attested among certain groups and regions within ancient Israel. For the possible development of Passover and its various rites, see Propp, *Exodus 1–18*, 427–58.

the characteristics common to both sheepshearing and Passover simply accrue to the latter? Or did the more licentious aspects of sheepshearing endure, finding expression elsewhere?

On this last note, Segal has suggested that because several features common to New Year's celebrations in the ancient Near East are present in the festivals of Passover and Purim together, these may have originated from a prior, perhaps Canaanite, springtime festival.[55] Segal's description of the contributions of this hypothetical celebration to the origins of Passover (the slaughtering of sheep, the despoiling of others, the release of slaves, etc.) and Purim (drunkenness, the sharing of portions from the flock, etc.) fit well with our observations regarding Israelite sheepshearings. In view of the Bible's own admission of paschal neglect for a large part of the monarchic period (2 Kgs 23:21–23; 2 Chr 30:1–18), as well as the biblical evidence that sheepshearing was a significant springtime celebration observed by royalty and wealthy clan leader alike during this same period, might it be that Israelite sheepshearing is the pastoral celebration hypothesized by scholars that contributed to aspects of Israel's Passover observances?

Given the nature of our sources, we will likely never know the full answer to this question. What is evident from the biblical text, however, is that sheepshearing was a major event in ancient Israel, a יוֹם טוֹב, where sheep were shorn and slaughtered, a feast was held, and drinking occurred to excess. Moreover, sheepshearing was a time for settling old scores. Therefore, if you weren't careful, you might find yourself deceived, despoiled, or even dead. This last observation highlights what must have been common knowledge during this season throughout ancient Israel: while sheepshearing is a time to let down one's hair, it is not a time to let down one's guard.

---

55. Segal, *Passover*, 147–48, 239–40.

"Plowing with a Heifer" in Judges 14:18: Tracing a Sexual Euphemism

SHALOM M. PAUL

The Hebrew University of Jerusalem

"Out of the eater came something to eat. Out of the strong came something sweet." This well-known riddle of Samson in Judg 14:14 has been subject to many interpretations,[1] as befits the riddle genre.[2] Here, however, I would like to focus on the finale of this chapter and Samson's response after realizing that he has been betrayed by Delilah who has disclosed to his "thirty companions" the answer to the riddle (v. 11). Samson responds: לולא חרשתם בעגלתי לא מצאתם חידתי 'Had you not plowed with my heifer, you would not have solved my riddle' (v. 18). It is very intriguing that Samson resorts to agricultural imagery and refers to Delilah as a "heifer"[3] with which they plowed a field. Yet the sarcastic subtlety of his comment actually conceals a deft double entendre, because the Hebrew verb employed here, חר״ש 'to plow', can also serve as a metaphor for sexual coition, attested as far back as Sumerian times. In one of the Inanna-Dumuzi love lyrics, the goddess compares her vulva to uncultivated land[4] on the steppe:[5]

Author's note: To Dick, dear friend and colleague.

1. Among the commentators in the past century, refer to H. Bauer, "Zu Samsons Rätsel in Richter Kapitel 14," *ZDMG* 66 (1912) 473–74; O. Eissfeldt, "Die Rätsel in Jdc 14," *ZAW* 30 (1910) 132–35; H. Gunkel, *Reden und Aufsätze* (Göttingen: Vandenhoeck & Ruprecht, 1913) 38–64. Consult the modern commentaries to Judges and in particular J. L. Crenshaw, *Samson: A Secret Betrayed, A Vow Ignored* (Atlanta: John Knox, 1978); Y. Zakovitch, *The Life of Samson* (Jerusalem: Magnes, 1982) 103–8 (Hebrew).

2. For the riddle genre, see Crenshaw, *Samson*, 99–120.

3. For the metaphor "heifer" (עגלה) as applied to peoples/nations, see Hos 10:11; Jer 46:20; 50:11. For a Ugaritic reference, see below, n. 15.

4. Compare EA 74:17–19, *eqlija aššata ša la muta mašil aššum bali errēšim* 'For lack of a cultivator/plowman, my field is like a woman without a husband'; J. A. Knudtzon, *Die El-Amarna Tafeln* (Aalen: O. Zeller, 1964); see also 75:15–17; 81:37–38; 90:42–44 (pp. 374, 378, 394, 428, respectively). Some read, however, *erēšim* (instead of *errēšim*) 'plowing'. For a study of this proverb, tracing its Canaanite elements, see D. Marcus, "A Famous Analogy of Rib-Haddi," *Journal of the Ancient Near Eastern Society* 5 (*Gaster Festschrift*; 1973) 281–86. On p. 281 n. 7, Marcus cites studies on the comparison of a wife to a field,

My vulva, a well-watered, a rising mount—
I, the maiden, who will plow[6] it?
My vulva, the wet and well-watered ground—
I, the young lady, who will station there the ox?

The desired answered immediately follows:

Young lady, the king will plow it for you.
Dumuzi, the king, will plow it for you.

To which she amorously responds:

To plow my vulva is for the man of my heart.

In yet another love lyric,[7] Inanna pleads with Dumuzi not to plow a foreign field nor to seek another wet ground, for she, Inanna, is his field and wet ground:

Do not dig a canal.[8] Your canal I shall be.
Do not plow a field. Your field I shall be.
Farmer, do not search for a wet ground.
Your wet ground I shall be.

---

especially the plowed earth, in agricultural societies. For an Egyptian reference, see J. B. Pritchard, *Ancient Near Eastern Texts Relating to the Old Testament* (3rd ed.; Princeton, NJ: Princeton University Press) 413; for the Qurʾān, sūra 2:223; and for an Ethiopian proverb, see Marcus, "Famous Analogy," 282. Likewise, compare the rabbinic expression, נסתחפה שדך 'Your field has been inundated', referring to one's wife (*m. Ketub.* 1:6); and Abaye's description of Esther as קרקע עולם 'immovable dormant ground' (*b. Sanh.* 74b), implying that she did not play any active role in submitting to Ahasuerus's sexual encounters with her. So, too, the Greek term ἄρουσα 'earth, ground' is employed as a metaphor for a woman receiving seed and bearing fruit; H. G. Liddell and R. Scott, *A Greek-English Lexicon* (Oxford: Clarendon, 1968) 245.

5. S. N. Kramer, "Cuneiform Studies and the History of Literature: The Sumerian Sacred Marriage Texts," *Proceedings of the American Philosophical Society* 107 (1963) 505–8, 519–20. For additional translations, see B. Alster, "Marriage and Love in the Sumerian Love Songs," in *The Tablet and the Scroll: Near Eastern Studies in Honor of William W. Hallo* (ed. M. E. Cohen, D. C. Snell, and D. B. Weisberg; Bethesda, MD: CDL, 1993) 24; Y. Sefati, *Love Songs in Sumerian Literature* (Ramat Gan: Bar-Ilan University Press, 1998) 90–91.

6. The Sumerian verb is ur_{11}-ru.

7. Alster, "Marriage and Love," 15, 20; Sefati, *Love Songs*, 91–92; Å. W. Sjöberg, "Miscellaneous Sumerian Texts, II," *Journal of Cuneiform Studies* 29 (1977) 22; Text II, 21ff., 24. In yet another love lyric there is reference to "plowing šuba (gem) stones" that according to Alster is also a metaphor for sexual intercourse. See Alster, "Marriage and Love," 18–19, 24; Kramer, "Cuneiform Studies," 493–95; W. G. Lambert, "Devotion: The Languages of Religion and Love," in *Figurative Language in the Ancient Near East* (ed. M. Mindlin, M. J. Geller, and J. E. Wansbrough; London: School of Oriental and African Studies, University of London, 1987) 31–34; V. Afanasjeva, "Zu den Metaphern in Einem Lied der 'Heiligen Hochzeit'," in *Societies and Languages in the Ancient Near East: Studies in Honour of I. M. Diakonoff* (ed. N. Postgate et al.; Warminster, England: Aris & Phillips, 1982) 15–21. For a different interpretation, see Sefati, *Love Songs*, 92, 197–98, 202.

8. For the euphemistic employment of "canal" in Egyptian poetry, see the reference cited in my "'Plural of Ecstasy' in Mesopotamian and Biblical Love Poetry," in *Solving Riddles*

The metaphorical usage of "plowing" to describe sexual intercourse is also attested in rabbinic literature. In *y. Yebam.* 1.1.2b it states that Rabbi Yossi, son of Ḥalafta, married his brother's wife in a levirate marriage: "He plowed five plowings (חמש חרישות חרש), had intercourse through a sheet,[9] and planted five plantings [sired five sons]." In the parallel account recorded in *b. Šabb.* 118b and *Gen. Rab.* 85,[10] the metaphor is made patently clear: "He had intercourse five times (חמש בעילות בעל)." Compare also its Aramaic interdialectal semantic equivalent, בעיא אנא ליה למירדי בגינתי רד"י ולא צבי 'I want him to plow in my garden, but he didn't want to'.[11]

Although the above statement in *y. Yebam.* 1.1.2b refers to five separate cohabitations (as does *b. Nid.* 64b, "I [Shemuel] could perform a number of acts of intercourse without causing bleedings"), it should be noted that in ancient Near Eastern literature there are several examples of multiple copulations:

1. *Sumerian*

The brother brought me into his house
And laid me down on a fragrant bed.
My precious sweet, lying by my heart,
One after another, "tongue-making,"[12] one after another,
My brother, of fairest face, made fifty times.[13]

---

and Untying Knots: Biblical, Epigraphic, and Semitic Studies in Honor of Jonas C. Greenfield (ed. Z. Zevit, S. Gitin, and M. Sokoloff; Winona Lake, IN: Eisenbrauns, 1995) 593 n. 30 = *Divrei Shalom: Collected Studies of Shalom M. Paul on the Bible and the Ancient Near East, 1967–2005* (Leiden: Brill, 2005) 248 n. 32.

9. So as not to derive any physical enjoyment from the act.

10. J. Theodor and C. Albeck, *Midrash Bereschit Rabbah* (3 vols.; Jerusalem: Wahrmann, 1965) 2:1038 (Hebrew).

11. M. Sokoloff and J. Yahalom, *Aramaic Poems from Eretz Israel of the Byzantine Period* (Jerusalem: Israel Academy of Sciences and Humanities, 1989) 136 line 3 (Hebrew). Line 4 continues: ואמר לי לית רדי תורא עם חמרא 'And he said to me, "An ox does not plow with an ass"', referring to the biblical injunction in Deut 22:10, which is interpreted as a metaphor for an incompatible marriage. See also Sir 25:8. M. Lambert ("Notes brèves," *RA* 76 [1982] 94) points out that the Akkadian *ittû* 'seeder plow' (*Chicago Assyrian Dictionary* I–J [Chicago: Oriental Institute, 1960] 312) is also listed in a text as a synonym for 'father'. See W. G. Lambert, "The Problem of Love Lyrics," in *Unity and Diversity: Essays in the History, Literature, and Religion of the Ancient Near East* (ed. H. Goedicke and J. J. M. Roberts; Baltimore: Johns Hopkins University Press, 1975) 112, ii:3–5; 114 n. 5. Greek ἀροτήρ 'plower' is a metaphor for "begetter, father," and ἄροτος 'plowing' serves as a metaphor for "procreation of children"; see Liddell and Scott, *Greek-English Lexicon*, 245.

12. For the Sumerian idiom e m e - a k 'to make tongue' with its specific sexual overtones, see my "Euphemistically 'Speaking' and a Covetous Eye," in *Hebrew Annual Review* 14 (1994; *Biblical and Other Studies in Honor of Reuben Ahroni on the Occasion of His Sixtieth Birthday*) 195–96 and nn. 12–14 = *Divrei Shalom*, 216 and nn. 24–26.

13. Kramer, "Cuneiform Studies," 509 lines 26–30. For the text and another translation, see T. Jacobsen, "The Sister's Message," *Journal of the Ancient Near Eastern Society* 5 (*Gaster Festschrift*; 1973) 200–202; idem, *The Treasures of Darkness: A History of Mesopotamian Religion* (New Haven: Yale University Press, 1976) 27–28.

2. *Akkadian*

[Like a ram eleven times], like a weaned ⟨sheep⟩ twelve times,
Like a partridge (?) thirteen times, [make love to me]!
[Like a] pig fourteen times, like a wild bull fifty ⟨times⟩,
Like a stag fifty ⟨times⟩.[14]

3. *Ugaritic*

He lay with her seventy-seven times.
She made him mount[15] eighty-eight.[16]

4. *Talmud*[17]

(a) *b. Yebam.* 103a = *b. Naz.* 23b

Rabbi Yoḥanan said: "That profligate (Sisera) fornicated (with Jael) seven times on that day."

Rashi explains the number seven by noting that the verbs שכב, נפל, כרע appear altogether seven times in Judg 5:27.

(b) *b. Sanh.* 22a

Abishag said (to David), "Let us marry." But he said, "You are forbidden to me" (since he already had the eighteen wives allotted to a king in marriage). She responded, "When strength fails the thief, he pretends to be virtuous" (thus taunting him with impotence). He then said to them (his servants), "Summon Bath-Sheba for me." . . . Rabbi Judah said in Rab's name: "On that occasion Bath-Sheba dried herself thirteen times (they had intercourse thirteen times)."

Thirteen times because, according to Rashi, 1 Kgs 1:15 ad loc., the verse referred to consists of thirteen words.

---

14. R. D. Biggs, *ŠÀ.ZI.GA: Ancient Mesopotamian Potency Incantations* (Locust Valley, NY: Augustin, 1967) 30, text no. 12, lines 18–19. See also p. 26, text no. 9, lines 4–6: "With the love[making of . . .], six times, with the lovemaking of a stag, seven times, with the lovemaking of a partridge (?), twelve times, make love to me!" Compare also the six days and seven nights' coital marathon of Enkidu and Šamḫat in Gilgamesh I.IV:21.

15. For the sexual employment of Ugaritic *ʿly* (here in the *shafʿel*: *šʿly*) and its etymological and semantic interdialectal equivalents in Akkadian *elû* and Hebrew על״י, see my "Two Cognate Semitic Terms for Mating and Copulation," *VT* 32 (1982) 492 = *Divrei Shalom*, 125–26. For another possible reference in a very fragmentary Ugaritic text, see *KTU*² 1.11:1–3: "[Baa]l was aroused and grasped her vagina. [Anat] was aroused and grasped him by the penis/testicles. [B]aal copulated by the thousand." This interpretation, however, has been contested by N. H. Walls, *The Goddess Anat in Ugaritic Myth* (SBLDS 135; Atlanta: Scholars Press, 1992) 134–39. See also P. L. Day, "Anat: Ugarit's 'Mistress of the Animals'," *JNES* 51 (1992) 184–85; and W. G. E. Watson, "Ugaritic and Mesopotamian Literary Texts," *Ugarit-Forschungen* 9 (1977) 277.

16. *KTU*² 1.5.V:19–21, describing the copulation of Baal with a 'heifer' (*ʿglt*).

17. I would like to thank Shamma Friedman for reminding me of some of these references.

(c) *b. Sanh.* 82b

Rabbi Naḥman said in the name of Rab (and here the verse from Prov 30:31 is cited), "that profligate (Zimri) cohabited four hundred and twenty-four times (with Kozbi) on that day." (Rashi: The *gematria* of the word זרזיר, which appears in this verse, totals 424.) Phineas waited for his potency to weaken (the word תַּיִשׁ in that verse is interpreted as being derived from תשש 'to weaken'). . . . In the *baraita* we learnt: "Sixty (times), until he became like an addled egg, while she became like a furrow filled with water."

Returning now to the Samson narrative, his euphemistic remark[18] was already correctly perceived by two medieval commentators: Ralbag (1288–1344) and Abarbanel (1437–1508). The former remarked, "Or he said this in order to show that he was suspicious that his wife had fornicated with his friends." And the latter commented, "He said, 'You plowed with my heifer', indicating that perhaps they committed adultery with her." Samson thus was subtly implying that his "friends" were able to guess the answer to his riddle, since they had "plowed" his "heifer."[19]

---

18. This has been all but overlooked by modern commentators, with the exception of Crenshaw, *Samson*, 119.

19. For fornication with a heifer in the Ugaritic Baal epic (*'glt*), see above, n. 16. S. Y. Friedman ("The Language of the Wise, the Language of the Commoners" [Hebrew; forthcoming]) has also applied this meaning to the enigmatic rabbinic expression חורש בגגות/ בגנות 'plowing on the roofs/in the gardens'. He concludes that the correct reading is the latter, בגנות, which he derives from the Greek γυνή 'woman'.

Aramean Skin Care:
A New Perspective on Naaman's Leprosy

Laura M. Zucconi

Richard Stockton College of New Jersey

Naaman's leprosy and conversion is not a typical healing story for the Hebrew Bible. It lacks a scene in which a foreign god is consulted for a cure, and a majority of the action plays out among servants rather than kings or other elites.[1] Naaman undergoes a therapeutic course, mostly in keeping with the popular medical culture of the ancient Near East; his healing and conversion occur in the context of the everyday world and highlight the need for all members of the Israelite community to maintain purity, not just kings and priests. This reading of 2 Kgs 5:1–19 combines two approaches: a historical comparison of medical practices that shows how Israelite healing both fits in the ancient Near Eastern medical culture and deviates from it, as well as a literary analysis in which Naaman represents everyone under the protection of Yahweh.[2] The historical accuracy of the common medical culture underscores the "every man role" of Naaman.

Basing a historical analysis of Israelite practices on the story of a prophet's miraculous cure is often seen as problematic; such passages tend to acquire the label "prophetic legend."[3] These have an ahistorical character, in addition to focusing on the prophet's role as miracle worker. But the case of Naaman does not entirely fit the model of a prophetic legend. Elisha's actions do not follow the expected norm of a miracle worker;[4] he does not

---

1. This idea deemphasizes the role of the monarch, in contrast to Cogan's claim that "for the author of Kings . . . the historical approach, the choice of events reported, and the manner of presentation are governed by a single idea: the loyalty of the monarch to the God of Israel as worshiped in Jerusalem determines the course of history." See Mordechai Cogan and Hayim Tadmor, *II Kings* (AB 11; New York: Doubleday, 1988) 3.

2. Cohn follows a tripartite division for 2 Kings 5: (1) Elisha vv. 1–14, (2) Naaman vv. 15–19, and (3) Gehazi vv. 20–27; see Robert Cohn, "Form and Perspective in 2 Kings V," *VT* 33 (1983) 171–84. A similar division can be found in Burke O. Long, *2 Kings* (Forms of the Old Testament Literature 10; Grand Rapids, MI: Eerdmans, 1991) 66–67. I am omitting the passages on Gehazi from this particular analysis without making further claims on the unity of 2 Kings 5 or the possible addendum of vv. 15–27.

3. G. M. Tucker, *Form Criticism of the Old Testament* (Philadelphia: Fortress, 1985) 39.

4. Long, *2 Kings*, 77.

invoke the name of Yahweh in an incantation nor does he physically manipulate Naaman by laying on hands or even waving them, against which Naaman complains (2 Kgs 5:11). The political relationship between Israel and Aram is an integral part of the story, further counteracting the assumption that it is just a prophetic legend.[5] The didactic function of the passage should not automatically disallow its historical elements as part of an analysis. Although a precise date cannot be given for 2 Kings 5, placing the action circa 850 B.C.E. should be acceptable when drawing comparisons with Iron Age medical practices throughout the ancient Near East.

The case of Ahaziah in 2 Kings 1 follows the pattern one would expect of medical issues in connection with the prophets. Ahaziah, injured from a fall, inquires about his health from the god Baal Zebub of Ekron only to have a messenger of Yahweh inform Elijah that Ahaziah will die. After Elijah delivers the prognosis of death, Ahaziah unsuccessfully sends soldiers to kill Elijah. Baal Zebub, in contrast to Yahweh, is proven ineffectual, not through Baal Zebub's failure to provide a prognosis or cure but because the captains and their men are consumed by fire from Yahweh. A connection is made between the impious act of inquiring of a foreign god and the king's subsequent death.

Ahaziah seeks a prognosis from the god Baal Zebub and follows the medical culture typical of the ancient Near East, which appears to be a mistake. The name Baal Zebub (Lord of the Flies) has been reconstructed as Baal Zebul (Lord, the Prince), a god invoked in medical incantations from Ugarit such as RIH I,16, 1–3 and KTU 1.82:38.[6] The act of seeking a prognosis from a god rather than a specific therapeutic measure was also widespread in the ancient Near East. The Diagnostic Handbook (TDP) is a collection of tablets containing symptoms and their prognosis; it was popular in Mesopotamia between the Middle Babylonian period (1595–1000 B.C.E.) and the Persian period (559–331 B.C.E.).[7] Letters from the archives of Esarhaddon and Assurbanipal also attest to kings seeking prognoses from an *asû* and/or *bārû*.[8] A similar situation can also be found in the Hebrew Bible when Isaiah gives prognoses to Hezekiah (2 Kgs 20:1–11). But Ahaziah makes the mistake of looking to Baal Zebub rather than Yahweh.

---

5. O. Eissfeldt, *The Old Testament: An Introduction* (trans. Peter Ackroyd; New York: Harper & Row, 1965) 295.

6. Wolfgang Herrmann, "Baal Zebub," in *Dictionary of Deities and Demons in the Bible* (Grand Rapids, MI: Eerdmans, 1999) 155.

7. René Labat, *Traité Akkadien de Diagnostics et Pronostics Médicaux* (Leiden: Brill, 1951).

8. Steven W. Cole and Peter Machinist, eds., *Letters from Priests to the Kings Esarhaddon and Assurbanipal* (SAA 13; Helsinki: Helsinki University Press, 1998); Robert H. Pfeiffer, *State Letters of Assyria* (American Oriental Series 6; New Haven: American Oriental Society, 1935); Robert F. Harper, *Assyrian and Babylonian Letters* (Chicago: University of Chicago Press, 1892).

Naaman differs from Ahaziah; the Aramean general does not seek a prognosis or a cure from Hadad Rimmon. He even seems quite content to live out his life with a skin affliction because it does not interfere with his service to the king of Aram. The impetus for seeking a cure comes from Naaman's Israelite maid servant (2 Kgs 5:3). This is the first indication that the healing of Naaman and his subsequent conversion do not follow an expected pattern. The recourse to a foreign god for medical purposes is not an issue and non-elites play an important role in the community formed by Yahweh.

But like the case of Ahaziah, there are elements of popular ancient Near Eastern medical culture germane to the story of Naaman. The use of a hierarchy of resort, the petition to the Israelite king for healing, the prophet not physically examining the afflicted, and bathing in a river are all features found in the medical practices of the ancient Near East. These elements of a common medical culture accentuate the significance of the non-elites in the Israelite community and the need for all members to maintain their purity.

The hierarchy of resort typically moves an afflicted person from the popular sector of health care to the professional sector.[9] A member of the popular sector initially recognizes a problem and labels an individual as sick.[10] Such practices existed in Mesopotamia in the labeling of workers as sick[11] and petitions to the king for healing.[12] The Israelite servant girl is the first character to mention that a cure for Naaman can be found with a prophet in Israel (2 Kgs 5:3). The identification of Naaman's skin affliction and a curative suggestion from a servant would not be out of the ordinary in the ancient Near East. The uniqueness of the situation is that the skin affliction signaled a significant problem for the Israelite, but apparently not for Aramean society. The Israelite slave labels Naaman, effectively placing him in the sick role from an Israelite perspective.[13] This is an important

---

9. Popular health care makes up the largest sector of health care in most societies. It consists of nonprofessionals and nonspecialists who initially define and treat the sickness; see Arthur Kleinman, *Patients and Healers in the Context of Culture* (Berkeley: University of California Press, 1980) 50.

Professional health care is an organized system of medicine sanctioned by the political, legal, and/or religious authorities in the community; see Kleinman, *Patients and Healers in the Context of Culture*, 53; Cecil G. Helman, *Culture, Health and Illness* (Boston: Butterworth Heinemann, 2000) 58.

10. N. J. Chrisman, "The Health Seeking Process: An Approach to the Natural History of Illness," *Culture, Medicine and Psychiatry* 1 (1977) 351–77; Kleinman, *Patients and Healers in the Context of Culture*, 49–70.

11. NBC 555 AS.01 and NBC 10891 AS.06.

12. K 577.

13. "A person is defined as being 'ill' when there is agreement between his perceptions of impaired wellbeing and the perceptions of those around him. In that sense, becoming

point for the coherence of the Israelite community. Yahweh acts through Naaman,[14] therefore the author of the passage must address the skin affliction as a sign of impurity.[15] But it is not a prophet or other elite that makes the initial diagnosis; rather, it is a lower member of society—a slave girl—who points out the problem. All members of the Israelite community should have a concern for purity regardless of whether their social station is a slave or a foreign general. If Yahweh acts through you, you are now part of His community. Naaman begins his slow shift from the broader medical and religious culture of the ancient Near East to the specific medical and religious culture of Israel.

Naaman seeks permission from his king who sends him to the king of Israel, and in turn the matter is forwarded to Elisha (2 Kgs 5:5, 8). As Naaman moves through the hierarchy of resort to the professional sector, he relies on petitioning the king, a therapeutic tactic common in the ancient Near East. First, a letter is sent to the king of Israel, "that you may remove him [Naaman] of his skin affliction" (2 Kgs 5:6). Petitions to the king for healing appear in Assyrian letters from the 7th century b.c.e.[16] Naaman acts in accord with ancient Near Eastern medical practices, but the Israelite king's response shows that Naaman must abandon his common assumptions about healing and power structures.[17]

Legitimation of Naaman's sick role (and consequent inability to work further for Yahweh) occurs when he and the Aramean king seek help from the king of Israel. When the story moves toward consultation with kings, Naaman's health care also switches to the professional sector (2 Kgs 5:4–5).

---

ill is always a *social* process which involves other people besides the patient . . . people who are so defined are temporarily able to avoid their obligations towards the social groups to which they belong . . . at the same time, these groups often feel obligated to care for their sick members . . ." (Helman, *Culture, Health and Illness*, 85). For further discussion of the sick role, see Howard Brody, *Stories of Sickness* (New York: Oxford University Press, 2003); Sol Levine and Martin A. Kozloff, "The Sick Role: Assessment and Overview," *Annual Review of Sociology* 4 (1978) 317–43; Talcott Parson, *The Social System* (Glencoe: Free Press, 1951).

14. "By him [Naaman] the LORD had given victory to Aram," 2 Kgs 5:1. Further indication that Naaman figures as part of an Israelite community can be seen in the phrase *ye'ĕsōp*, which Cogan notes as "'he will gather' describes the readmission of a suspected leper into society" (Cogan and Tadmor, *II Kings*, 64).

15. Cf. Leviticus 13.

16. K 577 is a plea from Nergal-sharrani that the king must act in order for his health to return. It is assumed that the king is to act as an intercessor with the divine realm on behalf of the afflicted man. The king's special position in society, to guide and protect the population as an intermediary with the gods (a priest *ex officio*), translates into the ability to help people with medical issues.

17. "And when the king of Israel read the letter, he tore his clothes and said, 'Am I god to cause death and to cause life that this (letter) is sent to me to remove a man from his skin affliction?'" 2 Kgs 5:7.

It is through this professional connection that Naaman comes to Elisha (2 Kgs 5:8). The formal character of their interaction comes through in the description of Naaman's horses and chariots as well as Elisha sending out a messenger (2 Kgs 5:9–10). These are hallmarks of a formal interaction between patient and medical practitioner. In the first half of the passage, the professional character of Elisha is authorized by the king of Israel. By the conclusion of the episode, the point is made that the religious authority, Yahweh, backs Elisha. Naaman has moved not only from the popular to the professional sector, but he also comes a step closer to the medical culture of ancient Israel and, consequently, to belief in the Israelite god.

From the outset, Naaman expects the setting of his cure to be the king's palace. Once the misunderstanding of who will handle Naaman's illness is corrected, Naaman proceeds to the house of Elisha, which sets up a series of important ironies. Typically, cases of prophetic healing have the prophet visit the afflicted rather than the other way around.[18] In this case, the prophet does not make a house call. The likely reason for this would be the fact that Naaman is an Aramean, a perceived (hostile) outsider. The irony is that the audience understands Naaman's role as an agent of Yahweh. The interaction between Naaman and Elisha does not take place in Elisha's home either. Naaman is kept outside, to be addressed only by a messenger (2 Kgs 5:10). This angers Naaman, who expected Elisha to come out and perform some miraculous act (2 Kgs 5:11), thus highlighting another ironic element to the story—Elisha behaves like other ancient Near Eastern healers. The Mesopotamian *asû* and *āšipu* would often treat patients without physically examining them or otherwise being near them. A letter between Esarhaddon and the *asû* Arad-Nana indicates that treatment measures could be carried out solely through correspondence.[19] Additionally, the prognoses in TDP are often based on events encountered by the *āšipu* before reaching the afflicted.[20] Just as Naaman begins to understand healing and power in Israel is not like Aram or anywhere else, Elisha reverts to a common healing strategy.

The prophet's ability to keep Naaman at bay reinforces the idea that Elisha, backed by the power of Yahweh, is superior to Naaman; it also places the men's servants, the common folk, in key roles. The messenger of Elisha behaves like a prophet; "say to him" is a directive usually given to prophets.[21] Similarly, the servants of Naaman convince him to obey the order to bathe in the Jordan. Like the Israelite slave girl earlier, these servants safeguard the purity of the community by advocating the treatment

---

18. Cf. 1 Kgs 17:17–24; 2 Kgs 4:17–37; 20:1–11.
19. K 532.
20. Labat, *Traité Akkadien de Diagnostics et Pronostics Médicaux*, 2–5.
21. Cf. 2 Kgs 1:3, 16.

of Yahweh's servant Naaman. The necessity of purity for those acting on behalf of Yahweh's community is not limited to the elite personages of kings and prophets. It is important for an Aramean general, not just an Is-raelite king, to be free of his skin affliction, and the common servant, not just the prophets, have the responsibility to identify and care for those af-flicted who also act on behalf of Yahweh.

Elisha's treatment of Naaman uses another therapeutic strategy com-mon to healers in the ancient Near East—bathing in a river. The advice to bathe in the Jordan only fuels Naaman's anger. From his perspective, if he's going to do such a common act, why not use the rivers Abanah and Phar-par? The use of running water in medical treatment can be found in the *namburbi* texts.[22] The power of the running water to trap and remove the malignancy derives not only from motion but also from the use of incan-tations, an important ritual element that Naaman notes is missing from Elisha's treatment.[23] The outward form of the healing ritual looks the same to Naaman because he does not yet understand that the efficacy of the cure derives from a different source than he would commonly expect. The Jor-dan, not the Abanah and Pharpar, is symbolically significant to the com-munity of Yahweh; its power comes directly from Yahweh rather than from a magical incantation. The meaning of Naaman's cure is that mortals do not control Yahweh or his healing ability. The medical practices may have many features in common with other cultures such as Aram and Mesopo-tamia, yet small (and significant) differences do exist.

Medical points unique to Israel are the king's inability to heal and the lack of an incantation to make a treatment effective. These differences in healing practices between Israel and Aram derive from the variations in the explanatory model of illness used by each culture. An explanatory model of illness is how one understands the conjunction of three elements: phys-iology, disease etiology, and treatment measures. In essence, it answers the questions: What is wrong? Why did it happen? How can it be fixed?[24] Aram and other ancient Near Eastern cultures have one set of answers to these questions, while the Israelites have another set.

The art and literature of Mesopotamia indicates how people of the an-cient Near East conceptualized the function of the human body. The votive statues of Tell Asmar attest to the idea that the human body functioned as

---

22. Richard Caplice, *The Akkadian Namburbi Texts: An Introduction* (Los Angeles: Un-dena, 1974) 9–10.

23. Cogan notes that "waving a hand" is an "expected rite of exorcism," but Cogan does not state whence this expectation derives; see Cogan and Tadmor, *II Kings*, 64.

24. Kleinman, *Patients and Healers in the Context of Culture*, 104–18; Helman, *Culture, Health and Illness*, 85.

a communicative object.[25] In addition to conveying a sense of the king's awe and power, many reliefs show the king as well as priests and even deities in the role of intercessor.[26] The role of intercessor similarly appears in texts such as the Code of Hammurabi, which declares that "When lofty Anum . . . and Enlil . . . determined for Marduk . . . the Enlil functions over all mankind . . . established for him in its midst an enduring kingship, named me to promote the welfare of the people. . . ."[27] A function of these works was conveying ideas about power; gods are the most powerful and, in turn, delegate some of that power to kings and priests. Such portrayals lead to the conclusion that physiology was inextricably linked to communicating with the divine. In terms of communication, illness is an instrument of the divine, prodding humans to behave in a particular manner.[28] The phrase *qāt* DN (hand of DN) is taken to mean that a god has directly touched or even smited the afflicted as a form of punishment. One need not commit a sin but merely neglect to act in a socially acceptable manner. Note that Enlil commands the *šuruppu* to send disease simply because the noise of men kept him awake, not because they were wicked.[29] Mesopotamians take a holistic approach in that illness, as they would say, grasps the whole person; it is not just localized, although a symptom may be confined to a specific area of the body. Consequently, treatments often target the whole person in the form of incantations or rituals.[30] The use of spells and rituals, it is hoped, shift the balance of power within the relationship between humans and the divine in order to gain an advantage for the patient that will eventually restore health.

For Israel, there is little relevant iconography from which to formulate ideas about human physiology.[31] The Song of Songs describes the ideal of

---

25. The body as communicative object with the gods is also evident in the divinatory practices of inspecting animal entrails.

26. André Parrot, *Arts of Assyria* (New York: Golden, 1961); André Parrot, *Sumer: The Dawn of Art* (New York: Golden, 1961); H. W. F. Saggs, *The Greatness That Was Babylon* (New York: Hawthorn, 1962) 475; Henri Frankfort, *Art and Architecture of the Ancient Orient* (New Haven: Penguin, 1995).

27. James B. Pritchard, *Ancient Near Eastern Texts Relating to the Old Testament* (Princeton: Princeton University Press, 1969) 164.

28. Hector Avalos, *Illness and Health Care in the Ancient Near East: The Role of the Temple in Greece, Mesopotamia and Israel* (Atlanta: Scholars Press, 1995) 134.

29. Atrahasis I, vii, 24–28.

30. K 2354, rev., col. III, 48–52; see R. Campbell Thompson, "Assyrian Prescriptions for Diseases of the Head," *American Journal of Semitic Languages and Literature* 24 (1908) 325–26.

31. The tradition of aniconism greatly restricted the representation of human figures until the 3rd century C.E. Humanoid representations from the Iron Age, whether clay figurines or inscriptions, do not provide enough evidence to substantiate significant theories of Israelite conceptions of physiology.

beauty with metaphors that emphasize the skin and pleasant odor.[32] Assuming that beauty is a corollary of health, these passages show that the appearance of one's skin is a hallmark of a healthy physiology. Leviticus's concentration on skin afflictions and discharges in terms of clean/unclean provides an indication as to how the biblical authors saw the relation between physiology, health, and the religious community when they developed an explanatory model of illness. By doing this, the Hebrew Bible links outward signs of health to public expressions of religiosity, namely, participating in cultic functions. According to the Hebrew Bible, physical restrictions on the priesthood (Lev 21:5, 16–21; 22:4–7) can apply also to the general Israelite population (Leviticus 12–15) and to sacrificial animals (Lev 22:21–25). Another Israelite conception of physiology is that a life force enters the body as a breath through the mouth and/or nose.[33] This indicates that the body is conceptualized as a whole. Much like the Mesopotamian ideas of sickness, an illness may be visible only in a particular place, such as the skin, but it is the entire body that suffers. Reports of illness in the Hebrew Bible are frequently connected to religious behavior, either as a consequence of transgression[34] or as a prohibition on participating in the religious community.[35] Yahweh alone is the deity that sends disease to the Israelites, and he is the only healer for the Israelites.[36] Treatments can take two forms. In one, the illness is healed by methods akin to the therapeutics found in Mesopotamia. This would consist of plasters, fumigations, amulets, the use of running water, and the like.[37] The second form of treatment would be that God simply removes the illness/punishment, without a physical enactment of treatment measures.[38] In the case of Naaman, the two possible treatment measures are combined: the common ancient Near Eastern therapy of bathing in a river is only effective because Yahweh has deemed it so.

The difference in explanatory models of illness between Aram/Mesopotamia and Israel accounts for why the Israelite king is incapable of healing Naaman and laments the request to do so. Yahweh has not delegated his healing power to a king, but the role of the prophet seems to carry with it

---

32. Song 1:12–13; 3:6; 4:3, 6–7, 11, 14, 16; 5:1, 5, 10, 13; 6:2; 7:9–10, 14.

33. Gen 2:7; 2 Kgs 4:34–35, etc.

34. 1 Kings 14; 2 Kgs 15:4–5, etc.

35. Leviticus 12–13, 15; Deut 23:2, etc.

36. Exod 15:26. For a discussion of Yahweh as healer, see Norbert Lohfink, "'I Am Yahweh, Your Physician' (Exod 15:26): God, Society and Human Health in a Postexilic Revision of the Pentateuch (Exod 15:2b, 26)," *Theology of the Pentateuch: Themes of the Priestly Narrative and Deuteronomy* (Minneapolis: Fortress, 1994) 35–95.

37. That such treatment strategies would be acceptable is demonstrated in Exod 21:18–19.

38. Cf. Jer 30:12–17.

some healing ability. This still leaves the question as to why an incantation is not necessary in healing Naaman. But the prophet does not need to shift the balance of power so that the afflicted may regain his health. Elisha as prophet is the spokesman for Yahweh and not acting on a delegation of power. Elisha, through a messenger, tells Naaman what to do for his skin condition, but Elisha does not make the Jordan an effective treatment. The role of messenger is highlighted, not by having the typical phrase "thus say to him," but by Elisha imparting the information through his own messenger. Here, the common person is a key to Naaman's cure. The action subsequent to Elisha's message reinforces the idea that non-elites are instrumental in the overall well-being of those acting on behalf of Yahweh (or his community). Naaman is upset that Elisha did not "call in the name of Yahweh his god," but his own servants point out that the message from the divine has been communicated: "if the prophet spoke a great word to you, would you not do it?" (2 Kgs 5:13). In essence, they are giving advice to look at the message, not the power of the messenger.

This advice runs throughout the story of Naaman's leprosy. Wise council comes from the Israelite slave girl, from the servants of the prophet and Naaman, and Naaman himself, a non-Israelite, all of whom act on behalf of Yahweh in one way or another. As an instrument of Yahweh, purity is of the utmost importance. Status within the community of Yahweh does not diminish its significance. Naaman slowly comes to realize the power of Yahweh and his role within the Israelite community as he begins to understand the subtle differences in Israelite medicine.

Abraham and Damascus in Some Greek and Latin Texts of the Hellenistic Period

JOHN A. EMERTON
University of Cambridge

According to the book of Genesis, Abraham[1] was born in Ur of the Chaldeans (11:26–31, 15:7; see also Neh 9:7), but he later moved to Haran and then to Canaan. It is nowhere said that he lived in Damascus; however, some Greek and Latin writers of the Hellenistic period offer a different account of events. One writer says that he was born in Syria, another possibly implies that he was born specifically in Damascus and was king there, and yet another that, although he was born farther east, he became king in Damascus. What is to be made of the discrepancy between these writings and Genesis?

The discrepancy is one of the arguments used by Giovanni Garbini[2] in relation to his theory that the original Greek translation of the first few books of the Hebrew Bible did not contain the book of Genesis, which was added only later, when the Septuagint version was made. The discrepancy is thus to be explained on the hypothesis that the relevant writers in the

---

Author's note: I am grateful to G. I. Davies for reading a draft of this article and making some helpful comments.

The present article had already been written and prepared for submission when I learned of, and read, Garbini's chapter "Abraham and Damascus," in his recent book, *Myth and History in the Bible* (JSOTSup 362; London and New York: Sheffield Academic Press, 2003) 22–35. I regret that it is no longer possible to discuss here his recent work on the subject, which presents some aspects of his theory more fully than in his earlier book (but does not add substantial new arguments). The arguments that I have advanced in my present article seem to me to remain valid.

1. It is convenient for the present purpose to use the spelling Abraham throughout (except in quotations) and to ignore the fact that his name is said originally to have been Abram.

2. In his book *Storia e ideologia nell'Israele antico* (Biblioteca di storia e storiografia dei tempi biblici 3; Brescia: Paideia, 1986). I give, however, quotations and references from the English translation by John Bowden, *History and Ideology in Ancient Israel* (London: SCM, 1988), adding also page references to the Italian original.

Hellenistic period either did not know the book of Genesis or at least preserved a tradition that originated before Genesis was known in Egypt.

Garbini appears to accept a date for the LXX "between the end of the third and the beginning of the second century BC" (p. 146; Italian, p. 200). He regards its preparation as part of an attempt to bring the religion of Jews in Egypt into line with the current Judaism in Jerusalem.

> It was not a matter of translating already known texts into Greek . . . the texts which were to be put into Greek at Alexandria were new texts which gave a new face to Judaism. . . . The Septuagint version was to introduce to Egypt the 'final edition' of the Jerusalem law. This had made many innovations, not only over Jewish origins and over Moses, but also over Abraham. (p. 140; Italian, p. 192)

Garbini does not claim that the belief that Abraham was born in Ur of the Chaldeans was entirely new, for he thinks that it originated in the time of Nabonidus in the 6th century (p. 145; Italian, p. 199; see also pp. 77–84; Italian, pp. 112–21). Nevertheless, it was new in the text that appeared in Genesis that was translated in the LXX, and "Genesis deliberately stresses the relationships of Abraham and his family . . . with Mesopotamia" (p. 144; Italian, p. 197).

The present article is not a discussion of Garbini's whole theory about the purpose of the LXX, a theory that is based primarily on arguments about the alleged earlier biblical translation into Greek and about the alleged beliefs of Egyptian Jews concerning the origin of their nation. The passages about Abraham and Syria in certain writings of the Hellenistic period raise questions in their own right without going into Garbini's wider theory in detail, and a discussion of such questions is the purpose of the present article. Reference will, however, be made (where appropriate) to the bearing of the present discussion on Garbini's theory as a whole.

Before the extrabiblical texts are examined, mention needs to be made of two passages in Genesis where there are references to Damascus in the context of the narrative about Abraham. The first is Gen 14:15, where it is said of Abraham that, after defeating the eastern kings in battle, he pursued them as far as Hobah, which is north of Damascus. The passage does not, however, speak of Abraham being in Damascus.

The second passage is in Genesis 15. Abraham is told by God in v. 1 that his reward will be great. In reply, Abraham asks (v. 2) what God will give him, because he is on the move, childless, and toward the end of his life. The verse continues with words that are obscure and difficult to translate. They say, literally, "and the son of *mešeq* of my house, he is (or, that is) Damascus Eliezer (or, of Eliezer)." The word *mešeq* is a *hapax legomenon*, and the phrase "Damascus Eliezer" or "Damascus (of) Eliezer" is strange. Some scholars have held that "Damascus" is a (mistaken) gloss on *mešeq*. If they are right, then "Damascus" was not an original part of the text. However, that is no more than a hypothesis. It is widely agreed that the verse is probably corrupt, and the problem of the original text and its meaning have never been explained in a way that has been found generally convincing. It is clear, however, from the following verse that v. 2 must be saying something about the person who will be Abraham's heir if he never has a son.

Whatever modern scholars may think about the problems of Gen 15:2, people in the Hellenistic period sought to make some sense of a verse that does not appear to have differed from the MT (and that included the word "Damascus"). Different renderings are found in the ancient versions. The LXX understands the Hebrew to refer to "the son of Masek, my home-born female slave," Aquila to "the son of him who gives drink to my house" (apparently associating *mešeq* with the participle *mašqeh*), Symmachus to "the kinsman of my house," and Theodotion to "the son of him who is over my house."

The targums, too, represent ways of interpreting the text. *Onqelos*, *Pseudo-Jonathan*, and the *Fragment Targums* understand the reference to be to the administrator of Abraham's house, while *Neofiti I* has "the son of my house." *Neofiti I, Pseudo-Jonathan*, and the *Fragment Targums* take Eliezer to be the subject of the clause. *Onqelos* renders "Damascus Eliezer" as "Eliezer of Damascus" (as also does the *Peshitta*). *Neofiti I, Pseudo-Jonathan*, and the *Fragment Targums*, however, separate the two words and say that by Eliezer's hands wonders were performed in Damascus. This appears to be a reference to Abraham's victory over the eastern kings in Genesis 14, interpreted in terms of a midrashic tradition. The numerical value of Eliezer's name is 318, and Gen 14:14 says that this was the number of Abraham's servants in the battle. *Gen. Rab.* 43.2 therefore records the comment of a rabbi on the victory that "It was Eliezer alone."

It cannot, of course, be assumed that all the interpretations found in the targums were current as early as the Hellenistic period. Nevertheless, the targums, like the ancient versions, illustrate the ways in which interpretations of biblical passages were offered, including a difficult text, which was part of sacred Scripture and needed to be explained, but which modern scholars think is corrupt and in need of different treatment. It is now time to examine the writers of the Hellenistic age who link Abraham with Syria and, in some cases, especially with Damascus.

Apollonius Molon, Pompeius Trogus, and Nicolaus of Damascus

The first writer to be considered is Apollonius Molon who, according to Garbini, wrote in the 1st century BC that Abraham had been born in a mountainous and desert region of Syria after his ancestors had been chased out of Armenia. (p. 140; Italian, p. 192)

The source for this statement is Eusebius of Caesarea, *Praeparatio Evangelica* 9.9.1–3. (See also Menahem Stern,[3] pp. 148–56, who gives an introduction to Molon and quotes the relevant passages with translations and notes.)

Molon's outline of events from "the survivor of the flood" (Noah's name is not mentioned) until Moses bears a general resemblance to that of Genesis and the beginning of Exodus. It begins with Armenia, and in Gen 8:4 the ark is said to have landed on Mount Ararat, although Genesis says nothing of Noah and his sons being expelled from the land. Abraham's legitimate wife is said by Molon to have born him a son whose name means "laughter"; and the LXX uses the same Greek word: *gelōs*. Sarah says that "The Lord has made laughter for me." There are, however, discrepancies in addition to the difference over Abraham's place of birth: Abraham is said to have been born after three generations, not ten as in Genesis 11; the etymology of Abraham's name, although possibly Semitic (see Stern, p. 151), differs from Gen 17:5; twelve sons, who settle in Arabia, are ascribed to Abraham and his Egyptian concubine, rather than to their son Ishmael; similarly, Gelos, rather than his son Jacob, is said to have been the father of twelve sons including Joseph; and Moses is said to have been the grandson of Joseph, rather than descended from his brother Levi as in Exod 2:1–10.

The LXX of Genesis was certainly in existence in the time of Molon, but the discrepancies between it and what he says make it unlikely that he had himself used it as a source, unless he was extremely careless. On the other hand, his information must ultimately have been derived from a Jewish source, which was either the book of Genesis in Greek or something very like it, and whose etymology of Abraham's name may have been Semitic. According to Josephus (*Ag. Ap.* 2.7 §§79–80), Molon was strongly anti-Semitic, and this suggests that Molon's source or sources may not have been directly Jewish. A possible hypothesis is that Molon's source was ultimately Jewish but was mediated to him through one that was gentile. Such a hypothesis does justice to both the similarities to and the differences from the book of Genesis in the LXX version.

The second writer, Pompeius Trogus, who wrote in Latin and lived toward the end of the same century as Molon and the beginning of the next, was the author of *Historiae Philippicae* (see Stern, pp. 332–43). Apart from

---

3. M. Stern, *Greek and Latin Authors on Jews and Judaism*, vol. 1: *From Herodotus to Plutarch* (Fontes and Res Judaicas Spectantes; Jerusalem: The Israel Academy of Sciences and Humanities, 1974).

the Prologue, the work has survived only in the form of the Epitome prepared by Justin (M. Iunianus Iustinus) in the 3rd or 4th century. The Epitome 1.9–3.9 of book 36 says that the "origin of the Jews was from Damascus," which received its name from King Damascus (2.1–2). The next kings were "Azelus, and then Adores, Abraham and Israhel." Israhel had ten sons and divided his people among them into ten kingdoms, and he "called them all Jews from Judas," one of the sons (2.3–5). The youngest son, Joseph, was sold by his brothers to merchants who took him to Egypt. There, he found "great favor with the king" (2.6–7) whom he warned of a coming famine and advised to store wheat (2.8–10). The Egyptians later expelled from Egypt Joseph's son Moses together with people suffering from scabies and leprosy. Moses led the exiles, taking with them the sacred utensils of the Egyptians; and the Egyptians, who wished to retrieve them by force, "were compelled by tempests to return home" (2.11–13). Moses led the people to Damascus, "his ancestral home," and "took possession of mount Sinai"; he also established the Sabbath on the seventh day each week "for a fast-day." Remembering that "they had been driven from Egypt for fear of spreading infection," the Jews "took care . . . to have no communication with strangers" (2.14–16). The son of Moses was Arruas,"—presumably Aaron is meant—who "was made priest . . . and soon after created king; and ever afterwards it was a custom among the Jews to have the same persons both for kings and priests," and "it is almost incredible how powerful they became" (2.16).

Much of this looks like a garbled account of the story in Genesis and other parts of the Pentateuch, combined with a story found in various forms among Hellenistic writers, that the Jews were expelled from Egypt for leprosy or some other disease. The names of Azelus and Adores, who are said to have been kings of Damascus before Abraham, have been compared with those mentioned in the Hebrew Bible (Stern, p. 339). The name Azelus has been compared with Hazael, the Aramean general who, in 2 Kgs 8:7–15, consulted Elisha and then murdered Ben-hadad as "the son of Ader" (4 Kgdms 8:7, 9). The Hebrew letters *dalet* and *rêš* are similar in appearance and are sometimes confused, even in manuscripts of the Hebrew Bible; for example, in Gen 36:39 and 1 Chr 1:50, the name of the same person appears as "Hadad" and "Harar" in variant readings. It is therefore possible that Adores in the narrative of Pompeius Trogus goes back ultimately to the second element in Ben-hadad's name. Incidentally, although Josephus (*Ant.* 9.4.6 §§87–93) calls the king whom Azaelos kills Adados, he ignores the first element of Ben-hadad's name. A different Hadad appears in 1 Kgs 11:14–22, which tells how an Edomite prince of that name escaped Joab's massacre of Edomite males and fled to Egypt. When King David died, Hadad sought and obtained the permission of the king of Egypt to return to his native land. Verses 23–24 go on to tell how Rezon (an "adversary" of Solomon, like Hadad in v. 14) and his men settled in Damascus and he became king there. The end of v. 25 in the MT says that Hadad reigns in Aram, but the LXX and the Peshitta say that it was in Edom. The LXX omits the account of Rezon's establishing himself in Damascus. This is not the place to discuss the problems of the text in detail, but it is widely held that the account of Rezon's doings has been inserted into the story of Hadad in the Hebrew text, and that v. 25 completes the account of Hadad's return to Edom and becoming its king. However, the insertion of the story of Rezon and his settlement in Damascus led a scribe into confusing Edom with Aram and substituting the latter for the former in the Hebrew text (see the commentaries). Be that as it may, it is easy to see how the present Hebrew text could be understood to say that a man named Hadad became king of Aram in Damascus. Incidentally, Josephus (*Ant.* 8.7.6 §§199–204) tells how the Edomite Aderos escaped to Egypt but returned to Idumea (i.e., Edom) after the deaths of David and Joab. However, since Idumea was occupied by Israelite garrisons, Aderos did not stay there but went to Syria. He joined forces there with Razos (i.e., Rezon) and his band of robbers and became king of that part of Syria. Josephus thus understood the biblical text to say that Aderos (i.e., Hadad) became king in Syria (i.e., Aram).

What conclusions may be drawn about the account given by Pompeius Trogus concerning Abraham and the events of his life, and about its probable origin? First, the resemblances between what he narrates and what is found in Genesis and elsewhere in the Pentateuch testify that the ultimate origin was probably the Pentateuch, but the differences make it most unlikely that he had direct access to it. The information came ultimately from a Jewish source, but it was probably mediated to him by some other source. Second, whatever its origin may have been, his belief that the Jews originated in Damascus may be compared with the statement by Apollonius Molon that Abraham was born in Syria. It is possible that Trogus supposed that King Damascus was the ancestor of the kings that followed him in the city that bore his name, because it is reasonable to suppose that Israhel was thought to be the son of Abraham. Further, the statement that "a progeny of ten sons made Israhel more famous than any of his ancestors" suggests that the ancestors were the earlier kings of Damascus. The narrative may imply that Abraham had been born in Damascus, which would be consonant with the statement that "the origin of the Jews was from Damascus." On the other hand, as will be seen below, Nicolaus of Damascus says that Abraham was king of Damascus, and also that he came from the land of the Chaldeans. Moreover, we have only Justin's Epitome and not the full account by Trogus himself. As Stern points out, "it may be that the full narrative of Trogus conformed more with Nicolaus" (p. 339). It is impossible to be certain, but it is possible that Trogus thought that Abraham was born in Damascus. Third, the story that the Jews were expelled from Egypt because they were lepers is a form of story told by a number of Hellenistic writers, and the source for it can scarcely have been Jewish. Fourth, the reference to Azelus as a king of Damascus has been interpreted as a reference to Hazael (Azaêlos in the LXX), and it has been suggested that Adores is to be identified with Ben-hadad, whom Hazael murdered and succeeded as king in Damscus. There may also have been influence from the story of the Edomite Hadad (Adados in Josephus, but Aderos in the LXX) who may be understood on one reading of the Hebrew to have become king of Aram. Such a hypothesis may need to be tentative, but it is plausible. If it is correct, Pompeius Trogus has turned into contemporaries of Abraham two kings of Damascus of a much later date.

The third writer is Nicolaus of Damascus who "was born at Damascus *c.* 64 B.C.E." and "entered the service of Herod by 14 B.C.E. at the latest" and "seems to have spent his last years at Rome" (Stern, pp. 227–28). His *Historiae* begin "with the ancient history of eastern monarchies" and the work "becomes more detailed as it approaches the author's own time" (p. 228). The account by Josephus of the reign of Herod the Great and also of earlier Jewish history owes much to Nicolaus. According to Josephus (*Ant.* 1.7.2 §§159–60), Nicolaus says that Abraham

> reigned (in Damascus), an invader who had come with an army from the country beyond Babylon called the land of Chaldees. But, not long after, he left this country also with his people for the land then called Canaan but now Judaea, where he settled, he and his numerous descendants. . . . The name of Abram is still celebrated in the region of Damascus, and a village is shown that it is called 'Abram's abode'. (Stern, p. 233, quoting H. St. J. Thackeray's translation)

Unlike Appollonius Molon, Nicolaus does not say that Abraham was born in Syria. His narrative is much closer to the record in Genesis than those of Molon and Trogus, although Genesis says nothing of Abraham's being king in Damascus, and its reference in 14:15 to his pursuit of the eastern kings as far as Hobah near Damascus places it after his settlement in Canaan. Since Nicolaus came from Damascus, it may be assumed that his reference to the celebration of Abraham's name in that city and to the village called "Abram's abode," is based on local knowledge.

It is reasonable to assume from this statement that there was a Jewish community in Damascus at the time of Nicolaus, and the presence of Jews in the city is recorded in the New Testament (Acts 9:1–25, especially vv. 19–22). Also, it may be suspected that the belief that Abraham was once king in Damascus was an extrabiblical tradition among Jews there, to whom it probably owes origin, as Stern suggests (p. 234).

Garbini notes the hypothesis that "a Jewish colony in Damascus in the Hellenistic period" was "the origin of the legend that had Abraham ruling in Damascus" (p. 141; Italian, p. 193). However, he maintains that the information given by Nicolaus "can hardly have been the product of late traditions, especially with its mention of a toponym said to be 'Abram's abode'." It is, he claims,

> quite difficult to suppose that a late tradition, connected with a group which certainly cannot have been the most authoritative in the city, succeeded in finding its way into Hellenistic historiography and creating a toponym.

We cannot be certain when the tradition originated, but Garbini's argument against a late date is unconvincing. If there was a village known by Jews as "Abram's abode" (possibly a place where a number of Jews lived), the relative unimportance of the Jewish community in Damascus is not evidence that the name cannot also have been known to, and possibly used by, gentiles in the region. The "Hellenistic historiography" to which Garbini refers is presumably the *Historiae* of Nicolaus, who was obviously interested in the Jews and their origins as well as having a direct knowledge of Damascus and its environs.

In his comments on this passage, Stern points out (pp. 233–34) that Abraham is called a "prince of God" in Gen 23:6, and he refers to "various midrashic traditions about Abraham as king" cited by Ginzberg.[4] Stern also compares Philo, who says of Abraham that

> by those among whom he settled he was regarded as a king, not because of the outward state which surrounded him, mere commoner that he was, but because of his greatness of soul, for his spirit was the spirit of a king.[5]

The statement that he was regarded as a king is based on the LXX of Gen 23:6, where he is said to be, not merely a prince but "a king (*basileus*) from God." These words are quoted by Philo in his account of what happened after Sarah's death.[6] The idea that Abraham was a king, as found in texts of the Hellenistic period, can thus plausibly be traced back to the LXX of Gen 23:6. However, the same idea can be found in a Semitic context at a later date in midrash. In *Midr. Gen. Rab.* 42:6 (see also 58:6), gentiles say to Abraham, "Thou art a king for us; thou art a prince over us;

---

4. L. Ginzberg, *The Legends of the Jews* (7 vols.; Philadelphia: The Jewish Publication Society of America, 1925–38) 5.216.

5. *De virtutibus* 39 §216, in F. H. Colson, *Philo* (10 vols.; Loeb Classical Library; ed. F. H. Colson et al.; Cambridge, MA: Harvard University Press / London: Heinemann, 1929–62) 8.297.

6. *De Abrahamo* 44 §261, in Colson, *Philo*, 6.127.

thou art God over us." Apparently, both "prince" and "God" are understood as separate epithets referring to Abraham, rather than as a phrase meaning a "prince of God." Understandably, Abraham wishes to dissociate himself from such a way of addressing him, for he replies: "The world does not lack its kings, and the world does not lack its God."

The Old Testament and
Abraham's Link to Damascus

It is not only in texts from the Hellenistic period or later that traditions linking Abraham with Damascus are alleged to be found. First, Garbini claims that

> The antiquity of the traditions which linked Abraham with Damascus finds interesting confirmation in the Old Testament itself. Genesis has a recollection of Abraham's journey to Damascus in the figure of Eliezer of Damascus who would have become Abraham's heir had not Isaac been born. (p. 141; Italian, p. 195)

He believes, no doubt correctly, that the text of Gen 15:2 is corrupt, and he concludes that "the corruption is ancient," and maintains that

> we cannot exclude the hypothesis that it [presumably, the corruption] was meant to make obscure a passage which should have clarified relations between the patriarch and the Syrian city. (p. 141, Italian, pp. 193–94)

However, to say that the hypothesis cannot be excluded is not the same as to say that it is probable. Moreover, to say that the corruption 'was meant to make obscure' (*che essa fosse voluta per rendere oscuro*) implies that Garbini has in mind deliberate editorial change rather than accidental scribal corruption of the text. If the purpose of the corruption had been to remove a reference to a connection between Abraham and Damascus, one would have expected the editor to have made the new meaning plain rather than to have made the text obscure; also, it would have been surprising if he had either added "Damascus" or even left it in the text. The verse's difficulties were discussed above near the beginning of the present article. The words "Damascus Eliezer" cannot be translated "Eliezer of Damascus" without emendation of the text, and it was noted that some scholars regard "Damascus" as a gloss. However, even if the original text said that Abraham's servant came from Damascus, that would tell us only of his place of origin, not that Abraham traveled to Damascus to obtain him as a servant or slave.

The second passage to which Garbini refers is Amos 7:9, in which "Isaac" and "Israel" appear in parallel "with a reference to the northern Hebrew kingdom" (p. 141; Italian, p. 194). According to Garbini, "Given the close connection between Isaac and Abraham, here we have explicit evidence of the presence of this patriarchal cycle in the kingdom of Israel, i.e. outside the typically southern ambience presented by Genesis." There is no mention of Damascus here, but Garbini understands the verse as associating Abraham, by implication through Isaac, with the Northern Kingdom rather than with that of Judah. That is scarcely suprising, if the probability is recognized that Northern and Southern traditions about the patriarchs had been combined by the time of Amos who, incidentally, was himself from Tekoa in the south, although he prophesied in the North. It is reading too much into the verse to claim that it implies the existence of a specifically Northern tradition about Abraham (and, in any case, the north of Israel is not the same as Damascus).

Amos 7:9 is one of the places in which Isaac's name is spelled with the letter *śîn* (as in Jer 33:26, Ps 105:9, and also Amos 7:16) instead of the more common spelling with *ṣādê*. The cognate verbs, spelled both ways, mean 'to laugh', hence Isaac's name is explained (Gen 17:17, 19; see also 18:12–13, 15). It is usually thought that the two spellings of Isaac's name are simply by-forms; perhaps the emphatic sibilant has been dissimilated to a non-emphatic sibilant under the influence of the emphatic consonant *qôp*. Garbini offers a different explanation:

> An attempt was made to eliminate the contrast between the information in Amos and that in Genesis by the later tradents of the text, who transformed the name Isaac by simply changing a consonant, so that it became a similar sounding word which meant 'laugh'.

Once again, Garbini finds here a deliberate attempt to remove a connection between Isaac (and through him Abraham) and the north. Not only is this hypothesis an unnecessary alternative to the view that we have here by-forms of the same name, but it also attributes to the editor an unrealistic hope that it was possible to lead readers to fail to recognize a reference to Isaac simply by changing the nature of one sibilant. If that was the hope, and if the spelling in Amos 7:9, 16 influenced the spelling in Isa 33:26 and Ps 105:9, it failed to mislead the authors of the verses in Isaiah and the psalm, who plainly had the patriarch in mind. It is unlikely that an editor who wished to lead readers into supposing that Amos 7:9 was not referring to Isaac would have been so incompetent as to resort to so inadequate a means as the substitution of one sibilant for another.

Third, Garbini refers to Amos 3:12 where, after a mention of Israelites, "a parallel is drawn between 'Samaria' and 'Damascus'" (p. 142; Italian, pp. 194–95). This is a difficult verse, which reads,

> As the shepherd rescues out of the mouth of the lion
> two legs or a piece (?) of an ear

So will the children of Israel be rescued,
who dwell in Samaria on the corner of a couch,
and in Damascus (??) a bed.

This rendering is possible only if the pointing is changed to read "Damascus"; and the relation of the emended word "Damascus" to "a bed" is obscure. Various emendations have been proposed, and the emendation suggested by Garbini reads: "those who are in Samaria a handful of tribes, and at Damascus ten (men)." It is rarely, if ever, wise to base an argument on a conjectural emendation of the text, especially when it is only one of a number of emendations that have been suggested (see the commentaries). Moreover, it is not clear why ten Israelites who happen to be in Damascus are selected for special mention, or how this verse is thought to supplement significantly the parallelism elsewhere between Isaac and Israel, or what bearing it has on the connection between Abraham and Damascus. Even the claim that Samaria and Damascus are parallel to each other is possible only when the vocalization of the MT is changed to introduce into the passage the name of the latter city.

Fourth, Gen 15:16 promises to Abraham's descendants "this land, from the river of Egypt unto the great river, the river Euphrates," which, as Garbini points out, "includes not only all Palestine but also all Syria" (p. 142; Italian, p. 195). He comments that the *Genesis Apocryphon* (1Qap Gen) 21:11–12 "is rather more complete from a geographical point of view," and is "a description of the whole region between Egypt and Mesopotamia," and that "this large area . . . from the summit of Mount Hazor, just north of Bethel . . . has its geographical centre in Damascus." This may be roughly true from a geographical point of view, though Damascus is not mentioned specifically in either text. However, this view of the extent of the promised land—which apparently represents, not historically achieved reality (whatever may or may not have been achieved by David), but Israelite hopes at some stage—does not specifically refer to Damascus. It offers little firm support for claims of an ancient tradition of Abraham's kingship over Damascus.

Fifth, Amos 5:27 speaks of God taking the people into exile beyond Damascus. It is usually thought that there is an allusion to this verse in references to those "who entered the new covenant in the land of Damascus" in the *Damascus Document*, CD-A VI 19, VII 21, and CD-B XIX 33–34; and CD-B XX speaks apparently of members of the sect who had apostasized and were to be "expelled from the congregation" and who had (11–12) "despised the covenant . . . and the compact which they had established in the land of Damascus, which is the new covenant." The phrase "new covenant" echoes the prophecy in Jer 31:31–33. Similarly, CD-A VII 18–19 refers to the "star" in Num 24:17 who comes from Jacob and says that "the star is the Interpreter of the Law, who will come to Damascus." According to Garbini, the "new covenant made at Damascus . . . will be 'the covenant of Abraham'," to which reference is made in CD-A XII 11 (p. 143; Italian, p. 196). He comments that

> This conception, quite original in identifying the place of exile with that of the making of the new covenant, is as it were a synthesis of Genesis, Jeremiah and Amos; however, it would have been very difficult to bring about had there not already been a tradition which linked Abraham with Damascus. (p. 143; Italian, p. 196)

It is questionable, however, whether the "new covenant made in the land of Damascus" is to be identified with "the covenant of Abraham." The context of the latter phrase is a prohibition against selling a slave, whether male or female, to foreigners; and it is said of the slaves that "they had entered with him into the covenant of Abraham"—and by "him" it presumably means the owner of the slave. This prohibition comes from a long series of laws, of which some appear to be concerned only with members of the sect, but others to be applicable to all Jews. The sale of Jewish slaves to foreigners was abhorrent to Nehemiah (see Neh 5:8), and it is regarded as "a violation of the laws of the country" by Josephus in *Ant.* 16.1.1 §1. There are two references in Genesis to God making a covenant with Abraham. One is in 15:18, where the land is promised to the descendants of Abraham; the other is in 17:7–14, 19, 21, where a covenant is established with Abraham and his descendants, which gives them the land and involves the circumcision of all male children and of other males (presumably slaves) whether "born in the house or bought with money of any stranger." That surely implies that female slaves too were brought into the covenant of Abraham. There is nothing to suggest that the slaves in the *Damascus Document* had joined the Qumran sect. Indeed, it can scarcely be supposed that the reference is to slaves, female as well as male, becoming members of the sect. The "covenant of Abraham" is the covenant made with the ancestor of the Jews, not the new covenant made in the land of Damascus.

It may also be questioned whether it would have been so difficult to speak of making a new covenant in the land of Damascus if there had not already been a tradition linking Abraham with the city. The Qumran sect sought to interpret Scripture in terms of the past and the present, especially in terms of the sect's own history, and to interpret events relevant to them in terms of Scripture. The making of the new covenant seems to have been an event of major importance in the history of the sect, and to have taken place in what could be described as "the land of Damascus," however precisely the phrase may have been interpreted. If that was so, and the past event recalled what had been said by Amos, it may be doubted whether the fact that Amos 5:27 speaks of the region beyond Damascus as a place of ex-ile would have deterred them from alluding to it, even without a tradition about Abraham and the city.

Further Comments on
Abraham's Connection with Syria

The discussion above focuses attention chiefly on the links alleged by Garbini between Abraham and Damascus in tradition before the Hellenis-tic period, and his arguments have been questioned. There is, however, something further to be said about Abraham's connections with Syria. The MT of Genesis states that Abraham was born in Ur of the Chaldeans, and, as was noted above, Garbini believes that the theory of a Babylonian origin goes back to the time of Nabonidus in the 6th century. He sees in some Jewish texts of the Hellenistic period a polemic against the ideas of Jews in Egypt where, in his opinion, many believed that the Jewish people had originated in Egypt, though the polemic also played down Abraham's links with Syria in general, and Damascus in particular.

Gen 11:28, 31, and 15:7 speak of Ur of the Chaldeans as the place from which Abraham's family came and in which he was born. This belief is found in passages ascribed to the J source by many scholars, apparently including Garbini (p. 145; Italian, p. 199). However, a number of penta-teuchal critics have argued that the references in J to Ur are secondary and are probably assimilations to the Priestly source. They suggest that Abra-ham was originally believed to have been born in Haran, in Syria.

According to the standard analysis of Genesis into sources, some of the passages relevant to the present discussion are ascribed to J, and some to P. Jews of the Hellenistic period were, of course, unacquainted with modern theories of source criticism, and for them the narrative was a unity. When Abraham wishes to find a non-Canaanite wife for his son Isaac, he sends his servant to "my country and my kinsfolk" (Gen 24:4). This appears to be a reference to the city of Abraham's brother Nahor (11:26–27; 24:10, 15, etc.), to which Abraham's servant then travels. It is said to be in Aram-naharaim (24:10). Rebekah, the daughter of Nahor's son Bethuel, agrees to go to Canaan to marry Isaac. Years later, when Rebekah's son Jacob's life is threatened by Esau, she urges him to flee to her brother Laban, whose home is said to be in Haran (27:43; see also 28:10 and 29:4), which is said (by P) to be in Paddan-aram (28:2, 5–7; see also 25:20). Laban is said to be an Aramean (25:20; 28:5; 31:20, 24), which is rendered in the LXX as "Syr-ian." Thus (even in P) Nahor's family lives in Syria, even though Nahor did not accompany Terah, Abraham, and Lot to Haran (11:26–31), and noth-ing is said about a later journey.

Although Abraham is said in the MT to have been born in Ur of the Chaldeans, he thus has links with Syria. The LXX does not render Ur as a place-name, but has "the land (*chôra*) of the Chaldeans." The reason for this is not certain. Perhaps Ur as the name of a place was unknown to the translator. According to Gadd,[7] the life of the city of Ur "ended in an age of gradual but finally completed disappearance some time between the 4th century B.C. and the beginning of our era" (p. 47). In contrast, Josephus (*Ant.* 1.6.4 §151) was better informed about the name of the city, which he calls *Ourê*. Even if the LXX translator did not recognize Ur as the name of a place, the fact that it is said to be "of the Chaldeans" testifies that it was recognized to be in Babylonia. It is, therefore, surprising that in 24:4 where, in the MT, Abraham instructs his servant to go "to my country and to my kinsfolk," the LXX has "to my country, where I was born," but he goes in 24:10 to Aram-naharaim, for which the LXX here has "Mesopotamia," but in 25:20 "Syrian Mesopotamia." Moreover, in the MT of 24:7, Abraham relates how "the Lord took me from my father's house and from the land of my kinsfolk," presumably referring to the command in 12:1 after the death of Abraham's father in Haran (11:31–32). In the LXX of 24:7, however, Abraham speaks of being taken "out of my father's house and out of the land where I was born." The LXX thus implies that Abraham was born in Haran, despite the fact that it elsewhere states that he was born in the land of the Chaldeans.

The existence of this anomaly in the LXX of Genesis does not easily fit Garbini's theory that the preparation and publication of the LXX was part of an attempt to impose on the Egyptian Jews the ideology of the Judaism of Jerusalem, including the belief that Abraham was born in the Ur of the Chaldeans and the tendency to minimize the links between Abraham and Syria, especially with Damascus. Anyhow, the LXX may be part, at least, of the origin of the opinion that Abraham was born in Syria, just as the LXX of Gen 23:6 helps to explain the tradition that he was a king. Moreover, much of the MT of the story of Abraham shows signs of a probable earlier stage in which Abraham was born in Haran, before it was modified to fit the Priestly view that his place of birth was Ur of the Chaldeans. Further, one is tempted to wonder whether the LXX translators, and perhaps even some of the writers of the Hebrew text, were somewhat uncertain about the geography of the region. Of course, they did not have access to anything like a modern biblical atlas; they were perhaps also not as well informed about the subject as some gentile writers of the period.

---

7. C. J. Gadd, "Ur," in *Archaeology and Old Testament Study* (ed. D. W. Thomas; Oxford: Clarendon, 1967) 87–101.

Conclusion

First, Apollonius Molon and Pompeius Trogus lived after the publication of the LXX Pentateuch, and their accounts of the early history of the ancestors of the Jews bear a general resemblance to the narrative in Genesis. However, the differences from Genesis are such that neither author is likely to have used the LXX of these books. The traditions based on Genesis have reached them through intermediaries, some but not all of whom were Jewish.

Second, belief that Abraham was a king can perhaps be traced back to the LXX of Gen 23:6; and Pompeius Trogus may have read back into the time of Abraham the names of later kings of Damascus, which are found in the books of Kings.

Third, the account of events by Nicolaus of Damascus is closer to that of Genesis, which he may well have read, and he records that Abraham came to Damascus from the east, not that he was born in Damascus. The statement that he was king of Damascus may, like that of Trogus, be dependent on the LXX of Gen 23:6. His reference to "Abram's abode" in or near Damascus is probably derived from Jews who lived there, and it is a plausible hypothesis that it was among them that the belief arose that Abraham had lived there, and that he was king of Damascus.

Fourth, although Garbini's arguments for an earlier link in the Hebrew Bible between Abraham and Syria and Damascus are not convincing, there is an older connection between Abraham and Haran in Syria. It is likely that the J document originally located Abraham's place of birth in Haran, but the text was modified to fit the Priestly writer's belief that he was born in Ur of the Chaldeans. Evidence remains in the MT that associates Abraham closely with Haran. The LXX goes farther and states that Haran was the place of Abraham's birth. This disagreement between the Hebrew text of Genesis and the LXX counts against Garbini's theory that the LXX of the Pentateuch was intended, as part of an attempt to bring Egyptian Judaism into line with that of Jerusalem, to promote the belief that Abraham was born in Ur of the Chaldeans.

It is a pleasure to join with other scholars in honoring my friend Richard Friedman, whose scholarly good judgement has contributed much to the study of the Pentateuch, as also of other parts of the Hebrew Bible.

Rethinking Sectarian Judaism:
The Centrality of the Priesthood in the
Second Temple Period

RISA LEVITT KOHN and REBECCA MOORE
San Diego State University

Pick up most traditional discussions of Second Temple Judaism and you are likely to come across a chapter called "The Diverse World of First-Century Judaisms,"[1] or "Palestinian Judaism in the Time of Jesus,"[2] or "Sectarianism in the Second Commonwealth."[3] The prevailing image is that of a world populated by competing theologies and feuding parties. The Sadducees, we are told, control the temple and the priesthood. The Pharisees, led by lay leaders, represent the "common people." The Essenes are eccentric renegades who live in relative seclusion, distancing themselves philosophically and geographically from the other groups. The Zealots are wild-eyed bomb-throwers, ready to install the first messiah who comes along. One gets the impression that if we could walk down the streets of 1st-century Jerusalem, we might easily identify and differentiate card-carrying Pharisees from Sadducees or spot visible distinctions between Essenes and Zealots.

Even though we find these rather neat and tidy labels convenient for describing what seems to be going on in 1st-century Judea, we also know they are historically anachronistic. In addition, the reality was clearly more complicated than traditional scholarly paradigms suggest. In fact, the situation may be better understood as one in which a variety of closely related groups view themselves as maintaining and protecting the tradition of biblical Israel.

---

1. Stephen L. Harris, *The New Testament: A Student's Introduction* (5th ed.; New York: McGraw Hill, 2006) 81.

2. Paula Fredriksen, *From Jesus to Christ: The Origins of the New Testament Images of Jesus* (2nd ed.; New Haven, CT: Yale University Press, 2000) 86.

3. Lawrence H. Schiffman, *From Text to Tradition: A History of Second Temple and Rabbinic Judaism* (Hoboken, NJ: Ktav, 1991) 98.

195

Postexilic Israel and
Communities of Interpretation

The successors of ancient Israel use the Hebrew Bible—Torah, the Prophets, and some Writings, such as the Psalms—as their guide to the true Israel. In essence, they are interpreting scripture, resulting in varied viewpoints and opinions that become manifest in a number of theological worldviews and behaviors. Within a single entity identifying itself as "Israel," we find a number of interpretive communities, each attempting to uphold traditions perceived as the embodiment of historical Israel in the face of changing historical circumstances.[4]

In this paper, we will first examine the sources generally used to identify the various forms of Judaism in the Second Temple period—including the accounts by Josephus, New Testament texts, and rabbinic literature—and consider how scholars usually describe Jewish "sects" of this period. We will then offer as an alternative paradigm for understanding Judaic religion the concepts of Torah, priesthood, and Temple, which all groups considered central to their life and practice. Three case studies in the interpretation of the priesthood—the Qumran community, the Pharisees, and the Jesus Movement—show the importance of priesthood within the lives and customs of these groups. What we find are competing communities of Torah interpretation that redefine or re-work the concept of the priesthood in ways that provide a sense of group identity on the one hand, but that do not necessarily make them "sectarian" on the other. Although the understanding of self as priest—or the community as a priesthood—helps to draw boundaries, with the exception of Qumran (and even that is questionable), these new "priests" maintained their own identity as part of their distinctive group but did not exclude themselves from the rest of Israel.

Earliest Sources Describing Sectarian Judaism

Josephus

The traditional sectarian picture is drawn from a number of texts written in the 1st through 6th centuries C.E. These include the writings of Josephus, the New Testament, and rabbinic literature.

Josephus, a Jewish military and diplomatic leader, provides the earliest account of the so-called Judean groups, which he calls "philosophies." Writing in Greek for a Roman audience, Josephus is both interpreter and apologist for the customs of the Judeans. In his accounts of the history of

---

4. On the importance of the Torah as both an interpretive tool and cultural symbol in the Second Temple period, see C. A. Newsom, *The Self as Symbolic Space: Constructing Identity and Community at Qumran* (Leiden: Brill, 2004) 23–25.

the Judeans—*Jewish Antiquities* (or perhaps more accurately, *Archaeology of the Judeans*)[5] and *The Jewish [Judean] War*—Josephus describes four philosophies. These four Judean groups have dominated scholarly evaluations of 1st-century Judaic religion since the Enlightenment.

"Let me describe the various schools of thought among the Judeans" (*Ant.* 18:1; *J.W.* 2:117). Josephus goes on to discuss the Pharisees, the Sadducees, the Essenes, and, perhaps, the Zealots. He says that the Pharisees,

> simplify their standard of living, making no concession to luxury. They follow the guidance of that which their doctrine has selected and transmitted as good, attaching the chief importance to the observance of those commandments which it has seen fit to dictate to them. . . . Because of these views they are, as a matter of fact, extremely influential among the townsfolk, and all prayers and sacred rites of divine worship are performed according to their exposition. (*Ant.* 18:12–15)

He also notes that the Pharisees believe that souls survive death, and are rewarded or punished based on moral conduct.

The Sadducees, in contrast, "hold that the soul perishes along with the body" (*Ant.* 18:16). In addition, the Sadducees "own no observance of any sort apart from the [written] laws" (*Ant.* 18:16). Josephus is rather critical of the Sadducees, saying they are somewhat argumentative and disputatious, although they are also "men of the highest standing" (*Ant.* 18:17). Elsewhere he notes that the Sadducees had the confidence of the wealthy alone, and no following among the populace (*Ant.* 13:297). As a result, they had to submit to the teachings of the Pharisees, "since otherwise the masses would not tolerate them" (*Ant.* 18:18). According to Josephus, the key theological conflict between the Pharisees and Sadducees is that the Pharisees

> had passed on to the people certain regulations handed down by former generations and not recorded in the Laws of Moses, for which reason they are rejected by the Sadducaean group, who hold that only those regulations should be considered valid which were written down (in Scripture), and that those which had been handed down by former generations need not be observed. (*Ant.* 13.197)

The third "philosophy" Josephus describes is that of the Essenes, who like the Pharisees believe in the immortality of the soul. Because they use a different purification ritual, they are barred from the temple sanctuary. They hold property in common, says Josephus, and live by themselves,

---

5. The Greek title is *'Ioudaike Archaiologia*. H. St. J. Thackeray, translator of the Loeb edition of Josephus, *Jewish Antiquities*, vol. 1 (Cambridge: Harvard University Press, 1961) states that *archaiologia* meant 'archaeology', in the sense of a history of the race, noting that Josephus undoubtedly borrowed his title from Dionysius of Halicarnassus, *Roman Antiquities* 9. *Archaiologia* is usually translated *Antiquities*.

without wives or slaves, establishing communities in cities and towns throughout the country. He discusses their form of community organization, their charitable endeavors, and—with particular emphasis—their piety, noting that "they are stricter than all Jews in abstaining from work on the seventh day," not even defecating on the Sabbath (*J.W.* 2.148).

Josephus does not mention Zealots by name when he describes the fourth philosophy, but scholars assume that this is the group he means. The Zealots agree with the opinions of Pharisees, "except that they have a passion for liberty that is almost unconquerable, since they are convinced that God alone is their leader and master" (*Ant.* 18.23). Subsequent scholars have identified this group as a revolutionary body that emerged shortly before the First Jewish War. Fredriksen calls this group the "Insurrectionists," Judeans who "focused on liberating Jerusalem and cleansing the Temple."[6]

New Testament Sectarians

The New Testament mentions Sadducees, Pharisees, and Zealots as well, and also mentions Samaritans, scribes, and elders, but it does not say anything about Essenes by name. We need to specify which New Testament writings we mean when we talk about the various groups that existed in the 1st century. For example, Paul's letters refer to Pharisees, but do not mention Sadducees, Samaritans, or Zealots. This probably reflects the fact that Paul is a Judean in Diaspora, and thus has no contact or knowledge of Sadducees and Samaritans. Furthermore, his audience consists of non-Judeans, whose interest in "Jewish philosophies" would be limited at best. Finally, Paul's letters were written before the Zealots even existed, at least according to current analyses of Judean conflict with Roman authority.[7]

The four Gospels—Matthew, Mark, Luke, and John—provide the most detail in the New Testament about 1st-century Judean groups. It is intriguing to read which groups they highlight and which they neglect. For example, one of Jesus' disciples, Simon, is identified as a Zealot (Mark 3:18 // Matt 10:4 // Luke 6:15).[8] This is the only reference to the Zealots contained in the Gospels, although during Jesus' trial there is a reference to insurrection (Mark 15:7 // Luke 23:25). The Sadducees also play a minor role, appearing only once in Mark and Luke, and not at all in John. Mark tells a story about them in regard to their lack of belief in the resurrection and their question to Jesus about a woman who dies with seven husbands

---

6. Fredriksen, *From Jesus to Christ*, 90–91.

7. See Richard A. Horsley and John S. Hanson, *Bandits, Prophets, and Messiahs: Popular Movements in the Time of Jesus* (Minneapolis: Winston, 1985).

8. James Tabor claims that "Simon the Zealot" was Jesus' younger brother, named after Judas the Galilean, the supposed founder of the Zealots, in *The Jesus Dynasty: The Hidden History of Jesus, His Royal Family, and the Birth of Christianity* (New York: Simon and Schuster, 2006) 104, 120.

(Mark 12:18 // Matt 22:23 // Luke 20:27). The inclusion of Sadducees in this pericope might have come from Josephus's discussion of Sadducean beliefs about the afterlife, since they merely serve as a framing device for Jesus' observations about resurrection.[9] In other words, the Sadducees, like the Zealots, play a minimal role in the Gospels.[10] Scholars explain this by stating that the Sadducees vanished with the destruction of the Temple in 70 C.E., and the Gospels—written at the end of the 1st century C.E.—reflect this loss.

The Gospels refer to the Pharisees (88 times) more than any other group—with the exception of priests (93 times)—and they depict Jesus both in conflict with them, and in conversation with them.[11] The Pharisees seem to be concerned with following written Torah and the traditions of the elders. They ask Jesus why his disciples violate the Sabbath by plucking some grain to eat and why they fail to wash their hands before eating. They get upset when Jesus heals a man on the Sabbath. The disciples ask Jesus why the Pharisees fast but they do not. The Pharisees also practice tithing and are committed to supporting the temple. In fact, priests and Pharisees are mentioned together seven times, which is seven times more than priests and Sadducees.

Another group the Gospels mention (62 times) is the scribes—the usual translation of *grammateis*—or teachers of the law (NIV). These people are not Pharisees; they are mentioned separately, although they seem to accompany both Pharisees and priests. "The scribes presented in the Synoptic Gospels are best understood as bureaucrats and experts on Jewish life," according to Saldarini. Although they may have acted as low-level administrators or copyists in the Galilee, they seemed to be associates of priests, "both in judicial proceeding and enforcement of Jewish custom and law, and ongoing business in the Sanhedrin."[12]

The last group the Gospels mention are the Samaritans. This is an unpopular group among the Judeans, or Jews, and even Jesus and his disciples disdain them. For example, Jesus tells his disciples not to go to any towns with Samaritans in them (Matt 10:5). But Jesus also tells the parable of the kindly Samaritan who took care of a mugging victim (Luke 10:30–27), and in John's Gospel, Jesus' first non-Judean believer is a Samaritan woman of ill repute who persuades her Samaritan community that Jesus is a prophet

---

9. Robert W. Funk et al., eds., *The Five Gospels: The Search for the Authentic Words of Jesus* (New York: Macmillan, 1993) 103.

10. Matthew pairs the appearance of Sadducees with Pharisees seven times.

11. Matthew exaggerates the role of the Pharisees, turning Markan scribes into Matthean Pharisees (or scribes *and* Pharisees) 4 times (Mark 2:16 // Matt 9:11; Mark 3:22 // Matt 12:24, 9:34; Mark 12:35 // Matt 22:45; Mark 12:38 // Matt 23:1, scribes *and* Pharisees).

12. Anthony J. Saldarini, "Scribes," *ABD* 5:1015.

(John 4). "Josephus was ambivalent toward them," writes Ferguson, "sometimes treating them as a Jewish sect but at other times regarding them as non-Jews."[13]

Rabbinic Literature on the Sectarians

A final source to consider when attempting to identify different Judaic groups in the 1st century is rabbinic literature. Like the New Testament, rabbinic texts such as the Mishna (200 C.E.) and the Talmuds (5th and 6th centuries) are compiled from oral traditions handed down over time. The rabbinic material contains stories about sages from the 1st century such as Hillel and Shammai, and also cites legal decisions attributed to these teachers. As with the writings of Josephus and the New Testament, stories of 1st-century rabbinic sages and the "laws" ascribed to them are used in rabbinic writings to put forward a specific religious point of view not necessarily in accord with historical reality.

There are several passages where these writings may directly allude to the Pharisees and Sadducees by name, but even here no specific theologies or interpretive strategies are outlined. In addition, there were those "on the second lowest rung" of the social ladder, according to Stemberger, who separated themselves from the *am ha-aretz* but were not actually Pharisees. "In this context . . . we are not necessarily dealing with Pharisees, but just with people who keep themselves separate (*porsin*) from less observant people."[14]

The Mishna puts *perushim* and *saddukim* together in one text where at least some scholars believe we are dealing with the Pharisees and the Sadducees.[15] M. *Yad.* 4:6–8 cites several disputes between *perushim* and *saddukim* relating primarily to ritual purity—corpse uncleanness and water flowing from a burial ground—and to an issue of civil law (the responsibility one has when an injury is caused by one's cattle). In *m. Parah* 3:7–8, the *perushim* want greater purity of the priest for the rite of the red heifer than the official ritual requires, and thus appear in conflict with the *saddukim*. In general, the Mishna discusses *perushim* more often than *saddukim*, and frequently shows the superiority of the *perushim* position: in other words,

---

13. Everett Ferguson, *Backgrounds of Early Christianity* (3rd ed.; Grand Rapids, MI: Eerdmans, 2003) 534.

14. Günter Stemberger, *Jewish Contemporaries of Jesus: Pharisees, Sadducees, Essenes* (trans. Allan W. Mahnke; Minneapolis: Fortress, 1995) 41.

15. Several scholars posit that the occurrence of these two groups together in a given text suggests reference to Pharisees and Sadducees. See for example, E. Rivkin, *A Hidden Revolution* (Nashville: Abingdon, 1978) 125ff.; and J. Lightstone, "Sadducees versus Pharisees: The Tannaitic Sources," in *Christianity, Judaism and Other Greco-Roman Cults: Studies for M. Smith* (ed. J. Neusner; Leiden: Brill, 1975); also Stemberger, *Jewish Contemporaries of Jesus*, 40.

the texts are polemical rather than historical in nature. With that said, however, the *perushim* appear infrequently in the Mishna, while the *saddukim* are even less visible.[16]

Second Temple "Judaisms"?

Based on the sources outlined above and others, scholars usually tell the story of Second Temple "Judaisms" as one of competing "sects" operating within an oppressive environment dominated by Hellenistic culture. The Sadducees are the upper class of society, linked directly with the priesthood and the office of High Priest at the temple in Jerusalem. The Pharisees represent the "masses" and the "middle class" and are the "democratizers" of priestly practice who extend traditionally priestly rites to nonpriests. The Essenes are a radical monastic group who break from the establishment entirely and live in total seclusion practicing their own idiosyncratic form of Judaism. Most of the other groups—such as Judeans in Diaspora, Samaritans, and Egyptians—are neglected as relatively minor characters in the story. The overarching view that one receives from this analysis is a society that is highly segmented and one that—with the exception of the Sadducees—is reacting to the corruption and Hellenization of the priesthood.

What this account fails to consider is the importance of the Torah as a unifying, cultural symbol of central social and political significance.[17] In effect, the Torah is all that tangibly remains of Israel after the Exile of 587 B.C.E. It was during the early Exile that the text is edited, redacted, promulgated, and read in a variety of public settings. Even once the temple is rebuilt, the text remains the guide for how to live as Israel, both inside and outside of Judea.

Because the Torah serves as the springboard from which all daily life and practice is determined, all of the "sects" in question would have accepted several basic principles vis-à-vis temple and priesthood. The first is that God appointed a hereditary priesthood to act as the conduit for communicating the will of God by interpreting God's law. Second, priests, via the practice of sacrifice, mediate that communication with God. Third, the Sabbath and festivals mark significant experiences in the community's relationship with God. They are set apart as times when special behavior was required. In addition, the Torah concept of God's dwelling among the Israelites requires that the environment be in constant worthiness of his holy presence. As a result, purity is a concern as Israel strives to continue to live as a holy people (Lev 19:1–2).

---

16. Stemberger, *Jewish Contemporaries of Jesus*, 50.
17. Newsom, *The Self as Symbolic Space*, 25.

The Torah is the primary—and at times, the only—remaining identity marker for the Israelites and the nation of Israel after the Exile. As a result, the principles listed above take on paramount importance in the life of different communities. Though the Torah discusses each of these issues in some detail, it provided few specifics with respect to behavior. It set out the fundamental principles, but implementation is left to interpretation. For example, the commandment to keep the Sabbath holy leaves much room for determining the nature and extent of that holiness. Before the Exile, there is little mentioned with respect to Sabbath observance, although Jeremiah prohibits carrying pots outside of one's house (17:21–24). After the Exile, however, there is great discussion and debate about proper observance. Nehemiah forbids buying and selling on the Sabbath (13:15–22), and 1 Maccabees discusses whether or not the army should fight on the Sabbath (2:29–42). Josephus also raises the question of fighting on the Sabbath (*J.W.* 1:145–47).

Many scholars posit a shift at this point in time (between Ezra in the mid-5th century B.C.E. to the Maccabean Revolt of 167 B.C.E.) from priestly to lay authority. A popular and influential group of non-priestly teachers supposedly move away from an emphasis on priestly religion and lead a democratization of Judaism.[18] This lay opposition to an unpopular priesthood is often correlated with a contrast between the autonomous synagogue and the hierarchical temple.

Extant Second Temple sources, however, provide little evidence to substantiate this vision. There is no textual support from this period to document a major shift of power and authority from priestly to lay hands. Rather, to the extent that any shifts take place, they occur between competing priestly groups or between increasingly specialized subgroups.[19] We are calling these subgroups—previously identified as sects—communities of interpretation.

Instead, what appears to have existed in the period of so-called Second Temple "Judaisms" is a central priesthood, located in the temple that interacts and responds to the various explanations of Torah that these different interpretive communities present. We are arguing against the traditional

---

18. For example, Ferguson writes that "The Pharisees appear to have been for the most part non-priests," 516. See also Shaye D. Cohen, *From the Maccabees to the Mishna* (Philadelphia: Westminster, 1987) 160–61. See additional notations and comments in S. Fraade, "'They Shall Teach Your Statutes to Jacob': Priests, Scribes and Sages in Second Temple Times," unpublished essay; see also S. Fraade, *From Tradition to Commentary: Torah and Its Interpretation in the Midrash Sifre to Deuteronomy* (Albany, NY: State University of New York Press, 1991) 72–73. The authors would especially like to thank Dr. Fraade for generously sharing his work with us.

19. Fraade, "Priests, Scribes and Sages in Second Temple Times"; see also *From Tradition to Commentary*, 73.

understanding of a shift in authority from the priesthood (Sadducees) to the laity (Pharisees) and to the ascetics (Essenes). On the contrary, it appears as though all three of these groups—and others as well—not only were comprised (at least in part) of priests, but also couch their so-called philosophies in priestly vocabulary and matrices. Indeed, they see themselves as operating within the priesthood as outlined in Torah and in continuity with the priesthood as depicted in the redacted Torah. As Fraade says:

> Those Second Temple groups that questioned or rejected the legitimacy or fitness of the Jerusalem Temple and its priesthood affirmed no less the principle that the descendants of Aaron and Levi were the authoritative purveyors of Israel's scriptures, their interpretation, and legal implementation. These groups to the extent that they distanced themselves from the Jerusalem Temple and its Priesthood, developed their own (from their perspective, more legitimate) priestly vision and praxis, including alternative or supplemental scriptures authenticated by their own priestly scribes and interpreters.[20]

In painting the political and theological picture of Second Temple "Judaisms," traditional scholarship emphasizes the sects themselves, highlighting their similarities and especially their differences. We contend, however, that a more accurate starting point for understanding the variety of Judaic religions is to focus on the temple and the priesthood. This lens allows us to see a number of competing interpretive communities as claimants to the same heritage. We can follow their shifting allegiances and alliances, which strengthens our perception that they all remain within the boundaries of what they believed to be biblical Israel, namely, their antecedents in Torah.

We begin our discussion by examining what our sources say, both about priests, the central figures of political and cultural authority, and about the Temple, their central institution in the wake of the Exile and the return.

Torah, Temple, and Priesthood

The primary roles of the priests in preexilic times are to communicate the will of God to the people and impart the laws and associated rituals to the people. Both activities are affiliated with the verb *torah* (instruct/instruction).

While the everyday tasks of officiating at sacrifices and discerning God's will are temporarily suspended during the Exile, there is little evidence to suggest that the priesthood continued as an empty vessel, defined solely through inherited identity. On the contrary, it is clear that at least some priests directed their energy toward compilation of, interpretation of, and

---

20. Fraade, "Priests, Scribes and Sages in Second Temple Times," pp. 4–6.

teaching of various texts. The book of Ezekiel (written by a priest, or priests more likely, in Exile) and the book of Ezra (which depicts a priest who brings the "Torah of Moses" back to Jerusalem) suggest that some priests were quite active in Babylon.[21]

Moreover, there is evidence that the priesthood continues to exist back home. Priests continued to conduct sacrifices at the ruins of the Jerusalem Temple, as well as throughout the land. Samaritans had developed their own temple and cult, possibly during the reign of Alexander the Great. Recent archaeological evidence, which identified the outlines of a sanctuary atop Mt. Gerizim substantially different from that of Jerusalem, actually pushes the date of construction into the Persian period.

In addition, priests and temples claiming ties to Israelite religion also exist in Diaspora, most notably in Egypt. The evidence from Elephantine, for example, indicates a sacrificial system that existed until the destruction of the Egyptian temple by the Persians in 410 B.C.E. Since Elephantine Judeans had written to the High Priest in Jerusalem, this suggests that they did not view themselves in opposition to the Jerusalem Temple. A second temple built in Leontopolis in Lower Egypt, however, apparently was constructed in explicit competition with the Jerusalem Temple. Confusing documentary evidence comes from Josephus, and while there is scholarly debate over this temple's origins, there is agreement that the temple was erected sometime between 163 and 145 B.C.E. as part of the political conflict between the Ptolemy and Seleucid empires. It was personal political ambition, though, rather than a concern about priestly purity or calendrical correctness, that led to its construction.

The text of Torah gives legitimacy to the priesthood, both by the heavenly institution of the office, and by virtue of the ability of the priests to correctly divine God's wishes. The absence of a central political lay leader, in addition to the lack of political independence, heightens the importance of the temple and its managers, which in turn increases the significance of Torah as the cultural symbol of Israel. In short, the Torah reinforces the priesthood, and the priesthood reinforces the Torah. Public reading of Torah buttresses national sentiment for a people lacking political means of identity. In the absence of a king, an army, or control over their land, the Torah serves as the ideological basis for national survival and identity. In other words, the Torah is a constitution, a history, and a source of authority.[22] Those who interpreted Torah had tremendous power derived from this interpretive authority.

---

21. There remains a rather large group of scholars who attribute the composition of the Priestly source as whole to the period of the Exile.

22. Newsom, *The Self as Symbolic Space*, 26.

The history of the priesthood from the return from exile in the late 6th century B.C.E. through the end of 1st century C.E. is fraught with conflict over maintenance of the temple apparatus and control of Torah interpretation. The books of the Maccabees detail some of this discord; Josephus relates conflicts; and the New Testament reports other disagreements. 1 Maccabees, for instance, describes the violent opposition to a Hellenized and corrupt priesthood mounted by traditionalist Judeans. The Maccabean Revolt of 167–164 B.C.E. resulted in a change of administration in the priesthood. Josephus recounts these events, as well as the slaughter of various parties who fell out of favor with ruling authorities and priests. Jesus, of course, is said to have faced priests at his trial, while his followers encountered the anger of priests in the New Testament book of Acts. One named Stephen, brought up before the council, is questioned by the High Priest. When Stephen retells the story of Israel (including Abraham, Moses, Aaron, and David in his account), the assembly is so outraged that they stone him (Acts 7). But elsewhere Acts says that "the word of God increased; and the number of the disciples multiplied greatly in Jerusalem, and a great many of the priests were obedient to the faith" (Acts 6:7). In other words, textual evidence from three rather different types of sources documents the ongoing importance of the priesthood.

Even before the Exile it is clear that the priest served as the interpreter of "Torah" in the sense of Torah as God's will and instruction.[23] For example, Lev 10:11 shows God commanding Aaron to "teach the people of Israel all the statutes which the Lord has spoken to them by Moses." Deuteronomy gives the "Levitical priests" extensive power to judge cases of homicide, assault, and legal rights, saying that the Israelites should do what the priests say, "and you shall be careful to do according to all that they direct you; according to the instructions which they give you, and according to the decision which they pronounce to you, you shall do" (Deut 17:8–11). In fact, the person who does not obey the priest shall die! Regarding the Levites (or more accurately, this was said of Levi): "They shall teach Jacob thy ordinances and Israel thy law," in addition to burning incense and making whole burnt offerings to the Lord (Deut 33:10).

After the Exile, we find allusions to the interpretive function of priests appearing in Josephus, Philo, and of course the Mishnah.[24] Josephus says that it is the priests, and especially the chief priest, who are entrusted with the administration of Israel's divinely ordained constitution, not just in the area of worship, but equally in matters of law and the training of the entire community. Philo similarly understands the priests, seeing their

---

23. Ibid., 29.
24. See Fraade, *From Tradition to Commentary*, chap. 3 n. 20.

consecration to God's service as providing both a bridge and a buffer between the divine and human realms. In the Mishna, the priests are the ones who bestow blessings over the congregation in the synagogue and who are given the honor of the first *aliyah* to the Torah.[25]

Although there is plenty of evidence to suggest the presence of conflicting ideas about who should run the temple and how it should be done, there is little evidence to suggest that any Second Temple Judaic groups would deny that the descendants of Aaron and Levi were the legitimate teachers and implementers of Torah in Israel. To the extent that they distance themselves geographically or theologically from the temple, these groups cultivate their own priestly visions and programs.

Qumran

The continued importance and prominence of the priesthood outside the realm of the Jerusalem Temple is clearly evident in the Dead Sea Scrolls. Priesthood at Qumran is a matter of descent. It is not understood metaphorically but in the very concrete sense of belonging to the "seed of Aaron."[26] The sectarian writings found at Qumran outline a community clearly organized with the Zadokite priests at the center.[27] The Levites appear in the scrolls in a manner similar to their depiction in the Torah: they serve as judges, officers, and leaders of the congregation. They are the mediators in a community that is comprised of both priests and lay people.[28] Similarly, the traditional Israelite distinction between priests, Levites, and laity is mentioned throughout the scrolls.

At the same time, it is clear that the Qumran community has at least temporarily removed itself from the temple and cult in Jerusalem. As a consequence, the "priests" at Qumran do not function as priests in quite the same way as their contemporaries at the temple. Most significantly, they do not officiate at or make sacrificial offerings, and as a result, they do

---

25. See *m. Ber.* 5:4; *m. Meg.* 4:5, 6, 7; *m. Soṭah* 7:6; *m. Tamid* 7:2; *m. Giṭ.* 5:8. Fraade, "Priests, Scribes and Sages in Second Temple Times."

26. F. García Martínez, "Priestly Functions in a Community without Temple," in *Gemeinde ohne Tempel/Community without Temple* (Tübingen: Mohr Siebeck, 1999) 303.

27. Fraade likens this organization to the model of the traveling wilderness camp "with its tabernacle and priests at the center and its rites for ensuring the purity of those who wished to dwell within, in proximity to the divine presence," in "Priests, Scribes, and Sages." See also L. Schiffman, *Reclaiming the Dead Sea Scrolls: The History of Judaism, the Background of Christianity, the Lost Library of Qumran* (Philadelphia: Jewish Publication Society, 1994) 113–14; "Community without Temple: The Qumran Community's Withdrawal from the Jerusalem Temple," in *Gemeinde ohne Tempel/Community without Temple,* 267–68.

28. "The sons of Levi shall serve each according to his position under the authority of the sons of Aaron to lead the whole congregation in and out. . . . The Levites shall serve as judges and officers according to the numbers of all their hosts under the authority of Zadok the priest" (1QSa 1:22–25).

not receive their share from such offerings.[29] They do, however, preside over the meals, blessing the bread and wine, observing a ritual that seems to parallel or replicate the sacrificial system in Jerusalem.[30]

The priests at Qumran also appear to assume, or rather resume, several important functions attributed to the Israelite priesthood.[31] Specifically, they teach, providing instruction in the laws of Torah (Deut 33:8–10). They make oracular pronouncements based on their use of the *urim* and *thumim*. They are also involved in the judicial process. For example, several texts mention the casting of lots in connection with priestly verdicts:[32]

> Only the sons of Aaron will have authority in the matter of judgment and of goods, and by their authority will come out the lot for all decisions regarding the men of the community and the goods of the men of holiness who walk in perfection. (1QS 9:7)

In addition, there are numerous references to the priestly teaching of Torah. The Teacher of Righteousness is a priest with the function of interpreting Torah.[33] Similarly, the Zadokites are assigned to:

> Swear with a binding oath to revert to the law of Moses, according to all that he commanded, with all [his] heart and all [his] soul, in compliance with all that has been revealed of it to the sons of Zadok, the priests who keep the covenant and interpret his will. (1QS 5:8–9)

They also practice the priestly function of invoking the blessings of God on the faithful, and so in the Community Rule it states, "And the priests will bless all the men of God's lot . . . And the Levites shall curse all the men of the lot of Belial" (1QS 2:1).[34]

In short, though not engaged in the sacrificial cult, the priests at Qumran continue to function as a clearly identifiable group with tasks specific to their hereditary positions. As such, they are set apart from the rest of the community at Qumran in terms of the authority they wield and the tasks they perform. At the same time, as we will see below, their so-called obsession with purity and other priestly concerns is not unique to their community. Certainly it is not markedly different from the concerns shared with priests at the temple in Jerusalem, though specific practices are distinct. Moreover, they share the same interests as the Pharisees and those in the Jesus Movement.

---

29. García Martínez, *Gemeinde ohne Tempel/Community without Temple*, 304.

30. "And when they prepare the table to dine or the new wine for drinking, the priest shall stretch out his hand as the first to bless the first fruits of the bread and the new wine" (1QS 6:4–5).

31. García Martínez, *Gemeinde ohne Tempel/Community without Temple*, 305.

32. Ibid., 308 citing 4QpIsa[d], and 1QS 6:16, 18–19, 21; 9:7.

33. Ibid., 309–10. See 1QpHab 2:2–3; 8–9; 7:5–6.

34. Ibid., 313–14.

The Pharisees

Notwithstanding the many difficulties we encounter in reconstructing their history and beliefs, the Pharisees appear at first glance to break away from the priestly model. They are most often described as the middle class, lay intelligentsia in opposition to the priests in Jerusalem. But there were Pharisaic priests. It is even possible that Pharisaic control of the priesthood during the Hasmonean period forced a group of Sadducean priests to withdraw from Jerusalem and found the community at Qumran.[35] The Pharisees actually influence and control the priesthood in key moments prior to the end of the 1st century C.E.

Josephus describes a few of these moments. For example, the Pharisees are extremely popular with John Hyrcanus (reigned 134–104 B.C.E.), enjoying feasts and festivals with him. When he asks them if they noticed him doing anything wrong, all the Pharisees praise him but one, who asks Hyrcanus to give up the high priesthood and simply be the political leader of the nation (*Ant.* 13.288–98). According to Josephus, this comment so enraged Hyrcanus that he joined the party of the Sadduceans. Yet Alexander Janneus, grandson of John Hyrcanus, reputedly begs his wife Alexandra on his deathbed to

> yield a certain amount of power to the Pharisees, for if they praised her in return for this sign of regard, they would dispose the nation favourably toward her. These men, he assured her, had so much influence with their fellow-Jews that they could injure those whom they hated and help those to whom they were friendly. (*Ant.* 13.400–408)

Alexandra becomes queen (reigned 76–67 B.C.E.) and follows Alexander's advice, permitting the Pharisees to do whatever they like and commanding the Judeans to obey them. "And so," Josephus concludes, "while she had the title of sovereign, the Pharisees had the power" (*Ant.* 13.409). They exercise that power by freeing prisoners, recalling exiles, and even urging the queen to take revenge for the deaths of Judeans killed by her husband. "In a word, [they] in no way differed from absolute rulers."

The Gospels also link Pharisees with the Jerusalem power structure, frequently showing the Pharisees and priests, or high priests, in close association. John's Gospel connects the Pharisees and chief priests several times:

> Then the temple police went back to the chief priests and Pharisees, who asked them, "Why did you not arrest him?" (John 7:32)

> The chief priests and the Pharisees called a meeting of the council, and said, "What are we to do? This man is performing many signs." (John 11:47)

---

35. Schiffman, "The Qumran Community's Withdrawal from the Jerusalem Temple," 268.

Now the chief priests and the Pharisees had given orders that anyone who knew where Jesus was should let them know so that they might arrest him. (John 11:47)

So Judas brought a detachment of soldiers together with police from the chief priests and the Pharisees, and they came there with lanterns and torches and weapons. (John 18:3)

While New Testament scholars frequently dismiss the historicity of the Gospels, in light of Josephus's earlier comments, it seems fair to assume that the Pharisees were a powerful group, closely aligned with the priesthood, if not always the priests themselves.

Although extant Second Temple sources for the Pharisees are all rather biased and difficult to reconcile with one another, it is still evident that the Pharisees share a number of priestly concerns with the community at Qumran. Both groups stress the importance of purity and observe purity practices in the most scrupulous and profound manner as the chief means of achieving holiness. The fact that they are consumed with the issues of purity and ritual (for example, Sabbath observance, tithes, food, and washing) also likens them to the priests of the temple and the preexilic priesthood. Their interests fall entirely in line with priestly concerns in general.

What differentiates the Pharisees from the temple priests on the one hand, and the priests at Qumran on the other, is that they extend priestly practices beyond the boundaries of the temple without entirely removing themselves from either the temple or the community.[36] They achieve this middle ground by legitimizing their practices and beliefs as coming from an authoritative body of teaching that exists in addition to the written Torah, namely, the "traditions of the elders." In place of genealogical ancestry, they claim an ancestral tradition that, in their minds, is equally authoritative, equally binding, and equally old, but not directly tied to the "seed of Aaron." The rabbis eventually trace these traditions back to Moses, but that does not occur until the mid-3rd century C.E.[37]

The Pharisaic extension of the boundaries of purity beyond the temple, along with their allegiance to extra-Torah tradition earns them the reputation in traditional scholarship as being champions of the right to holiness and extending it to "all Jews equally."[38] In other words, some scholars believe that the Pharisaic program was aimed at making everyone a

---

36. While it is true that some Essene communities lived within and among cities and their inhabitants, they lived communally in a way that differed markedly from that of the Pharisees.

37. This occurs in the so-called "Chain of Tradition" in *m. ʾAbot* 1:1, which scholars generally date to the mid-3rd century.

38. Jacob Neusner, "Judaism in a Time of Crises," *Judaism* 21/3 (1972) 322. See also Cohen, *From the Maccabees to the Mishna*, 218.

"priest."[39] There is, however, no evidence that this was their intent, nor that it even occurred.

> Rather it makes more sense to assume that the Pharisees, like the Qumran sectaries, undertook these supererogatory purity practices in order to distinguish themselves from, and to elevate themselves above, the rest of Israel, and to define for themselves a status approaching, but not equaling, that of priests.[40]

The Pharisees cannot break away from the priesthood because they are committed to Torah. However, by behaving more piously (in their opinion) than the temple priesthood and by justifying this behavior as "ancient," they establish for themselves a liminal position between the temple and Qumran, that is, between two other competing groups of priests. Although traditionally the Pharisees have been viewed as the lay leaders of Second Temple Judaism, and as departing from the confines of traditional Israelite priestly religion, this is a gross exaggeration of what appears to have been the case. They cannot be a part of Israel without accepting the precepts of the Torah, which included the priesthood and all of the ritual and practices attached to it. But they can add the "traditions of the elders" to the Israelite people and thereby rationalize their priestly actions as entirely logical and, moreover, absolutely requisite in order to be faithful to Torah.

The Jesus Movement

Although patristic writers and their successors downplay the significance of the Levitical priesthood—focusing instead on the mysterious priest-king Melchizedek (Gen 14:18–22, Ps 110:4, Hebrews 7)—it is clear that the concepts of priesthood, temple, and Torah remain important for those in the early Jesus movement.[41] We see New Testament writers transforming these concepts in two main ways: by identifying Jesus as priest and temple; and by identifying believers as priests and temple. In both instances, the traditional priesthood is abandoned in favor of a new and "improved" priesthood.

---

39. Oscar Skarsaune, *In the Shadow of the Temple: Jewish Influences on Early Christianity* (Downer's Grove, IL: InterVarsity, 2002) 120.

40. Fraade, "Priests, Scribes, and Sages." See also E. P. Sanders, "Did the Pharisees Eat Ordinary Food in Purity?" in *Jewish Law from Jesus to the Mishnah* (London: SCM, 1990) 244–45; and Daniel Schwartz, "Kingdom of Priests: A Pharisaic Slogan?" in *Studies in the Jewish Background of Christianity* (Wissenschaftliche Untersuchungen zum Neuen Testament 60; Tübingen: Mohr, 1992) 57–80.

41. Indeed, the Gospels tell us that John the Baptist and Jesus were both descended from priests, and in fact John's father was a priest of the order of Abijah, while his mother, Elizabeth, was a descendant of Aaron (Luke 1:5, 3:23–38).

In the Johannine literature, Jesus is identified as the temple of God, or the place where God "dwells."[42] John's Gospel sees Jesus' body as the locus for the "dwelling" of the Logos (John 1:14) but also as the temple itself (John 2:19–22). This interpretation corresponds to Torah, since the temple (and before it, the tabernacle) *is* the dwelling place of God in biblical Israel. In his apocalyptic vision, John of Patmos says, "I saw no temple in the city, for its temple is the Lord God the Almighty and the Lamb" (Rev 21:22). Revelation 21 alludes to John 1:14, when it says, "See, the home of God is among mortals. He will dwell with them; they will be his people, and God himself will be with them" (Rev 21:3–4).

If John sees Jesus as the temple and tabernacle, the book of Hebrews (probably written between 60 and 100 C.E.) views Jesus as the High Priest. The author of Hebrews assumes the centrality of priesthood and temple, but totally reinterprets them. The temple is subsumed by the tabernacle (chap. 9). Indeed, there is no temple at all, but rather the tent/tabernacle of meeting as described in the Torah (Exod 25:10–40, 26:31–33; Lev 24:5–9, etc.). Jesus appears as the "high priest of the good things that have come, then through the greater and more perfect tent (not made with hands, that is, not of this creation)" (9:11). This more perfect tent is the body of Jesus. We cannot assume that the author of Hebrews knew the Gospel of John, or vice versa, so the fact that both texts use the language of tent, tabernacle, and temple seems significant. The author asks if the sprinkling of bull's blood sanctifies the impure, "how much more shall the blood of Christ, who through the eternal Spirit offered himself without blemish to God, purify your conscience from dead works to serve the living God?" (9:14). So Jesus becomes the priest, the temple, and the sacrifice.

Paul redefines the temple as the community of believers who individually are the temple of God. His only explicit mention of the priesthood occurs in his final letter, which he concludes by saying that he was a minister of Christ Jesus to the Gentiles "in the priestly service of the gospel of God, so that the offering of the Gentiles may be acceptable, sanctified by the Holy Spirit" (Rom 15:16).[43] Paul ties together the idea of priesthood and sacrifice with the notion of Gentile inclusion into the Jesus movement. For him, what was important was the temple that exists in the hearts of believers. "Do you not know that you are God's temple and that God's spirit

---

42. For more details, see Risa Levitt Kohn and Rebecca Moore, "Where is God? Divine Presence in the Absence of the Temple," in *Milk and Honey: Essays on Ancient Israel and the Bible* (ed. S. Malena and D. Miano; Winona Lake, IN: Eisenbrauns, 2007) 133–53.

43. The relative absence of priests in the Pauline corpus may reflect the fact that Paul lives in Diaspora and is preaching outside of Jerusalem to a Gentile audience: priest and temple are distant, while pagan sacrifices are not.

dwells in you" he asks. "If anyone destroys God's temple, God will destroy that person. For God's temple is holy, and you are that temple" (1 Cor 3:16–17). Paul makes similar comments elsewhere in 1 Corinthians as well as in 2 Corinthians. For him, the temple exists in the heart.

It seems a short step to go from the believers being God's temple, to seeing the community of God's people as the priests of the temple, as later New Testament literature does. Exod 19:6 provides the point of departure in Torah for this interpretation: "For you shall be for me a priestly kingdom and a holy nation." 1 Peter, probably written at the end of the 1st century to a community undergoing persecution by the Romans, reminds the people that they are "a chosen race, a royal priesthood, a holy nation, God's own people" (1 Pet 2:9). Revelation—probably written around the same time during the same persecution—also describes a "kingdom of priests serving his God and Father" (Rev 1:6); and later on, "You have made them to be a kingdom and priests serving our God, and they will reign on earth" (5:10). Near the conclusion of the apocalypse the author declares, "Blessed and holy are those who share in the first resurrection. . . . They will be priests of God and of Christ, and they will reign with him a thousand years" (20:6). Revelation describes a new Jerusalem coming down out of heaven, with the home (lit., "tabernacle") of God coming down with it.

These New Testament writings indicate a development in the thought of the early church. On the one hand, the priesthood and the temple are transferred to Jesus, who has become the new central "institution" in the minds of his followers. On the other, the priesthood and the temple are transferred to the community, an institution that was growing in importance in the delay of Jesus' return. Paul argues that believers are the temple of God in order to exhort Gentiles to be holy and to reject their former paganism. The authors of 1 Peter and Revelation go further, adopting and adapting the language of Exodus to apply it to all believers: all are holy, because they are a kingdom of priests. We see, therefore, that the importance of the priesthood remains in the New Testament, although in modified forms. Indeed, eventually it is extended to the community of believers.[44]

Competing Communities of Priests

This brief survey illustrates how the concept of priesthood, clearly defined in the Torah, becomes a rather contested concept in the first centuries B.C.E. and C.E. Determining who had legitimate claims to the priesthood, however it is identified, encompasses the much larger issue of which

---

44. In this sense it is the Jesus movement and not the Pharisees who universalize the priesthood so that holiness is accessible to all.

group or groups could claim true Israelite inheritance in terms of both theological identity and interpretive Torah authority. The image of the priesthood, so clearly established and central to the preexilic Israelite cult, is still viewed as a central institution in the postexilic communities. Grossman notes, "As guardians of the sanctuary and administrators of ritual practice, the ancient Jewish priesthood served as a reminder of the covenant, a visible link between God and his community."[45] Priestly behavior and interests served as platforms for contested ideas about the leadership, authority, and maintenance of the true Israelite tradition. "'Priesthood,' as a concept," Grossman continues, "provided language for arguments about which community was maintaining the ancient covenant (or enacting a new one to replace one that had become corrupted) . . . and those who had somehow gone astray."[46]

The concept of priesthood, along with that of temple and Torah, is a useful way to understand various Judaic groups that existed roughly between 200 B.C.E. and 200 C.E., and indeed is preferable to thinking along sectarian lines. Schiffman criticizes the identification of various "Judaisms" of this period, saying that this view "ignores the vast body of commonality which united them around adherence to the law of the Torah. . . . [W]hat brought them together as a nation, civilization, and religion far outweighed the differences, which tended to be exaggerated in the sources."[47] The sources that discuss the various groups—from Josephus and the New Testament, to the Qumran literature and rabbinic writings—are all polemical texts, written with theological or tendentious purposes in mind.

What is truly remarkable is how all of these texts indicate the centrality of priesthood, Torah, and temple to self-identity and self-understanding across time, space, and social location. As the descendants of biblical Israel, claiming to be the rightful heirs to the covenantal tradition, the Qumran community, the Pharisees, the Jesus Movement, and others employ the same strategy: namely, to claim the markers of Israel for themselves.

---

45. M. Grossman, "Priesthood as Authority: Interpretive Competition in First-Century Judaism and Christianity," in *The Dead Sea Scrolls as Background to Postbiblical Judaism and Early Christianity* (ed. J. Davila; Leiden: Brill, 2000) 117.

46. Ibid., 122.

47. Schiffman, *From Text to Tradition*, 98.

Part 4

The Bible and Archaeology

In Defense of Forgery

BARUCH HALPERN

Pennsylvania State University

For many years, I have lived in a world in which archaeologists denounce people who collect antiquities and refuse to associate with those who buy or sell them. They argue that the open market in antiquities encourages looting. They argue that unprovenanced objects—relics with no documented geographical, geological, residential, or other context—are of no scientific value. They argue that without a market there would be no displacement of ancient objects from their source contexts.

This attitude rings hollow, self-righteous, and hypocritical: self-righteous, because archaeologists are the people who rarely publish what they themselves dig up. In fact, one archaeologist, in a rare publication that was supported by a grant from collectors, had the gall and the bad taste to excoriate the people who had made it possible for her to present her material. This is typical scholarly self-overestimation. A number of archaeological and other scholarly societies and journals have also announced—without always enforcing—policies against the publication of collected artifacts. This is, again, the Yeti of stupidity. The job of the scholar is to produce information about the civilizations or subcultures of the past. In no proper science does one turn two blind eyes to information pertinent to the subject. Instead, one evaluates its intrinsic implications in light of the limits of how the data was obtained.[1]

There is also a certain hypocrisy at work because the reality of archaeology almost never matches the rhetoric. In the Near East, truly scientific field excavation (in any recognizable sense) is rare. This is a laboratory in which control is lacking, partly because of dependence on hired or volunteer labor. Specialists direct excavation rather than excavating themselves. It is as though a heart surgeon, or a surgical team, invited high school students to perform the operations for which they had contracted. Sure, it can be done, but there would be a certain degree of sloppiness and, possibly,

---

1. Naomi J. Norman, "Editorial Policy on the Publication of Recently Acquired Antiquities," *American Journal of Archaeology* 109 (2005) 135–36; for documentation of the hysteria behind this view, see Matthew Bogdanos, "The Casualties of War: The Truth about the Iraq Museum," *American Journal of Archaeology* 109 (2005) 477–526.

the rate of patient attrition would rise. Although archaeologists do not usually kill people, they do murder remains, rather than sifting, sampling, storing, and being careful with them. Archaeologists have been the barber-surgeons of the last two centuries.

A second element of hypocrisy in this dismissal of "unprovenanced" objects is that in fact whole scholarly industries have been based on unprovenanced objects. The earliest Dead Sea Scrolls, for example, were bought on the open market and brought to the attention of scholars by the dealers who bought them. Later excavation, of a rather unscientific nature, brought similar materials to light at Qumran (and also at Massada). Thus, looting leads scholars to sites in the same way that wolves lead ravens to offal. Another area of scholarship based primarily on unprovenanced objects is the art history of Cycladic figurines. I am of the mind that up to three of these are genuine, but they certainly have encouraged professional exploration of the prehistory of the Aegean.

The final element of hypocrisy to mention here is the fact that some of the worst culprits in the story are members of the professional guild of archaeology. Looting is of course reprehensible; but some of the worst vandalism is committed by those who excavate whole sites without publishing them—admittedly, very recently, the profession has moved, albeit at a glacial pace, to acknowledge and in a few cases to address the problem. But the day of the archaeologist who excavates every year for twenty-five years while holding a day job teaching at a university has not yet passed into oblivion. In fact, perhaps the strongest argument against looting and for the publication of looted objects is the enthusiasm it stirs among archaeologists to go treasure-hunting and to measure themselves in terms of finds rather than by contributions to knowledge.

Originally, the issue concerning nonprovenanced artifacts revolved around the sense of archaeologists' being in control—although, again, archaeologists sometimes pass around a bit of taffy about how much control they have. The important thing is in fact that the ostensible provenance be on the record, so that it can be subject to dispute. Oddly, however, the unprovenanced artifact also is prone to be redated, placed in various imagined original locations, and so on. It is just that the archaeologists do not have a starting point with which to take issue, or a locality to which to limit the dispute about an object's stratification or location on site (which, in the case of collectibles, may often be secondary). That is, archaeologists tend to be very jealous of control: this is why very few excavations publish regular full reports on their findings, reflecting a preference to hoard rather than to share knowledge. Indeed, objects discovered on surveys lack any stratigraphic provenience whatever—they are surface finds or, sometimes, they are finds in sections created by erosion or bulldozers. Yet these are not discarded precisely because they have a local association. Never mind that quarrying for road-bedding led to the distribution of Roman pottery all over the highways of England, such that taphonomic processes confused researchers for decades. At a more limited scale, the same sometimes goes on in stratified excavation. Note, however, that the dialectic of publication and refutation can sometimes resolve confusion.

This leads to an issue that is only secondarily intertwined with that of provenience from a "scientific" excavation: the issue of forgery. In recent years, "respectable" archaeologists—that is, those who insinuate themselves socially into the official hierarchies of various professional societies —have gradually withdrawn from the business of authenticating artifacts for antiquities dealers and collectors, as they had (overall) been wont to do until about 1990. They also frequently were collectors themselves. At the same time, in line with the policies outlined above, they have been increasingly vocal about the publication of artifacts from private collections, in many cases going so far as to bar such publication from the journals, and, recently, to protest the endowment of archaeological centers by collectors—a shockingly short-sighted and self-righteous position.[2] Two claims are used to justify this trend in policy: first, private collection encourages looting from sites; and second, one cannot count on the authenticity of objects with no clear provenience in an excavation—even looted objects lose value, goes the codicil to this argument, when removed from a stratified context. Indeed, in 2005 at the annual convention of the American Schools of Oriental Research, a full "Presidential Forum" was dedicated to the issue of forgery.[3] The same arguments were naturally rehearsed there.[4] Reform, said Roscoe Conklin, is the final refuge of a scoundrel.

From the other standpoint, such mavens as Hershel Shanks, the editor of *Biblical Archaeology Review*, and many leading epigraphers, prefer to see materials authenticated when there is some, but not glaring, doubt. One might argue that the desire is emotional rather than rational, or that the (completely unconscious) desire to maintain access to private sources of epigraphic or artistic objects and to collectors connected with suppliers influences epigraphers. So many objects have now been exposed as forgeries that archaeologists finally have learned to doubt the authentications that

2. See "$200 Million Gift for Ancient World Institute Triggers Backlash," *Science* 311 (2006).

3. *American Schools of Oriental Research Newsletter* 55/4 (2005) 1.

4. Christopher Rollston, "Non-Provenanced Epigraphs I: Pillaged Antiquities, Northwest Semitic Forgeries, and Protocols for Laboratory Tests," *Maarav* 10 (2003) 135–93; "Non-Provenanced Epigraphs II: The Status of Non-Provenanced Epigraphs within the Broader Corpus of Northwest Semitic," *Maarav* 11 (2004) 57–79; cf. *BAR* on the subject, e.g., 29/3 (2003) passim; 28/6 (2002); 28/4 (2002); 22/2 (1996); 18/5 (1992); 30/3 (2004) 4848–62; 30/4 (2004) 4; 30/5 (2004) 52–56; 30/6 (2004) 52–59; 31/6 (2005) 20–25.

textualists provide. The situation is reminiscent of those many reviews of Toynbee's *A Study of History* in which scholars wrote, "In my field, this is not very good. But in every other subject, it is brilliant." Where humanists have the expertise to enter into disputes—and many scholars defend their turf by defining others out of it—they do dispute their colleagues' conclusions and often their methods. Where they lack the expertise, they rely, naturally, on the views of specialists in other fields. But many archaeologists cite divided opinion among textual scholars to cast doubt on any sense of quality in the study of epigraphs or art.

The flaws in these arguments are massive and to a degree, contradictory. First, collecting and looting are mutually reinforcing, to be sure, but one does not stop the trade in antiquities by banning information from journals. Both phenomena considerably antedate the development of journals—relics have been collected certainly since the early Christian era, culminating in the wholesale purchase of pieces of the true cross and the collection of saints' bones no later than the Byzantine era. (Scholarly journals, in contrast, originated in the 17th century.) In reality, the trade in antiquities is probably considerably older even than the time of Queen Helena. From the 1st century C.E., there is a ring inscribed in crude Aramaic characters with the name of Ahab, king of Israel. It is of course vaguely possible that this name was thought to summon demonic or other powers, but it is more likely that it was sold to a collector familiar with Israelite tradition. Jezebel, after all, used Ahab's signet seal to authorize the men of Jezreel to frame Naboth. So the ring, with Ahab's name on it, might have substantial sentimental value.[5]

Even in remote antiquity, kings' imaginations were fired by encounters with legends of the past, especially the distant monuments of distant predecessors. This is one reason why Assyrian scribes collected inscriptions in the countryside—including boundary-markers or *kudurrū*—as well as systematically copying transmitted classics, such as Gilgamesh or the Enuma Elish, from the traditional scribal curriculum. Such collections, the ancient predecessors to Theodor Mommsen's epigraphic survey of Italy, were not cultural isolates in the period. They came along with pseudepigraphs—works attributed to figures of hoary antiquity and great authority. Such works were aimed at implementing or at least inspiring changes in contemporary practice—such as subventions to particular temple establishments—under the guise of returning to older, more authentic conventions.

---

5. See Christoph Uehlinger, "Ahabs Koenigliches Siegel? Ein antiker Bronzering zwischen Historismus und Reliquienkult, *Memoria* und Geschichte," in *Peregrina Curiositas: Eine Reise durch den orbis antiquus* (ed. Andreas Kessler, Thomas Ricklin, and Gregor Wurst; Novum Testamentum et Orbis Antiquus 27; Freiburg: Universitätsverlag, 1994) 77–116.

Essentially, by the 7th century B.C.E. in Jerusalem, and by the 6th century in Babylon, the royal court was confronted by the problem not only of collecting but also of forgery.[6] After all, where there are collectors, there is forgery.

It is, in this sense, too late for publication of an object substantially to affect its market value. Authentication of it, perhaps sometimes implicit in uncritical publication, might raise the value somewhat. But the publication that really matters—not just biblical but of ancient texts and ancient history more broadly—is already done. So the real nexus is between collecting and forgery.

So long as ancient figures command the historical imagination of elite members of the public, there will always be a market for antiquities. What archaeologists perhaps rightly object to is ostensibly or professedly the removal of such objects from stratified contexts. But in reality, their problem has to do with their inability to assess the objects and the significance of the objects. Archaeology is hierarchical, unforgiving, almost military in nature. The person who commands a site commands a team, hires experts (who are the ones who deal with objects), and assumes responsibility for interpretation. However, when the object or evidence is unstratified, archaeologists are out of their element.

Again, an often forgotten principle of the sciences is that one evaluates rather than discards evidence. Archaeologists, whose work is often ignored by those who do not understand it, have sometimes retaliated by the heuristic device of assessing the past on archaeological evidence alone. But this is no better scholarship (and possibly worse) than the adverse school of thought. Worse, because in historical archaeology, texts must be evaluated carefully and judiciously in order to associate the archaeological data with particular times. For example, when P. L. O. Guy found the Megiddo gate (now attributed to stratum VA–IVB by most scholars; to stratum IVA by David Ussishkin) back in the 1920s, he assigned it to Stratum III, and assigned that stratum to Solomon. This means that in hindsight, the dirt at the site was improperly stratified, and it was only architectural reconstruction that permitted some semblance of sequencing. As a result, further analysis revealed that the gate was associated with stratum IVA; and Solomon moved with the gate, now tied to the stables of Solomon, referred to in 1 Kings 10. Thereafter, however, critics divorced the gate from

---

6. See Peter Machinist and Hayim Tadmor, "Heavenly Wisdom," in *The Tablet and the Scroll: Near Eastern Studies in Honor of William W. Hallo* (ed. Mark Cohen, Daniel Snell, and David Weisberg; Bethesda, MD: CDL, 1993) 146–51; Gonzalo Rubio, "Scribal Secrets and Antiquarian Anxiety: Writing and Scholarship in Cuneiform Traditions," in *Denkschrift Jeremy Black* (ed. H. D. Baker, E. Robson, and G. Zolyomi; Alter Orient und Altes Testament; Münster: Ugarit-Verlag, forthcoming).

Stratum IVA, based again on architectural remains, and attached it to an earlier Stratum VA–IVB. Solomon again moved with the gate, and this stratum became 10th century. Perhaps we should say that the centuries moved with the association with Solomon. But all this movement made an orphan of the stables, and they subsequently became the stables of Ahab, who fielded 2,000 chariots at the battle of Qarqar in 853. It is doubtful, today, that these are stables at all, as results from the current Megiddo excavations will show.

But the same principle applies to "found" evidence, namely, that one needs to evaluate it rather than discarding it. Unfortunately, with textual evidence, few archaeologists are capable of such evaluation. And the argument that specialists in epigraphs or in art or in the natural scientific testing of objects differ is no less self-serving than the argument that archaeologists themselves differ, as in the case of the Megiddo stables, and that therefore antiquity should be reconstructed exclusively from texts.

In any case, forgeries will always be with us whether for profit, amusement, ideological justification, or all of the three. One has to learn the epistemologies of the tests scholars not in one's own field apply. Only if one can evaluate the arguments in cognate fields can one fruitfully introduce results into one's own. This is a challenge to all groups of scholars who evaluate the authenticity of unprovenanced artifacts—archaeologists, epigraphers, and natural scientists alike. Over time, however, forgeries tend to be exposed, because forgers cannot often anticipate developments or discoveries in scholarship beyond a limited span of years.[7] Simple forgeries, such as coins or pots, have a longer half-life; but anything complex or important is bound to hit the wall of credibility over time. The only damage such forgeries do in the long run is to the reputations of credulous analysts.

There is also an argument to be made on behalf of forgery. It is, in fact, the only answer to widespread looting. It is far easier to concoct a forgery that will pass muster on the market—not for huge sums, but for modest ones—than it is to dig a site in the hope of encountering a saleable object. Coinage has been particularly susceptible to this art because, once one has cut the dies, one can stamp out numerous examples, using base metals if one is not pitching to the higher end of the market. Back in the 1970s, the coin collection of the Harvard Semitic Museum was riddled with forgeries, with tell-tale seams on silver coins, but also on the bronzes, around the coins' rims; this is something one does not encounter in stratified ancient coins.

---

7. See, for example, Peter Hopkirk, *Foreign Devils on the Silk Road: The Search for the Lost Treasures of Central Asia* (Oxford: Oxford University Press, 1980).

Another medium of choice is bullae. Their forgery has now been documented particularly by Benny Sass and Yuval Goren. Although one forger committed the misstep of using fima instead of clay (for the bulla of "Berekyahu son of Neriyahu"), forgeries of bullae are, in the absence of expensive laboratory testing, undetectable except by the identification of the forger's ductus or by errors in the script, orthography, or onomasticon. While one must cut a seal of some sort in order to forge bullae (and one ought not, therefore, forge the bullae of known figures all too often from a single seal), the skilled forger can create a stamp relatively quickly, and evidently does.

The class of arrowhead inscriptions also falls into this category. After the discovery of a few inscribed Iron I arrowheads at Raddana, the number of such objects on the market proliferated. Odds are that at least some of these are forgeries. Again, the forgeries are undetectable if a patina is cultivated or if a dealer claims that he has cleaned the objects, obliterating the patina.

Forging inscriptions successfully requires at least a modicum of training. However, there is certainly a pool of underemployed epigraphers to draw from, as well as a pool of practical jokers. The students or scholars who, however, forge elaborate inscriptions—the Joash inscription, though unsuccessful, being a prime example—always leave traces that a dedicated scholar can trace, whether these are syntactical, semantic, or merely paleographic. The simple forger (of coins or of pots) can be more successful, if not more profitable. Still, forgeries can also represent superb historical reconstructions, if done appositely, like Cycladic figurines.

Given the state of looting in traditional archaeological sites, teaching looters how to forge simple objects makes perfect sense. And fooling scholars is both monetarily and emotionally rewarding—emotionally, because they overstate their certainty about their conclusions, which is what scholars try to do to one another. Adopting a market solution to the problem of looting may involve fooling some scholars, who will, like Hugh Trevor-Roper, be shamed later by other scholars. Still, economically it is the only practical approach. Scholars must choose between incentives to loot and incentives to forge, and they must understand that practitioners of either activity will never desist. It is better, scientifically, to tilt that balance in the direction of forgery and against certain (usually temporary) personal reputations than in the direction of the destruction of authentic remains. Indeed, the deliberate marketing and then exposure of forged objects would even have a deleterious impact on trade in antiquities generally.

There is one other argument for encouraging forgery. The challenge of forgery actually sharpens scholarship—and the same holds, clearly, for the challenge of all unprovenanced objects and for many with a provenience.

Anthony Grafton has argued that modern scholarship developed out of the need for collectors to discern the difference between forgeries and authentically antique objects.[8] Today, of course, as a result we have the sorts of tests that exposed the fraudulence of the Vinland map. And the prospects for natural scientific testing expand every year. Without the threat of forgery, would we so sharpen our tools? Forgery improves scholarship, ironically, and does so for the advancement of knowledge.

Squawks over collecting, looting, dealing and forging are too idealistic in their degree. In the near future, we will not be hanging collectors, nor the usually impoverished folk who loot, nor forgers. Forgery, to be sure, is a form of fraud, at least when done for money, and there is no doubt that one could drive dealing underground. (What would that have done to the Dead Sea Scrolls?) Still, when all is said and done, it seems better to grapple with reality than to deny it. This is called the art of scholarship.

---

8. Anthony Grafton, *Forgers and Critics: Creativity and Duplicity in Western Scholarship* (Princeton: Princeton University Press, 1990).

Can Archaeology Serve as a Tool in Textual Criticism of the Hebrew Bible?

WILLIAM G. DEVER

University of Arizona

In the last decade or so, we have reached a crisis in Israelite historiography. As the title of a recent volume of essays by European biblical scholars puts it, *Can a History of "Israel" Be Written?* Practically speaking, most authors said no—at least not a history that most of us would recognize as a real "history of events"—detailed, balanced, and satisfying.[1]

The "Revisionist" Manifesto

The prevailing skepticism actually began long ago (one might even say with the beginnings of modern literary critical methods in the last century), but it surfaced specifically in 1992 with the provocative work of Sheffield University's Philip R. Davies, *In Search of "Ancient Israel."* Davies distinguished three Israels: (1) "biblical" and "ancient Israel," which were simply intellectual and social "constructs" of biblical scholars ancient and modern, mostly Jewish and Christian, that is, literary fictions designed to enhance their own self-identity; and (2) a "historical Israel," which might have existed in the Iron Age of Palestine, but is unrecoverable because all the biblical texts are Hellenistic in date and therefore "irrelevant"; and archaeology, while theoretically useful, is largely "mute."[2]

There soon emerged in Europe a deliberate, self-conscious school of biblical "revisionists" who systematically wrote what I shall call here "ancient Israel" out of history altogether. Keith Whitelam's 1996 book caught the nihilist agenda of this movement in its title, *The Invention of Ancient Israel*, as did Thomas L. Thompson's 1999 work, *The Mythic Past: Biblical*

---

1. L. L. Grabbe, ed., *Can a "History of Israel" Be Written?* (JSOTSup 245; Sheffield: Sheffield Academic Press, 1997). See also other "revisionist" works cited in nn. 2–6.

2. P. R. Davies, *In Search of "Ancient Israel"* (JSOTSup 148; Sheffield: Sheffield Academic Press, 1992). There is only one reference to the standard handbook—A. Mazar, *Archaeology of the Land of the Bible 10,000–586 B.C.E.* (New York: Doubleday, 1992)—and that is to dismiss the entire archaeology of the Iron Age as irrelevant to Davies's "Persian period Bible" (*In Search of "Ancient Israel,"* 24).

Archaeology and the Myth of Israel (although I assure readers that the latter has nothing to do with archaeology). As Thompson and his colleague Neils Peter Lemche at Copenhagen had put it earlier: "The Bible is not history, and only recently has anyone ever wanted it to be."[3] Thompson's final manifesto:

> There is no more ancient Israel. History has no room for it. This we know. And now, as one of the conclusions of the new knowledge, 'Biblical Israel' was in its origin a Jewish concept.[4]

The reason that this particularly virulent form of "political correctness" denies ancient Israel any historicity rests on its fundamental presupposition that the Hebrew Bible, the only source for history writing the revisionists accept, is a product of Judaism's identity crisis in the Hellenistic era. The Bible is a free literary composition, fictitious throughout, and little more than the original Zionist myth, as Lemche argues in his 1998 book, *Israel in History and Tradition*.[5] The Hebrew Bible is thus a late Hellenistic phantasmagoria, the product of the perfervid imagination of a beleaguered Jewish community; in effect, it is a "literary hoax" that has misled countless generations until it was unmasked by the intrepid revisionists. It therefore has no real-life historical context.

Elsewhere, I have attacked the revisionists' caricature of archaeology and anthropology. I have also undermined the revisionist position by showing that it rests upon an easily discredited postmodern epistemology, which would deny us any knowledge of the past; on a "deconstructionist" approach to the biblical texts, which robs them of any truth or meaning; and ultimately on the nihilism of Nietzsche a hundred years ago, who declared that "there are no facts, only interpretations."[6]

---

3. N. P. Lemche and T. L. Thompson, "Did Biran Kill David? The Bible in the Light of Archaeology," *JSOT* 64 (1994) 18.

4. T. L. Thompson, "A Neo-Albrightian School in History and Biblical Scholarship?" *JBL* 114 (1995) 697.

5. N. P. Lemche, *The Israelites in History and Tradition* (Library of Ancient Israel; Louisville: Westminster John Knox, 1998) 163–66. The political agenda is even more obvious in idem, "Ideology and the History of Ancient Israel," *JSOT* 14/2 (2000) 165–93. For the original proposal for a Hellenistic date, see idem, "The Old Testament—A Hellenistic Book?" *JSOT* 7/2 (1993) 163–93. Yet the only evidence here is a single footnote arguing that the closest parallels to biblical historiography are to be found in Pliny (see Lemche, ibid., 183 n. 39).

6. W. G. Dever, *What Did the Biblical Writers Know and When Did They Know It? What Archaeology Can Tell Us about the Reality of Early Israel* (Grand Rapids, MI: Eerdmans, 2001); see especially 23–52 and references there. For other mainstream critiques of revisionism, see B. Halpern, "Erasing History: The Minimalist Assault on Ancient Israel," *Biblical Research* 11/6 (1995) 26–35, 47; J. Barr, *History and Ideology in the Old Testament: Biblical Studies at the End of a Millennium* (Oxford: Oxford University Press, 2000); Z. Zevit, "Three Debates about Bible and Archaeology," *Bib* 83 (2002) 11–27.

Here I intend to attack their basic assertion that the Hebrew Bible cannot contain any useful history of ancient Israel because it was written long after the events in question (in the Persian or Hellenistic period) and reflects only the social context of that era. I will show, on the contrary, that archaeological data prove that the core of the crucial biblical narratives—the Deuteronomistic History in Joshua, Judges, Samuel, and Kings—consists of stories that are set in and only in the Iron Age of Palestine. If that can be demonstrated, then the final editors of the literary tradition enshrined in the Hebrew Bible as we now have it, however late, had genuine earlier historical sources, both oral and written, some of them contemporary with the events described. With that datum, the entire revisionist house of cards collapses. Richard Elliott Friedman, an esteemed colleague and friend for many years, wrote some years ago to ask "Who wrote the Bible?" I hope to corroborate his seminal work by asking, *"When* did they write it?"

How Archaeology Can Provide a Specific Historical Context for Many Biblical Narratives

An earlier generation of biblical archaeologists sought confidently to "prove the Bible true" by focusing on the great public events posited by the final redactors of the biblical tradition as formative: the migrations of the patriarchs, the descent into Egypt, Moses and Yahwistic monotheism, the Israelite exodus and conquest of Canaan, the promise of the land, and Israel's uniqueness as a people during the monarchy. Today, however, archaeology has vindicated none of these biblical "stories," and ironically it is we archaeologists who have written the truly "revisionist" histories of the eras in question, not the revisionists, for all their bravado.[7]

I intend to take a more modest approach here to the problem of supplying an archaeological context for the Hebrew Bible by looking at everyday life in ancient Israel, especially by "reading between the lines" in specific texts. This is because here the final redactors had less reason to tamper with their sources or to introduce their own tendentious theological biases. Sometimes they have inadvertently described a real, not an "ideal," Israel, so that the essentially historical character of the original narrative can be separated out. The result is what I call a "historical core," which must go back at least to the monarchy, and some of it possibly even to the pre-monarchical era.

---

7. See, for instance, W. G. Dever, *Who Were the Early Israelites and Where Did They Come From?* (Grand Rapids, MI: Eerdmans, 2003); idem, *Did God Have a Wife? Archaeology and Folk Religion in Ancient Israel* (Grand Rapids, MI: Eerdmans, 2005).

The goal of this enterprise, which unfortunately archaeologists have rarely systematically undertaken, is to provide a *true* Sitz im Leben—a real-life setting for the bulk of the Deuteronomistic History—not merely a *Sitz im Literatur.*[8] And by providing external evidence for a preexilic rather than Persian-Hellenistic date, archaeology greatly enhances the Hebrew Bible's value as a source for history writing. It is *archaeological context* that provides the methodological clue to dating and thus "rescuing" obscure passages as potential historical sources.

Some Case Studies of the Convergences between Text and Artifact

Good historians, who still take history writing seriously and who are methodologically rigorous, avail themselves of all available classes of data, critically sifting out reliable material and in particular looking for what we may call "convergences."[9] For our purposes here, convergences would be points at which a particular biblical text would be independently corroborated by material culture remains or vice versa. Thompson dismisses this sort of comparison of sources as typical of biblical archaeology's "harmonistic presuppositions";[10] but such cavalier assertions only reveal how unacquainted Thompson is with sound historical method.

The Era of Solomon

The supposed "Golden Age of Solomon" is one of the revisionists' favorite whipping boys. Lemche and Thompson, for instance, leave no doubt about their nihilism:

> Our argument is not that the Bible exaggerates the exploits of David, nor is it that Solomon was never as rich as the Bible makes him out to be. We are not dealing with issues of skepticism here. Rather, we are trying to argue that the Bible's stories about Saul, David and Solomon are not about history at all.[11]

My point is that, while much of the biblical account of "Solomon in all his glory" is indeed fiction, behind the fantastical elements and obvious theological propaganda there is a substantial core of truth, precisely be-

---

8. Some years ago, Rolf Knierim lamented the lack of "societal settings behind the texts," but concluded that "we have never had such a comprehensive picture"; see "Criticism of Literary Features, Form, Tradition and Redaction" in *The Hebrew Bible and Its Modern Interpreters* (ed. D. A. Knight and G. M. Tucker; Philadelphia: Fortress, 1985) 144. This has prompted my characterization of a mere *Sitz im Literatur,* as well as a call for many years now for a program to make up for Knierim's missing "societal setting."

9. This is the central theme of my *What Did the Biblical Writers Know?*

10. Thompson, "Neo-Albrightian School?" 696.

11. Lemche and Thompson, "Did Biran Kill David?" 18.

cause the later biblical editors were drawing on some traditions that archaeological data prove were older and almost certainly authentic.

My first case study is not the famous but now much-disputed gates of Hazor, Megiddo, and Gezer but the well-known list of Solomon's district administrators in 1 Kings 4.[12] This list has often been discussed by biblical scholars but rarely by archaeologists. Yet today we can say that, of the roughly 15 regional centers listed in this text, 13 have been identified with known archaeological sites and have been reasonably well investigated archaeologically. Several of them—Hazor, Tell el-Farʿah/Tirzah, Yoqneam, Megiddo, Gezer, and Beth-shemesh—have yielded evidence of centralized planning and monumental architecture that would indeed qualify them to have been administrative centers in the 10th century B.C.E. What is perhaps most significant is that nearly all of these towns are conspicuously lacking in Hellenistic (or even Persian) period remains, having long been abandoned and all but forgotten. How could biblical writers centuries later have possibly "invented" this list—as the revisionist scenario would require—and gotten it right?

But can we be more precise on the date of the original sources of 1 Kings 4? I think that we can. Some towns listed here were probably not "Israelite" at all in the 10th century B.C.E. and possibly not even extensively occupied that early. Dor, for instance, remained largely Phoenician until relatively later in Israel's history. "Ramoth-gilead," almost certainly Tell er-Rumeith in northern Transjordan, may not have been an Israelite site at all. I would suggest therefore that the Deuteronomistic editors of 1 Kings 4 must have worked with some older, genuinely historical sources but that their revised version is best dated to about the 7th century B.C.E. and understood as reflecting largely the political realities of that time. That would tend to confirm mainstream biblical scholarship, but with external data.

A second footnote in the biblical narratives is the reference in passing in 1 Kgs 11:40 and 2 Chr 12:2–4 to a raid of the Egyptian pharaoh "Shishak" in the 5th year after Solomon's death. This is clearly Sheshonq of the 22nd Dynasty, whose campaign of ca. 925 B.C.E. is described on a stele found on the walls of the Temple of Amun at Karnak.[13] The Shishak stele lists more

---

12. Fuller discussion and references will be found in my *What Did the Biblical Writers Know?* 138–44. On the Solomonic era generally, see my "Archaeology and the 'Age of Solomon': A Case-Study in Archaeology and Historiography," in *The Age of Solomon: Scholarship at the Time of the Millennium* (ed. L. K. Handy; Leiden: Brill, 1997) 217–51.

13. For the latest and most authoritative treatment, see K. A. Kitchen, "The Shoshenqs of Egypt and Palestine," *JSOT* 93 (2001) 3–12. For the archaeological implications (although somewhat too skeptical), cf. I. Finkelstein, "The Campaign of Shoshenq I to Palestine: A Guide to the 10th Century BCE Polity," *Zeitschrift des deutschen Palästina-Vereins* 118 (2002) 109–35; but see n. 14 for the chronology. The revisionists simply ignore the Shishak datum, the foundation for the chronology of the United Monarchy (not

than 150 sites that the Pharaoh claims to have destroyed in Palestine. Some 25 of these can be identified with known archaeological sites that have been excavated and that give evidence of destruction levels dated by distinctive hand-burnished pottery to the mid–late 10th century B.C.E. We even begin to have some carbon 14 dates that support the conventional 10th century B.C.E. chronology (rather than Finkelstein's idiosyncratic "low chronology").[14] Again, we must confront the obvious implication. Shishak had been forgotten by the Hellenistic era, along with his victory stele in Egypt; and Egyptian hieroglyphic had become a dead script, not to be rediscovered and deciphered until the 19th century A.D. Did the late biblical editors "invent" the Shishak raid and by accident get it right?

The Divided Monarchy

The revisionists grudgingly admit to a "minimalist" history of later Israel in the Divided Monarchy, although in their view this consists of little more than the king-lists contained in the deuteronomic literature. And even there, they base their position largely on several references in extrabiblical Neo-Assyrian and Neo-Babylonian texts, discounting most of the biblical materials as fanciful. Thompson, for instance, describes the king-lists as "based on hypothetical but otherwise unknown dynastic lists," despite the occurrence of the names of most of the prominent kings in cuneiform records.[15] Or again, Thompson acknowledges not an "Israel," but a northern entity called "Samarina" (following the usage of the Assyrian texts) and a people whom he designates as "the Iron Age population of Syria's marginal southern fringe."[16] Despite the biblical witness, there cannot have *been* a real "ancient Israel," since that would be inconvenient for revisionist theories.

My first test case concerns the biblical portrait of Arameans and Phoenicians penetrating into northern Israel in what we now know would be the 9th century B.C.E. The biblical account may be partly influenced, of course,

---

surprisingly). Thus Lemche: "None of the places mentioned by Shoshenq in his list, however, refer to the central part of Israel or Judah" (*History and Tradition*, 56).

14. The literature on the vexed problem of 10th–9th centuries B.C.E. chronology is now enormous. But for a recent assessment, with references to earlier literature, see my "Histories and Non-histories of Ancient Israel: The Question of the United Monarchy," in *In Search of Pre-Exilic Israel* (ed. J. Day; London: Continuum, 2004). Add now I. Finkelstein, "Recent Radiocarbon Results and King Solomon," *Antiquity* 77 (2003) 771–79; A. Mazar, "Greek and Levantine Iron Age Chronology: A Rejoinder," *IEJ* 54 (2004) 24–36. See also n. 22 below.

15. T. L. Thompson, *Mythic Past*, 15; for the extrabiblical texts, see my *What Did the Biblical Writers Know?* 160–67.

16. T. L. Thompson, "Defining History and Ethnicity in the South Levant," in *Can a History of "Israel" Be Written?* (ed. L. L. Grabbe; JSOTSup 245; Sheffield: Sheffield Academic Press, 1997) 185–87. So also Lemche (*History and Tradition*, 52–54).

by the southern or Judahite bias of the deuteronomic writers. But does it nevertheless contain some reliable historical information? Several lines of evidence suggest that it does.

First, we now have a number of northern sites that betray a clear "non-Israelite" ethnic character. Moshe Kochavi's Iron II site of Hadar, just north of Israelite 'Ein-gev on the eastern shore of the Sea of Galilee, excavated in 1987 onward, has close material cultural affinities with Aramean sites in southern Syria, thought unique at the time.[17] In the 1990s, however, excavations began at nearby Beth-Saida, and they brought to light what is probably another 10th–8th century B.C.E. "Aramean" site, replete with a monumental gate shrine featuring a unique moon goddess that has no parallels at demonstratively Israelite sites (but is Aramean).[18] A site with several Phoenician material culture features has been found by Zvi Gal at Cabul in lower Galilee.[19] By coincidence (?), this site is mentioned in 1 Kgs 9:13 as having been ceded to Solomon by Hiram (cf. 2 Chr 8:2), king of Tyre, as a Phoenician enclave or more likely as a trading entrepôt. The major remains of the site, however, suggest that Ahab, rather than Solomon, is the king in question—well known, of course, for his love of things Phoenician (including his queen, Jezebel).

Second, the writers and editors of the Hebrew Bible profess to know of Aramean cultural and economic influences in northern Israel, such as the reference to *ḥūṣṣôt* 'bazaars' in 1 Kgs 20:34, which Ahab could erect in Damascus as the Arameans under Ben-hadad and his father had likewise erected in Israel. At Tel Dan on the northern Israelite border, Avraham Biran has brought to light a number of 9th–8th-century B.C.E. structures located atypically outside the city gate, which he interprets as 'bazaars'— in this case a sort of 'free port' area that would suit the meaning of the Hebrew term *ḥūṣṣôt* ('outside structures') admirably.[20] Incidentally, there can be no doubt about Aramean presence at Dan as early as the 9th century B.C.E., because there was recently found there a fragmentary mid–9th-century monumental victory stele inscribed in Aramaic.[21] The revisionists dismiss the stele as a modern forgery; so much for "honest scholarship"!

---

17. M. Kochavi, "Hadar, Tel," *New Encyclopedia of Archaeological Excavations in the Holy Land* (ed. E. Stern; 4 vols.; Jerusalem: Israel Exploration Society and Carta / New York: Simon & Schuster, 1993) 2:551–52.

18. R. Arav, "Bethsaida 2003," *IEJ* 55 (2005) 101–6 and references; and on the moon-god stele, see O. Keel, "A Sanctuary of the Moon God at the City Gate of Et-Tell (Bethsaida)?" *Goddesses and Trees, New Moon and Yahweh: Ancient Near Eastern Art and the Hebrew Bible* (JSOTSup 261; Sheffield: Sheffield Academic Press, 1998) 115–20.

19. Z. Gal and Y. Alexandre, *Horbat Rosh Zayit: An Iron Age Storage Fort and Village* (Israel Antiquities Authority Report 8; Jerusalem: Israel Antiquities Authority, 2000) 196–201.

20. A. Biran, "Two Bronze Plaques and the Hussot of Dan," *IEJ* 49 (1999) 43–54.

21. The literature on the Dan inscription has burgeoned; see, most recently, H. Hagelia, "The First Dissertation on the Tel Dan Inscription," *JSOT* 18/1 (2004) 135–46,"

Needless to say, Jews living in the Hellenistic era and writing the Bible then could scarcely have made up a story about the ancient Arameans and their relations with Israel in the Iron Age—especially with regard to such specific institutions as reciprocal trade concessions like the Dan bazaars.

Finally, the biblical accounts of wars with the Arameans and Aramean destructions in the early Divided Monarchy can be corroborated not only by the clear evidence in the Tel Dan stele of a victory there ca. 840 B.C.E. but also by other destructions. At Tel Rehov in the upper Jordan Valley near Beth-shan, Amihai Mazar has recently brought to light a massive destruction layer that the University of Arizona radiocarbon laboratory has dated with an extremely narrow margin of error to ca. 840 B.C.E.[22] This is not only the exact date of the events of the Tel Dan stele but also the date required by all that we now know of the Israelite-Aramean wars in the 9th century B.C.E. Were these "stories" invented by the biblical writers; or did they know something, something that, thanks to archaeology, we too now know?

My second case study concerns an auxiliary palace of the Judean kings, probably located at "Beth-Haccherim," identified with the small mound of Ramat Rahel just north of Bethlehem. Beth-Haccherim is not mentioned by name but is apparently alluded to in Jer 22:13–19, where the prophet denounces Jehoiakim, the son of Josiah, for defrauding the poor to "build his house by unrighteousness." This palace does not appear, however, to be the main palace in Jerusalem; but it may be, like Jezreel, a country estate or retreat. The palace is described as "a great house, with spacious upper rooms," having "cutout windows" and paneled with cedar and "painted with vermillion" (Jer 22:14).

The site of Ramat Rahel, situated on a prominent hilltop overlooking terraced vineyards with Jerusalem visible on the horizon, was excavated by Yohanan Aharoni between 1954 and 1962. It was founded in the 9th century B.C.E. and was then occupied principally in the later Iron Age and the Persian periods. The major structures belonged to Str. VB of the 8th century B.C.E. and Str. VA of the late 7th/early 6th century B.C.E. A large perimeter wall with its own gate enclosed an area of ca. 800 square meters, most of it apparently not built up. The single structure inside the walls was a large multiroomed citadel with its own casemate walls, a large central court, and many adjoining rooms. The construction was unusually fine, featuring dressed ashlar masonry laid in header-stretcher style—the only

---

mentioning more than 170 publications. For the notion that it is a forgery (still not re tracted in print), see Lemche and Thompson, "Did Biran Kill David?

22. Cf. Dever, "Histories and Non-histories" 73–74; H. Bruins, J. van der Plicht, and A. Mazar, "^{14}C Dates from Tel Rehov: Iron Age Chronology, Pharaohs, and Hebrew Kings," *Science* 300/5617 (2003) 315–18. See also references in n. 14 above.

known example of this sort of royal masonry after the 10th–9th centuries B.C.E. As with ashlar buildings elsewhere, at Ramat Rahel there were palmette or Proto-Aeolic capitals. A unique find was a stone window balustrade with several short palmette columns with drooping fronds, topped with stylized palmette capitals joined to form a continuous window rail. That this was originally a window balustrade is shown by almost identical windows and balustrades on typically 8th–7th centuries B.C.E. Phoenician ivories—often with a woman leaning over the balustrade, which is apparently meant to depict the second story window of a palace or temple. Significantly, the columns and capitals bore traces of red paint.[23]

Here the *convergence* between the description of a royal palace in Jeremiah 22 and the archaeological evidence from Ramat Rahel is striking. The Str. VB-A enclosure and principal structure are certainly palatial, built on far too grand a scale and embodying too costly construction to be of domestic character. The ashlar masonry alone makes this a "royal establishment." The fenestrated window and balustrade fit the biblical description of a "cutout window" astonishingly well, just as the traces of red paint correspond to the house "painted in vermillion." All of these architectural features had disappeared, were buried and long forgotten after the destruction at Ramat Rahel by the Babylonians in the early 6th century B.C.E. A Persian administrative building occupied the hilltop later, but it cannot possibly have given rise to the detailed biblical description of a "great palace" of the kings of Judah. Once again, it defies credulity to suppose that the biblical writers or editors in the Hellenistic or Persian period "invented" the Iron Age palace at Ramat Rahel.

My third case study from the Divided Monarchy has to do with city gates, numerous examples of which are mentioned in the Hebrew Bible and have been excavated. Kyle McCarter and Baruch Halpern have noted the expression "the *yad* ('hand') of the gate" in 1 Samuel 4, the story of the prophet Eli falling to his death while seated somewhere in the city gate at Shiloh.[24] This phrase is usually translated "by the side of the gate," but by looking at the actual plan of many city gates excavated in Israel and Judah, one may suggest that the "hand" of the gate is the typical projecting tower. These towers probably were multiple-storied and certainly had slits or windows, so it is easy to picture Eli sitting at the window or possibly on the

23. Y. Aharoni, "Ramat Rahel," *New Encyclopedia of Archaeological Excavations in the Holy Land* (ed. E. Stern; 4 vols.; Jerusalem: Israel Exploration Society and Carta / New York: Simon & Schuster, 1993) 4:1261–67.

24. P. K. McCarter, *I Samuel* (AB 8; Garden City, NY: Doubleday, 1980) 114; B. Halpern, "Text and Artifact: Two Monologues?" in *The Archaeology of Israel: Constructing the Past, Interpreting the Present* (ed. N. A. Silberman and D. Small; JSOTSup 237; Sheffield: Sheffield Academic Press, 1997) 332.

roof, anxiously awaiting news of the capture of the Ark; and upon hearing the bad news from the messenger, the old man tumbled to his death.

Once again, archaeology not only reveals the fact that the Deuteronomistic editors of Samuel lived in a time when these towered gates were prevalent but it enables us to date their sources more precisely. Although the story of Eli is set in what we now know would have been the mid–11th century B.C.E., it cannot have been written that early because the type of gate in question originated only in the 10th century B.C.E. (or the Solomonic era; cf. the gates of Hazor, Megiddo, and Gezer). Its life-span then continues into the last days of Judah in the early 6th century B.C.E. But these distinctive city gates disappeared thereafter, and they are never found in Palestine in the Hellenistic period (apart from a possible Maccabean reuse of the gate at Gezer). The Eli narrative is thus another story that has its real-life setting in the Iron Age and *only* in the Iron Age. Halpern is inclined to place the original source as early as the 10th century B.C.E., contemporary with the earliest towered gates, but it could be somewhat later, perhaps 7th century B.C.E.[25]

A fourth and final case study, drawn from Samuel, fixes the date of a biblical story precisely in the 7th century B.C.E. 1 Sam 13:19–21 relates how the oppressed Israelites in the days of the Judges were forced to apply to the Philistines to repair and sharpen their metal implements, because of the latter's monopoly on metallurgy. The price for this service is said to have been one *pîm*, a word that occurs only here in the Hebrew Bible and whose meaning had long been unexplained until the advent of modern archaeology. The King James translation, for instance, guessed that it meant a "file" for sharpening! But we now know from the discovery of dozens of small stone sheqel-weights (for weighing out silver in balance pans) that a *pîm* was equivalent to about 2/3 of the standard Judean sheqel. We have 42 examples, inscribed *pîm* in Hebrew, averaging 7.815 grams. And the significant point is that all of these and the other numerous sheqel weights that we now have belong exclusively to the late 8th and mostly 7th centuries B.C.E. and are found almost exclusively in Judah.[26] It is therefore certain that this story, although ostensibly set in the 12th–11th centuries B.C.E., was written down in Judah in the late 8th or more likely the 7th century B.C.E.—precisely the date to which most biblical scholars would assign the earliest redaction of the Deuteronomistic redaction, including the book of Samuel. A "Hellenistic Story"? Hardly, for then it would certainly refer not

---

25. Halpern, "Text and Artifact," 332–35.

26. On the sheqel weights in general, as well as the *pîm* datum, see further my *What Did the Biblical Writers Know?* 221–28. The standard work is R. Kletter, *Economic Keystones: The Weight System of the Kingdom of Judah* (JSOTSup 176; Sheffield: Sheffield Academic Press, 1988).

to sheqel-weights but to coins. Incidentally, most scholars link the rise of the Deuteronomistic school with the reforms of Josiah in the late 7th century B.C.E., which would also provide a suitable context for the spread of standardized weights and measures, that is, the economic reforms for which the prophets called.

Archaeology and Dating the Sources for the Hebrew Bible

   In my recent book *What Did the Biblical Writers Know, and When Did They Know It?* I have collected dozens and dozens of convergences like those just discussed, in every case analyzing the textual and the artifactual remains independently and as objectively as possible. This is neither a "minimalist" nor a "maximalist" approach; it is simply sound comparative and historical method. It does not hold the Bible either "innocent until proven guilty" or, as the revisionists would have it, "guilty until proven innocent." As a secular archaeologist and historian, my aim is not to prove anything about the Hebrew Bible, certainly not to vindicate its theological claims, but simply to inquire honestly whether one can glean from it any reliable historical information. The results should help to date some of the individual biblical sources themselves, as well as the larger literary traditions into which they are finally integrated (the various so-called schools of J, E, D, and P). We are obviously then in a better position to evaluate these materials as sources for writing any history of ancient Israel.

   I do not dispute the majority opinion that much of the biblical narrative, including Joshua through Kings, was edited in the postexilic period or that its portrait of earlier Israel is highly selective, idealist, and theocratic. I am simply arguing that the final editors had early genuinely historical sources at their disposal; and more often than most have suspected, we can isolate and date some of the sources by re-placing them in their original Iron Age archaeological context. Archaeology then becomes, as I suggested in the beginning, a powerful tool in textual criticism, particularly in redaction history. The implication is, of course, that we need much more dialogue between biblical scholars and archaeologists if we are to get past the current impasse in Israelite historiography. Otherwise, the real history of ancient Israel will continue to elude us, and even theological studies will be impoverished.

Conclusion

   The archaeological case studies that I have offered here, and many more, point to a date no earlier than about the late 8th–7th centuries B.C.E. for the original composition of the Deuteronomistic History. This is precisely the first era when we have adequate archaeological evidence for widespread literacy in Israel and Judah, that is, relatively numerous ostraca, seals, tomb inscriptions, graffti, inscribed pottery, and even fragments of monumental inscriptions.[27] As an archaeologist, I would suggest that the traditional 10th–9th centureis B.C.E. dates for J and E should also be lowered to the late 8th–7th centuries B.C.E., when there is a more plausible Sitz im Leben. But in any case, older materials survived and were no doubt incorporated.

Throughout this discussion, I have sought to show that in many cases archaeological context can be used to date sources lying behind the composition of the Deuteronomistic History, thereby helping to isolate a historical core of ancient Israel. But why should this matter to anyone except a few professional biblical scholars?

In my judgment it matters because if there is not some real *history of events*—events whose interpretation formed the basis of Israel's faith and moral vision—then the supposed experience is fiction, only a social construct, and the Hebrew Bible becomes nothing more than a pious fraud. On the other hand, if the writers and editors of the Hebrew Bible were typical historians of their time, freely translating genuine historical sources into the basis for truths of a higher order, then this literature does not constitute a pious fraud but reflects a creative spirit that we moderns can understand and with which we can live. Furthermore, there is then a history *behind* the biblical history—a real history of a real Israel in the Iron Age—from whose historical experience we can draw instruction, inspiration, and hope.

Finally, I raise a question often implied in all this controversy but rarely posed directly: What would a "Hellenistic Bible" look like?[28] The texts would certainly reflect the milieu of the Greek worldview—rational, empirical, and "Western," rather than the Hebrew Bible's pervasive Oriental and mythopoeic outlook. It would reflect the everyday life of the Greek *poleis*; of cities planned *de novo* in Hellenistic Palestine; of cosmopolitan tastes in science, philosophy, literature, religion, and the arts, not to mention the spread of the Greek language. Yet there is not a *trace* of any of these Greek ideas or institutions in the Hebrew Bible. Its relatively isolated world is still that of villages and small walled towns atop the old Bronze Age mounds. The Hebrew Bible knows nothing of the complex multiethnic and multicultural mix of Hellenistic Palestine; it reflects rather the old Iron Age population of Israelites, Philistines, Canaanites, Phoenicians, Arameans, and finally Samaritans. In any case, the revisionists would scarcely recognize this Greek world—the period of the emergence of Judaism in Late Antiquity—

---

27. For a convenient survey of the development of literacy and literary traditions in ancient Israel, see now W. M. Schniedewind, *How the Bible Became a Book: The Textualization of Ancient Israel* (Cambridge: Cambridge University Press, 2004). Schniedewind opts, as I do, for the 8th century B.C.E. as the earliest possible date for the beginnings of the *written* traditions in the Hebrew Bible (pp. 89–90).

28. See further my *What Did the Biblical Writers Know?* 275–79.

since their publications show not even a minimal acquaintance with the vast literature of the era. As for the Persian period preferred by some, this is convenient since it is a relative "Dark Age" into which one can dump al-most anything[29] (and again, the revisionists are ill informed about what little we do know).[30]

---

29. The most comprehensive handbook is now E. Stern, *Archaeology of the Land of the Bible*, vol. 2: *The Assyrian, Babylonian, and Persian Periods (732–332 BCE)* (New York: Doubleday, 2001) 353–82.

30. This essay was completed in 2005 and could not be updated to include later litera-ture—especially on the continuing "10th/9th-century" controversy and new C[14] dates.

"You Shall Make for Yourself No Molten Gods": Some Thoughts on Archaeology and Edomite Ethnic Identity

THOMAS E. LEVY

University of California, San Diego

From an anthropological perspective, when conducting Iron Age archaeology in the southern Levant, it is essential to use the Hebrew Bible as an ethnohistorical document to penetrate the murky waters that cloud the identity of the peoples who lived in the region during the 2nd millennium B.C.E. The Bible, along with other ancient Near Eastern texts such as inscriptions, papyri, scrolls, cuneiform tablets and so on, provide the key historical data for elucidating the ethnic identity of the peoples whose material remains make up the archaeological record of the "Holy Land" (Schniedewind 2005). However, ethnicity is reflected in material culture in terms of symbols, food consumption patterns, settlement patterns, and other domains. Just how much history is embedded in the Hebrew Bible, other ancient Near Eastern texts, or ancient historical texts in general is a contentious debate that goes beyond the scope of this chapter (Halpern 2001; 2005; Levy 2000; Moreland 2001; Thompson 1999). However, by viewing the Bible as ethnohistory—an approach that uses both historical and ethnographic data as its foundation—a more robust picture of the past is possible, one that addresses both the historicity of parts of the Hebrew Bible as well as some of the anthropological processes that may have shaped the past. From an archaeological perspective, examining the Bible as an ethnohistorical document paves the way for bridging text and archaeology.

Ethnohistory uses historical methods and materials that go beyond the standard approach to the analyses of books and manuscripts by weaving

---

Author's note: This paper is offered in honor of my dear friend and colleague Richard Elliott Friedman to mark his 60th birthday. I am grateful to Bill Propp for discussing this paper with me and his erudite insights on biblical history. Thanks also to Alina Levy for many useful conversations concerning the Iron Age and Edom. However, the author is responsible for any errors herein.

together a variety of source materials including any material evidence of the past such as maps, music, paintings, photography, folklore, oral tradition, ecology, site exploration, archaeological materials, museum collections, folk customs, language, and place names (Axtell 1979). In many respects, ethnohistory is similar to the interdisciplinary approach that characterizes the French *Annales* school of historiography (Braudel 1976), an approach that is particularly useful for historical archaeologists (Knapp 1992; Levy and Holl 1998; Stager 1988). According to N. Lurie (1961), ethnohistorians utilize the special knowledge of the group, linguistic insights, and the understanding of cultural phenomena in ways that make for a more in-depth analysis of the past than more normative historical approaches that are based solely on written documents produced by and for one group. It is in this context that we will dip into the Hebrew Bible and examine a passage from Exodus that has bearing on the ethnogenesis of ancient Israel and their neighbors, the Edomites. In what follows, I suggest that Edomite ethnogenesis was an evolving process that began as early as the 13th–12th centuries B.C.E. when the inhabitants of Edom were known as Shasu by the ancient Egyptians and continued throughout the Iron Age when the Edomites interacted with the Israelites, Judeans, Assyrians, and other cultural groups in the region.

A Glimpse of Ethnogenesis in the Southern Levant

Exodus 34:17   You shall make for yourself no molten gods. (RSV)

אֱלֹהֵי מַסֵּכָה לֹא תַעֲשֶׂה־לָּךְ

How do we make the leap from Exod 34:17 to Edomite identity? We begin by touching on the notion of *ethnogenesis*, a concept that refers to the construction of group identity as well as the revival or perseverance of cultural features of a people undergoing rapid change (Seymour-Smith 1986). It may also be used to refer to a new ethnic system emerging out of an amalgamation of other groups. Ethnogenesis is a powerful conceptual model that can help explain the emergence of ancient Israel in Canaan (Faust 2006; Levy and Holl 2002), because it focuses on viewing ethnicity as a form of *resistance* to other cultural groups. The role of resistance in ancient Israel's ethnogenesis has been carefully studied in a recent volume by A. Faust (2006), where he argues that resistance to other social groups played a key role in the formation of a separate Israelite identity.

I suggest that early Israel's prohibition on making molten metallic gods was part of the ethnogenesis process that involved a myriad of new cultural behaviors that were aimed at creating a separate (Israelite) ethnic identity. This is not to say that the Israelite decision to embrace aniconism happened out of the blue. As discussed by T. N. D. Mettinger (1995) and

W. H. C. Propp (2006), aniconism was common in the ancient Near East. However, the production of molten metal images of god(s) (Negbi 1976) was part and parcel of other contemporary peoples' ethnic identity, from which the ancient Israelites were struggling to separate themselves. The prohibition on making molten images of god(s) is part of what some scholars refer to as the "Cultic Decalogue" (found in Exod 34:17–28), which establishes a number of decrees concerning sacrifice, pilgrimage, and other behaviors that contribute to making ancient Israel a separate ethnic entity. As Faust (2006) points out, Israelite resistance to the Philistines, a group they acknowledged as having a monopoly on iron production, is emblematic of how important it was for the Israelites to distance themselves from metal production and metalwork. The Philistine monopoly of production of iron tools and weaponry is seen in the following Biblical text:

> *1 Samuel 13:19*   Now there was no smith to be found throughout all the land of Israel; for the Philistines said, "Lest the Hebrews make themselves swords or spears." (RSV)
>
>

19 וְחָרָשׁ לֹא יִמָּצֵא בְּכֹל אֶרֶץ יִשְׂרָאֵל כִּי־(אָמַר) [אָמְרוּ] פְלִשְׁתִּים פֶּן יַעֲשׂוּ הָעִבְרִים חֶרֶב אוֹ חֲנִית

>

This is not to say that metallurgy of some kind was never practiced by Israelite groups (Muhly 1976; 1984; Waldbaum 1999). For example, in the 12th–11th-century B.C.E. levels at Tel Dan, an assemblage of stone circles and ash pits associated with tuyeres, crucibles, slag, and metal pieces were discovered in Courtyard 7026 in Stratum VI and Courtyard 7061 in Stratum V, generally associated with the latter part of the 12th century B.C.E. following the assumed conquest of Laish (Biran 1994). According to the archaeometallurgist S. Shalev (1993), this industry consisted of the production of copper-based tin-bronze objects. The presence of numerous broken bronze artifacts in the area around crucibles, as well as the tin content in the metal objects compared to the tin content in the slag, indicated remelting of scrap. According to Shalev (1993), this was a simple recycling system of metal work that did not even rely on imported metal ingots for manufacturing prestige and/or luxury objects. An important small-scale 9th-century B.C.E. iron smithy workshop was found recently by Shlomo Bunimovitz and Zvi Lederman at Tel Beth Shemesh in the upper Shephela (Bunimovitz and Lederman 2003). However, while some metal production took place in Israel to produce utilitarian goods, the numerous allusions to the prohibition of using metal (and other materials) to make idols (for example, Exod 20:4; 34:17; Deut 9:12; 27:15; Judg 17:3, 4; 18:17; and others) and the rarity of metal production evidence from sites in ancient Israel add weight to the idea that metal production was not a significant part of ancient Israel's economy or identity.

According to Friedman (2001: 292), "Only after the golden calf incident is the commandment added: Don't make molten gods (*massekah*)! If there was any doubt about their permissibility before, there is none now. In the wake of that event, no such statue is ever to be made again." For Friedman, after the golden calf episode, no molten icon is ever to be made again. While the antiquity of the Hebrew Bible in its present form is generally accepted to date from ca. 7th–6th centuries B.C.E. (Friedman 1988), the deep-time stories that relate to Israel's formative period at the end of the Late Bronze/Iron Age I period reflected in Exod 34:17 and 1 Sam 13:19 represent what W. G. Dever (2001) refers to as *convergences* between the Hebrew Bible and the archaeological record of the southern Levant, as noted above. The situation in neighboring Edom concerning metallurgy is markedly different from its neighbor to the northwest.

Metal Production and Identity in Ancient Edom

Edom, the region generally associated with the area south of the Wadi Hasa, east of the Wadi Arabah, and north of the Wadi Hisma in southern Jordan, represents the territory of one of ancient Israel's most important neighbors. In the Hebrew Bible, the word *Edom* is mentioned some 99 times and *Seir* 39 times. While often antagonistic, the relations between Edom and Israel were rooted in their common ancestry (Bartlett 1989). Excavations and surveys carried out by the University of California, San Diego, and Department of Antiquities of Jordan in the lowlands of Edom, in the copper ore rich Faynan district some 50 km south of the Dead Sea, have revealed significant new data concerning the evolution of Iron Age societies in Edom. These new data that have a direct bearing on the formation of Edomite ethnic identity and indirectly on that of ancient Israel (figs. 1–2). Some of the most important data come from excavations in the Iron Age cemetery at Wadi Fidan 40 that suggest that the buried population represents a nomadic pastoral group, possibly related to the Shasu nomads known from contemporary and older ancient Egyptian texts (Kitchen 1992; Levy, Adams, and Shafiq 1999; Levy 2004). Long ago, R. Giveon (1969–70; 1971) suggested that the early Israelite tribes had their origin in the social group known to the ancient Egyptians as the *Shasu*—an Egyptian term very similar to the generic concept of *Bedouin*—but linked specifically to the geographic region of Seir/Edom (Ward 1972). For reasons too long to detail here, I accept this hypothesis, as does A. Rainey (2001; and others). Here, I would like to emphasize that the Israelite prohibition of making molten gods or images of God may originate in the process of ethnogenesis—an attempt by earliest tribal Israel to form a separate ethnic identity, distinct from its ancestral roots in the supratribal confederation of Shasu nomads from whence they emerged somewhere in northwest Arabia/

southern Jordan. As part of the Shasu "supra-chiefdom," the hypothesis proposed here views ancient Israel as one of the tribal or chiefdom organizations known from the Hebrew Bible that may have included interrelated nomadic groups such as the Kenizzites, Midianites, Horites, Qenites, and others that lived in this part of northwest Arabia (Rothenberg 1999; Weinfeld 1987). While we have provisionally labeled the ethnic affiliation of the population buried in the WFD 40 cemetery as "Shasu," as more research is carried out in the Faynan district, it may be possible to discover epigraphic data with the name or term that the local people themselves used to refer to their ethnic identity. What is important to bear in mind here is the fact that the massive WFD 40 cemetery demonstrates the presence of a large Iron Age population of pastoral nomads inhabiting the copper ore rich Faynan district. In addition, this district is a part of the region of Seir/Edom from whence the god *Yah* emerged, possibly the same god called Yʜᴡʜ by ancient Israel (Giveon 1971). If this linkage is correct, it implies that ancient Israel had significant roots among the tribal nomadic peoples that inhabited northwest Arabia, that they adopted the god Yʜᴡʜ into their tradition from this region, but that they distanced themselves from metalworking, which was such a central part of the cultural world of the Iron Age inhabitants of Edom.

Evidence of Iron Age metal production in the lowlands of Edom was suggested long ago by N. Glueck (1940) based on his surveys in Transjordan, and more thoroughly demonstrated through systematic surveys and excavations by the author and others in the Faynan district such as the German Mining Museum, Council of British Research in the Levant (CBRL) (Barker et al. 2000), the Jabal Hamrat Fidan (JHF) (Levy et al. 2003; Levy et al. 2004), and the new UCSD–Department of Antiquities of Jordan Edom Lowland Regional Archaeology Project (ELRAP; Levy and Najjar 2006; Levy, Najjar, and Higham 2005). Here I will highlight two metallurgical discoveries from our excavations at the largest Iron Age metal production site in the Faynan district (and the southern Levant) called Khirbat en-Nahas, located on the south bank of the Wadi al-Guwayb and carried out as part of the JHF and ELRAP projects[1] (figs. 1–2). These finds add important data in support

1. I am grateful to the 2002 excavation team: Co-Principal Investigator Russell Adams (and ceramic analyst); Co-Director Mohammad Najjar; Senior Surveyor James Anderson; Area Supervisors Yoav Arbel, Lisa Soderbaum, and Elizabeth Monroe; GIS specialist and ceramics analyst Neil Smith; Archaeozoologist Adolfo Muniz; Administrator Alina Levy; Camp Manager Aladdin Mahdi; and the many other staff, students, and Bedouin workers who helped on the project. These excavations were part of the 1997–2002 Jabal Hamrat Fidan project sponsored by the University of California, San Diego, and the Department of Antiquities of Jordan. I would like to thank Dr. Fawaz al-Khraysheh, Director General of the Department of Antiquities of Jordan, and Dr. Pierre Bikai, former Director of ACOR, Amman, Jordan, for their logistical support. Finally, I am grateful to the C. Paul Johnson Family Charitable Foundation (Chicago and Napa, CA) for their generous support. For the

Fig. 1. The Iron Age Four-Chamber Gate excavated at Khirbet en-Nahas, Jordan, in 2006. Excavations carried out as part of the Jabal Hamrat Fidan Project, UCSD–Department of Antiquities of Jordan. Photo by T. E. Levy—Levantine Archaeology Laboratory, UCSD.

of the hypothesis that metallurgy was a key attribute in the ethnogenesis of the inhabitants of Edom, whose character traits the earliest Israelites were keen to distance themselves from in their own process of ethnogenesis.

I would like to offer the hypothesis that there is a convergence between the biblical passages related to the 9th-century Judean king Jehoram, generally dated to ca. 848–841 B.C.E. (Rogerson 1999: 128–29), and the archaeological record at Khirbat en-Nahas. Accordingly, in 2 Kgs 8:20 we learn that during the reign of Jehoram (also called Joram)

> In his days Edom revolted from the rule of Judah, and set up a king of their own. (RSV)

²⁰ בְּיָמָיו פָּשַׁע אֱדוֹם מִתַּחַת יַד־יְהוּדָה ²¹ וַיַּמְלִכוּ עֲלֵיהֶם מֶלֶךְ

2006 ELRAP excavations, I am grateful to my colleague and codirector, Mohammad Najjar, and research collaborators Lisa Tauxe, Andreas Hauptmann, and Tom Higham. Thanks especially to field staff members: Yoav Arbel, Adolfo Muniz, Neil Smith, Erez Ben Yosef, Marc Beherec, Kyle Knabb, Aaron Gidding, Caroline Hebron, Alina Levy, and Mohammad Defala. Funding was provided by NSF Grant 0636051, National Geographic Society grant 8095-06, Jerome and Mariam Katzin, Institute for Aegean Prehistory, Ramesh Rao, and the California Institute of Telecommunications and Information Technology (*Calit2*) at UCSD.

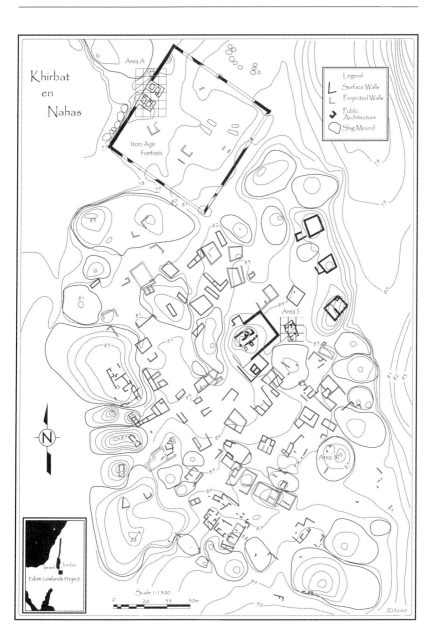

Figure 2. Topographic map and overview of the Iron Age architecture visible on the site surface at Khirbet en-Nahas, Jordan. The fortress is visible in the upper portion of the map and Area S in the middle. Source: Levy, Adams, Najjar, et al. 2004.

The point of drawing on this biblical passage concerning the 9th-century Edomite revolt is that one of the revolt's end products may have been to encourage Edomite metallurgical intensification as a way of solidifying their economic and political independence. In the same way that the prohibition of making molten images and subsequent paucity of Israelite metal production was a hallmark of their ethnogenesis, the Edomites—living in the richest copper ore resource zone of the southern Levant—enthusiastically embraced metal production. This is an archaeological interpretation based on the distribution of Iron Age metal production sites in the lowlands of Edom as well as evidence for the production of metal idols mentioned below.

In a recent in-depth study of the ceramics from Khirbat en-Nahas, both the 10th- and 9th-century B.C.E. assemblages are dominated by local "Edomite" styles and fabrics (Smith and Levy forthcoming). Given the overwhelming indications of an "Edomite" material culture in the 9th century B.C.E., one can assume that the reorganization of the site at this time was significantly connected to this cultural group.

How is it possible to identify archaeological evidence of a social process, such as a revolt, against an oppressor? Y. Arbel (2005) has outlined a wide range of archaeological correlates for the first Jewish Revolt (ca. 66–73 C.E.) against the Romans in Palestine. However, there are detailed and numerous descriptions of that revolt in the writings of Josephus (1976). In the case of the 9th-century B.C.E. Edomite revolt against Judah, we are left with only a one-line allusion to a major formative "historical" event mentioned in the Hebrew Bible concerning the formation or reconstitution of the Edomite Kingdom. However, we are at liberty to refer to the Edomite revolt as a historic event because, as B. Halpern has shown in *The First Historians* (1988), the biblical writers "had authentic antiquarian intentions" and adhered to the sources they had (cf. Dever 2001: 271). Further, Halpern (1988: 111–13) argues that the Deuteronomists were as much authentic "historians" as Herodotus, Thucydides, and other ancient writers. When examining the Hebrew Bible for issues of historicity, historical data especially reveals itself when dealing with the mundane (Levy et al. 2005). Thus, there is no reason for the biblical writers to record a loss or in this case a failure of one of the Judean kings unless it was indeed a historic event. What then would be some of the archaeological correlates of the Edomite revolt against their Judean overlords?

The 9th-Century B.C.E. Reorganization of Metal Production at Khirbat en-Nahas

The 2002 excavations at Khirbat en-Nahas (KEN) focused on two major areas at this massive copper metal production center: the fortress (Area A) and one of the buildings devoted to processing slag and other metallurgical activities (Area S) [fig. 2]. Following his surveys in Edom during the 1930s, N. Glueck (1940: 60–61) attributed the construction of the fortress at Khirbat en-Nahas to King Solomon. Over 60 years later, and in spite of the modern systematic surveys and excavations carried out at the site, this hypothesis remains both speculative and in need of further testing. Indeed, the historicity of Solomon remains a highly contentious issue (cf. Levy et al. 2005). That said, as a working hypothesis, let us assume that the fortress was constructed by 10th-century B.C.E. Israelites who, as Glueck (1940) suggested, may have used the fortress as a large prison camp to work the mines. According to the patristic literature, during the Late Roman period, slaves (both Christians and criminals) were forced to work the mines in the Faynan district. In this context, the new archaeological data from KEN for the 9th century B.C.E. provide possible convergences between text and Iron Age material culture. A total of 21 radiocarbon dates from 9th-century B.C.E. strata were processed for both the fortress and Area S building at the Oxford and Groningen radiocarbon laboratories (Levy et al. 2004; Levy et al. 2005). Here we will only discuss the results from the fortress excavations. The Iron Age fortress at KEN measures 73 × 73 meters and is one of the largest in the southern Levant desert zone (Levy et al. 2005). Originally constructed in the 10th century B.C.E. (Stratum A3), the Four-Chamber Gate passageway was sealed and the guard rooms (only 2 have been excavated to date; fig. 1) were reused for smelting copper during the 9th century B.C.E. (Strata A2b and A2a). As shown by the radiocarbon dating and associated Bayesian analysis of the dates from the stratigraphic deposits associated with the gate (Higham et al. 2005), Stratum A2b (that follows the gate construction in Stratum A3) represents intensified metal production activities that appear to have begun after the mid-9th century B.C.E. (890–860 B.C.E. [37.1% probability] or 855–830 B.C.E. [31.1%]).[2] Our team modeled the spans of time associated with each of the strata excavated in Area A and found that each was relatively brief (fig. 3). Stratum A3, for example, spanned only 0–10 years (at 68.2% probability) and indicates that the actual use of the monumental fortress was quite short. Both Strata A2b and A2a, like the preceding A3, appear to be relatively brief phases of activity (see fig. 3b; Higham et al. 2005). Our analysis indicates that activity in this part of the site, as represented by the uppermost boundary probability distribution, ended before the first few decades of the end of the 9th century B.C.E. (i.e., before 835–795 B.C.E. [68.2%]). The most recent (2006) excavations and analyses of radiocarbon dates from Khirbat en-Nahas support the

2. I want to thank Tom Higham for his help with the radiocarbon dating project of Khirbat en-Nahas. The Bayesian statistical study referred to here was carried out by Higham.

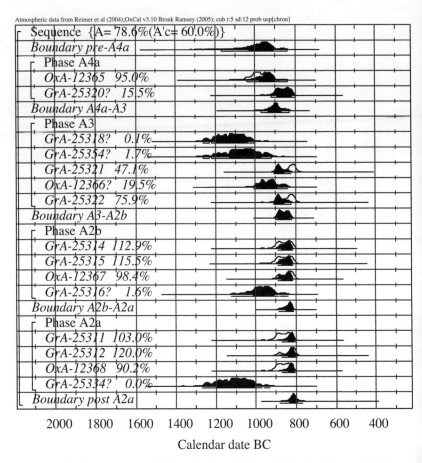

Fig. 3a. Final Bayesian model for the Area A Four-Chamber Gate at Khirbat en-Nahas, Jordan. Note: the calibrated B.C.E. dates are listed along the X axis (2002 excavations, source: Higham et al. 2005: 170).

2002 excavation results (Levy et al. forthcoming). Most important for our considerations here is the evidence for intensive industrial-scale Iron Age metal production during both the 10th and the 9th centuries B.C.E.

According to the working hypothesis suggested here, the monumental Iron Age fortress at KEN may have been intentionally sealed and decommissioned by the Edomites following their revolt against Jehoram, generally dated to ca. 848–841 B.C.E. There was no need for penal architecture in the new Edomite order. The Edomite decision to abandon using the fortress as a military/penal installation may have been tied to the Edomites' desire

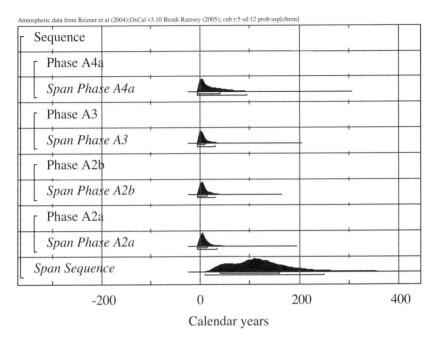

Atmospheric data from Reimer et al (2004);OxCal v3.10 Bronk Ramsey (2005); cub r:5 sd:12 prob usp[chron]

Fig. 3b. Probability distributions for the span of time in years for each of the four phases in the Area A fortress at Khirbat en-Nahas (2002 excavations, source: Higham et al. 2005: 171).

to put all energy and resources into expanding the mid-9th-century B.C.E. copper industry at KEN as quickly as possible while the Judean oppressors licked their wounds back in Judah following their retreat from Edom in the wake of the revolt. It is important to note that, to date, the slag mounds investigated by the German Mining Museum at KEN have been radiocarbon dated to two main phases of production—the 12th–11th and 10th–9th centuries B.C.E. (Hauptmann 2000)—and that our excavations have produced similar results. However, given the fact that (1) the Area S metallurgical processing building excavated by our team (Levy et al. 2005), (2) the nearby building excavated by V. Fritz under the auspices of the German Mining Museum (Fritz 1996), and (3) the decommissioning of the fortress noted here are all linked to the mid-9th century B.C.E., the proposed large-scale increase in metal production at this time is reasonable.

The rapid pace of the expansion in metal production at KEN during the 9th century B.C.E. is also marked by evidence of the production of molten images of what appears to be a goddess (fig. 4a and b). Although only a

Fig. 4a (left). Area S Stratum S1—mid-9th century B.C.E.—*Clay figurine mold for casting molten image, L. 317 (B. 6323 EDM #70879). Found in association with metallurgical processing building. Only a fragment of the open mold containing the anthropomorphic figure is preserved. Length = ca. 7 cm, Width = ca. 7 cm, Thickness = ca. 4 cm.*
Fig. 4b (right). Plastic cast of the mold interior. Shows face of woman with a large nose, hair, earring, and headdress. This could represent a south Levantine goddess such as the goddess Astarte, Ishtar, Kubaba, Atargatis, or some other.

fragment of a clay mold has been found in a courtyard associated with copper metal processing in Area S at the site, it is remarkable that the expansion in industrial-scale metal production was accompanied by a desire to produce what must represent a molten image destined for household consumption. When considered with other artifacts that point to ethnic identity such as food consumption patterns, ceramic assemblages, and architecture, this ideological artifact may mark a clear separation from earlier (possibly) outside managers of production at KEN to local Edomite managers. Accordingly, following their revolt against Jehoram, the formation or re-formation of the Edomite Kingdom was associated not only with the mass production of copper for a burgeoning 9th-century B.C.E. metals market but also with household material culture ritual objects—molten images of gods—that both reflected and defined their separate ethnic identity. In this context, the quotation from Exod 34:17 that opened this essay can be seen as a significant marker in the ethnogenesis of both ancient Israel and Edom. Alternative historical reconstructions have recently been proposed by I. Finkelstein; however, these are based on misinterpretations of the archaeological record related to the fortifications at Khirbat en-Nahas (Finkelstein 2005) outlined by Levy and Najjar (2006) and on inappropriate methods of averaging and working with the radiocarbon dates from our excavations (Finkelstein and Piasetzky 2008) highlighted by our research team (Levy et al. forthcoming).

I hope that by taking an ethnohistorical perspective of the Hebrew Bible and the history of Edom, we will be able to identify some of the convergences between text and archaeology. The new archaeological excavations at Khirbat en-Nahas challenge previous assumptions about the centrality of the 7th- and 6th-century B.C.E. Assyrians (Bienkowski 1995; Bienkowski and van der Steen 2001) as responsible for the emergence of the Edomite Kingdom. Instead, the archaeological data reflect more traditional historical reconstructions by scholars such as Bartlett and others (Bartlett 1989; 1992; Kitchen 1992); however, to test convergences adequately between the Hebrew Bible and Iron Age Edom—beyond the level of proposing hypotheses as outlined here—more large-scale excavations are needed at Khirbat en-Nahas and other sites in this part of southern Jordan.

Reference List

Arbel, Y.
    2005   *The Historical Impact and Archaeological Reflection of Intense Religious Movements.* Ph.D. diss., University of California, San Diego.
Axtell, J.
    1979   Ethnohistory: An Historian's Viewpoint. *Ethnohistory* 26: 1–13.
Barker, G. W., et al.
    2000   Archaeology and Desertification in Wadi Faynan. *Levant* 32: 27–52.
Bartlett, J. R.
    1989   *Edom and the Edomites.* JSOTSup 77. Sheffield: JSOT Press.
    1992   Biblical Sources for the Early Iron Age in Edom. Pp. 13–19 in *Early Edom and Moab,* ed. P. Bienkowski. Sheffield: Collis.
Bienkowski, P.
    1995   The Edomites: The Archaeological Evidence from Transjordan. Pp. 41–92 in *You Shall Not Abhor an Edomite for He Is Your Brother: Edom and Seir in History and Tradition,* ed. D. V. Edelman. Archaeological and Biblical Studies 3. Atlanta: Scholars Press.

Bienkowski, P., and van der Steen, E.
 2001 Tribes, Trade, and Towns: A New Framework for the Late Iron Age in Southern Jordan and the Negev. *BASOR* 323: 21–47.
Biran, A.
 1994 *Biblical Dan*. Jerusalem: Israel Exploration Society.
Braudel, F.
 1976 *The Mediterranean and the Mediterranean World in the Age of Philip II*. New York: Harper & Row.
Bunimovitz, S., and Lederman, Z.
 2003 Notes and News—Tel Beth Shemesh. *IEJ* 53: 235–37.
Dever, W. G.
 2001 *What Did the Biblical Writers Know and When Did They Know It?* Grand Rapids: Eerdmans.
Faust, A.
 2006 *Israel's Ethnogenesis: Settlement, Interaction, Expansion and Resistance. Approaches to Anthropological Archaeology*. London: Equinox.
Finkelstein, I.
 2005 Khirbet en-Nahas, Edom and Biblical History. *Tel Aviv* 32: 119–25.
Finkelstein, I., and Piasetzky, E.
 2008 Radiocarbon and the History of Copper Production at Khirbet en-Nahas. *Tel Aviv* 35: 82–95.
Friedman, R. E.
 1988 *Who Wrote the Bible?* London: Jonathan Cape.
 2001 *Commentary on the Torah: With a New English Translation and the Hebrew Text*. San Francisco: HarperSanFrancisco.
Fritz, V.
 1996 Ergebnisse einer Sondage in Hirbet en-Nahas, Wadi el-ʿAraba (Jordanien). *Zeitschrift des deutschen Pälestina-Vereins* 112: 1–9.
Giveon, R.
 1969–70 The Shosu of the Late XXth Dynasty. *Journal of the American Research Center in Egypt* 8: 51–53.
 1971 *Les Bédouins Shoshou des Documents Égyptiens*. Documenta et Monumenta Orientis Antiqui 18. Leiden: Brill.
Glueck, N.
 1940 *The Other Side of the Jordan*. New Haven, CT: ASOR.
Halpern, B.
 1988 *The First Historians: The Hebrew Bible and History*. 1st ed. San Francisco: Harper & Row.
 2001 *David's Secret Demons: Messiah, Murderer, Traitor, King*. Grand Rapids: Eerdmans.
 2005 David Did It, Others Did Not: The Creation of Ancient Israel. Pp. 422–38 in *The Bible and Radiocarbon Dating: Archaeology, Text, and Science*, ed. T. E. Levy and T. Higham. London: Equinox.
Hauptmann, A.
 2000 *Zur frühen Metallurgie des Kupfers in Fenan*. Vol. 11 of *Der Anschnitt*. Bochum: Deutschen Bergbau-Museum.

Higham, T. J.
    2005   Radiocarbon Dating of the Khirbat-en Nahas Site (Jordan) and Baye-
            sian Modeling of the Results. Pp. 164–78 in *The Bible and Radiocarbon
            Dating: Archaeology, Text, and Science*, ed. T. E. Levy and T. Higham.
            London: Equinox.
Josephus, F.
    1976   *The Jewish War [by] Josephus: Translated with an introduction by G. A.
            Williamson.* Baltimore: Penguin Books.
Kitchen, K. A.
    1992   The Egyptian Evidence on Ancient Jordan. Pp. 21–34 in *Early Edom
            and Moab: The Beginning of the Iron Age in Southern Jordan*, ed. P. Bien-
            kowski. Sheffield Archaeological Monographs 7. Sheffield: Collis.
Knapp, A. B.
    1992   Archaeology and Annales: Time, Space, and Change. Pp. 1–21 in *Ar-
            chaeology, Annales, and Ethnohistory*, ed. A. B. Knapp. Cambridge:
            Cambridge University Press.
Levy, T. E.
    2000   The Mythic Past Biblical Archaeology and the Myth of Israel. *Science*
            289: 145.
Levy, T. E.; Adams, R. B.; Anderson, J. D.; et al.
    2003   An Iron Age Landscape in the Edomite Lowlands: Archaeological Sur-
            veys along the Wadi al-Guwayb and Wadi al-Jariyeh, Jabal Hamrat Fi-
            dan, Jordan, 2002. *Annual of the Department of Antiquities of Jordan* 47:
            247–77.
Levy, T. E.; Adams, R. B.; Najjar, M.; et al.
    2004   Reassessing the Chronology of Biblical Edom: New Excavations and
            14C Dates from Khirbat en-Nahas (Jordan). *Antiquity* 78: 863–76.
Levy, T. E.; Adams, R. B.; and Muniz, A.
    2004   Archaeology and the Shasu Nomads: Recent Excavations in the Jabal
            Hamrat Fidan, Jordan. Pp. 63–89 in *Le-David Maskil: A Birthday Trib-
            ute for David Noel Freedman*, ed. W. H. C. Propp and R. E. Friedman.
            Biblical and Judaic Studies from the University of California, San Di-
            ego 9. Winona Lake, IN: Eisenbrauns.
Levy, T. E.; Adams, R. B.; and Shafiq, R.
    1999   The Jabal Hamrat Fidan Project: Excavations at the Wadi Fidan 40
            Cemetery, Jordan (1997). *Levant* 31: 293–308.
Levy, T. E.; Higham, T.; Bronk-Ramsey, C.; et al.
  forthcoming   High Precision Radiocarbon Dating and Historical Biblical Ar-
            chaeology in Southern Jordan. *Proceedings of the National Academy of
            Science.*
Levy, T. E., and Holl, A.
    1998   Social Change and the Archaeology of the Holy Land. Pp. 2–10 in *The
            Archaeology of Society in the Holy Land*, ed. T. E. Levy. 2nd ed. London:
            Leicester University Press.
    2002   Migrations, Ethnogenesis, and Settlement Dynamics: Israelites in
            Iron Age Canaan and Shuwa-Arabs in the Chad Basin. *Journal of An-
            thropological Archaeology* 21: 83–118.

Levy, T. E., and Najjar, M.
    2006   Some Thoughts on Khirbat en-Nahas, Edom, Biblical History and Anthropology: A Response to Israel Finkelstein. *Tel Aviv* 33: 3–17.
Levy, T. E.; Najjar, M.; and Higham, T.
    2005   How Many Fortresses Do You Need to Write a Preliminary Report? or Response to Edom and the Early Iron Age: Review of a Recent Publication in *Antiquity*, 12 May 2008. http://www.wadiarabahproject.man .ac.uk/titlepage/news/Antiquity/Response-KEN.pdf.
Levy, T. E.; Najjar, M.; van der Plicht, N. G.; et al.
    2005   Lowland Edom and the High and Low Chronologies: Edomite State Formation, the Bible and Recent Archaeological Research in Southern Jordan. Pp. 129–63 in *The Bible and Radiocarbon Dating: Archaeology, Text and Science*, ed. T. E. Levy and T. Higham. London: Equinox.
Lurie, N. O.
    1961   The Voice of the American Indian: Report on the American Indian Chicago Conference. *Current Anthropology* 2: 478–500.
Mettinger, T. N. D.
    1995   *No Graven Image? Israelite Aniconism in Its Ancient Near Eastern Context*. Stockholm: Almqvist & Wiksell.
Moreland, J.
    2001   *Archaeology and Text: Duckworth Debates in Archaeology*. London: Duckworth.
Muhly, J. D.
    1976   Supplement to Copper and Tin: The Distribution of Mineral Resources and the Nature of Metals Trade in the Bronze Age. *Transactions of the Connecticut Academy of Arts and Sciences* 46: 77–136.
    1984   Timna and King Solomon. *Bibliotheca orientalis* 61: 275–92.
Negbi, O.
    1976   *Canaanite Gods in Metal: An Archaeological Study of Ancient Syro-Palestinian Figurines*. Tel Aviv: Tel Aviv University Institute of Archaeology.
Propp, W. H. C.
    2006   *Exodus 19–40*. AB 2a. New York: Doubleday.
Rainey, A. F.
    2001   Israel in Mereneptah's Inscription and Reliefs. *IEJ* 51: 57–75.
Rogerson, J.
    1999   *Chronicle of the Old Testament Kings: The Reign-by-Reign Record of the Rulers of Ancient Israel*. London: Thames & Hudson.
Rothenberg, B.
    1999   Archaeo-metallurgical Researches in the Southern Arabah 1959–1990, Part 2: Egyptian New Kingdom (Ramesside) to Early Islam. *Palestine Exploration Quarterly* 131: 149–75.
Schniedewind, W. M.
    2005   Problems in the Paleographic Dating of Inscriptions. Pp. 405–12 in *The Bible and Radiocarbon Dating: Archaeology, Text and Science*, ed. T. E. Levy and T. Higham. London: Equinox.
Seymour-Smith, C.
    1986   *Macmillan Dictionary of Archaeology*. London: Macmillan.

Shalev, S.
1993   Metal Production and Society at Tel Dan. Pp. 57–65 in *Biblical Archae-ology Today, 1990. Pre-Congress Symposium: Supplement*, ed. A. Biran. Jerusalem: Israel Exploration Society.
Smith, N. G., and Levy, T. E.
forthcoming   The Iron Age Pottery from Khirbat en-Nahas, Jordan: A Pre-liminary Study. *BASOR*.
Stager, L. E.
1988   Archaeology, Ecology, and Social History: Background Themes to the Song of Deborah. Pp. 221–34 in *Jerusalem Congress Volume*, ed. J. A. Emerton. VTSup 40. Leiden: Brill.
Thompson, T. L.
1999   *The Mythic Past: Biblical Archaeology and the Myth of Israel*. New York: Basic Books.
Waldbaum, J. C.
1999   The Coming of Iron in the Eastern Mediterranean. Pp. 27–45 in *MASCA Research Papers in Science and Archaeology*, vol. 16: *The Archae-ometallurgy of the Asian Old World*, ed. V. Pigott. Philadelphia: The University Museum, University of Pennsylvania.
Ward, A. A.
1972   The Shasu "Bedouin": Notes on a Recent Publication. *Journal of the Economic and Social History of the Orient* 15: 35–60.
Weinfeld, M.
1987   The Tribal League at Sinai. Pp. 303–14 in *Ancient Israelite Religion: Es-says in Honor of Frank Moore Cross*, ed. P. D. Miller Jr., P. D. Hanson, and S. D. McBride. Philadelphia: Fortress.

Female Infanticide in Iron II Israel and Judah

Beth Alpert Nakhai

University of Arizona

The Problem

Ezekiel 16 describes Yahweh caring for Jerusalem, a city likened to a baby girl who had been abandoned even before she was cleansed and swaddled. In vv. 4–6, Yahweh addresses the baby, saying:

> As for your birth, when you were born and your navel cord was not cut, and you were not bathed in water to smooth you; you were not rubbed with salt, nor were you swaddled. No one pitied you enough to do any of these things for you out of compassion for you; on the day you were born, you were left lying, rejected, in the open field. When I passed by and saw you wallowing in your blood, I said to you: "Live in spite of your blood." Yea, I said to you: "Live in spite of your blood."

Even as the passage continues by focusing on salvation, the prophet's blasé attitude toward an act of thwarted infanticide seems startling. One wonders whether that was so because the killing of newborns was a common occurrence in the Judah that Ezekiel knew.[1] This essay explores the problem of infanticide and more specifically, of female infanticide, the murder of newborn girls, in Iron Age Israel and Judah (1000–587 B.C.E.). It begins with a general consideration of infanticide and, more specifically, of female infanticide. Next, it examines the biblical legitimization of violence against women and children. Then, it turns to the problem of child

---

Author's note: It is with pleasure that I dedicate this paper to Dick Friedman, outstanding scholar, great friend, and colleague on the Biblical Colloquium West Executive Committee. Early versions of this paper were presented at the Western Jewish Studies Association meeting (2001), the Pacific Coast Region Society of Biblical Literature (2003) and the American Schools of Oriental Research Annual Meeting (2003).

1. While Ezekiel's prophecy dates to the early Exilic Period, his upbringing was Jerusalemite (Boadt 1992: 713–14). That his imagery is drawn from historical reality is documented in multiple sources. See, for example, Ackerman 1989 on the prophet's accurate descriptions of Judean cultic practice; Davies 1994 for archaeological validation of elements within Ezekiel 13; and Vanderhooft 1999: 166–67 on Ezekiel's accurate portrayal of Babylonian administrative procedures.

sacrifice in Israel and Judah. Finally, it explores the unfortunate occurrence of female infanticide in Israel and Judah.

Infanticide: A Global Perspective

Why Does Infanticide Take Place?

It is a fact that infanticide was practiced in many societies in antiquity; the practice has continued into modern times (Langer 1974; Scrimshaw 1984; Wicker 1998: 213–16; Milner 2000). Culturally sanctioned infanticide (not to be confused with neonaticide associated with postpartum depression) is best understood as "consciously calculated to achieve economic and cultural as well as biologically-based goals" (Hrdy 1992: 409; see also Rega 1997: 238; Williamson 1978; Benedictow 1985: 20; E. Scott 1999: 72; Milner 2000). Infants with disabilities or illnesses, those who lack well-functioning families or whose paternity is questioned, and sometimes twins are also at risk regardless of their sex (Schwartz and Isser 2000: 23; Ball and Hill 2003).

Infanticide is possible because the very young are the most expendable and it is they in whom the least, whether food resources, education, or emotional commitment, has been invested. Even wanted newborns and infants may succumb to disease, poor nutrition, and other health stressors (Goodman and Armelagos 1989; E. Scott 1999: 30–32). The death rate for children under five years of age in antiquity (and in modern underdeveloped countries) reached 40% and more. At the same time, the many births required to sustain the desired population size placed women at increased risk of childbirth-related morbidity and mortality. Skeletal analysis indicates that the average woman in the Iron Age died at age 30, some ten years before her male counterpart (Genovés 1970: 441; Meyers 1988: 112–13).

Female infanticide is linked to a number of factors, most often related to economic viability. It is used to control population growth, avoid starvation, and prevent social disruption. It is found in patriarchal societies, because "infanticide is a reflection of the deadly consequences for females of the cultural domination of patriarchal values and culture" (Hom 2001: 139; see also Divale and Harris 1976: 525–26; S. Scott and Duncan 2002: 271). Female infanticide exists in patrilocal societies in which survival depends on close cooperation among male members who are engaged in farming and animal husbandry (Hughes 1981). It is also present when sons are the primary source of sustenance for aging parents (E. Scott 2001: 7; S. Scott and Duncan 2002: 271). Finally, in times of war, the need for warriors and for the maintenance of a militarized society encourages a preference for boys, which can be actualized only through selective female infanticide and the long-term neglect of baby girls (Divale and Harris 1976).

How Is Infanticide Perpetrated?

Infanticide is perpetrated in two basic ways. The first is postpartum murder. Newborns may be strangled, suffocated, buried alive, drowned, beaten to death, poisoned, or abandoned to starve or be eaten by predatory animals (Williamson 1978: 64; Scrimshaw 1984; Schwartz and Isser 2000: 32–34). The second is underinvestment, that is, the sustained neglect or abuse of newborns, infants, and even children, which results in their eventual death (see Ford 1945: 72–74; Johansson 1984; Martin 2000; E. Scott 2001: 16–17). In modern times, neglect leading to death as a way of eliminating unwanted children is more common than infanticide and it especially threatens young girls (Scrimshaw 1984: 452).

Who Is Killed?

Infanticide is a practice that most commonly disadvantages girls.[2] Female infanticide has taken place in myriad times and locations, including but not limited to the Paleolithic Near East and western Europe, Neolithic and Imperial China, Japan, Hellenistic Greece, Mesopotamia, Rome, Viking Scandinavia, medieval Norway, the pre-Christian Inuit Arctic, Amazonia, aboriginal Australia, New Guinea, Oceania, parts of Africa, Sweden in the 18th and 19th centuries, Russia and western Europe from the Middle Ages through the 19th century, the pre-Hispanic American Southwest, and more (Ford 1945: 72–74; Langer 1974; Divale and Harris 1976: 78–79; Williamson 1978; Dickemann 1979; Johansson 1984; Benedictow 1985; Defleur 1987 cited in Hayden 1992: 37; Hrdy 1992; Wicker 1998; Martin 2000: 286; Schwartz and Isser 2000: 26–38; Hom 2001: 139; and references therein). In North America, female infanticide was practiced from the Colonial era, during which time girls died at twice the rate of boys, through the 19th century (Schwartz and Isser 2000: 31–32). Most recently, the preference for sons over daughters has led to selective abortion and neonatal murder in India, Bangladesh, and China (Schwartz and Isser 2000: 26; E. Scott 2001: 3–7). An analysis of recent census data concludes that 60 million women are "missing" in Asia, while another 40 million are "missing" throughout the rest of the world (Kristof 1991).[3]

Iron Age Israel

Violence against Women

There is, by now, extensive scholarship documenting the poor treatment of women in ancient Israel. It is the Bible itself that forces the discussion,

---

2. In some rare instances, boys rather than girls are killed (Williamson 1978: 74 n. 33).

3. Another demographic study suggests 22 to 40 million "missing" girls and women (S. Scott and Duncan 2002: 271).

since so many passages indicate that women were considered fair targets for emotional abuse and physical violence. The many examples of violence against women perpetrated by both men and God reveal a society in which women were neither equal partners nor fully valued. In consequence, the extensive discourse of violence by men against women at home, on the battlefield, and in courts of law cannot be dismissed. Violence against women is seen in stories of humiliation, rape, and murder (Trible 1984; Bal 1987). Women were forced into prostitution and subjected to a legal double standard for sexual acts and transgressions (Frymer-Kensky 1992: 187–98; Bird 1997: 244–47). They were killed or taken captive as war booty (Divale and Harris 1976; Washington 1998). The biblical citations for these and similarly horrific events are too numerous to list here.

Many prophets expressed misogynist attitudes toward women and sanctioned violent acts against them. In many instances, they depicted Yahweh himself as the perpetrator of this violence, and they rationalized their vision by portraying the woman as the symbol of an errant Israel, Judah, or Jerusalem (Magdalene 1995; Exum 1996). Some modern readers comment on the relationship between their violent imagery and pornography (Galambush 1992: 161–63; Halperin 1993; P. Day 2000b; L. Day 2000; Malamat 2002). The book of Ezekiel is the parade example of attitudes of this sort (Galambush 1992; Weems 1995; Dempsey 1998; P. Day 2000a; L. Day 2000).

Socially sanctioned violence against women is most common in patriarchal societies such as Israel. According to H. Washington, "The role of violence in the discursive production of the engendered subject . . . runs deeper than the simple association of masculinity in the Hebrew Bible with the practice of warfare. The biblical representation of sexual violence, too, demonstrates that violence against a feminine object is elemental to normative masculinity" (1997: 331). In short, Iron Age Israel was a society in which women were objectified through violent pornographic imagery, threatened, damaged by psychological brutality, physically harmed, and sometimes murdered. Since these portrayals of gendered violence were composed by a number of authors over the course of centuries, they are understood to reflect conditions in Israel and Judah throughout the Iron Age and beyond. The fact that biblical authors found it acceptable to portray even God as a perpetrator of violence against women substantiates this interpretation. Their willingness to allow and even laud such deplorable behavior by both men and God reflects their Sitz im Leben in the Near East. From Old Babylonian law to Neo-Assyrian palace reliefs, there is no evidence to suggest that the men of Israel and Judah were different from those in the world around them.

Birth, Liminality, and Death

The point at which a baby is considered human is important in the discussion of infanticide.[4] As N. Finlay notes, "Until accepted into society, the infant often has no social persona and forms an ambiguous class of individual" (2000: 418; see also Ford 1945: 75–77; E. Scott 2001). In ancient times, there was no technology for identifying the moment of conception, but even early pregnancy has symptoms that are hard to miss (Ford 1945: 43–44). Though the Bible is mute on the topic of abortion, it includes legislation designed to penalize men whose violent actions caused miscarriage (Exod 21:22–23), suggesting that in Israel, social value accrued to the developing fetus. While the ritual of circumcision (Lev 12:3) joined a baby boy to the community on his 8th day of life, there was no comparable ceremony for girls. Already at risk from postpartum complications and disease, their continuing liminal status rendered them expendable when family and society were confronted with inadequate food and other resources. It may be that the period of extended bonding between mothers and newborn daughters, twice as long as that between mothers and newborn sons (Lev 12:1–5), was instituted to avert the tragedy of female infanticide, since babies with whom their mothers are closely bonded are more likely to be cared for and raised (inter alia, Scrimshaw 1984: 461).[5]

The Role of Children

A key element in the discussion of female infanticide is the role children played in Israelite society. The study of childhood in antiquity is rather new, but it is already clear that it cannot be divorced from gender studies because home and family are the traditional setting for both women and children. As anthropologists know, childhood is a social category and not an absolute stage in life, and thus it is understood variously in different societies (Ariès 1962: 411–15; Sofaer Derevenski 1994, 1997; Blenkinsopp 1997: 66–69; Baxter 2005: 27–37).

What can be said of the biblical child? Many stories underscore the longing for children and particularly for male heirs. Rachel's desperate plea to her husband Jacob, "Give me children, or I shall die" (Gen 30:1) is mirrored in Sarah's suffering the pain of giving her husband to a second wife (Gen 16:1–3) and in Hannah's willingness to relinquish her son to Yahweh

---

4. For the relationship between a society's understanding of when life begins and its definition of infanticide, see Scrimshaw 1984: 440–41; Hrdy 1992: 436–37.

5. In addition, women who were considered unclean were unavailable for sexual intercourse and therefore unable to become pregnant (see Ford 1945: 66–69; Hrdy 1992: 424–25 for taboos against postpartum intercourse). Statistics indicate that the children of mothers who become pregnant within three months of their delivery are much more likely to die than are children whose mothers defer pregnancy (Benedictow 1985: 48).

if only she could bear and nurse him (1 Sam 1:24–28). Overall, though, children figure little in the Bible other than as vehicles through which Yahweh's plans for Israel can be realized. A recent study of biblical language for childhood indicates that three terms, ʿōlēl, ʿōlal, and yōnēq refer to nursing infants, while gāmûl or gĕmûlâ refer to the weaned child. Most often, passages that refer to young children illustrate the trauma to which they were subjected. J. Blenkinsopp notes that in the Bible, "twenty-two of the thirty occurrences of terms for infants refer to their being violently destroyed" (1997: 68).

Cross-culturally, access to wealth (whether in goods or land) is among the most important factors in determining the viability of baby girls. In particular, the transmission of land through patrilineal descent is critical to the decision about whether baby girls will be allowed to live. Both the income-earning potential of boys and their responsibility for caring for elderly parents mean that they will be better fed and cared for, and consequently they will survive longer than girls (Dickemann 1979: 333; see also Chen, Huq, and D'Souza 1981: 66; E. Scott 2001). According to the Bible, sons were essential in the formation and preservation of Israel's primary social groups, the mišpāḥâ and the šēbet. These familial and clan groups, defined by patrilineal descent, controlled economic, marital, and other fundamental aspects of life. It was through sons that the patrimonial holdings remained within the control of the familial group, and it was to them that parents turned in their old age (Stager 1985; Blenkinsopp 1997). Israelite acceptance of gender-biased infanticide is one consequence of these factors.

The Exposure of Infants

The deliberate exposure of newborns is one way in which infanticide is perpetrated. According to M. Malul, child abandonment was common in Mesopotamia of the 2nd and 1st millennia B.C.E. (1990: 104–5). To the baby girl apotheosized as Jerusalem, Ezekiel states, "you were thrown out (wattušlĕkî) over the open field (ʿal pĕnê haśśādeh) in your own filth on the day of your birth" (16:5). "Over the open field" describes those who were abandoned in a location outside normal inhabited areas and therefore had to fend for themselves against the wrath of Yahweh (Kohn 2002: 65). The word hišlîk 'expose' or 'abandon' is a technical term used when abandoning someone with whom one is unable to deal (Cogan 1968).[6] In Mesopotamia, abandonment sometimes served as the prelude to adoption, in which case the newborn was left unwashed so that the adoptive father

---

6. The only abandoned baby in the Bible is the girl in Ezekiel 16. The other narratives about abandonment, which also use a form of the verb hišlîk, describe events in the lives of boys or men (Ishmael in Gen 21:25; Joseph in Gen 37:17b–24; and Jeremiah in Jer 38:1–7).

could wash—and thereby legitimize—his new child (Malul 1990: 109–13). The parallel between Mesopotamian foundlings and the bloody infant in Ezek 16:4–7 is obvious, but in Mesopotamia as in Israel, not every abandoned baby was later adopted. The popular literary motif in which an unusual birth and abandonment foreshadowed a brilliant future (Sargon I, Romulus and Remus, Ishmael, Moses, and more) only worked because the threat of actual abandonment underlay the tale (Lewis 1980: 150, 266; Redford 1967).

The story of the baby Moses is filled with unexpected and amazing reversals (Exum 1983). The Pharaoh who condemned an Israelite baby unwittingly raised him, a pampered prince became the unlikely spokesman for God, a bold prince became a humble man, slaves were freed, and the mighty were vanquished. Pharaoh's decree of death for Israel's baby boys set up yet another startling reversal of the norm.

> The king of Egypt spoke to the Hebrew midwives, one of whom was named Shiphrah and the other Puah, saying, "When you deliver the Hebrew women, look at the birthstool: *if it is a boy, kill him; if it is a girl, let her live.*" The midwives, fearing God, did not do as the king of Egypt had told them; they let the boys live. (Exod 1:15–17; italics mine)

The story continues.

> Then Pharaoh charged all his people, saying, *"Every boy that is born you shall throw into the Nile, but let every girl live."* (Exod 1:22; italics mine)

Despite the Bible's often terse style of story telling, the command to *let every girl live* is stated twice within the course of six verses, thereby emphasizing the extent to which it represents the transformation of all reasonable expectations. Rather than girls, in the story of Moses it was, surprisingly, the boys who were to be killed.

The Sacrifice of Children

Child sacrifice is best understood as a form of infanticide that operates in the public domain rather than in the domestic realm (E. Scott 1999: 81–89).[7] For Israel and Judah, as elsewhere, child sacrifice was a phenomenon that in many ways paralleled female infanticide. Both were the means to attain economic goals and regulate population growth. In 4th–3rd-century Carthage, child sacrifice served to ensure that large estates were not subdivided (Stager 1982: 162–63), and this may have been the case in

---

7. For an overview of child sacrifice in other regions and times, see Williamson 1978: 71–72. For an exhaustive study of human sacrifice in the ancient Near East, see Green 1975. For studies of child sacrifice in biblical Israel, see Mosca 1975; Ackerman 1992: 117–43; Levenson 1993: 3–17; Delaney 1998: 71–104; Doyle 1999; and Smith 2002: 171–81. For the Carthage *tophet*, with its archaeological evidence for child sacrifice, see Stager 1982; Stager and Wolff 1984. For a discussion that includes Second Temple, talmudic, and later rabbinic commentaries, see Landers 1991.

Israel and Judah, as well. The child sacrificed was often past infancy since sacrifice had worth only when value accrued to the object sacrificed—and the older the children were, the more "valuable" they became.[8]

In Israel, people resorted to child sacrifice only at times of extreme danger, such as when a city was under siege and its king had to enlist the help of his god (Smith 2002: 181). S. Ackerman highlighted the relationship between rites of child sacrifice, rituals to ensure fertility, and the maintenance of the cult of the dead (Ackerman 1992: 117–43). Child sacrifice had a place within the Yahwistic cult, fulfilling normative religious goals (Ackerman 1993; Smith 2002: 171–72 and references therein). The first of the Bible's child sacrifices, that of Jephthah's adolescent daughter (Judg 11:29–40), took place during a time of military crisis.[9] In Israel, children were sacrificed during Hoshea's reign, in the difficult years leading up to the Assyrian destruction (2 Kgs 17:17). In Judah, children were sacrificed during the reign of Ahaz, when Rezin of Aram and Pekah of Israel placed Jerusalem under siege (2 Kgs 16:3). They were also sacrificed during the reign of Manasseh, when the people of Judah struggled to recover from Sennacherib's devastating attacks (2 Kgs 21:6). The practice continued throughout the 7th century and well into the 6th, despite the efforts of Josiah (2 Kgs 23:10) and various prophets (Jer 7:31–32; 19:5–6; 32:35; Ezek 16:20–21, 36; 20:31; 23:37–39; Isa 57:5) to eliminate it.

Isa 30:27–33 and Ezek 20:25–26 claim that Yahweh required the sacrifice of firstborn sons as punishment for Israelites who did not obey God's law. Lest anyone doubt God's capacity to carry out this sort of penalty, the smiting of Egypt's firstborns (Exod 4:22–23, 11:4–6, 12:29–30) proved the point (Num 3:13, 8:16–17). In contrast, the deuteronomists (Deut 12:31, 18:10–12) and the priests (Lev 18:21, 20:2–5) argued against child sacrifice and developed counterrituals for redeeming firstborn sons (Exod 13:1–2, 11–15; 22:28–29; 34:19–20; Num 18:15; see also Gen 22:1–14). In one iteration, the dedication of the Levites served as a substitute for the sacrifice of firstborn sons (Num 3:11–13, 40–51; 8:14–19). Nonetheless, the witness of Isa 57:5 suggests that children were sacrificed well into the Exilic Period.

Female Infanticide in Israel

Mortuary Evidence

In Iron II Israel, children were buried in cemeteries and under house floors, in jars and in graves, in primary and secondary burials, and by cre-

---

8. See also Nakhai 2001: 39–44 for a discussion of the economy of sacrifice and the requirement that goods offered in sacrifice be valuable, the product of the labor of those individuals making the sacrifice.

9. The son of the king of Moab was similarly sacrificed in wartime (2 Kgs 3:26–27). See Steinberg 1999: 120 for further discussion.

mation, most commonly alongside their parents (Bloch-Smith 1992: 65–71). While it is sometimes possible to identify infanticide in the archaeological record, determining the sex of immature skeletons is less feasible, making gender bias difficult to demonstrate (Wicker 1998; Arnold and Wicker 2001). Children who were abandoned or otherwise murdered are unlikely to have been accorded funeral rites (Smith and Kahila 1992), and so it is no surprise that evidence for infanticide has not been uncovered in excavations in Judah and Israel.

The Historical Context for Judean Infanticide

As noted above, the factors that most often cause people to abandon or murder healthy infants, especially girls, include population pressure, loss of home, the tensions surrounding the division of family estates, poverty, famine, and warfare. In Iron II Israel, there were two periods in which these problems were particularly intense. The first was the late 8th century. Consequent to the Assyrian onslaught that began with Tiglath-pileser III in 734 and continued unabated through the reigns of Shalmaneser V and Sargon II, Israel was destroyed and much of its population killed. Many other people were displaced. Some were forcibly exiled from their homeland to other locations in the Near East, while others fled south from Israel to Judah and, most notably, to Jerusalem (Stern 2001: 3–13).

Judah, too, suffered serious damage. As a result of two waves of immigration, one from the north after the Assyrian destruction of Israel and one from the Judean hinterland after Sennacherib's major campaign of 701, Jerusalem doubled in size (Broshi 1993). The Assyrian administrative presence at Ramat Rahel, just outside Jerusalem, meant that Judah was not free of its obligations to its overlord until late in the 7th century, even as it was ruled by its own native kings (Naʾaman 2001: 270–75). The ongoing economic and psychological burden thus placed on an already stressed population was daunting.

The second period of societal trauma was the early 6th century, when Nebuchadnezzar, the king of Babylon, and his army were on the march. Towns and villages throughout Judah were destroyed. Jerusalem, too, was sacked and its elite forced into exile, resulting in the demise of the quasi-independent nation of Judah (2 Kgs 24:8–25:26). Excavations throughout the land document the extensive destruction caused by the Babylonian military offensives (Stern 2001: 303–31). Having witnessed some (Ezekiel; cf. Boadt 1992: 713–14) or all (Jeremiah; cf. Lundbom 1992: 684–90) of these devastating onslaughts, these two informants on child sacrifice and female infanticide were both forced from their homeland.

In both of these eras, extensive and long-term military crises uprooted people from their ancestral lands, created migratory populations, and caused famine, poverty, and death. Demographic studies of contemporary and historical societies demonstrate that, in times of social stress, women and children are particularly vulnerable to malnutrition and disease (Martin 2000: 272). Pregnant women and nursing mothers suffer and die in especially large numbers, because they have higher nutritional requirements than do other cohorts within the population. This causes high rates of morbidity and mortality for infants and small children (Scott and Duncan 2002: 143–59). When men are engaged in (or lost to) military conflict or to market production or to urban reconstruction, then women bear the heaviest burden for food production. At times such as these, there is a risk to pregnant women and their fetuses and an increase in infant mortality (Benedictow 1985: 52–53). One consequence of all this is a greater household investment in boys than in girls, which may include killing unwanted newborn daughters or keeping them alive without providing them with adequate food, clothing, and other resources (Johansson 1984: 484). Of all the suffering during these difficult years, then, none was as great as that of Israel's female population, and its youngest fared the worst.

Conclusions

In prophetic and historical passages, the Bible claims that, in times of crisis, both boys and girls could be sacrificed to God. Still, the only story about a child who was sacrificed is that of a girl, Jephthah's daughter. Likewise, both boys and girls could be abandoned, but again, the only abandonment with an unhappy outcome was that of a girl, Ezekiel's metaphoric Jerusalem, a city that the prophet had seen brutally plundered and destroyed in his own lifetime. The Bible reflects uneasiness about so much morally ambiguous behavior. The priests and the deuteronomists legislate against child sacrifice and provide a mechanism to prevent the offering of one's firstborn son to God. This did little to bypass the death of baby girls, who were considered of limited value in times of military tension and economic duress. They were offered to God or simply left to die, in order to ensure the future of their families and nation.

References Cited

Ackerman, S.
    1989   A *Marzeah* in Ezekiel 8:7–13? *Harvard Theological Review* 82: 267–81.
    1992   *Under Every Green Tree: Popular Religion in Sixth-Century Judah.* HSM 46. Atlanta: Scholars Press.
    1993   Child Sacrifice: Returning God's Gift. *Bible Review* 9/3: 20–29, 56.
Ariès, P.
    1962   *Centuries of Childhood: A Social History of Family Life,* trans. R. Baldick. New York: Knopf.

Arnold, B., and Wicker, N. L., eds.
2001   *Gender and the Archaeology of Death.* Walnut Creek, CA: AltaMira.
Bal, M.
1987   *Lethal Love: Feminist Literary Readings of Biblical Love Stories.* Bloomington: Indiana University Press.
Ball, H. L., and Hill, C. M.
2003   Reevaluating "Twin Infanticide." *Current Anthropology* 37/5: 856–63.
Baxter, J. E.
2005   *The Archaeology of Childhood: Children, Gender, and Material Culture.* Gender and Archaeology Series 10. Walnut Creek, CA: AltaMira.
Benedictow, O. J.
1985   The Milky Way in History: Breast Feeding, Antagonism between the Sexes and Infant Mortality in Medieval Norway. *Scandinavian Journal of History* 10/1: 19–53.
Berlin, A., and Brettler, M. Z., eds.
2004   *The Jewish Study Bible: Jewish Publication Society TANAKH Translation.* Oxford: Oxford University Press.
Bird, P. A.
1997   Translating Sexist Language as a Theological and Cultural Problem. Pp. 239–47 in *Missing Persons and Mistaken Identities: Women and Gender in Ancient Israel.* Overtures to Biblical Theology. Minneapolis: Fortress.
Blenkinsopp, J.
1997   The Family in First Temple Israel. Pp. 48–103 in *Families in Ancient Israel*, ed. L. Perdue, J. Blenkinsopp, J. Collins, and C. Meyers. Louisville: Westminster John Knox.
Bloch-Smith, E.
1992   *Judahite Burial Practices and Beliefs about the Dead.* JSOTSup 123. ASOR Monograph 7. Sheffield: Sheffield Academic Press.
Boadt, L.
1992   Ezekiel, Book of. Pp. 711–22 in vol. 2 of *ABD.*
Broshi, M.
1993   The Population of Iron Age Palestine. Pp. 14–18 in *Biblical Archaeology Today, 1990, Proceedings of the Second International Congress on Biblical Archaeology. Precongress Symposium: Population, Production and Power, Jerusalem, June 1990. Supplement.* Jerusalem: Israel Exploration Society.
Chen, L. C.; Huq, E.; and D'Souza, S.
1981   Sex Bias in the Family Allocation of Food and Health Care in Rural Bangladesh. *Population and Development Review* 7/1: 55–70.
Cogan, M.
1968   A Technical Term for Exposure. *Journal of Near Eastern Studies* 17: 133–35.
Davies, G. I.
1994   An Archaeological Commentary on Ezekiel 13. Pp. 108–25 in *Scripture and Other Artifacts: Essays on the Bible and Archaeology in Honor of Philip J. King*, ed. M. D. Coogan, J. C. Exum, and L. E. Stager. Louisville: Westminster John Knox.

Day, L.
2000   Rhetoric and Domestic Violence in Ezekiel 16. *BibInt* 8: 205–30.
Day, P. L.
2000a   Adulterous Jerusalem's Imagined Demise: Death of a Metaphor in Ezekiel XVI. *VT* 50: 285–309.
2000b   The Bitch Had It Coming to Her: Rhetoric and Interpretation in Ezekiel 16. *BibInt* 8: 231–54.
Delaney, C.
1998   *Abraham on Trial: The Social Legacy of Biblical Myth.* Princeton: Princeton University Press.
Dempsey, C. J.
1998   The "Whore" of Ezekiel 16: The Impact and Ramifications of Gender-Specific Metaphors in Light of Biblical Law and Divine Judgment. Pp. 57–78 in *Gender and Law in the Hebrew Bible and the Ancient Near East,* ed. V. H. Matthews, B. M. Levinson, and T. Frymer-Kensky. JSOTSup 262. Sheffield: Sheffield Academic Press.
Dickemann, M.
1979   Female Infanticide, Reproductive Strategies, and Social Stratification: A Preliminary Model. Pp. 321–67 in *Evolutionary Biology and Human Social Behavior: An Anthropological Perspective,* ed. H. A. Chagnon and W. Irons. North Scituate, MA: Duxbury.
Divale, W. T., and Harris, M.
1976   Population, Warfare, and the Male Supremacist Complex. *American Anthropologist* 78/3: 521–38.
Doyle, R.
1999   Molek of Jerusalem? Pp. 171–206 in *Zion, City of Our God,* ed. R. S. Hess and G. J. Wenham. Grand Rapids, MI: Eerdmans.
Exum, J. C.
1983   "You Shall Let Every Daughter Live": A Study of Exodus 1:8–2:10. Pp. 63–82 in *The Bible and Feminist Hermeneutics,* ed. M. A. Tolbert. Semeia 28. Atlanta: Scholars Press.
1996   Prophetic Pornography. Pp. 101–24 in *Plotted, Shot, and Painted: Cultural Representations of Biblical Women.* JSOTSup 215. Gender, Culture, Theory 3. Sheffield: Sheffield Academic Press.
Finlay, N.
2000   Outside of Life: Traditions of Infant Burial in Ireland from *Cillín* to Cist. *World Archaeology* 31: 407–22.
Ford, C. S.
1945   *A Comparative Study of Human Reproduction.* Yale University Publications in Anthropology 32. New Haven, CT: Yale University Press.
Frymer-Kensky, T.
1992   *In the Wake of the Goddess: Women, Culture and the Biblical Transformation of Pagan Myth.* New York: Free Press.
Galambush, J.
1992   *Jerusalem in the Book of Ezekiel: The City as Yahweh's Wife.* Atlanta: Society for Biblical Literature.

Genovés, S.
    1970   Estimation of Age and Mortality. Pp. 440–41 in *Science in Archaeology: A Survey of Progress and Research*, ed. D. Brothwell and E. Higgs. New York: Praeger.

Goodman, A. H., and Armelagos, G. J.
    1989   Infant and Childhood Morbidity and Mortality Risks in Archaeological Populations. *World Archaeology* 21 (*Archaeology of Public Health*): 225–43.

Green, A. R. W.
    1975   *The Role of Human Sacrifice in the Ancient Near East*. ASOR Dissertation 1. Missoula, MT: Scholars Press.

Halperin, D. J.
    1993   *Seeking Ezekiel: Text and Psychology*. University Park, PA: Pennsylvania State University Press.

Hayden, B.
    1992   Observing Prehistoric Women. Pp. 33–47 in *Exploring Gender through Archaeology: Selected Papers from the 1991 Boone Conference*, ed. C. Claassen. Monographs in World Archaeology 11. Madison: Prehistory Press.

Hom, S. K.
    2001   Female Infanticide in China: The Human Rights Specter and Thoughts toward (An)Other Vision. Pp. 138–46 in *Femicide in Global Perspective*, ed. D. E. H. Russell and R. A. Harmes. New York: Teachers' College Press.

Hrdy, S. B.
    1992   Fitness Tradeoffs in the History and Evolution of Delegated Mothering with Special Reference to Wet-Nursing, Abandonment, and Infanticide. *Ethology and Sociobiology* 13: 409–42.

Hughes, A. L.
    1981   Female Infanticide: Sex Ratio Manipulation in Humans. *Ethology and Sociobiology* 2: 109–11.

Johansson, S. R.
    1984   Deferred Infanticide: Excess Female Mortality during Childhood. Pp. 463–85 in *Infanticide: Comparative and Evolutionary Perspectives*, ed. G. Hausfater and S. B. Hrdy. New York: Aldine.

Kohn, R. L.
    2002   *A New Heart and a New Soul: Ezekiel, the Exile and the Torah*. JSOTSup 358. London: Sheffield Academic Press.

Kristof, N. D.
    1991   Stark Data on Women: 100 Million Are Missing. *The New York Times*, Nov. 5, 1991. Pp. C1, C12.

Landers, S.
    1991   Did Jephthah Kill His Daughter? *Bible Review* 17/4: 28–31, 42.

Langer, W. L.
    1974   Infanticide: A Historical Survey. *History of Childhood Quarterly* 1: 353–65.

Levenson, J. D.
1993   *The Death and Resurrection of the Beloved Son: The Transformation of Child Sacrifice in Judaism and Christianity.* New Haven, CT: Yale University Press.
Lewis, B.
1980   *The Sargon Legend: A Study of the Akkadian Text and the Tale of the Hero Who Was Exposed at Birth.* ASOR Dissertation 4. Cambridge, MA: American Schools of Oriental Research.
Lundbom, J. R.
1992   Jeremiah. Pp. 684–98 in vol. 3 of *ABD.*
Magdalene, F. R.
1995   Ancient Near Eastern Treaty-Curses and the Ultimate Texts of Terror: A Study of the Language of Divine Sexual Abuse in the Prophetic Corpus. Pp. 326–52 in *A Feminist Companion to the Latter Prophets,* ed. A. Brenner. The Feminist Companion to the Bible 8. Sheffield: Sheffield Academic Press.
Malamat, A.
2002   The Politics of Bipolarity in the Guise of Sexual Relations: The Case of Ezekiel 16 and 23. Pp. 355–57 in *Sex and Gender in the Ancient Near East: Proceedings of the 47th Recontre Assyriologique Internationale, Helsinki, July 2–6, 2001,* Pt. 2, ed. S. Parpola and R. M. Whiting. Helsinki: The Neo-Assyrian Text Corpus Project of the University of Helsinki.
Malul, M.
1990   Adoption of Foundlings in the Bible and Mesopotamian Documents: A Study of Some Legal Metaphors in Ezekiel 16:1–7. *JSOT* 46: 97–126.
Martin, D. L.
2000   Bodies and Lives: Biological Indicators of Health Differences and Division of Labor by Sex. Pp. 267–300 in *Women and Men in the Prehispanic Southwest: Labor, Power, and Prestige,* ed. P. L. Crown. Santa Fe, NM: School of American Research Press.
Meyers, C.
1988   *Discovering Eve: Ancient Israelite Women in Context.* New York: Oxford University Press.
Milner, L. S.
2000   *Hardness of Heart/Hardness of Life: The Stain of Human Infanticide.* Lanham, MD: University Press of America.
Mosca, P. G.
1975   *Child Sacrifice in Canaanite and Israelite Religion: A Study in Mulk and Mlk.* Ph.D. dissertation. Harvard University.
Naᵓaman, N.
2001   An Assyrian Residence at Ramat Rahel? *Tel Aviv* 28: 260–80.
Nakhai, B. A.
2001   *Archaeology and the Religions of Canaan and Israel.* ASOR Books 7. Boston: American Schools of Oriental Research.

Redford, D.
  1967   The Literary Motif of the Exposed Child (cf. Ex. ii 1–10). *Numen* 14:
          209–28.
Rega, E.
  1997   Age, Gender and Biological Reality in the Early Bronze Age Ceme-
          tery at Mokrin. Pp. 229–47 in *Invisible People and Processes: Writing
          Gender and Childhood into European Archaeology,* ed. J. Moore and
          E. Scott. London: Leicester University Press.
Schwartz, L. L., and Isser, N. K.
  2000   *Endangered Children: Neonaticide, Infanticide, and Filicide.* Pacific Insti-
          tute Series on Forensic Psychology. Boca Raton, FL: CRC.
Scott, E.
  1999   *The Archaeology of Infancy and Infant Death.* British Archaeological
          Reports, International Series 819. Oxford: Archaeopress.
  2001   Killing the Female? Archaeological Narratives of Infanticide. Pp. 3–
          21 in *Gender and the Archaeology of Death,* ed. B. Arnold and N. L.
          Wicker. Walnut Creek, CA: AltaMira.
Scott, S., and Duncan, C. J.
  2002   *Demography and Nutrition: Evidence from Historical and Contemporary
          Populations.* Oxford: Blackwell Science.
Scrimshaw, S. C. M.
  1984   Infanticide in Human Populations. Pp. 439–62 in *Infanticide: Com-
          parative and Evolutionary Perspectives,* ed. G. Hausfater and S. B. Hrdy.
          New York: Aldine.
Smith, M. S.
  2002   *Early History of God: Yahweh and the Other Deities in Ancient Israel,* 2nd
          ed. Grand Rapids, MI: Eerdmans / Dearborn, MI: Dove.
Smith, P., and Kahila, G.
  1992   Identification of Infanticide in Archaeological Sites: A Case Study
          from the Late Roman–Early Byzantine Periods at Ashkelon, Israel.
          Journal of Archaeological Science 19: 667–75.
Sofaer Derevenski, J.
  1994   Where Are the Children? Accessing Children in the Past. *Archaeolog-
          ical Review from Cambridge* 13/2: 7–20.
  1997   Engendering Children, Engendering Archaeology. Pp. 192–202 in
          *Invisible People and Processes: Writing Gender and Childhood into Euro-
          pean Archaeology,* ed. J. Moore and E. Scott. London: Leicester Uni-
          versity Press.
Stager, L. E.
  1982   Carthage: A View from the Tophet. Pp. 155–66 in *Phönizer im Wes-
          ten,* ed. H. G. Niemeyer. Madrider Beiträge 8. Mainz am Rheim: von
          Zabern.
  1985   The Archaeology of the Family in Ancient Israel. *BASOR* 260: 1–35.
Stager, L. E., and Wolff, S. R.
  1984   Child Sacrifice at Carthage: Religious Rite or Population Control?
          BAR 10/1: 30–51.

Steinberg, N.
  1999 The Problem of Human Sacrifice in War: An Analysis of Judges 11. Pp. 114–35 in *On the Way to Nineveh: Studies in Honor of George M. Landes*, ed. S. L. Cook and S. C. Winter. Atlanta: Scholars Press.
Stern, E.
  2001 *Archaeology of the Land of the Bible*, vol. 2: *The Assyrian, Babylon and Persian Periods, 732–332 BCE*. New York: Doubleday.
Trible, P.
  1984 *Texts of Terror: Literary-Feminist Readings of Biblical Narratives*. Overtures to Biblical Theology. Philadelphia: Fortress.
Vanderhooft, D. S.
  1999 *The Neo-Babylonian Empire and Babylon in the Prophets*. HSM 59. Atlanta: Scholars Press.
Washington, H. C.
  1997 Violence and the Construction of Gender in the Hebrew Bible: A New Historicist Approach. *BibInt* 5/4: 324–63.
  1998 "Lest He Die in the Battle and Another Man Take Her": Violence and the Construction of Gender in the Laws of Deuteronomy 20–22. Pp. 185–213 in *Gender and Law in the Hebrew Bible and the Ancient Near East*, ed. V. H. Matthews, B. M. Levinson, and T. Frymer-Kensky. JSOTSup 262. Sheffield: Sheffield Academic Press.
Weems, R. J.
  1995 *Battered Love: Marriage, Sex and Violence in the Hebrew Prophets*. Minneapolis: Fortress.
Wicker, N. L.
  1998 Selective Female Infanticide as Partial Explanation for the Dearth of Women in Viking Age Scandinavia. Pp. 205–21 in *Violence and Society in the Early Medieval West*, ed. G. Halsall. Woodbridge, England: Boydell Press.
Williamson, L.
  1978 Infanticide: An Anthropological Analysis. Pp. 61–75 in *Infanticide and the Value of Life*, ed. M. Koh. Buffalo, NY: Prometheus.

Part 5

Religion and Religious Studies

Elements of Popular Piety in Late Medieval and Early Modern Jewish Psalms Commentary

ALAN COOPER

Jewish Theological Seminary

While the ancient liturgical functions of the individual psalms, as well as the manner of their musical performance, remain matters of scholarly interest and speculation, it seems clear that the biblical book of Psalms was not compiled primarily for liturgical use. The oldest Jewish liturgies incorporate only a few psalms, notably the 6 psalms of the original *pesuqei de-zimra*, the 7 daily psalms, and the 6 psalms that comprise the festival Hallel. And even now, only about 45 psalms (that is, fewer than a third) turn up in the standard liturgies, some of them infrequently, and many of them relative latecomers to the prayer books. The present shape of the book of Psalms (organized, like the Pentateuch, into five books) suggests that the texts were expected to be objects of meditation, contemplation, and study. And while the book is framed in such a way as to support eschatological interpretation,[1] it also seems clear that, like the Torah, the book of Psalms was intended to serve as a guide to proper living.[2]

As such, the psalms have played a vital role in popular religion, although this use of psalms has diminished considerably among mainstream North American Jews. It has been an axiom of Jewish piety for two millennia that the recitation of psalms can keep evil at bay. The psalms are effective against all the demons that beset people, both literal and figurative, whether they originate in the outside world or within a tormented soul:

With God's protection,
You need not fear the terror by night,
or the arrow that flies by day,

---

1. See David C. Mitchell, *The Message of the Psalter: An Eschatological Programme in the Book of Psalms* (JSOTSup 252; Sheffield: Sheffield Academic Press, 1997).

2. See J. Clinton McCann Jr., "The Psalms as Instruction," *Interpretation* 46 (1992) 117–28. For a survey of the various themes that have been alleged to unify the book of Psalms, see John C. Crutchfield, "The Redactional Agenda of the Book of Psalms," *Hebrew Union College Annual* 74 (2003) 21–47.

the plague that stalks in the darkness,
or the scourge that ravages at noon (Ps 91:5–6).[3]

In this vein, one also thinks of the use of psalms in healing rituals or the practice of reciting psalms over a corpse during the night prior to its burial.

In the old *Jewish Encyclopedia*, there is a marvelous article entitled "Bibliomancy" about the magical use of biblical texts.[4] The article includes three tightly packed columns of *shimmush tehillim*, practical uses to which psalms can be put. The best-known collection of these, compiled by the great 18th-century mystic Chaim Azulai (Chid"a), is still available in bookstores that cater to a pious Jewish clientele. One learns that Psalm 3 will cure a headache or pain in the shoulders, Psalm 35 will provide relief from mischievous busybodies, Psalm 93 will help to win a lawsuit, and so on.

The magical protective properties of psalms figure in innumerable Jewish tales. In a charming story of Moroccan origin, for example, a pious rabbi named Shmuel urgently needs to go abroad. He finds a ship that is about to embark, but since he has no money, the captain will not let him on board. Undaunted, the rabbi sets his sleeping mat down on the water, sits on it, and begins to recite psalms. When the ship sets sail, Rabbi Shmuel sails right alongside on his mat, saying psalms all the while. The captain is now anxious to have this wonder-worker for his passenger and offers the rabbi free passage. "God be praised," the rabbi replies, "I'm happy where I am and better off than I'd be on your ship." After the story becomes known, everyone calls Rabbi Shmuel "Abuhatzeira," which means "Mat Man."[5]

In a more somber tale (the Eastern European disposition tends to be more somber), it is reported that in the year 1772, a poor, pious old man died in a certain town. He was neither learned nor distinguished in any way. Imagine the local rabbi's surprise, then, when during the month of mourning following the man's death the fellow appeared to the rabbi in a dream, cloaked in his burial shroud and carrying a book. "Aren't you the guy we just buried?" asks the rabbi, "and what is that book?" "I am," the man replies, "and it is the book of Psalms. I have come to admonish you to warn all of the Jews in town to flee for their lives. For as long as I was alive, reciting the entire book of Psalms each and every day, the town was secure. But now there is no one to protect it."

The rabbi immediately publicized the warning, and, sure enough, the Jews who fled saved themselves, while those who remained suffered griev-

---

3. Biblical texts are cited according to NJPSV, except where modification is required by the context. All translations of rabbinic and medieval texts are my own.
4. *Jewish Encyclopedia* (ed. I. Singer; New York: Funk & Wagnalls, 1925) 3:202–5.
5. See Pinchas Sadeh, *Jewish Folktales* (New York: Doubleday, 1989) 253–54.

ously. From the day of his vision onward, the rabbi began a regimen of reading the book of Psalms. And in case the reader missed the moral of the story, the storyteller spells it out: "All those who faithfully read Psalms will keep all sorts of evil at bay, protecting not only themselves, but the members of their family and others as well, and eliciting the benefits of God's love, mercy, and blessing for themselves and for others."[6]

There are many texts that prescribe beneficial regimens of psalm-reading.[7] The most common take the reader through the entire book either weekly or monthly. One variation of the weekly regimen entails one reading of the book on weekdays, and a second on the Sabbath. Another kind of regimen recommends particular psalms for specific occasions or times of the year. And then there is a mystical regimen of ten daily psalms corresponding to the ten *sefirot*, a sequence that is allegedly replete with significance and power: "three psalms of rebuke [79, 80, 137] . . . three of penitence [25, 51, 90] . . . three of comfort [89, 98, 107] . . . and then a tenth psalm [96] concerning the redemption that is at hand, for then the whole world will recognize the Kingdom of the Almighty."[8]

The recurrent themes in the popular use of psalms are power and control—gaining power over one's environment and assuming control of one's life. The psalms are believed to heal the sick, protect the vulnerable, comfort the bereaved, empower the weak, and enfeeble the oppressor. They have these capabilities not because of any inherent qualities but because they embody a single overarching principle: "The Lord watches over all who love Him, but all the wicked He will destroy" (Ps 145:20); "The Lord watches over the stranger; He gives courage to the orphan and widow, but makes the path of the wicked tortuous" (Ps 146:9).

In his book, *The Art of Biblical Poetry*, Robert Alter perceptively characterizes the psalms as instances of "poetic form used to reshape the world in the light of belief."[9] In late medieval and early modern Jewish Psalms commentaries (by which I mean commentaries written ca. 1500–1800), the task of the commentator is to describe that world—a world in which the believer, sometimes against all odds, confidently asserts, "Happy are all who take refuge in [the Lord]" (Ps 2:12, reiterated about three dozen times in other psalms).[10] The burden of commentary is to show how the psalms

---

6. Cited from Simcha Abraham Hashlag, ספר תפילות דוד בן ישי (Bnei Brak: Merkaz torani . . . Ashlag, 1994) 219.

7. Conveniently collected in Hashlag, ספר תפילות דוד בן ישי, passim.

8. Isaiah Horowitz [Shela"h], שני לוחות הברית (5 vols.; Jerusalem: Oz ve-hadar, 1993) 3:343–45 (quotation on p. 343).

9. Robert Alter, *The Art of Biblical Poetry* (New York: Basic Books, 1985) 133.

10. On the root חסה 'to take refuge' as a key word in the shaping of the book of Psalms, see Jerome F. D. Creach, *Yahweh as Refuge and the Editing of the Hebrew Psalter* (JSOTSup 217; Sheffield: Sheffield Academic Press, 1996).

convey a fundamental truth: that "David" (the surrogate for the believer) gains control of his life not by the exercise of military or political might but through devotion to God in the form of prayer, penitence, and observance of the commandments.

Psalm 27 is a text that is rich in interpretive potential, not only because of its content but also due to its liturgical function as the penitential psalm of the New Year season. This application of the psalm seems to have been a relatively late development in Ashkenazi prayer.[11] As the usage spread, it also became productive for popular Psalms commentary. Two examples from the 17th–18th centuries will illustrate my point. The first is a homily by Pinchas Halevi Horowitz collected in פנים יפות (an anthology of Horowitz's Psalms interpretations drawn from his various writings), a tour de force in which Horowitz relates the psalm to the period from the beginning of the month of Elul (the month immediately preceding the New Year) until Shemini Atzeret.[12] Adding up the numerical value of the letters of the first three words of the psalm, he notes, yields the same total as the Hebrew words זכרון plus כפורים (639), which designate Rosh Hashana and Yom Kippur, respectively. In like manner, the phrase מעוז חיי ('stronghold of my life', v. 1) hints at Sukkot because it is numerically equivalent to the words ימי סוכה ('days of *sukkah*'). David's request to "live in the house of the Lord" in v. 4, according to Horowitz, is an allusion to dwelling in the *sukkah*, where one hopes to be worthy of receiving the Divine Presence (שכינה).[13] The petition, "Do not subject me to the will of my foes" (v. 12), he suggests, refers to Shemini Atzeret, "when the chits are handed in" and the penitential season is concluded.

With comparable ingenuity, Chaim Katz, in his Psalms commentary ארץ החיים, observes that the word לולא at the beginning of v. 13 is an anagram for the month name Elul, "because in Elul it is possible to repair what has been spoiled" during the year. The three clauses of v. 14, then, refer to the High Holiday season: "Look to the Lord" on Rosh Hashana; "Be strong and of good courage" during the Ten Days of Repentance; and "Look to the Lord" on Yom Kippur.[14]

---

11. I am grateful to my colleague Menahem Schmelzer for this information.

12. ספר תהלים עם פירוש פנים יפות השלם (Jerusalem: Makhon haflaʾa, 1994) 99–107. Horowitz was born and educated in Poland but served prominently as a rabbi in Frankfurt from 1771 until his death in 1805. In his youth, Horowitz came under the influence of some of the founders of Hasidism; later on, as a champion of Neo-Orthodoxy, he preached against the Jewish Enlightenment (*haskala*). See *EncJud* 8:999–1001.

13. In *Pesiq. Rab Kah.* Sup. 2.1 (ed. Bernard Mandelbaum; 2 vols.; New York: Jewish Theological Seminary, 1962) 2:453, the *sukkah* of Ps 27:5 provides protection for the righteous on the Day of Judgment.

14. Avraham Chaim Cohen, ארץ החיים (Constantinople, 1750) 39a. While Avraham Chaim Cohen is the name on the title page of the book, the author seems also to have

The liturgical use of the psalm is based on a well-known passage in the midrash *Leviticus Rabbah* that is frequently cited in later commentary. Commenting on v. 1, "The Lord is my light and my help," the midrash states, "my light on Rosh Hashana, and my help on Yom Kippur."[15] That statement comes in the concluding section of a long homily on Psalm 27 and is a prime example of rabbinic midrash. The starting point of the midrash is Lev 16:3. At the beginning of the priestly ritual that is traditionally associated with Yom Kippur, the instruction reads, בזאת יבא אהרן אל הקדש 'with this shall Aaron come into the sanctuary'. The ambiguous demonstrative בזאת[16] ('with this') serves as the stimulus for the midrash, which seeks to identify the thing (the 'this') that Aaron requires and finds a ready correlation between בזאת in Lev 16:3 and the same word in Ps 27:3, in the phrase בזאת אני בוטח 'in this I trust'. Whatever induces confidence in the psalmist, even when enemies surround him, also accompanies Aaron into the sanctuary on Yom Kippur.

The correlation of the two texts occasions a four-part homily on Psalm 27, relating the psalm sequentially to the Exodus from Egypt, David's encounter with Goliath, David's war against Amalek, and a New Year judgment scene. The midrash is structured both chronologically and symmetrically: it moves from the distant past to the homilist's present, and it is arranged in an A B B A pattern, with two stories about the salvation of the Jewish people framing two stories about remarkable victories of David. The midrash thus actualizes the rabbinic dictum that everything in the book of Psalms applies to David, to all Israel, and to all times.[17]

The chronological movement, moreover, signifies a conceptual movement from the historical level to a timeless, mythic plane. The exodus and the story of David and Goliath are concretized in the psalm through networks of intertextual allusions, designed to fix in the reader's mind the connection between the psalm and the stories. This sort of intertextual connection is a prominent feature of historical and biographical Psalms

---

been known as Chaim Katz. Adding to the confusion, a brief notice in *EncJud* 6:1159 dubs him Hayyim (Abraham) Ben Samuel Feivush (Phoebus). The online catalogue of the Jewish Theological Seminary Library, incidentally, describes ארץ החיים as "Bible. Psalms. Hebrew," with no mention of Katz/Cohen, or his commentary!

15. *Lev. Rab.* 21:4, in מדרש ויקרא רבה (ed. Mordecai Margulies; Jerusalem: Wahrmann, 1972) 473–80 (quotation on p. 478). Cf. the parallel in מדרש תהלים (ed. Buber), 1:112b (p. 224).

16. See Betty Rojtman, *Black Fire on White Fire: An Essay on Jewish Hermeneutics, from Midrash to Kabbalah* (trans. Steven Rendall; Contraversions 10; Berkeley: University of California Press, 1998) 15–67.

17. *Midr. Ps.* on Ps 18:1, in מדרש תהלים (ed. Solomon Buber; 2 vols. in 1; Vilna, Poland: Romm, 1891) 1:68a (p. 135). Also *Midr. Ps.* on Ps 4:1 (ed. Buber; 1:20b [40]): "Everything that David said refers to himself and to all Israel."

interpretation, both in the midrash and in later commentary. (It may also have given rise to some of the Psalms' superscriptions.)[18]

When the midrash discusses Amalek and the Day of Judgment, however, the connections are established more by assertion than through proof texts. Already in the Bible, Amalek has an ambivalent status, appearing both as a historical entity and as the archetypical enemy. In postbiblical literature, of course, Amalek takes on an entirely symbolic character.[19] And thus Amalek provides a fitting transition in the midrash to the final judgment scene, where the guardian angels of the nations level charges of perfidy against the Jews, and God rebuffs the would-be prosecutors:

> These are idolaters, and those are idolaters; these engage in illicit sex, and those engage in illicit sex; these shed innocent blood, and those shed innocent blood. Why, then, do these descend to Gehinnom while those do not? "It is they, my foes and enemies, [who stumble and fall]"[20] (Ps 27:2): there are 365 days in the solar year, but the numerical value of "the Satan" (השטן) is 364. All year, Satan prosecutes; on Yom Kippur, however, Satan does not prosecute.

The midrash concludes with the language of Ps 27:3 embedded in a prayer of thanksgiving (the additions are italicized): "'Should an army *of the nations of the world* besiege me, my heart would have no fear; should *the nations of the world* arise against me, in this I trust'—in what you promised me [in saying] 'with this shall Aaron come [into the sanctuary],'" returning at last to the Leviticus text that prompted the midrash.

The *Leviticus Rabbah* text provides an excellent example of two kinds of flexibility in Psalms interpretation, with respect to chronology (past and present) and the identity of the psalmist (the individual David and the corporate Israel). Late medieval and early modern commentary manifests both the survival of the midrashic methods and greater concern for the spiritual development of the individual who is praying or contemplating the psalm. I will illustrate those two aspects of later Psalms commentary with texts from the 16th–18th centuries.

The historical/biographical mode of interpretation is perpetuated in the 16th-century commentary of Ovadia Sforno.[21] Sforno provides introduc-

---

18. See Brevard Childs, "Psalm Titles and Midrashic Exegesis," *JSS* 16 (1971) 137–50; Eliezer Slomovic, "Toward an Understanding of the Formation of Historical Titles in the Book of Psalms," *ZAW* 91 (1979) 350–80. For the argument that the superscriptions facilitate readerly identification with "David," see Susanne Gillmayr-Bucher, "The Psalm Headings: A Canonical Relecture of the Psalms," in *The Biblical Canons* (ed. J.-M. Auwers and H. J. de Jonge; Leuven: Leuven University Press, 2003) 247–54.

19. See Elijah Judah Schochet, *Amalek: The Enemy Within* (Los Angeles: Mimetav, 1991).

20. That is, the would-be prosecutors ("the nations of the world") will "stumble and fall" instead of the Jews.

21. תהלים . . . עם פירוש . . . רבינו עובדיה ספורנו (ed. Aaron Walden; Vilna, Poland: Romm, 1876). On Sforno, see Ephraim Finkel, *R. Obadja Sforno als Exeget* (Breslau: Schatzky, 1896);

tory rubrics for most psalms, clarifying the direction that his interpretation will take. These introductory comments usually are either historical or eschatological in character: his "David" either reflects on the past or prophesies concerning the future. On Psalm 27, Sforno comments, "In this psalm, [David] prayed when he was fleeing from Saul that he might not fall into his hand, nor into the hand of idolaters, and that he might not learn from their actions while he was in their midst."[22] It is not difficult to see the first part of that rubric as reflecting an historical interest and the second as addressing a contemporary concern—Sforno admonishing his readers not to "learn from" the "idolaters" among whom *they* were living.

When he comments on the body of the psalm, Sforno glosses it with historical information. On v. 1, for example, "'the Lord is my light' in anointing me by means of Samuel; 'and my salvation' from the lion and the bear and Goliath." On the word יסתירני in v. 5, "'he sheltered me' when Amalek attacked Ziklag." And in v. 12, the "foes" who are mentioned are "those who incite Saul against me."

Sforno reads other psalms as messianic prophecies. For example, on Psalm 24: "In this psalm [David] prayed concerning Israel that they all be worthy of the Messianic Era and life in the world to come."[23] Similarly, in Psalm 30, the "house" that is to be dedicated in the superscription, according to Sforno, is the one "that will be built, speedily in our day."[24]

Occasionally, Sforno moves directly from the historical dimension to the lesson that the contemporary reader is supposed to draw from the psalm. A good example is his rubric for Psalm 34:

> It already has been explained [in the superscription] that David composed this psalm when he "feigned madness in the presence of Abimelech." What arises from it is that it is not fitting for a person in distress to protest against God, but to bless God, because all of God's ways are love and truth. One should pray concerning the distress, and the Merciful One undoubtedly will come to the rescue.[25]

This rubric displays the tendency toward personalization of the message of the psalm, which becomes increasingly prominent in later commentary. Sometimes (as in Sforno), the historical element is retained, and other times it is not. Two commentaries from later in the 16th century exemplify both of these styles of interpretation.

Joseph Volk, הפרשן־ההומניסט, ר' עובדיה ספורנו, in ניייגר ספר (ed. A. Biram; Jerusalem: Hachevra le-cheqer ha-miqra be-yisraʾel, 1959) 277–302.

22. Sforno, תהלים, 19b.
23. Ibid., 18a.
24. Ibid., 21b.
25. Ibid., 24b.

Moses Alshekh introduces his commentary on Psalm 27 with an anthropological statement:

> It is well known that the person (אדם) is the soul (נפש), not the flesh (בשר). The flesh is referred to as "human flesh" (בשר אדם) because it is flesh and not spirit (רוח). Therefore, in speaking about his soul, [David] said "my light and my help, etc." In speaking about his flesh, he said, "to eat up my flesh."[26]

The notion that the psalmist differentiates between physical and spiritual enemies is in an interpretation cited by Abraham Ibn Ezra: "There are those who say, 'my light' concerns matters of the soul, and 'my help' matters of the body; 'stronghold of my life' is the conjoining of soul and body, and he does not fear that any person can sunder them."[27]

Many commentators, like Alshekh, distinguish the longing for material success from the yearning for spiritual well-being. Their view, naturally, is that only the latter represents the psalmist's true desire. Joseph Jabez, a Spanish commentator of the generation of the Expulsion (d. 1507), prefaces his interpretation of Psalm 27 with the remark "Our perfect Torah enables us to acquire spiritual well-being (הצלחת הנפש) essentially and primarily, and material well-being (הצלחת הגוף) accidentally and secondarily."[28] According to Samuel Laniado of Aleppo (d. 1605), the reason the psalmist does not fear his enemies is that "whatever evil they might do to me is to the flesh, not to the essence of my person [i.e., my soul, עצמות נפשי]; they have the power only 'to devour my flesh.'"[29]

Immediately following his opening comment, Alshekh identifies the existential crisis in David's life that gave rise to the psalm:

> He was prophesying about a particular incident; that is, he was still suffering the consequences of the Bathsheba incident.[30] His enemies still insisted that, as an adulterer, he ought to be put to death, and they vexed him even in his house of study. It is well known that prior to the Bathsheba incident, he had asked God for permission to build the Temple, and God had not responded. Some time afterwards, the Bathsheba incident occurred, giving rise to the purpose of this psalm.

---

26. ספר רוממות אל על תהלים לרבינו האלשיך הקדוש (ed. David Ohayon; 2 vols.; Bnei Braq: pub. by the author, 1992) 1:217–24. On Alshekh, see Shimon Shalem, רבי משה אלשיך: לחקר שיטתו הפרשנית והשקפותיו בעניני מחשבה ומוסר (Jerusalem: Ben-Zvi Institute, 1966).

27. מקראות גדולות הכתר: תהלים חלק א׳ (Ramat-Gan: Bar Ilan University, 2003) 83.

28. Samuel Halpern, ed., תהלים עם פירוש יוסף יעבץ . . . יוסף יעבץ (London: pub. by the editor, 1952) 151. On Jabez, see *EncJud* 9:1173

29. Chaim Kutainer, ed., ספר תהלים עם שלשה פירושים נפלאים (Jerusalem: n.p., 1985) 44. On Laniado, who was a rabbi and communal leader in Aleppo, see *EncJud* 10:1423.

30. *Pesiq. Rab Kah.* 5.3 (ed. Mandelbaum; 1:84) places Ps 27:1 before the Bathsheba incident.

After giving that "historical" setting for the psalm, Alshekh takes note of its broader application, recalling the anthropological comment with which he introduced the psalm. He writes:

> A person generally has two kinds of enemies. One is the enemy of the soul, that is, the evil inclination and all the forces of uncleanness that are brought into being by transgressions—each one of which is like a warrior attempting to drag him into additional sin, ultimately to destroy his soul. The second is the enemy of the body, such as those kings who would conduct wars against him and his kingdom and try to kill him.

David, it transpires, "had yet a third kind of enemy: those enemies roundabout him such as Doeg and Ahitophel, who humiliated him and vexed him." Alshekh continues:

> As for the first and second kind of enemies, David said that he was not worried about them: with God as his help, he need not fear any affliction of his soul or his body. As for the third kind, however, he declared that if only God would grant his prior request, and allow him to build the Temple, he would withdraw from human affairs and reside every day in the Temple—returning home each evening and then resuming his station in the Temple the following morning every day of his life. Then his enemies would see and be ashamed, for God would have vindicated him in allowing him to build God's house, and to become a member of God's household. Only then would [David] have respite from their rebuke.

Two aspects of this opening section of Alshekh's commentary are anticipated in earlier commentary but assume greater prominence in later writings. The first is his move toward interiorizing the enemy of the psalmist, identifying the "enemy of the soul" with the "evil inclination." The second is the notion that David's principal desire—the "one thing" that he asks of God in v. 4—is to retire from worldly affairs to a contemplative life. The same idea is found earlier, for example, in Menachem Meiri's Psalms commentary. Meiri writes:

> David apparently uttered this psalm as a general prayer for protection against his enemies, and as an acknowledgement of his trust in God. It is also to acknowledge that his intention was not the attainment of power and victory, or honor and pleasure, but the perfection of his soul by means of perpetual service of God.[31]

Or, as Samuel Laniado puts it, "I am not concerned with the give and take and the dealings of my everyday life in this world, but with 'my dwelling in the house of the Lord.'"[32]

---

31. מקראות גדולות הכתר: תהלים חלק א׳ (Ramat-Gan: Bar Ilan University, 2003) 83.
32. ספר תהלים עם שלשה פירושים נפלאים, 44.

When he comes to v. 2, Alshekh offers a striking interpretation of the phrase צרי ואיבי לי. His David declares that these "enemies and foes" are the "destroyers [משחיתים] that were created by my transgressions." They are "mine" [לי] in a possessive sense, in the same sense as "every occurrence of לי in Scripture that denotes 'belonging to me' [שלי]." The meaning of this pronouncement is not only David's acknowledgement of guilt and responsibility; it also provides a valuable lesson for the penitent reader:

> When a person who has created destroyers by sinning repents out of love, the Gemara asserts that the sins have been transformed into virtues and the prosecutors into defenders.[33] As R. Shimon b. Levi said, "Great is the power of repentance, in that faults become like virtues" because the prosecutors are turned into defenders and lovers.[34]

Turning "David" into the prototypical penitent gives Alshekh a powerful tool for analyzing the progress of the psalm. He summarizes the development of thought in his commentary on v. 14. Although David explicitly requests only "one thing" of God in v. 4, according to Alshekh he actually petitions God for three things in sequence, "as is the way of the humble penitent." The first is that God should allow David access to the Divine Presence (v. 8); the second is that God should not deprive David of that beneficent Presence for any reason (v. 9); and the third is that God should "instruct him and conduct him on the path of piety beyond the letter of the law" (v. 11). The three clauses of v. 14, then, represent the supportive and encouraging response of the "Holy Spirit" to David's three petitions.

In contrast with Alshekh, his contemporary (and fellow student in the yeshiva of Joseph Taitazak in Salonika), Moses Almosnino, offers an exposition of Psalm 27 in which the historical references recede into the background, while the psalmist's response to adversity is exemplary for the contemporary audience. This exposition appears in the first sermon in Almosnino's collection, ספר מאמץ כח.[35] The theme of the sermon is divine providence; the gist of it is that God knows what is best for people, including the right time to inflict suffering on them.

Almosnino asserts that there are two things that the psalm imparts from the outset. The first is that one requires "a teacher to show the path that one should take, who illuminates it against the darkness" of the enemy. The second is that even if one should be overtaken by the enemy, God will

---

33. Alshekh paraphrases and expands the statement in *b. Yoma* 86b attributed to Resh Laqish: גדולה תשובה שזדונות נעשות לו כזכיות.

34. The Resh Laqish quotation in the Talmud is attributed to Shimon b. Levi in *Yal. Shim.* 2:530.

35. ספר מאמץ כח (Venice, 1588) 8a (bot.)–12b. On Almosnino, see Meir Bnaya, משה אלמושנינו, איש שלוניקי: פועלו ויצירתו (Tel-Aviv: Tel-Aviv University, 1996) esp. 93–105 on מאמץ כח.

provide help. "Concerning both of them," Almosnino writes, "'The Lord is my light and my help, whom should I fear': this means that God is my light, providing light by which I might discern my enemies, and God is my help, rescuing me even if they should attack me."

When he comes to v. 2, Almosnino relates the psalm explicitly to the theme of his sermon. One should bear in mind that Almosnino was preaching in Salonika to a congregation comprising refugees from Spain and Portugal and their children:

> We have witnessed many perfected individuals[36] who have experienced many evil hardships, despite no transgression or sin on their part. Likewise, King David himself, against whom many arose, which is why he said, "when evil men assail me, etc." This means that when the evil things approached me, it was in order "to devour my flesh"—not my soul, for they have no power to touch my soul.

The evil things that befall the righteous person, "David" recognizes, are "for my own benefit, in that they suppress the material so that the 'form' might be elevated [שיכניעו החומר ותגבה הצורה] and the soul strengthened."[37] When David says צרי ואויבי לי, according to Almosnino, "he means that [those enemies] are for my benefit and for my own good, as is indicated by the word לי, as in לך לך, 'for your benefit and for your own good'"—citing Rashi's famous comment on the call of Abram in Gen 12:1. In like manner, the "enemies roundabout" in v. 6 are a metaphor for "my corporeal faculties" (כחותי הגשמיות). The soul is capable of overcoming these "enemies," and this provides an occasion for offering songs of praise (also in v. 6).

The "one thing" that David requests of God, for a post-Maimonidean like Almosnino, can mean only the attainment of knowledge of God (ההשגה האלהית),[38] to which he finds metaphorical reference in v. 4. A lengthy discussion of this point is preceded by observing that, for Aristotle, "perfect love" should have only a single object, as exemplified by David's requesting only "one thing."[39] This discussion is typical of Almosnino's

---

36. שלמים, the philosophical term denoting individuals who have attained the highest intellectual and spiritual attainment that is possible for a human being. See, e.g., Yehuda Halevi, *Kuzari* 1.1; Maimonides, *Guide of the Perplexed* 3.54.

37. Almosnino alludes to the standard philosophical contrast between matter and form, referring to corporeality and spirituality, respectively.

38. Following Maimonides, *Guide* 3.54 (end): שלמות האדם אשר בו יתהלל באמת הוא להגיע אל השגת האלוה כפי היכולת 'the human perfection in which one may glory is to attain knowledge of God in accordance with one's capacity'.

39. Samuel Laniado makes a similar point without reference to Aristotle: "A person might petition for one thing with the purpose in mind of attaining something else in addition, so that his one petition is actually two, a single petition with a dual purpose. David, however, said, 'one thing I ask of the Lord,' not two, and the one thing that I ask is for the purpose 'that I seek,' and nothing else" (ספר תהלים עם שלשה פירושים נפלאים, 45).

popular philosophizing: he regularly incorporates simple philosophical ideas into his sermons with pedagogical intent.

The upshot of the first six verses of the psalm, then, is that "while God sometimes treats me with strict justice because of my wickedness, it is for my own good, and in fact everything is derived from God's mercy." The rest of the psalm, according to Almosnino, entails "the recounting of what happened to [David] in the past and in the present, and what might happen to him in the future."

After expounding the psalm at length, with felicitous interpretations of many details,[40] Almosnino addresses his congregation directly:

> Now every one of us, collectively and individually, who dwell in this city, can recite this psalm about ourselves. And so I say about myself, "the Lord is my light and my help, whom should I fear," because God has been a light for me, and has led me on my way. God surely has rescued me, so that I need not fear the multitude of people. With God as the "stronghold of my life, whom should I dread?" From now on, "when evil men assail me to devour my flesh"—as has been the case until now, when they stood ready to destroy us[41] with persecutions and calumny—I will be avenged, and my foes and my enemies will stumble and fall.

When the psalmist petitions, "Show me your way, O Lord" (v. 11), Almosnino glosses the 'way' (דרך) as "the way of spiritual perfection, namely the true discernment that may be described as God's way."

This discernment should be complemented by right action (the "level path" of v. 11), which will confound those "false witnesses" (v. 12) who think that the psalmist is interested in material success rather than spiritual attainment. And finally, "I continually say to myself, 'Look to the Lord; be strong and of good courage': . . . God will requite me for my righteousness and innocence . . . and will repay the wicked for their evil." The world is predictably reshaped in the light of belief.

I now move on to the two later commentaries that I mentioned previously in connection with the liturgical use of Psalm 27. Here we find two more instances of the identification of the biblical "enemies" with the evil inclination, as well as prescriptive lessons arising out of that identification. In an isolated comment on Ps 27:2, Pinchas Halevi Horowitz contends that the evil inclination, like the "idolaters who enslave Israel," ultimately will be subjected to divine judgment. He writes:

---

40. For example, a detailed analysis of the distinction between 'fear' (יראה) and 'dread' (פחד) in v. 1; also a fine interpretation of v. 5 as a description of the all-encompassing nature of divine protection.

41. שהיו עומדים עלינו לכלותינו, borrowing the language of the Passover *Haggadah*.

Accordingly, when David says "when the evil assail me to devour my flesh" [v. 2], he means to say that even though they have been permitted "to devour my flesh," eventually "my foes and enemies will be mine," in the sense that they will be judged, and will "stumble and fall."

In a lengthier homily on the same text, Horowitz echoes Alshekh's (and the Rabbis') notion that when people sin, they cause destructive powers to be arrayed against them. These 'prosecutors' (מקטריגים, based on the language of 'Abot 4.11), "vex (משטינים) humans from on high, and demand justice against them." When David says, "My foes and my enemies"— namely, those foes and enemies who seek judgment against him, it is they who will "stumble and fall."

Horowitz also follows Alshekh in dividing the psalmist's enemies into three categories. Horowitz's categories, however, unlike Alshekh's, are divorced from the circumstances of the historical David and relate solely to the contemporary reader. First is the existential enemy, the nations among whom the Jews live in exile. Second are the "prosecutors" I just mentioned, "who are born out of transgression." And third is the evil inclination, "the enemy within that dwells in the heart." Relating his three enemies to the language of the psalm, Horowitz writes:

Accordingly, "when evil men assail me" (v. 2) should be interpreted in relation to the idolatrous rulers who vex the Jews with torments in exile. These arise on account of the transgressions of the Jews, as Scripture says, "You were sold off for your sins" (Isa 50:1), and they [i.e., their sins] become the prosecutors against the Jews who continue to torment them. . . . As for these second enemies that are created out of transgressions and surround people, he said "my heart would have no fear" (v. 3), because as long as one directs one's heart towards heaven, [the transgressions] cannot hold sway. When he said "should war beset me" (v. 3), that refers to the third enemy, namely the evil inclination that dwells within and rises up and incites. Concerning this, he said, "in this (בזאת) I am confident," namely in Yom Kippur, about which it is said, "with this (בזאת) shall Aaron come," when the [evil inclination] has no power to incite, as is explained in the midrash.

Horowitz's commentary can be distilled down to three essential elements of personal piety that he seeks to convey to his reader through the medium of the psalm. The first is comparable to one of Almosnino's main points: that the goal of prayer is to seek not personal gain but the illumination of God's presence. That is the "one thing" the psalmist requests in v. 4. Horowitz focuses his teaching on the New Year season: "On Rosh Hashana and Yom Kippur we make many petitions, but the substance of all of those petitions is just one thing—to serve God, and to receive God's presence joyfully."

His second important idea, which we have noted already, is that God offers protection against all kinds of enemies, including those from within as well as those from without. And the combination of the first two propositions leads him to his concluding argument, which is also reminiscent of one of Almosnino's themes, namely, that God's deliverance may be achieved through suffering. Commenting on v. 9, Horowitz writes:

> We must further explain what [David] means by "Do not hide your face from me," because there is a face of good will and a face of wrath. . . . A person should not err with regard to the face of wrath that provides benefit in this world, thinking that it is the face of affection; on the contrary, one should accept suffering with love, as we find in Egypt, when the hardship of slavery was decreed against [the Israelites] in order to hasten their redemption.

When David appeals to "God, my deliverer" (אלהי ישעי) at the end of the verse, his use of the divine name *Elohim*, which traditionally denotes strict justice, indicates that David actually sought out suffering as the means of attaining deliverance.[42] The lesson for the reader of the psalm is clear: "How good is suffering in life if one accepts it with love, recognizing that it is for one's benefit."

The identification of the psalmist's enemies with the evil inclination, also with reference to the midrash, figures in Chaim Katz's Psalms commentary, ארץ החיים, which was written in the late 17th century and published in Constantinople around 1750.[43] Katz's primary distinction seems to be that he was the great-grandson of Joshua Falk, the author of standard commentaries on the normative Jewish law code, the *Shulchan Arukh*. In his biographical work שם הגדולים, Chaim Azulai (Chid"a) describes Katz by his filiation. He also mentions that, late in life, Katz came to Hebron, where "he comported himself in a pious manner."[44]

Katz's little-known Psalms commentary turns out to be filled with interest. On Ps 27:3, "should an army besiege me," he offers a virtuosic elaboration of the ambiguous demonstrative of *Leviticus Rabbah*:

> This means the army of the evil inclination. Even though it declares war against me—since the evil inclination of a person gains daily in strength, particularly in the disciples of the wise . . . "in 'this' I trust," namely in the holy covenant[45] that is called "'this' is the sign of the

---

42. Cf. *b. Sanh.* 107a–b.

43. I have not seen Katz's work cited in any recent scholarly discussion, although it is excerpted in Aaron Walden's collection of Psalms commentary, מקדש מעט (4 vols.; Warsaw: Baumritter and Genscher, 1889–1897) 1:175b–176a (350–51).

44. Chaim Azulai, ספר שם הגדולים השלם (Jerusalem: Otsar ha-sefarim, 1992) 220, §142. Azulai occasionally cites ארץ החיים in his own Psalms commentary, חומת אנך. See, e.g., תהלים :א הרחיד"א אוצרות ספר (Jerusalem: Or torat har. chida, n.d.) 36a–b.

45. That is, circumcision. Cf. Rojtman, *Black Fire on White Fire*, 64.

covenant" (Gen 9:12, 17), and the Torah, which is called "'this' is the Torah" (Deut 4:44), and the *Shekinah*, which is called "this." . . . "The fool does not understand 'this'" (Ps 92:7), but David said, "with 'this' I know that you have favored me" (Ps 41:12).

When the psalmist petitions God to "shelter me in his *sukkah*" (v. 5), Katz comments, "This means that God should providentially protect me against the evil inclination in this world, which is called a *sukkah*, since it is a temporary dwelling—the seven days [of Sukkot] corresponding to the seventy years [of a normal lifespan]."

Like Almosnino and Horowitz, Katz betrays the deep pessimism that pervades much early modern Jewish homily. Their writings reflect both anxiety about the condition of the Jewish people and despair about human nature. If even those who are "perfected" experience misery in their lives, how much worse it must be for ordinary people. There is only one source of comfort: that the suffering that one endures during one's brief life in this world is both beneficial and providential, leading to vindication in the world to come. The existential enemies of the Jews are deconstructed into mere figments, "prosecutors" born out of Jewish sin, and are therefore subject to destruction by acts of piety. Through prayer, repentance, and observance of the commandments, believers can gain at least an illusion of control over their destiny.

I will conclude with a sample of 18th-century commentary in which these themes appear in a kabbalistic context. This interpretation is from the חידושי תהלים of Rav Yeivi (Jacob Joseph of Ostrog), one of the "sages of the *kloyz*," a circle of kabbalists in Brody.[46] Rav Yeivi deviates immediately from most earlier commentary in joining the superscription לדוד to the psalm proper. He writes:

It is well known that the *Shekinah* is called "David," and that when "David" and Adonai are conjoined [i.e., לדוד יי, the first two words of the psalm], there is unity [יחוד] on high. Then Adonai is my light, granting continual illumination to me, that I might know the right path to walk, as it is written, "the commandment is a lamp, the teaching is a light" (Prov 6:23).[47] A person who is walking in the dark might fall into a pit, but one who has a lamp to light the way sees the pit and avoids falling

---

46. ספר רב ייבי (Brody: M. L. Hermelin, 1874) 54b–55b. On the *kloyz*, see *EncJud* 10:554.

47. Cf. *Zohar* 3:119a: "'The Lord is my light and my help': When a person cleaves to the luminary that is on high, and God sends forth his illumination upon him, he need fear nothing in the upper or lower world, as it is written, 'But upon you the Lord will shine, and his glory will be seen over you' (Isa 60:2). 'The Lord is the stronghold of my life': When God is united with a person, he need fear none of the angels of judgment in that world." In a sermon for the Sabbath of Repentance (the Sabbath that falls between Rosh Hashana and Yom Kippur), Isaac Chaber (Wildmann; 1789–1853; the sermon is dated 1848) relates the preternatural illumination of the Zohar to the judgment scene in

into it. In like manner, the divine commandment provides light for the one who fulfills it, so that one will not fall into the pit of Gehinnom. The Torah comprises all of the commandments that illuminate the way for a person, so that one will not transgress the commandments and fall into the pit of Gehinnom. "My help" [ישעי] refers to those times when a person knows the right way, but commits a transgression nevertheless, because the evil inclination prevailed. It says "my help" because God provides help against the evil inclination.

To amplify that last point, Rav Yeivi draws on the psalmist's military metaphor in v. 3:

> David taught our fellow Jews to serve God, and not to fear any of the evil prosecutors who would impede that service. Just as a prince who is surrounded by a mighty army that protects him from all harm naturally fears no one, so too the righteous person is called a "warrior" and is surrounded by a mighty army brought into being through observance of the commandments, as the sages said, "one who fulfills a commandment acquires a defender."

Even if the army is invisible to the believer, faith is still possible—the certainty that "the *Shekinah*, who is called 'this,' together with her legion, surround and protect" the penitent.

Rav Yeivi twice asserts the significance of the number 91, as well as the theurgic power of human action, in his comments on vv. 1 and 5:

> [on v. 1:] Then the psalmist says "whom [ממי] shall I fear." The numerical value of ממי plus one [the *ʾalep* of the next word, אירע] is 91 [40 + 40 + 10 +1], the equivalent of אדני / ה"והי [26 + 65—two different spellings of the divine name]. Because of that unity, a person must fear the Exalted One. The reason is that all of the unities that are attained on high are by virtue of the good deeds that the righteous perform below.

> [on v. 5:] Everything that a person does in this world is preserved and stored away [צפון, from the same root as יצפנני] for the world to come, whether for good or for ill, as recompense. How good it is for a person to be righteous and devoted to God, storing up [יצפון] good deeds that will provide reward in the world to come! . . . The interpretation of the verse, כי יצפנני בסכה is that what I store away [מצפין] every day for the world to come are the good deeds by which I establish unity between the Holy One and the *Shekinah*, as is indicated by the numerical value

---

Leviticus Rabbah: "'My light' on Rosh Hashana, namely, the spark of revealed supernal light in the place of darkness below—that was on Rosh Hashana, by means of the blowing of the shofar, which suppresses Satan. And [God] is 'my help' on Yom Kippur against Satan, so that [Satan] cannot prosecute at the time when sins are forgiven." See ספר שיח יצחק (2 vols.; Kaidan: S. Movshovitz, 1939) 1:43.

of סוכה [*sic*] = 91, equivalent to הוי״ה / אדני.[48] Then on an evil day God "will protect me in his tent," namely by the *Shekinah*, which is called "tent."

For all its kabbalistic trappings, the simple piety underlying Rav Yeivi's interpretation is easy to discern: by their good deeds, the righteous earn God's protection.

I believe it is appropriate to conclude with the strong theurgic impulse behind these last texts. In fact, I like to think of the retrieval of these obscure but fascinating commentaries as my own "good deed." Late medieval and early modern commentators probe the religious expression of the biblical psalms to profound homiletical effect. Eschewing the more down-to-earth approach of the "canonical" commentaries (Rashi, Ibn Ezra, Radaq), these authors seek to forge an intimate connection between the text and the inner life of the pious reader. In doing so, they cast a fascinating (if occasionally oblique) light on the psalms themselves.

---

48. Another member of the *kloyz* group, Moses Ostrer, proves that the *sukkah* of v. 5 denotes the *Shekinah* by observing that the letters preceding those in the word בסכה (i.e., אניד) can be rearranged to spell the divine name אדני. See Ostrer's דרש משה (ed. Aaron Ostrer; Lemberg: Carl Budweiser, 1879) 58a. In his commentary on v. 4 (57b), Ostrer cites a Lurianic tradition that takes the 'one thing' (אחת) David requests of God as an acronym connoting three things: the Land of Israel (ארץ ישראל), life in the world to come (חיי העולם הבא), and Torah (תורה). David makes this request of "Adonai" because that divine name connotes the divine attribute of mercy. Thus, David is asking that he receive those three benefactions out of God's love, and "not by means of suffering."

The Biblical Icon

STEPHEN COX

University of California, San Diego

Richard Friedman concludes *Who Wrote the Bible?* by saying, "The question, after all, is not only who wrote the Bible, but who reads it."[1] I agree; but I would add a phrase. I would say, "who reads it, and why they want to do so."

What shall we say about the Bible's hold on individual readers? What shall we say, in particular, about the biblical passages to which readers perennially return for inspiration, instruction, or confirmation of preexisting ideas? Very few Jews or Christians base their religious views on a systematic study of every book in the canon, but virtually all of them recall the temptation in Eden, the attempted sacrifice of Isaac, the salvation at the Red Sea, and the giving of the law at Sinai. What shall we make of the ties that bind believers to these episodes?

Questions such as these bring up the embarrassingly nonscientific issue of the "greatness" and "richness" of literary texts. They also bring up a problem that Dorothy Sayers, the mystery writer, identified as a serious hindrance to discussion of the Bible's status as literature: people's tendency to believe that there are two kinds of writers, "real writers" and "Bible writers," the latter being utterly distinct from the former.[2] This tendency isn't limited to untrained, unanalytical readers; it's a marked characteristic of professional students of the Bible, both secular and religious.

Few "real" writers, however, have forgotten the emotional and therefore the literary power of the Bible's salient passages. William Blake once started to recite the prodigal son, a story he knew by heart, "but at the words, 'When he was yet a great way off, his father saw him,' could go no further; his voice faltered, and he was in tears."[3] But Blake, like other "real" writers, knew how to exploit the biblical passages that overpowered him. After the

---

1. Richard Elliott Friedman, *Who Wrote the Bible?* (New York: Harper & Row, 1987) 245.

2. Dorothy Sayers, "A Vote of Thanks to Cyrus," *Christian Letters to a Post-Christian World: A Selection of Essays* (Grand Rapids: Eerdmans, 1969) 53.

3. Alexander Gilchrist, *Life of William Blake* (ed. Ruthven Todd; rev. ed.; London: Dent, 1945) 302.

final lines of his climactic work, *Jerusalem*, he engraved a symbolic picture of the story of the prodigal, adapted to his own highly individual mythology. His earlier work contains dozens of other representations of the story.

Taking Sayers's comment to heart, I don't want my own discussion of the Bible's literary qualities to be based entirely on the Bible itself, as if it were actually something distinct from "writing." I'll take my next example of a salient passage from another work of ancient literature, the *Odyssey*.

In Book 13, Homer's hero has returned to his homeland but has not yet resumed his role as king. Obstreperous guests are still camping out in his palace, and he has to devise a way of ousting them. On the beach at Ithaka, he meets his patron, Athena, disguised as a young man, to whom Odysseus, ever wary, tells a long, lying story about who he is. At last, the goddess reveals her identity, laughingly complimenting him on his craftiness. A trickster herself, she appreciates trickery in others. The two friends exemplify their cleverness by hiding the treasure that Odysseus has brought home with him. Then they proceed to business:

> [U]nder the old grey olive tree those two
> sat down to work the suitors death and woe.[4]

Concentrated in this little episode are many of the poem's most important features: its assumption of the distinctness, yet the likeness, of humans and their gods; its insistence on the importance of clever thought and action, with an emphasis on clever thought; the excitement that the poet takes in narrating risky adventures, together with the assurance he offers that everything will turn out right; his ability to embody his conceptions in a panoply of images, both subtle and dramatic. It's no accident that Odysseus and Athena sit down together, chatting familiarly, in the shade of an olive tree. Clever people—male or female, mortal or immortal—belong together; and their sign is the olive, Athena's tree, the symbol of wealth derived from the clever use of natural resources. The translator, enjoying the scene, adds a picturesque detail, making the olive "old" and "grey." That, of course, comports with Homer's view that good things are old: wisdom is old; Athena is old (indeed, immortal); and Odysseus's claim to Ithaka is old, although it remains as precious as the olive tree, as "sacred" (that is Homer's word for the olive, *hieros*) as the wit of two old friends who understand each other.

This is how the motivating ideas of Homer's world are presented, connected, and rendered memorable in the original poem and in translation. If someone asked you for a conceptual summary of the *Odyssey*, you might suggest this passage. When one thinks about the *Odyssey*, one recalls not

---

4. Homer, *Od.*, 13.372–73 (trans. Robert Fitzgerald; New York: Farrar, Straus, and Giroux, 1998) 239, 242.

an outline of abstract ideas but a series of richly evocative episodes. There ought to be a word for literary features like this, and I believe there is one: the scene on the shore of Ithaka is a literary *icon*.

Like a painted icon, the episode is a vivid presentation and interpretation of its subject—a presentation that invites further interpretation, because its figures and objects express ideas that are as interesting as they are important. Like a painted icon, the scene is rich enough in suggestion to be studied in abstraction from its surroundings; like a painted icon, it invites its audience to revisit it and keep finding new suggestions of meaning inside its borders. Described in this way, an icon, whether it is painted or written, is both an intellectually attractive and an intellectually slippery thing, potent both in its sense of self-assurance and in its incitement to interpretation.

It was not merely Homer's felicitous phrases and his instructive tone that kept the ancients reading and quoting him; it was the pungency of his iconic passages. Similarly, iconic episodes and sayings incite people to read and quote the Bible. Few Christian preachers think of scheduling a five-part sermon sequence on Paul's epistle to Philemon, or even on the Council of Jerusalem passages of Acts, as important as they are to the evolution of Christian doctrine. Sermons are based on iconic passages, from the descent of the herald angels out of the skies of Bethlehem to the descent of the New Jerusalem out of the heaven of John's Apocalypse. Of course, preachers never pronounce the word "icon"; rather, when they find an iconic passage, they say to themselves, "There! That's it. That'll preach." Bible readers don't pronounce the word either, but when they are looking for inspiration or instruction, they turn to the same kind of passages that preachers like: clear and simple statements of belief (e.g., John 3:16) or richly iconic presentations of their religious worldview.

The term *icon* does exist in literary studies, but it has been significantly undersold. It is used almost exclusively in scholarship influenced by logical or linguistic theories, such as those of C. S. Peirce, who regarded an "icon" as a word or phrase that resembles its referent.[5] An icon might be a word like *growl*, which sounds somewhat like the thing it denotes, or it might be a set of words that appear to do what they talk about doing, as in Alexander Pope's lethargic verse about a lethargic verse, a line of poetry that "like a wounded snake, drags its slow length along."[6] A slow line is like a slow line. It is therefore "iconic." But this, frankly, is a trivial use of the concept,

---

5. For clear accounts of the concept of "iconicity" or "iconism" in contemporary scholarship, see Earl R. Anderson, *A Grammar of Iconism* (Madison: Fairleigh Dickinson University Press, 1998; and Max Nänny and Olga Fischer, eds., *Form Miming Meaning: Iconicity in Language and Literature* (Amsterdam: John Benjamins, 1999).
6. Alexander Pope, *An Essay on Criticism*, 2.157.

at least in comparison to the one suggested by W. K. Wimsatt in his once famous book, *The Verbal Icon*. Wimsatt briefly recognizes that "the term *icon* is used today by semeiotic [*sic*] writers to refer to a verbal sign which *somehow* shares the properties of, or resembles, the objects which it denotes," adding that "[t]he same term in its more usual meaning refers to a visual image and especially to one which is a religious symbol." Then he suggests, much as I am suggesting, that "[t]he verbal image which most fully realizes its verbal capacities is that which is not merely a bright picture (in the usual modern meaning of the term *image*) but also an interpretation of reality in its metaphoric and symbolic dimensions. Thus: *The Verbal Icon*."[7]

The phrase "bright picture" is appropriate. An iconic passage emerges distinctly and intensely in the memory, as if it were a picture with a bright line around it—a color illustration facing a page of ten-point type. "Interpretation of reality" is also a good phrase. It captures the intellectual quality of the icon, its apparent attempt to teach. "Metaphoric and symbolic dimensions" is a little hazier, but no one would deny that iconicity is involved with symbolism. An icon is separable from the work that surrounds it—at least it *can* easily be separated, in memory and in exposition—but an icon can also be understood as representing meanings that are implicit elsewhere in the work and elsewhere in life, and this kind of representation is a function of symbolism. When a work of literature is applauded for its reach, its intensity, its concentrated force of meaning, the presence of verbal icons probably has much to do with it.

Strangely, the remarks just quoted are virtually all that *The Verbal Icon* has to say about verbal icons. Wimsatt immediately abandons any specific concern with iconicity, turning instead to a defense of "literature as a form of knowledge" and to some very general and diffuse concerns with the role of "poetry" in "Christian thinking." No one else seems to have picked up the thread. If we want to make sense of "iconicity" in the way in which he mentioned it, we have to rely on ourselves to expand and exemplify the concept.

One way to start is by recognizing that verbal icons are nothing strange or exotic. Everyone has had the experience of creating and recreating them. All that is needed is the bright line of identification, the will to discover intense significance in a pattern of words. Everyone has had a conversation like this:

"I don't know why she said that."
"Neither do I. It's a Rosebud situation."

---

7. W. K. Wimsatt Jr., *The Verbal Icon: Studies in the Meaning of Poetry* (Lexington: University of Kentucky Press, 1954) xii, 266–79.

That one word, "Rosebud," is enough to evoke the great iconic passages in *Citizen Kane* ("He just said 'Rosebud,' and then he dropped the glass ball and it broke on the floor"), together with all the problems of human knowledge and motivation that those passages suggest. Say the special word, and the icon recurs, carrying with it either the original set of meanings or an ironic or paradoxical "interpretation of reality." Suppose that what "she said" was not one word but a five-paragraph speech. Ironically, it might still be as opaque as Charles Foster Kane's single word, and opaque in similar ways. Citation of the icon from *Kane* would then become an invitation to reassess both Kane and "her" and all those secret similarities that lurk beneath the surface of apparently dissimilar lives.

The creation and recreation of icons is aptly illustrated by a scene in J. F. Powers's great work of religious realism, *Wheat That Springeth Green*. It is the story of Father Joe, a Roman Catholic priest, and his young assistant, Bill, both of whom have trouble negotiating the relationship between Christianity and the everyday world. When Bill enters the rectory and finds Joe, who is overweight and alcoholic, preparing food and drink, Joe likes to remark, "This isn't for me." The phrase becomes "a family joke, something to say when making another drink, when not declining dessert, or having a second dessert."[8] It becomes both an expression of community (a saying that means something only to Bill and Joe, the priestly insiders) and an assertion of personal integrity (an assertion that, appearances to the contrary, Joe is self-conscious about his eating and drinking and is therefore a fit model for the younger generation). It shows that Joe is able to laugh at himself (a little bit); it also shows that he maintains control of the way in which "family jokes" should be directed.

These are some of the ways in which the expression is meaningful for the characters. For readers, it gradually becomes iconic in other respects. Once you understand the author's hints that Joe's habits of consumption are indeed out of control, you recognize "this isn't for me" as a symbol of his failure to confront his flaws, of his unfitness to serve as a model for anyone, and of the whole complex of moral problems arising from the conflict between soul and body, authority and the individual, the church and the world. The icon doesn't just identify certain ideas or problems; it also gratifyingly identifies the people who are capable of appreciating them—the cunning author, first of all, and then we ourselves, the cunning readers. For very cunning readers, it may even symbolize the skill that we all possess in detecting the sins of other people (such as Father Joe), while congratulating ourselves on our own membership in the community of the sinless: "This isn't for me."

---

8. J. F. Powers, *Wheat That Springeth Green* (New York: Washington Square, 1990) 180.

Clearly, the act of citing or even thinking about a literary icon can give
it a significance that the words themselves would not otherwise possess.
"This isn't for me" is a perfectly inane set of words. It gains resonance and
complexity only when Joe quotes and requotes it, and attentive readers follow his example, giving it their own imaginative interpretations. Allusion
has an icon-making and an icon-changing power. The study of icons calls
for the kind of distinction that E. D. Hirsch has drawn between *meaning*,
the original sense and purport of a text, the sense that one can reasonably
assume is understood by an author or a character, and the *significance* that
later readers may attach to it.[9] One way (though of course not the only or
the perfect way) of charting the development of Judaism and Christianity
is to see them as constant and unending responses to biblical icons, interpretive responses that, themselves iconic, do the work of converting Bible
"meaning" into religious "significance."

Nothing in the Bible is more iconic than the scenes in Genesis in which
God makes his covenant with Abram. God doesn't simply make a promise;
he intensifies its literary effect with colorful words and spectacular symbols. "Get out of here!" he says; "leave your father's house, and I will make
a great nation out of you; everyone will be blessed in your name" (Gen
12:1–3). "Count the stars," he says, "if you are able to; I will make your seed
as many as those stars." He says this, then he paints a prophetic picture of
the lives of Abram's descendants, the beneficiaries of the covenant, and he
emphasizes the power of covenant by a miraculous appearance of heat and
light amidst what the King James Version impressively calls "an horror of
great darkness" (Gen 15:4–21). Again, he gives his covenant and prophecy,
enriching the icon of covenant with permanent symbols of relationship: he
changes Abram's name to Abraham and Sarai's name to Sarah, and he man-
dates the circumcision of Abraham and his household (Gen 17:1–16).

These scenes and symbols, gathered by memory and reflection into a
single but complex iconic picture, figure largely in the rest of Scripture. In
Exodus, God himself remembers them and imbues them with new significance as a motive for current action: "Depart, go up hence, you and the
people whom you have brought up out of the land of Egypt, to the land of
which I swore to Abraham, Isaac, and Jacob, saying, 'To your descendants
I will give it'" (Exod 33:1).[10] David reemphasizes the icon's significance as
an explanation of Israel's history (1 Chr 16:7–36; cf. Psalm 105). Jehoshaphat makes the icon the basis of a theology and a plea for divine assistance
for the covenant people (2 Chr 20:5–20). Ezekiel reverses this sense of the

---

9. E. D. Hirsch Jr., *Validity in Interpretation* (New Haven: Yale University Press, 1967);
idem, *The Aims of Interpretation* (Chicago: University of Chicago Press, 1976).

10. Unless otherwise indicated, Scripture quotations and chapter and verse numbers
are derived from the Revised Standard Version.

icon's significance, turning it into a complaint against Israel for its failure to resemble its ancestor Abraham, to whom the covenant was originally given (Ezek 33:23–29). Micah uses the icon to prophesy a restoration of Israel, joining it with an allusion to that other optimistically iconic scene, the exodus from Egypt. For him, each icon signifies the promise of its own renewal: "As in the days when you came out of the land of Egypt I will show them marvelous things. . . . Thou wilt show faithfulness to Jacob and steadfast love to Abraham, as thou hast sworn to our fathers from the days of old" (Mic 7:14–20). The book of Nehemiah reiterates the two icons, now so crucial to Israel's self-understanding, restages their action, and stresses their significance to the great historical narrative stretching from the creation of the world to the recovery of Israel's homeland after the Babylonian Exile (Neh 9:6–37).

Finally, Paul gives the icon of the covenant a revolutionary twist, using it to establish the independence of the Christian church from the nation of Israel. If Abraham, he argues, was the friend of God, despite his failure to practice obedience to the Law (the Law not having yet been given), and he was nevertheless considered righteous because he believed God's covenant promises, then justification comes not by works of Law but by faith and grace (Gal 3:5–18, citing Gen 15:6). This is certainly not a meaning that anyone had hitherto discovered in the iconic episodes in Genesis; it is the assignment of an entirely new significance. But without this resignification, Christianity would be missing much of its theological foundation, and Paul would be missing much of his ability to respond to the arguments of those who maintained that the rabbi of Galilee represented no decisive break with Israel's past.

I leave to people more expert than I in the Hebrew Scriptures the job of tracing its own many patterns of iconic repetition and resignification. My chief concern in this essay is the way in which the recurrence of biblical icons shapes the New Testament and later Christian literature. Yet I doubt there is any fundamental difference between the essential functions that icons serve when they are remembered and reused in the Hebrew Scriptures, on the one hand, and in Christian literature, on the other. Three of these functions can easily be identified.

Most obviously, icons are used for *explanation*. This is Paul's purpose when, in Galatians, he returns to the scene of the Abrahamic covenant and makes it part of his interpretation of God's dealings with humanity. That is Jesus' purpose when he tells his former neighbors in Nazareth that he has begun a new work. "Today this scripture has been fulfilled in your hearing," he says, citing the vivid words of Isaiah 61 to explain his mission and its divine authorization (Luke 4:16–21). That is Peter's purpose at the feast of Pentecost, when he uses an iconic passage from the prophecy of Joel to describe what is happening at the foundational event of the Christian church:

> But this is what was spoken by the prophet Joel: "And in the last days it shall be, God declares, that I will pour out my Spirit upon all flesh, and your sons and your daughters shall prophesy, and your young men shall see visions, and your old men shall dream dreams; yea, and on my menservants and my maidservants in those days I will pour out my Spirit; and they shall prophesy. And I will show wonders in the heaven above and signs on the earth beneath, blood, and fire, and vapor of smoke; the sun shall be turned into darkness and the moon into blood, before the day of the Lord comes, the great and manifest day. And it shall be that whoever calls on the name of the Lord shall be saved." (Acts 2:16–21, citing Joel 2:28–32)

Explanation ordinarily includes resignification. One of the purposes of the book of Acts is to explain the separation of the Christian church from Israel. In line with that purpose, Peter's speech omits an important part of Joel's icon of prophetic agitation: "For in Mount Zion and in Jerusalem there shall be those who escape" (Joel 2:32). Joel emphasizes the importance of national Israel; Peter does not, and his omission alters the significance of the passage as a whole.

Elaboration is a second function of iconicity—a function that may also involve a radical resignification of a literary passage. Isaiah prophesies that a young woman will bear a son, whom she will call Immanuel, "God with Us." It is a powerful image in its original form, but it is vastly elaborated in the Christian interpretations that begin with Isaiah's prophecy and end with the child who, in the words of the 19th-century hymn, is worshiped as "the Virgin's Son, the God incarnate born" (Isa 7:14, Matt 1:23).[11]

Elaboration can exist on its own, as the single function of a quoted icon. We see this in the 80th Psalm's beautiful extension of the iconic imagery of Exodus:

> Thou didst bring a vine out of Egypt; thou didst drive out the nations
> and plant it.
> Thou didst clear the ground for it; it took deep root and filled the land.
> The mountains were covered with its shade, the mighty cedars with its
> branches;
> it sent out its branches to the sea, and its shoots to the River.
> (Ps 80:8–11)

Elaboration can also be linked with explanation, as in the episode of Philip's conversion of the Ethiopian eunuch, the court official who is

---

11. Matthew Bridges and Godfrey Thring, "Crown Him with Many Crowns" (1852, 1874).

riding in his chariot, reading the "suffering servant" passages of Isaiah and wondering what they mean (Isaiah 53, Acts 8:26–39). Philip asks him, "Do you understand what you are reading?" No, he answers. Philip then explains the great iconic scene in Isaiah ("As a sheep led to the slaughter . . .") by elaborating its connection with "the good news of Jesus." Though anchored to the images of Isaiah, the New Testament conversion scene develops its own iconicity as a set of symbols that explains, comprehensively, what it means to be an active Christian. Among other things, the episode demonstrates that a person such as this

1. maintains close connections with the Hebrew Scriptures;
2. is proficient in the *kerygma*, the basic story of Christ, and is able to explain its relationship to preexisting stories: "beginning with this scripture [in Isaiah] he told him the good news";
3. is constantly ready to be commissioned by God: "And the Spirit said to Philip, 'Go up and join this chariot.' So Philip ran to him";
4. is always ready to change, whenever God demands change: "And as they went along the road they came to some water, and the eunuch said, 'See, here is water! What is to prevent my being baptized?' . . . and he baptized him."

In summary, the passage argues (5) that Christians should be the kind of readers who, like Philip or the Ethiopian eunuch, can spot an iconic passage, seek its meaning—or its new significance—and put themselves in the story it tells.

Quite possibly, the author of Acts, who is a very clever writer, intends the resonant phrase "Do you understand what you are reading?" to resonate in just this way, as an invitation to self-examination on the part of his Christian audience. Certainly he could have narrated the episode without recording that particular remark. In fact, he could have dispensed with all the iconic features of the incident, saying only that Philip preached the gospel to a Jewish proselyte from Ethiopia, whom he thereby converted: end of story. But in that case, the story would have been a supremely *un*memorable literary moment. As it stands, the passage both elaborates the significance of Isaiah 53 and explains the Christian life. But it has another function: it is an *expression* of Christian identity, a means of saying "what we do" and "who we are." Icons offer more than intellectual meanings or occasions for discovering new kinds of intellectual significance; they also give the people who produce and reproduce them a way of expressing themselves more intensely than they could by other literary means.

According to the Gospels, Jesus doesn't simply wander from place to place, saying that he has a commission from God. He expresses himself much more vividly than that, both by repeating iconic passages from Scripture, as at the synagogue in Nazareth, and by reenacting them, as in his role as Suffering Servant (John 12:37–38). Jesus creates his own iconic scenes, in his parables and in the episodes of his life that have no apparent biblical precedents. One example is his transfiguration. It is a visible expression of his relationship to Israel's past:

> And behold, two men talked with him, Moses and Elijah, who appeared in glory and spoke of his departure, which he was to accomplish at Jerusalem.

of his relationship to Israel's God:

> And a voice came out of the cloud, saying, "This is my Son, my Chosen; listen to him!"

and of his relationship to his loyal but uncomprehending followers, who haven't yet learned to understand the significance of the iconic scenes in which they participate or even to recognize that the scenes are iconic:

> [T]hey saw his glory and the two men who stood with him. And . . . Peter said to Jesus, "Master, it is well that we are here; let us make three booths, one for you and one for Moses and one for Elijah"—not knowing what he said. (Luke 9:28–36)

Like the calling of the Ethiopian eunuch, the transfiguration became a means of self-expression by later Christians, who found a dramatic significance in its every detail. The Gospel of Luke says that "when [God's] voice had spoken, Jesus was found alone" (Luke 9:36; see also Matt 17:8, Mark 9:8). The picture of "Jesus alone" is endlessly repeated in Christian literature. It appears in the high prophetic mode of Blake, who engraved the words, in Greek, above *Jerusalem's* first lines of verse ("of the passage through / Eternal Death! and of the awaking to Eternal Life").[12] It appears in the demotic mode of 19th-century hymns and gospel songs:

> I must tell Jesus! I must tell Jesus!
> Jesus can help me, Jesus alone.[13]

And it appears in the still more popular mode of today's internet devotions:

> No one else. Jesus alone with them. They alone with him.
> This brief, bright, surprise of the Christ touching them. Saying, be
>   without fear.
> Saying, be what you are. Saying, be what you see.[14]

---

12. William Blake, *Jerusalem*, 4.1–2, *The Complete Poetry and Prose of William Blake* (ed. David V. Erdman; rev. ed.; Garden City, NY: Doubleday, 1982) 146.

13. Elisha Hoffman, "I Must Tell Jesus" (1893).

14. "Bill" in "Today at Meetingbrook Archives," n.p. [cited 23 Feb. 2002]. Online: http://www.meetingbrook.org/blogger/today.asp?2002-02-17-archive.html.

If nothing else, these examples illustrate the difference between the original meaning of a passage and the new kinds of significance that can develop when it is used as a means of religious self-expression. There is nothing in the Gospel accounts of the transfiguration that emphasizes the idea of being alone with Jesus or embracing "Jesus alone." Yes, the disciples are left alone with him, but nothing in the text suggests that this is an important point of the story. *That* is the icon-creative significance that later readers have attached to it.

The New Testament authors' own self-expressive qualities, though seldom a focus of interest in scholarly research and theory, are frequently evident in their creation or identification of icons. Paul can always think of Scripture passages the quotation of which can give intensity to his ideas and ethos: "Who shall separate us from the love of Christ? . . . As it is written, 'For thy sake we are being killed all the day long; we are regarded as sheep to be slaughtered'" (Rom 8:35–36, citing Ps 44:22). The book of Revelation is a treasury of Old Testament allusions, many of them reiterations of iconic passages and many of them simultaneously expansive, explanatory, and expressive. When the intensely visual and dramatic 11th chapter of Revelation alludes to the intensely visual and dramatic 12th chapter of Daniel, citing especially the idea that 1,260 days must pass before the sufferings of God's people are ended, it *explains* the curious relationship of eternal providence to temporal events, portraying it as a matter of God's permitting evil but also establishing its limits (Dan 12:7, Rev 11:2–3). Meanwhile, the Revelator *expands* the story of God's providence, showing its relevance both to Israel and to the Christian church, his allusion to Daniel implying that providence always acts in similar ways and even in accordance with similar divisions of time ("1,260"). By implication, also, the Revelator uses Daniel to *express* his confidence that his own prophetic moment is more advanced than any described in the Hebrew Scriptures. Daniel says that he "heard" the prophetic message but failed to divine its meaning; he complains about the lack of explanation vouchsafed to him and is informed that the prophecy will remain "sealed until the time of the end," when the "wise shall understand" (Dan 12:8–10). The Revelator, having discovered a new significance in Daniel's vision of a threatened temple and a persecuted people, suggests that the "wise" who "shall understand" have now appeared and are people like himself. He emphasizes this favorable comparison between Daniel's degree of knowledge and his own by using a similar numerology and similar pictures of holy people beset by adversaries, then embedding it all in a self-confident vision ("sweet as honey in my mouth," Rev 10:10) of conclusive contemporary events, the events between the birth of Christ and the consummation of his kingdom that provide the key to Daniel's prophecy (Revelation 10–12).

This is one illustration of Christianity's ability to express itself by creating new literary icons and resignifying icons already present in Scripture. The process continues wherever Christianity continues. It ordinarily involves an intensifying combination of the three functions of iconicity within a single literary event. Events such as these—remembered, enjoyed, repeated, and often resignified—provide much of the intellectual and emotional basis of popular Christianity.

Of course, there are many other influences, among them, systematic Bible study and the teachings of the various Christian churches. But anyone who has ever participated in a dialogue between people of different denominations will remember what happens when somebody names a doctrine taught by his or her home institution. "Oh," the members of the other churches say, "we believe in that too, don't we?" Probably they do, but it's clear that their Christianity does not entail a minute comprehension of doctrine. Reference to such richly doctrinal episodes as the Council of Jerusalem (Acts 15) elicits curiosity rather than recognition. But concerning the big iconic scenes of the New Testament, no questions arise. Everyone knows about the night at Bethlehem, the morning at the empty tomb, and the day on which "the trumpet shall sound, and the dead shall be raised incorruptible" (1 Cor 15:52, KJV). These are the things that all Christians know, the things to which all Christians recur in their private readings and private thoughts.

The two main sources for their knowledge of the Bible's iconic passages are probably sermons and hymns. Although the latter source is badly neglected by most writers on popular Christianity, it may be more influential than the former. Few sermons (or daily meditations, or devotional tracts, or works of systematic theology) are as memorable as "Once in Royal David's City." The preachers in *Elmer Gantry* complain, with good reason, that their sermons are forgotten almost as soon as delivered, but everyone remembers the hymns.[15] A good hymn *lasts*. Open the hymn book in any church, and you will find hundreds of literary works that have lasted for centuries. Virtually all of them are tissues of allusion to biblical icons.

To see how icons are identified, resignified, reedited, and accommodated to other icons, consider a hymn that has been in general use in Protestant churches during the past century and a half, "From Every Stormy Wind That Blows" (1828). It is one of the hundred or so early 19th-century songs that still commonly appear in hymnals in English-speaking countries. Thousands of other poems of that era have perished, so far as popular culture is concerned, including virtually all the lyrics of Blake and Byron,

---

15. Sinclair Lewis, *Sinclair Lewis: Arrowsmith, Elmer Gantry, Dodsworth* (New York: Library of America, 2002) 547, 676–77, 754, etc.

Wordsworth and Coleridge, Shelley and Tennyson. But this poem survives, a witness to the strength of the Bible icons on which it is based and to its author's imaginative feel for their potential. The iconicity of the hymn begins with Exodus, gathers strength from the Septuagint, the Psalms, the Gospel of Luke, and the book of Hebrews, gains new emphasis from Reformation translations of the Bible, and culminates in the author's own writing and editing. Here is the hymn:

> From ev'ry stormy wind that blows,
> From ev'ry swelling tide of woes,
> There is a calm, a sure retreat;
> 'Tis found beneath the mercy-seat.
>
> There is a place where Jesus sheds
> The oil of gladness on our heads;
> A place than all beside more sweet;
> It is the blood-stain'd mercy-seat.
>
> There is a spot where spirits blend,
> And friend holds fellowship with friend;
> Tho' sunder'd far, by faith they meet
> Around one common mercy-seat.
>
> Ah! whither could we flee for aid,
> When tempted, desolate, dismay'd,
> Or how the hosts of hell defeat,
> Had suffering saints no mercy-seat?
>
> There, there on eagle-wing we soar,
> And time and sense seem all no more;
> And heaven comes down our souls to greet,
> And glory crowns the mercy-seat.
>
> Oh! may my hand forget her skill,
> My tongue be silent, stiff, and still;
> My bounding heart forget to beat,
> If I forget the mercy-seat.[16]

Hugh Stowell (1799–1865), the author of these lines, was a priest of the Church of England—the state church, and a church notorious at the time for its chilly devotion to ritual. His personal commitments were warmly evangelical. He was, in fact, one of the most popular preachers of the evangelical movement. When his neighbors in Salford, a suburb of Manchester, grew concerned that he might go elsewhere to preach, they went deeply in debt to build a new church for him. The edifice seated 1,300 people, and

---

16. Hugh Stowell, "From Every Stormy Wind That Blows," hymn 216 in *A Selection of Psalms and Hymns, Suited to the Services of the Church of England* (3rd ed.; Manchester: Sowler, 1833) 266–67.

apparently the seats were full. During the 1830s, a railway terminal was built nearby, and the parish promptly developed into something that has been called "The Classic Slum." Stowell became a vigorous advocate of missions and of education among the poor. Though he was hated by hierarchs and ritualists in the church, his death was succeeded by "incredible funeral scenes," including a procession "a mile long."[17]

But Stowell is not remembered for his good works, his weekly sermons, or the essays he wrote on diverse subjects, including the literary value of the Bible.[18] The sad truth is that when one finishes an essay by Stowell, it is virtually impossible to remember anything he said. On one occasion, however, his enthusiasm was dramatically focused by a biblical icon, and a memorable hymn emerged.

The central iconic reference of "Every Stormy Wind" is to the tabernacle and its furnishings, as described in the Pentateuch, and especially to the "mercy seat," as briefly described in Exodus 25 and 37 and Leviticus 16. Here is an important variant on iconicity. None of the tabernacle descriptions can be accounted great literature. They are exactly the kind of passages that most readers happily skip over, until a rabbi or minister draws a bright line around them by discoursing on their significance or until a reader finds the page in a Bible commentary or dictionary that attempts to illustrate what the tabernacle and its furnishings looked like. Then the details unite in a single, iconic object, and the tabernacle can be seen as believers from Philo to modern adventists have seen it—as a complex symbol of the relationship between humanity and divinity.[19]

This tabernacle is a set of sacred enclosures—the outer court, the Holy, the Holy of Holies, and within that innermost room, the innermost object, the ark of the covenant. By these enclosures, the mysteries of God are progressively set apart from his people, signifying the remote perfection of his holiness. Yet the iconic object is set amid the people; the tent is pitched beside their tents; and provision is made for the representatives of the people,

---

17. Arthur J. Dobb, *Like a Mighty Tortoise: A History of the Diocese of Manchester* (Durn Mill, Littleborough, England: Upjohn & Bottomley, 1978) 19, 21–22. My biographical information on Stowell is largely dependent on pp. 19–22.

18. Among them, Hugh Stowell, "The Bible Self-Evidential," "The Wonders of the Bible," and "The Glory of the Old Testament," *Exeter Hall Lectures* 5 (1849–50) 1–44; 8 (1852–53) 1–48; 10 (1854–55) 114–40.

19. Philo, *Moses* 2.71–108; Ellen G. White, *The Great Controversy between Christ and Satan: The Conflict of the Ages in the Christian Dispensation* (Mountain View, CA: Pacific Press Publishing Association, 1911) chap. 23; Charles Taze Russell, *Tabernacle Shadows of the "Better Sacrifices": A Helping Hand for the Royal Priesthood* (Brooklyn: International Bible Students Association, 1911). The history of tabernacle interpretations in the ancient world is chronicled by Craig R. Koester, *The Dwelling of God: The Tabernacle in the Old Testament, Intertestamental Jewish Literature, and the New Testament* (Washington: Catholic Biblical Association, 1989).

the priests, to enter the tabernacle and approach the divinity on the people's behalf. Remoteness and accessibility are usually in opposition, but the tabernacle demonstrates that conditions can be created in which they are intimately, perhaps miraculously, joined. From a literary point of view, it is pointless to wonder whether there ever was a place such as the tabernacle or whether its essential features were faithfully reiterated in the Jerusalem temple. The literary point is that the text, without saying so overtly, has created an icon of God's relevance to humanity.

This icon points to other icons, behind and beyond itself. The tabernacle, we are told, was modeled after a plan that God revealed to Moses in their colloquies on Sinai (Exod 25:9). So, what we see in Scripture—and in our mind's eye—is an iconic representation of an iconic place of worship, which is itself a representation of an iconic picture in God's own mind. Representation follows representation, allusion follows allusion; and the reiteration continues, with subtle revisions, in the biblical descriptions of Solomon's temple and in the Septuagint's rendering of the pentateuchal concepts.

The revision that interests me at present has to do with the *kappōret*, the cover of the ark of the covenant, the sacred furnishing of the Holy of Holies. The *kappōret* was a table of gold, to which were attached the golden effigies of two cherubim. While it may have been conceived as the "footstool" of the deity,[20] Scripture also likens it, by implication, to his throne: "O Lord the God of Israel, who art enthroned above the cherubim" (2 Kgs 19:15). Annually, at *yom kippur*, the high priest sprinkled sacrificial blood upon and near the *kappōret*. The word *kappōret* has been pronounced "untranslatable, so far," although its apparent derivation from *kippēr* 'purge'[21] licenses terms such as 'place of purgation'. In the Hebrew Scriptures, the object itself appears only once after the Pentateuch (1 Chr 28:11).

But this is not the end of its story. In the Septuagint translation of the Pentateuch into Greek, *kappōret* was rendered as *hilastērion* 'place of propitiation', thus broadening its significance. The word now explicitly evokes

---

20. Jacob Milgrom, *Leviticus 1–16: A New Translation with Introduction and Commentary* (AB 3; New York: Doubleday, 1991) 1014, referring to the possibility that *kappōret* is a development of an Egyptian word for "sole of the foot." Milgrom rules out an original association with "throne," as does C. L. Seow, "Ark of the Covenant," *ABD* 1:388–89, 392. Seow is favorable to the "footstool" idea (though not in respect to P's references to the ark). He observes that the ark was not a convenient place to sit. But during Israel's history the ark came to be regarded as a symbolic throne, as is indicated by several passages of Scripture that Seow himself cites, including: 1 Sam 4:4 and 2 Sam 6:2. Michael M. Homan, *To Your Tents, O Israel!: The Terminology, Function, Form, and Symbolism of Tents in the Hebrew Bible and the Ancient Near East* (Brill: Leiden, 2002) 97, acknowledges both throne and footstool.

21. Milgrom, *Leviticus*, 1014. Milgrom (pp. 1079–84) traces the development of *kippēr*'s religious associations in Israel.

the concept not simply of purgation but of a God who invites pleas for help and ordains a place to hear them. The idea is a natural complement to other ideas, cherished by Jews and Christians, about God's care and mercy. This is the significance that Protestant translations associate with *hilastē-rion* as it is used in the New Testament book of Hebrews (9:5). While the Vulgate stays conservatively close to its original (*propitiatorium*), and Douay-Rheims-Challoner profits from the example ("propitiatory"), Luther decides on *Gnadenstuel*, and Tyndale follows with "seat of grace,"[22] thus specifying the Pauline theology of grace triumphant. Finally, the most potent translation of them all, the King James Version, offers "mercy seat" (or "mercyseat"), the reading generally adopted in English translations of both Old Testament and New Testament references. It's a mistranslation, but it makes iconic sense; indeed, it completes the icon of the tabernacle. The building as a whole suggests the distance, yet the presence, of a personal God. Now its central object, the ark and its covering, invokes the paradoxical union of God's two primary interests, law and mercy—distanced, objective judgment and sympathetic love. The ark contains the stones on which the laws of God were written (Exod 25:21, 31:18), and God, who is now clearly envisioned as *seated* on the thronelike ark, metes out justice in accordance with law. Yet the result of his lawful rule is mercy; his very throne is the seat of mercy; mercy is transcendent over law. So the original icon is resignified and, in a literary sense, improved. The *kappōret* leaves behind its limited or uncertain meanings; now it is rich with lessons for believers.

Already, long before the modern translator went to work on the subject, the book of Hebrews had provided a crucial resignification of the icon of the tabernacle. Without the literary contribution of Hebrews, the structure, furnishings, and ceremonies of the tabernacle and its successor, the Jerusalem temple, might well have lost their iconicity for Christians, becoming from their perspective mere antiquarian lore. The writer of Hebrews resignifies the icon by interpreting the high priest as a symbol of Christ, and the high priest's annual entrance into the Holy of Holies as a symbol of Christ's entrance into heaven with the fruits of his redeeming sacrifice. In this picture, Christ enters "the holy place," the tabernacle of heaven, with "his own blood," which he sprinkles before the *hilastērion* (Heb 9:12, KJV).[23] It is a literary picture of great power and beauty—a curi-

---

22. F. F. Bruce, *The Epistle to the Hebrews* (rev. ed.; Grand Rapids: Eerdmans, 1990) 116. Bruce (pp. 78–79) reviews the associations that, for Jews and Christians, naturally surrounded *hilastērion*, its textual sources, and its verbal relatives, and mentions part of its history in modern translation. Philo, *Moses* 2.95, follows the Septuagint in using *hilastērion*.

23. In considering Stowell's sources, I quote the King James Version, the translation Stowell used.

ous beauty, since it actualizes not just "the cherubims of glory shadowing the mercyseat," as King James's translators saw it (Heb 9:5, KJV), but the bloody results of crucifixion. The image is a concrete expression of the writer's view of the Christian life as a scene of suffering opening directly to the realms of glory.

That view is also Stowell's. He begins where Hebrews leaves off, with the psychological implications of the story that the New Testament book developed out of Exodus and Leviticus. He is not concerned with analyzing the theological significance of the tabernacle icon; that has already been done by Hebrews. He dwells instead on the tabernacle's privacy, mystery, and glory. In Hebrews, the Holy of Holies is resignified as spiritual and symbolic; it is God's shrine in heaven. Stowell accepts this resignification and commends it as an expression of Christians' invisible community with one another. The tabernacle is the hidden place where, mysteriously, "spirits blend." Speaking to those who are on the "inside" of the community but may not always remember that they are, Stowell reminds them that there is a place where they can withdraw from the world and enter the spiritual Holy of Holies, an inner room where "time and sense seem all no more."[24]

Chapter 4 of Hebrews urged Christians to "come boldly unto the throne of grace, that we may obtain mercy" (v. 16, KJV); the King James translation of chap. 9 created a concrete image of God's grace by naming his throne the "mercyseat." Stowell adds an emphasis on the personal characteristics that allow believers to make God's mysteries their own: explicitly, faith ("Tho' sunder'd far, by faith they meet"); implicitly, the ability to respond to biblical icons and to place oneself imaginatively inside them. Meanwhile, his emphasis on the believer's emotions takes him far past the tabernacle passages in the Pentateuch or even in Hebrews. His invocation of "glory" is appropriate to Hebrews' reference to "the cherubims of glory," but the effulgence of light that suddenly "crowns the mercy seat" is inspired less by Hebrews than by the dramatic pictures of glory, and of glorious crowns, in the book of Revelation, with probable assistance from Isa 62:3 and 1 Pet 5:4. The idea that "heaven comes down our souls to greet," in answer to private devotion, is less the product of Exodus or Leviticus than of Jesus' parable about the prodigal son, whose father sees him struggling up the path toward home and runs to meet him (Luke 15:20).

Nor is "the oil of gladness" anything that the Hebrew Scriptures especially associates with the tabernacle and its rites. That part of the picture, as Stowell renders it, comes from the psalmist's magnificent iconic picture of the divinely favored king ("God, thy God, hath anointed thee with the oil

---

24. Thomas Hastings, writer of the impressive tune with which Stowell's hymn is almost inseparably associated, read the poem well: he called his tune *Retreat* (1842).

of gladness above thy fellows") and from the resignification of that icon in the book of Hebrews, which applies its words to Jesus (Ps 45:7, KJV, Heb 1:9). The explicit connection of gladness with the mercy seat is Stowell's own contribution, as is his use of another Bible icon to reemphasize the importance of a personal, emotional response to spiritual conflict. His final stanza is his version of the psalmist's picture of mourning for the beloved city: "If I forget thee, O Jerusalem, let my right hand forget her cunning. If I do not remember thee, let my tongue cleave to the roof of my mouth" (Ps 137:5–6, KJV). Stowell transforms this determination not to forget a physical place into a determination not to forget a spiritual experience. Thus are Bible icons resignified into terms that would seem literally incredible to their original authors.

Yet even fidelity to an original icon can produce a dramatic resignification. The strongest line of Stowell's hymn is undoubtedly "It is the bloodstain'd mercy seat." Here is a warmly imaginative response to Leviticus's literal descriptions of the high priest's yearly ritual. When the high priest entered the Holy of Holies to sprinkle blood upon the *kappōret*, it would already be stained by the blood of earlier offerings (Lev 16:14–15). But while this is a natural deduction from the text, it is something that the text never mentions. We would not expect it to: bloodstains are hardly effective images of purgation, which is the point of the ritual that Leviticus describes. Stowell, however, has another point to make. He wants to picture the relationship between spiritual exaltation and earthly suffering—the suffering of Christ and his disciples, the "saints" of stanza 4. To do this, he insists on the continued presence of the reminders of suffering, the blood stains on the mercy seat.

This particular way of shaping the picture seems to have occurred to Stowell only when he reread his own poem and saw more deeply into the icon he was crafting. In the poem's first published version (1828), he used a conventional image: "the blood-bought Mercy Seat."[25] "Blood-bought" was a familiar adjective in Christian sermons and songs.[26] It was the kind of adjective that may already have lost its force. Worse, it was theologically confused in the context in which Stowell used it. According to Christian theology, Jesus' blood "buys" salvation, but it does not "buy" the source of salvation, God's "mercy seat." Soon after the poem's first publication, Stowell issued a revised version, in his *Selection of Psalms and Hymns* (1831–1864), which resolved both the literary and the theological problem by returning to the literal object inside the tabernacle. He knew that the "mercy

25. Hugh Stowell, "The Mercy Seat," in *The Winter's Wreath: Or a Collection of Original Contributions in Prose and Verse* (London: Whittaker, 1828) 239–40.

26. Such as the famous hymn by William Cowper, "There Is a Fountain," in the *Olney Hymns* (1779).

seat" in the Pentateuch must have been blood-stained. He also knew that the book of Hebrews dwells on the similarity between the heavenly and the earthly tabernacles (Hebrews 9). He saw the literary potential: the spiritual shrine to which true Christians "retreat" could be pictured as bearing the same indelible marks of suffering as the literal and historical shrine. By 1833, he had replaced "blood-bought" with "blood-stain'd," and he kept it that way through the last edition published in his lifetime.[27] This revision greatly strengthened the line, and it strengthened the rest of the poem, too. The hymn now makes the daringly paradoxical claim that "sweet," and sweeter "than all beside," is the "blood-stain'd" object at the center of the awe-surrounded shrine.

This strong version of the poem was reprinted in such popular offerings as *The Methodist Sunday-School Hymn-Book* and the nondenominational *Songs of Grace and Glory*.[28] It continues to appear in prominent hymn books.[29] But most editors who have used Stowell's work have performed their own revisions, returning by preference to the poem's weak, early version—not, apparently, because it is the only version they can find (the 1828 printing was much less widely circulated than the twelve later printings in Stowell's *Selection*), or because they respect the author's first intent (most of them accept his smaller revisions of the 1828 poem), but because they reject his graphic emphasis on suffering. Even editors of Stowell's own denomination have found this hard to accept. In 1871, the American Episcopal *Hymnal* ran the poem without the 4th and 6th stanzas and with the weak reading of stanza 2, leaving only "calm," "gladness," "fellowship," and other pleasant things. Wiser heads prevailed in the 1892 *Hymnal*; stanzas 4 and 6 were still left out, but "blood-bought" was again replaced by "blood-stained." Unfortunately, the 1940 *Hymnal* continued the omissions of 4 and 6 and substituted "the blessed mercy-seat" for "the blood-stain'd mercy seat," thus preferring platitude to paradox. Even this jejune phrase is omitted from the current *Hymnal*, because the hymn itself is omitted.[30] In this way, the icon that Stowell identified, revised, and

27. Hugh Stowell, *A Selection of Psalms and Hymns, Suited to the Services of the Church of England* (Manchester: Edwin Slater, 1864) 266–67.

28. *The Methodist Sunday-School Hymn-Book*, compiled by direction of the Wesleyan-Methodist Conference (London: Wesleyan-Methodist Sunday-School Union, 1879), hymn 268; *Songs of Grace and Glory* (ed. Charles B. Snepp; new and rev. ed.; London: James Nisbet, 1873) hymn 834.

29. Such as the popular "ecumenical" book published by the Orthodox Presbyterian Church, *Trinity Hymnal* (Philadelphia: Great Commission Publications, 1961, 1976) hymn 528.

30. *Hymnal: According to the Use of the Protestant Episcopal Church in the United States of America* (Philadelphia: Lippincott, 1871) hymn 381; *The Hymnal: Revised and Enlarged . . . 1892* (New York: Henry Frowde, n.d.) hymn 481; *The Hymnal of the Protestant Episcopal*

resignified was revised and resignified by his coreligionists, then finally rejected—a mainstream denomination's last critical response to an overzealous preacher.

What moral shall we derive from the adventures of this Bible icon? One of the most plausible conclusions we could reach is that iconicity is merely in the eye of the beholder. Not everyone can spot an icon; not everyone wants to; and those who do identify biblical icons feel free to interpret them in any way they please. The original version doesn't matter much; iconicity is a random walk through a luxuriant forest of potential resignifications. As a wise critic once said, "A carload of bricks doesn't make a mason."[31] People respond to literature as their culture, beliefs, and temperament lead them to respond; the Bible may contain a carload of iconic bricks, but that doesn't mean that readers will know what to do with them or that any two readers will do the same things.

Yes, this is a plausible conclusion. But we should not forget that the Bible story that caught William Blake's imagination was the story of the prodigal son, not the story of Ananias and Sapphira; and it was the Pentateuch's descriptions of the tabernacle that Stowell and the author of Hebrews identified as iconic, not its descriptions of Israel's dietary laws. Even a good mason has to have a supply of bricks, and bricks have to possess certain qualities for masons to be able to use them. What are the literary qualities that an icon needs to possess if later authors are to identify, exploit, and perhaps resignify it?

Several of these qualities have become fairly obvious. A literary icon needs to be concrete enough to attract the imagination but suggestive enough to allow allusion and resignification in a variety of new contexts. It must have "a local habitation and a name," but it must be capable of developing something more than local relevance. It must also have, or be capable of developing, intense emotional associations.

I doubt that the story of the prodigal son would ever have been taken as iconic if the sinful young man had been described as gradually finding out, through a long course of psychotherapy, that there are certain ethical issues that he had hitherto neglected to clarify in his own mind, issues about which he might not have taken entirely appropriate action; or if he had been described as revisiting a father who merely sat with him in the family room and made some improving comments about forgiveness and love.

Church in the United States of America 1940 (New York: Church Pension Fund, 1961) hymn 421; *The Hymnal, 1982: According to the Use of the Episcopal Church* (New York: Church Hymnal Corp., 1985).

31. Isabel Paterson, "Turns with a Bookworm," *New York Herald Tribune "Books"* (Feb. 8, 1931).

No, the Prodigal sins greatly, suffers greatly, and suddenly and dramatically "comes to himself." He rushes back to his father; and his father, seeing him, runs out, falls on his neck, kisses him, and orders a public celebration. It doesn't take much thought to find the intensity in Jesus' parable; it's right there in the text. It does take thought to appreciate the iconic potential of the *kappōret*; but that potential is also really there, in the biblical descriptions of the tabernacle: enclosure upon enclosure, then the innermost room, the jewellike splendor of the cherubim, the offering of blood, the climactic approach to God. Across the centuries, these features have been richly and diversely resignified, but they have not been random creations of any reader's subjectivity. They, too, are in the text, as assuredly present as the cherubim of gold atop the wooden box.

For the responsive reader, the discovery of passages and features such as these is a joyful event, one that ensures the interest and confirms the importance of the act of reading. For "people of the Book," they are frequently the core of literary as well as religious experience. Perhaps I am merely resignifying the resignifier, but whenever I hear Stowell's hymn, I am reminded not only of the glory of the mercy seat, as he and the author of Hebrews evoke it, but also of the sudden glory that comes to readers when they find a great literary passage, and to literary craftsmen when they find a text out of which they can fashion something new and great. It's a sense of discovery, and a sense of power—the power of God, indeed, but also the power of art. Wherever historical research on the Bible may take us, we should never forget the glory and the power that people find in it. To resignify, once again, Richard Friedman's memorable remark, the question isn't who wrote the Bible but who reads it, and glories in the reading.

Walter Rauschenbusch, the Social Gospel Movement, and How Julius Wellhausen Unwittingly Helped Create American Progressivism in the Twentieth Century

STEVEN CASSEDY

University of California, San Diego

In *Stride toward Freedom* (1958), the story of the Montgomery bus boy-cott, Martin Luther King speaks of the moment in his seminary years when he discovered an intellectual foundation for his struggle against "social evil." The book he credits is *Christianity and the Social Crisis*, by Walter Rauschenbusch.[1] The name of this author has appeared over the years in the writings of Jim Wallis, founder of the left-wing Christian organization Sojourners and author of *God's Politics* (2005). In *Stealing Jesus* (1997), an angry denunciation of American fundamentalism, Bruce Bawer devoted an entire chapter to Rauschenbusch, crediting him with helping liberal Prot-estants during the 20th century build a "Church of Love" and noting Rau-schenbusch's influence on Gandhi, King, and Desmond Tutu. But Bawer lamented that almost no Christians of his day would even recognize the name.[2]

So it might come as a surprise to many Americans today that a century ago a certain Walter Rauschenbusch, his books, and the movement he represented were immensely famous. Rauschenbusch (1861–1918) came from a long line of German Lutheran pastors. He was born in the United States, carried out his studies both here and in Germany, became a Baptist minister to a German-speaking congregation in New York City, and fin-ished his career as a professor of church history at the Rochester Theo-logical Seminary, where his father had served on the faculty for many

---

1. Martin Luther King Jr., *Stride toward Freedom: The Montgomery Story* (New York: Harper & Row, 1958) 91. King included the story two years later in "Pilgrimage to Non-violence," *Christian Century* 77 (1960) 439–41; and five years later in *Strength to Love* (New York: Harper & Row, 1963) 137–38.

2. Bruce Bawer, *Stealing Jesus: How Fundamentalism Betrays Christianity* (New York: Crown, 1997) 91–107.

years. He was a leading figure in what came to be called the Social Gospel movement.

That movement has its own story. In its standard version, it goes something like this: after the Civil War, with the accelerating rise of industrialism and its attendant social ills, American Protestantism gave birth to a spirit of social reform. Leading representatives of the new spirit were moved by the spectacle of human misery among the working classes in American cities and by the belief that capitalism had helped create a climate in which greed and corruption had produced great suffering. They were moved even more by the belief that the solution to the great social problems of the Gilded Age lay in a rejuvenated Christianity. This Christianity bore two essential features designed to set it apart from what liberal pastors saw as an ossified and lifeless form of religious practice: (1) its faithfulness to the "true," "original" spirit of Jesus and (2) its emphasis on *community* and *solidarity* over *individual salvation*.

In notoriety, authority, and influence, Rauschenbusch certainly surpassed other members of the movement. Arthur Schlesinger Jr. described him years ago as "the most searching theologian of the Social Gospel," identifying the movement as a central shaping force in Theodore Roosevelt's progressive social philosophy. He named Rauschenbusch, too, as a major influence on Norman Thomas, thus on American socialism in the early years of the New Deal and the presidency of Franklin Delano Roosevelt.[3]

The work that made Rauschenbusch almost a household word after the turn of the century was the one that King named. It would be inaccurate to say of the central ideas in *Christianity and the Social Crisis* (1907) either that they were entirely new in the Social Gospel movement or that they were new even in Rauschenbusch's pastoral career. What the book offered that set it apart from others of the era was the scholarly grounding in history that the author gave those ideas.

The ideas can be quickly summarized. Rauschenbusch's program contained a call to action and a theological basis for that call. First, the historical conditions that inspire the call to action: capitalism is the great culprit because in practice it has fostered poverty and inequality. The moral fault of capitalism stems from its promotion of economic individualism and competition. Rauschenbusch spent much of his mature life observing in the gritty slums of New York City the true human cost of an economic system that promoted profits at the expense of all else.

If there's a moral truth in Rauschenbusch that subsumes all others, it's that poverty is unacceptable and that a society not dedicated to its eradica-

---

3. Arthur Schlesinger Jr., *The Crisis of the Old Order, 1919–1933* (Boston: Houghton Mifflin, 1957) 23, 206–7.

tion is not worth much. Chapter 5 of *Christianity and the Social Crisis*, titled "The Present Crisis," could have been written by someone of any faith or by someone of no faith at all. There we read a dialogue between "the Spirit of the Nineteenth Century" and "the Spirit of the First Century." Having at first boasted of the progress he has witnessed, the Spirit of the Nineteenth Century is finally obliged to make this concession to his opponent: "My great cities are as yours were. My millions live from hand to mouth. Those who toil longest have least. My thousands sink exhausted before their days are half spent. My human wreckage multiplies. Class faces class in sullen distrust. Their freedom and knowledge has only made men keener to suffer."[4] The call to action is primarily to end poverty and inequality.

The theological basis for Rauschenbusch's program can be encapsulated in one phrase: the kingdom of God. Rauschenbusch did not invent the phrase, of course, nor was he responsible for introducing it into the lexicon of the Social Gospel. But he popularized it and, in *Christianity and the Social Crisis*, gave it a scholarly foundation different from what we find in the writings of his contemporaries. Rauschenbusch considered the kingdom of God to be *the* central concept in the teaching of Jesus. Christian tradition over the centuries, he thought, had perverted the meaning of the concept, and his task was to restore it to its state of primal purity—to tell the world what he thought *Jesus* understood by "the kingdom of God."

The kingdom of God, for Rauschenbusch, did not refer to the millennium or the "hidden life with God."[5] For Jesus himself, Rauschenbusch insists, the kingdom of God referred to *this* world. As *kingdom*, it had to do with "that social justice, prosperity, and happiness for which the Law and the prophets called, and for which the common people always long." As kingdom *of God*, it meant "the consummation of the theocratic hope."[6] As *kingdom*, it was a this-worldly concept; as kingdom *of God*, it denoted an ideal world (but *this* world) that reflects God's justice.

As Rauschenbusch tells the story in *Christianity and the Social Crisis*, the character of the kingdom of God is inextricably tied to two essential features of Judaism in Palestine during the historical period of Jesus. The first is political: it is the Roman occupation and the lack (going all the way back to the fall of the monarchy) of a Jewish nation. The second is religious: it is the dominance, in this era, of the priestly element in Judaism and the consequent emphasis, among powerful religious leaders, on ritual, law, and proper worship. In this account, Jesus' response was a campaign to restore

---

4. Walter Rauschenbusch, *Christianity and the Social Crisis* (New York: Macmillan, 1907) 212–13.

5. Ibid., 54–55.

6. Ibid., 57.

the traditions of the Prophets, whose teachings he considered—as did Rauschenbusch—antithetical to those of the priests.

This is where Julius Wellhausen enters the scene. In 1891, Rauschenbusch had produced a manuscript titled *The Righteousness of the Kingdom*. He never sent it to a publisher. It was discovered only after his death and published in 1968. The central chapter is devoted to the kingdom of God. In this early work, Jesus appears at the end of a continuous tradition of Hebrew prophecy, beginning with Elijah and stretching to the era of the Roman occupation (though Rauschenbusch names very few prophets). In 1894, Wellhausen published his *Israelitische und jüdische Geschichte* (History of Israel and Judaism). Sometime between then and 1907, Rauschenbusch read this popular book, which included many of the findings of Wellhausen's earlier *Prolegomena zur Geschichte Israels* (1883) but reflected the author's growing interest in Christianity and took Jewish history up through Jesus of Nazareth.

It is clear that the book transformed the way Rauschenbusch viewed both Jesus' place in history and the genesis of the kingdom of God. If Rauschenbusch found in Wellhausen a congenial spirit from the outset, it was no doubt because the German biblical scholar represented a method that he, Rauschenbusch, so admired. Rauschenbusch was a passionate supporter of modern science, from the theory of evolution to the fledgling field of sociology to what he called "historical science." He describes this last field as being a century old, as being solidly founded on the concept of organic growth, and as being largely a product of Germany.[7]

What now entered the historical picture for Rauschenbusch was the priestly period in Jewish history—according to the way *Wellhausen* viewed that period, chronologically. Thus Rauschenbusch, like Wellhausen himself and like so many readers of Wellhausen, incorporated into his work the "brilliant mistake" that Eduard Reuss had made back in 1833 and that plays such a pivotal role in Richard Friedman's *Who Wrote the Bible?*[8] He viewed the period in Jewish history when the Law dominated as *subsequent* to the prophetic period (and, like Wellhausen, treated the "prophetic period" as its own distinct entity). The result for *Rauschenbusch* was a story line that was no longer characterized by unbroken continuity between the prophets and Jesus. The new story line included a rupture in the prophetic tradition and an image of Jesus as a prophet who, in establishing the kingdom of God on earth, sought to restore a pure version of that tradition— thus an image of Jesus as a singularly rebellious prophet. The story line

7. Ibid., 194; and "The Influence of Historical Studies on Theology," *The American Journal of Theology* 11 (1907) 111–27.

8. Richard Elliott Friedman, *Who Wrote the Bible?* (1987; repr. San Francisco: HarperSanFrancisco, 1997) 161–73.

about the priestly period was Wellhausen's unwitting contribution to the Social Gospel movement in America.

Rauschenbusch dutifully divides the history of Israel before Jesus into three broad periods: (1) the period of primitive religion, characterized by its emphasis on sacrifice; (2) the period of the prophets; and (3) the priestly period. For Rauschenbusch, the prophetic phase contains all that is holy in Judaism and all that by rights should have been retained (but was not) over the centuries by the Christian churches. Prophetic religion is national, ethical, humane, and focused on justice. With the fall of Jerusalem and the destruction of the temple in the early 6th century B.C.E., the Jewish religion begins its turn toward the personal. But a change in direction that might have proved fruitful, leading to a system of belief in which the individual seeks salvation "not as a member of his nation, but as a man by virtue of his humanity," is steered off course by the priestly class.[9] The culprit here, as in Wellhausen, is Ezekiel, who, in this view, shifted the emphasis in Judaism from justice to the mere mechanics of cultic ceremony.

This is essentially the way Wellhausen tells the story, though Rauschenbusch has done some condensing and selecting. He's also done some borrowing that borders on outright plagiarism. Many passages in the sections of *Christianity and the Social Crisis* that tell the story of the transition from "primitive" Judaism to the prophetic period and from the prophetic to the priestly period are translated almost word for word from Wellhausen's book, without attribution. (The one footnote reference to the book comes in connection with an ancillary point about Jesus, many pages after the central portions of the story have been told.)

The borrowing is particularly pronounced when it comes to the transition from the prophetic to the priestly. Here (in my translation) is what Wellhausen says about Ezekiel: "The ideal is not justice but holiness. As early as the lists of sins that occupy so much space in the first part of his book, it emerges what excessive value Ezekiel places on cultic worship [*Kultus*]."[10] Here is Rauschenbusch: "Ezekiel dwelt on the sins of man against God, especially idolatry. Not justice but holiness had become the fundamental requirement, and holiness meant chiefly ceremonial correctness."[11]

Rauschenbusch relied heavily on Wellhausen, too, for the later parts of the story. Wellhausen describes John the Baptist and Jesus like this: "They welcomed the conflict with the Romans. The question was what the outcome would be. It was the same question that had posed itself to Amos and Jeremiah as the conflict with the Assyrians and the Chaldeans threatened.

---

9. Rauschenbusch, *Christianity and the Social Crisis*, 28.

10. Julius Wellhausen, *Israelitische und jüdische Geschichte* (9th ed.; Berlin: de Gruyter, 1958) 147.

11. Rauschenbusch, *Christianity and the Social Crisis*, 30.

. . . The prophecy of the impending advent of the kingdom of God coincided with the prophecy of the impending destruction of the temple and of the holy city."[12] Here is Rauschenbusch's version: "As Amos and Jeremiah foresaw the conflict of their people with the Assyrians and the Chaldeans, so Jesus foresaw his nation drifting toward the conflict with Rome, and like them he foretold disaster, the fall of the temple and of the holy city."[13] To highlight the supremacy of Jesus, Wellhausen used a comparison with the scribes: "As a teacher [Jesus] is compared with the scribes, but he was able to do it better than they, and he also did it differently."[14] Rauschenbusch is more extravagant, comparing Jesus with the prophets: "In the poise and calm of his mind and manner, and in the love of his heart he was infinitely above them all [the prophets]."[15]

There has been some debate over whether Wellhausen was a Hegelian thinker.[16] However one might choose to settle that debate, it's clear that, in *Israelitische und jüdische Geschichte*, he applied at least a rudimentary Hegelian logic to the story of Jesus. Rauschenbusch followed his predecessor's lead but diverged on an important point. In Wellhausen's account, the progress from (1) the prophets through (2) the priestly to (3) Jesus of Nazareth follows a fairly neat Hegelian pattern. So, to use a scheme that Hegel's followers introduced, if Jesus represents the synthesis to the "thesis" of prophecy and the "antithesis" of priestliness, he brings about a condition that transcends/cancels out (*aufheben*) the legalistic and the theocratic while elevating individual, private freedom. Wellhausen's kingdom of God thus substitutes universalism (a kingdom for Jew and Gentile alike) for a nationalist theocracy (a state for Jews alone) and Jesus' individual freedom for the priests' individual ceremonial correctness.

But Rauschenbusch never abandoned the idea of theocracy. In *The Righteousness of the Kingdom*, he had vigorously and unabashedly promoted the idea of "Messianic Theocracy." In *Christianity and the Social Crisis*, he continued to insist (a bit confusingly) that for Jesus the restoration of the Jew-

---

12. Wellhausen, *Israelitische und jüdische Geschichte*, 359–60.

13. Rauschenbusch, *Christianity and the Social Crisis*, 53.

14. Wellhausen, *Israelitische und jüdische Geschichte*, 360. The earlier editions lack this sentence.

15. Rauschenbusch, *Christianity and the Social Crisis*, 53. This is the sentence to which Rauschenbusch supplies a footnote reference to Wellhausen's book.

16. Lothar Perlitt, claiming that religion and philosophy are identical for Hegel, argues against classifying Wellhausen as Hegelian, since Wellhausen, in Perlitt's eyes, wrote *Profangeschichte* ('profane history'). See Lothar Perlitt, *Vatke und Wellhausen: Geschichtsphilosophische Voraussetzungen und historiographische Motive für die Darstellung der Religion und Geschichte Israels durch Wilhelm Vatke und Julius Wellhausen* (Berlin: Alfred Töpelmann, 1965) 232, 239. Arnaldo Momigliano is less troubled by the claim that Wellhausen was a Hegelian thinker. See "Religious History without Frontiers: J. Wellhausen, U. Wilamowitz, and E. Schwartz," *History and Theory* 21 (1982) 49–64.

ish nation was a primary goal but one that Jesus modified significantly. This is the point on which he most diverges from Wellhausen. In Wellhausen's view, the transformation that Jesus brought about in Judaism consisted in his no longer regarding the temple and the holy city as a necessary foundation for the kingdom of God. Instead, Jesus emphasized "individual conditions/qualifications" [*individuelle Bedingungen*] for admission into the future kingdom. "[These conditions] became for him [Jesus] so much the chief issue that his preaching about them lost the character of prophecy, for the fulfillment of the conditions was already possible in the present."[17] In the earlier editions of the book, Wellhausen added that the kingdom of God "extended into the present," but only in the sense that it was "inwardly constituted" (that is, within the individual).[18] Rauschenbusch insists that Jesus never ceased being a prophet. For him, the kingdom of God, as Jesus conceived it, was already present and "always but coming."[19] How to explain this? Rauschenbusch has recourse to an organic image. Jesus, amusingly represented here as a kind of proto-Hegelian, saw the kingdom in this way:

> It was like the seed scattered by the peasant, growing slowly and silently, night and day, by its own germinating force and the food furnished by the earth . . . Jesus had the scientific insight which comes to most men only by training, but to the elect few by divine gift. He grasped the substance of that law of organic development in nature and history which our own day at last has begun to elaborate systematically.[20]

In more explicit language: "[The kingdom's] consummation, of course, was in the future, but its fundamental realities were already present," he says.[21]

Thus, in Wellhausen's account, the coming fall of Jerusalem and the Second Temple to the Roman armies was to be a positive development for Jesus, preparing the way for the less earthly kingdom of God. In Rauschenbusch's account, this predicted fall was to be disastrous for Jesus, since it represented the end of Jewish national aspirations. But the result that *should have occurred*, namely the establishment of an *earthly* kingdom of God, a result continually subverted during two thousand years of misdirected rule in the Christian churches, *would have represented* a fitting synthesis for Rauschenbusch's historical scheme. The scheme shows that

---

17. Wellhausen, *Israelitische und jüdische Geschichte*, 360.
18. Wellhausen revised the book for the fifth edition (1904). This language still appeared in the fourth edition (Berlin: Georg Reimer, 1901) 381.
19. Rauschenbusch, *Christianity and the Social Crisis*, 421.
20. Ibid., 59.
21. Ibid., 62.

Rauschenbusch was a committed Hegelian but that, at the same time, he thought the history culminating in Jesus betrayed a kind of fractured logic.

How? To begin with, whereas for Wellhausen the priestly seemed a natural (though unpleasant) phase in the progress toward Christianity, for Rauschenbusch it was clearly an aberration. In fact, it is precisely when he speaks of the abnormality of the priestly phase that he adopts his most explicitly Hegelian language, in order to show how Hegelian logic was *violated*. With the destruction of the First Temple and the consequent loss of a Jewish nation, Rauschenbusch says (closely following Wellhausen's account of Jeremiah), religion retreated inward. As he puts it, "The death-pangs of the national life were the birth-pangs of the personal religious life" (possibly echoing a footnote in which Wellhausen said, "The Jewish church arose as the Jewish state was sinking").[22] This could and should have been a favorable development. "But every new religious synthesis should contain all that was good and true in the old. If the religious value of the individual was being discovered, why should the religious value of the community be forgotten?"[23] So what in fact happened was not what *should have* happened. The period following the end of Jewish national life under the monarchy *should have* presented the perfect Hegelian synthesis of community and individuality. Instead, Ezekiel came along and turned the entire religion into a hollow shell of perfunctory ritual observance. And later, after Jesus came to *restore* the prophetic period in a grand synthesis with the new spirit of individuality, it was the Christian churches that once again disrupted natural historical progress by diverting their followers from communal to private and individual concerns.

And yet this argument ultimately serves Rauschenbusch's purposes, for two reasons. First it is consistent with a view that Rauschenbusch had long held, namely, that Jesus was a revolutionary. Wellhausen's chronology, in which the priestly period follows the prophetic, both altered this view and gave it added force for Rauschenbusch. In *The Righteousness of the Kingdom*, Jesus was the successor to the prophets, and if he was a revolutionary ("Christianity Is Revolutionary" was the title of the first chapter of this work), it was because *all* the prophets were by nature revolutionaries in their own times.[24] The earlier prophets rebelled against kings and dynasties. Jesus' rebellion was more fundamental. He came into a Jewish world dominated by priests and rebelled specifically against the prevailing *religious* powers in his own day.

---

22. Ibid., 28; Wellhausen, *Israelitische und jüdische Geschichte*, 169 n. 1.

23. Rauschenbusch, *Christianity and the Social Crisis*, 29.

24. Walter Rauschenbusch, *The Righteousness of the Kingdom* (ed. Max L. Stackhouse; Nashville: Abingdon, 1968) 70–71.

Second, if the Christian churches for almost two thousand years have hindered the neat Hegelian logic of Jewish history by interrupting what *could* have been a grand synthesis brought about by Jesus' correction of the *previous* aberration in Jewish history, then it is up to Rauschenbusch's readers, in 1907, to complete that logic by rallying the spirit of Christian solidarity in the fight against the selfishness and greed of modern capitalism. American men and women in this progressive era can now correct history, can make the previous 1,900 years appear as only a hiatus separating the conception of Jesus' grand idea from its realization.

In the final analysis, despite the differences between the two accounts, Wellhausen supplied Rauschenbusch with a story line that firmly emphasized the urgent need for *restoration*. Wellhausen was a historian; Rauschenbusch was a political activist. Wellhausen's interest, at least in *Israelitische und jüdische Geschichte*, ends with the period of the Gospels; Rauschenbusch's extends to modern times and the future. Wellhausen, an admirer of Bismarck, would have been most surprised to see that his historical method and the documentary hypothesis had an impact on the radical politics of another country.

"Starving" the Patient:
A Jewish Perspective on Terry Schiavo and the Feeding Tube Controversy

RANDY LINDA STURMAN ל"ז

University of Georgia

The recent Florida case of Terry Schiavo has stirred much debate over the right to die versus the right to live. Ms. Schiavo's heart stopped, causing her to sustain irreversible brain damage and remain in a persistent vegetative state for 13 years. The core of the debate between her husband and her parents is whether or not she should be removed from her feeding tube, which would result in her death. Her case has generated not only a multitude of legal battles and philosophical discussions but also the intervention of the governor and the Florida legislature. Her husband appeared on Larry King Live, the event was discussed on the *New York Times* editorial pages, and countless popular (and not-so-popular) journals have commented on her case and the cause.

Why has this case generated so much publicity? Aside from the moral, legal, medical, and ethical issues, why has Terry Schiavo become a focal point for politicians to rally for their causes and for religious leaders to argue over the morality of allowing her to suffer—for some, by refusing to allow her to go to her grave peacefully, for others, by "starving" her to death? The answer lies in our ambiguity over the use of feeding tubes and our discomfort with what it means to allow someone to die from lack of nourishment.

I spent a year in Jerusalem interviewing individuals who were involved in making end-of-life decisions, including family members, physicians, nurses, rabbis, and social workers. In one case, a woman with ALS (Lou Gherig's disease) was paralyzed from the neck down. She and her family discussed at what point life would no longer be worth living and how decisions such as these are made. In another case, a pregnant woman went into a coma, and her family disagreed with the physicians about what should happen to the fetus. A judge was called in to decide the case. In yet another case, a young man who had virtually no chance of recovery was aggressively treated by his physicians, who could not bear to let him die. My aim was to examine the legal, medical, ethical, and cultural issues that arise from these cases. Israel, being an extraordinary mixture of cultures, proved to be an ideal setting within which to address these issues of universal concern.

The issue of whether or not to remove a feeding tube came up on several occasions. What interested me was why individuals who had no difficulty disconnecting someone from a respirator, or not placing a person on one in the first place, were extremely reluctant to disconnect a feeding tube. Why the difference, especially in cases in which the patient is so close to death, with no realistic chance of recovery? Why are individuals, even doctors, comfortable with removing a respirator when no reasonable hope is left, yet removal of a feeding tube presents such an emotional dilemma? I present here two of my cases, which I hope will shed light on the subject.

The Case of Sarah:
How Does One Define the Term Heroic Measures?

By the time I met Hannah, her mother Sarah had already died. She grieved for her mother, but even more, she had self-recriminations for how her mother had spent her last few days of life and whether she should have fought harder to stop the doctor from inserting a feeding tube into her mother as she lay dying.

Sarah was born in Poland, and in 1933 she married and moved to Mexico. When the Holocaust broke out, she was able to obtain only one visa to save a member of her family by bringing this person to Mexico. Her brother was married, her sister was single. The sister got the visa and lived; the rest of the family perished.

Move forward about 65 years. Sarah moved to Israel, following her daughter Hannah. She spent the last few years of her life in a nursing home with a progressively worsening case of pulmonary disease. By the time she entered Hadassah Hospital in Jerusalem in January of 1998, her lung disease could no longer be treated; she was days away from death.

The question arose as to how aggressively Sarah should be treated. Hannah informed the doctors that her mother had clearly stated that she did not want any "heroic measures" to be used to save her life. She had come to this conclusion when she saw her husband suffering near the end of his life with tubes being inserted into his body to prolong his life. The problem was what constituted "heroic measures."

The first doctor to treat Sarah was comfortable with not placing her on a respirator; however, he did not consider a feeding tube to be heroic measures. He tried once and failed to insert a tube, but when Hannah objected, he agreed not to try again. Another doctor then took over the case. She would not agree to allow Sarah to die without placing her on a feeding tube. Hannah did not agree with the doctor but was reluctant to object too strenuously as she was Orthodox and was afraid of violating any religious requirements. The nurse disagreed with the doctor but agreed to try once to insert the tube. (The doctor was a secular Jew, the nurse quite religious.) She was able to place the feeding tube down Sarah's throat and Sarah died later that day, unaware of the controversy surrounding her death.

The Case of Fanny:
Can a Mind Function without a Body?

Fanny has a disease most people would dread. It has left her with a completely functional mind and no use of her body from the neck down. She cannot bathe herself or wipe her own nose. She cannot turn the pages of a book. She can still talk, but someday she will also lose this ability. She is suffering from amyotrophic lateral sclerosis (ALS), commonly known as Lou Gherig's disease. It is a degenerative disease that causes people gradually to lose control of their muscles, eventually the muscles involved in respiration, and the final result is death.

I first became aware of Fanny's case when I met her daughter, Maya, who was the drama teacher in my daughter's elementary school. As often happens when one is conducting research overseas, I was not making sufficient contacts, my research was not progressing as fast as it should, and it appeared that I would have to leave the country without enough data to write my book. One day, I decided to put my work aside and go on a Tu'B'shevat tree-planting field trip with my daughter's school. Through the shouting and singing on the school bus (I still remember the song *Ani tsiltsel b'telephone* 'I call you on the telephone'), I managed to strike up a conversation with Maya. She asked me what my research was about and then proceeded to say, "I would be the perfect subject for you." It turned out that she and her sister had been struggling for years with their mother's terminal illness.

Maya told me of her mother's initial weakness, progressive deterioration, and, finally, her diagnosis of a terminal illness. The diagnosis was kept from her mother but revealed to Maya by the neurologist as the two walked down the corridors of the hospital together.

Maya related their struggles to help her mother through her progressively worsening condition, and then she told me of her mother's hospitalization when she began having trouble breathing. It was during this hospitalization that a decision was made to surgically implant a feeding tube into Fanny. Everyone, including her Orthodox Jewish doctors at

Shaare Tzedek hospital (the more religious of the hospitals in Jerusalem) agreed that it was pointless to place Fanny on a respirator. Yet, when it came to inserting a feeding tube, the doctors and Fanny's daughters agreed that it should be done. Some time after the feeding tube was inserted, Fanny's condition improved, and she was able to leave the hospital. When I met her, she was paralyzed from the neck down and received her nourishment through the feeding tube that had been surgically implanted in her stomach. She was completely coherent and mentally alert. Although she is not happy with her present condition, she did appear to be resigned to her fate and did not speak of wanting to end her life.

Discussion:
The Feeding-Tube versus the Respirator

I now return to my initial question: why are individuals who have no problem disconnecting someone from a respirator, or not placing a person on one in the first place, so reluctant to disconnect a feeding tube? Why is such a clear distinction drawn between a lack of food and lack of breath? Why the emotional reaction to removing a feeding tube? Why the reference to "starving" a patient when, in fact, one will die as surely from the removal of a respirator as from being taken off a feeding tube? The answer lies in a complex analysis of social, psychological, and religious variables.

In the cases of both Fanny and Sarah, references were made to the pain associated with not eating. The doctor in Sarah's case told me that she "shouldn't be starved. Fluid and food are basic to life" and "you have to understand that this is the 90s. We don't starve people to death." Similarly, in Fanny's case, her daughter Maya stated that she "didn't want to starve" her mother. In both cases, failing to insert a feeding tube was seen as actively allowing a person to die, even implying that it would be a painful type of death. In contrast, failing to insert a respirator is equated with allowing a person to die of natural causes. Even in Sarah's case, in which she was clearly dying and was unable to eat because her bodily functions were shutting down, the understanding of the doctor was that she had an active duty to intervene and that providing food was part of basic medical care. This is the perception: that not feeding equals actively killing (i.e., starving), while not helping one to breathe equals allowing one to die. Understanding this perception helps to explain individuals' attitudes about the difference between the two interventions.

In fact, this perception that it is painful for a dying person to be deprived of food is not true. In interviewing Dr. Ray Fink, the founder of the hospice movement at Hadassah Hospital, he told me that when a person is dying and is no longer able to digest foods, it is often more painful to force them to eat than to follow the body's natural shutting down process. He further stated that, unlike a healthy person who has been deprived of food, once the body is in the process of dying, there is little pain associated with the cessation of food, so long as the person is given small amounts of fluids. I personally witnessed this phenomenon when a good friend of ours had to place his dying mother in a hospice. This patient, who was over 80 years old and suffering from end stage cancer, was being force-fed intravenously in the hospital after she was unable to swallow food by mouth. Once she was moved to the hospice, they stopped feeding her. Her condition improved, she showed fewer signs of pain, and she lived another month, well beyond the prediction of the hospital physicians.

Breathing is seen as something that is done automatically and cannot be controlled, whereas food can be given or withheld at will. Breathing is simple. One either breathes or does not breathe. Eating is a complex process that involves both biological needs and psychological and social rewards that also encompass cultural elements. Eating is a social activity involving sharing and giving. There are tasty foods and not-so-tasty foods, foods that are considered "clean" and those that are considered not so clean. Food can be associated with love, particularly in the Jewish tradition (hence, the stereotype of the Jewish mother as one who constantly urges her children to eat). This distinction between breathing, which is considered a purely involuntary, biological process, and eating, which is a highly complex, voluntary activity that fulfills not only a biological need but a myriad of social and psychological needs as well, must influence people's understandings of the difference between the two.

For an individual who keeps kosher, food is a constant reminder of one's religious affiliation and commitment. At every meal, one's choice of foods, combination of foods, and desistance from eating forbidden foods serves to reinforce one's Jewishness. It connects us to our ancestors and to Jews the world over. It reminds us that we are a distinct people.

Judaism plays yet another role in distinguishing between a feeding tube and a respirator. In traditional Jewish religious terms, breath is equated with life. Whereas the less religious use brain death to determine the time of death of a patient, many religious Jews still determine the time of death by the cessation of the heart and breath. There are references to this idea of equating life with breath as far back as the Hebrew Bible. For instance, in the biblical story of Noah, the Bible refers to the death of "all in whose nostrils was the breath of life" (Gen 7:22). When creating man, God "breathed into his nostrils the breath of life: and man became a living being" (Gen 2:4). There are linguistic connections as well between the two in both biblical and modern Hebrew. Often, the words for breath and for life are interchangeable. The Hebrew word *neshama* means soul or breath. It is the same root as the word *linshom,* to breathe, and the term *mechonit hanshama,* meaning respirator (literally, breathing machine or device). The Hebrew word *ruach* means spirit, wind, breath, or respiration. The Hebrew word *nefesh* means life, soul or person, but its Semitic root meaning is to breathe. Thus, there is a powerful religious connection between breath/respiration and life that must influence why people view the lack of respiration as a natural cause of death whereas they see the lack of an ability to eat or digest food as unnatural and needing to be corrected.

When the issues are examined in this context, one can see why individuals, especially those who are emotional and vulnerable because they are dealing with the death of a loved one, react so differently to the removal of a feeding tube than to the removal of a respirator. It is not a logical distinction, but it does not have to be. Death itself is not logical. It is not logical for a person to be there one day but gone the next; it is not logical to accept that someone we love, someone we held and talked to and laughed with, is no more. In the case of Terry Schiavo, it does not seem logical that a young woman in the prime of her life would simply stop functioning, that she can look directly at her mother yet in reality not acknowledge her or know that she is there.

Perhaps this is why we react to these issues more with our emotions and our hearts than with our intellect. We cannot breathe into the lungs of a dying mother but we can try to comfort her, to show her love in the way we know how, by giving her nourishment. End-of-life decisions raise moral, ethical, and religious concerns, but when feeding tubes are involved, morality and emotion intersect. It reminds us of our desire to care for our loved ones, and this care includes providing food, especially at a time when they are most in need of comfort. While breath is life, food is love and warmth and caring and a connection to our heritage, past and present. Perhaps this is what makes the choice so difficult.

Index of Authors

Index of Scripture

New Testament

Deuterocanonical Literature